Graced by the Seasons

Spring and Summer in the Northwoods

John Bates is the author of

Trailside Botany

A Northwoods Companion - Spring and Summer

A Northwoods Companion - Fall and Winter

Seasonal Guide to the Natural Year: Minnesota, Michigan, and Wisconsin

River Life - A Natural and Cultural History of a Northern River

Praise for

Seasonal Guide to the Natural Year for Minnesota, Michigan, and Wisconsin

"There are the rare outdoor books that are so jam-packed with interesting stuff that you find yourself reaching for it whenever you get a spare minute to yourself. You find yourself taking it with you camping, hiking, fishing, even just walking. And the darn thing is so well written that you don't mind – in fact, you pick it up as much for the pleasure as you do for the information. Wisconsin outdoor writer John Bates has just published such a book."

—Russell King, Council for Wisconsin Writers

River Life: The Natural and Cultural History of a Northern River

Of the many books that have been written about American rivers, most are quite forgettable, but occasionally one comes along that is outstanding . . . Now you can add another to the relatively short list: Naturalist John Bates' "River Life".

—Mike Svob – *Silent Sports* Magazine

[Bates'] storytelling is so complete and enrapturing and his understanding of aquatic biology is so sophisticated that the book should be incorporated into environmental studies and high school curriculums throughout the state.

—Scott Froehike – River Alliance of Wisconsin

Bates leads the way with tantalizing stories and factoids as he presents the diverse ecological communities that can be experienced along the way . . . an excellent resource for presenting examples of natural history and ecology or for highlighting the biodiversity of northern temperate rivers.

—CHOICE

Graced by the Seasons

Spring and Summer in the Northwoods

By John Bates

Illustrated by Terry Daulton

Manitowish River Press
Mercer, Wisconsin

Graced by the Seasons: Spring and Summer in the Northwoods

Published by: Manitowish River Press
4245N Hwy. 47
Mercer, WI 54547
Phone: (715) 476-2828
Fax: (715) 476-2818
E-mail: manitowish@centurytel.net
Website: www.manitowish.com

ISBN 978-0-9656763-5-9

Printed in the United States on 30% recycled paper.

Editor: Greg Linder
Illustrations: Terry Daulton
Cover photography: Jeff Richter
Book design: Pat Bickner, anewleaf-books.com
Cover design: Pat Bickner

Publisher's Cataloging in Publication Data
Bates, John, 1951-
Graced by the Seasons: Spring and Summer in the Northwoods
written by John Bates ; illustrated by Terry Daulton
Includes index.
ISBN 978-0-9656763-5-9 (softcover)
1. Natural History
2. Seasons
3. Nature Study
Library of Congress Control Number: 2006926752
0 9 8 7 6 5 4 3 2 1

My deep thanks go to the following people for making the production of this book possible: Terry Daulton, Greg Linder, Mary Burns, Pat Bickner, Callie Bates, and Stephany Freedman.

****

This book is dedicated to all the people in the Northwoods who have fought, and continue to fight, to keep the North the North and to redefine the term "progress."

And to Mary. Thank you, thank you, thank you.

It's all about joy.

Contents

Introduction 11	March 17	April 69
May 117	June 177	July 245
August 327	Appendix 386	Index 428

Introduction

I think of spring as the primary season of "firsts": When does the first robin return? The first red-winged blackbird? The first great blue heron? When does the first trailing arbutus bloom, the first hepatica, the first hazelnut? When does the ice go off the lakes, the frost go out of the ground, the river reach spring flood level? When do the first spring peepers sing, the first chipmunks emerge, the first mosquitoes buzz in your ear? And so on.

Spring is the best season in which to study the orderly timing and progression of natural events, or what is known as phenology. Some folks get a little creative with the pronunciation of phenology, adding an "r" to make it into "phrenology." Unfortunately, phrenology has everything to do with the pseudo-science of studying bumps on people's heads to determine personality, and nothing to do with observations of the natural world. Still, there's some similarity: Phenology is a close look at landscape. It's a study of the lay of the land and of all its bumps in order to learn the personality of a place. What you ultimately see and experience reflects both your internal psychological landscape and the external physical landscape.

Requirements for becoming a practicing phenologist are simple – a healthy curiosity, a willingness to pay attention, and a doggedness in keeping clear records. But phenology is much more than simply keeping track of dates on where and when events occur. Phenologists work to understand the whole array of relationships that occur between living organisms and the non-living physical environment. They ask questions like: What is the relationship between climate and periodic biological events? Which leads to questions like, if the average melting date of lake ice is getting earlier every year, are waterfowl returning earlier every year as well?

Phenologists also observe relationships between living organisms. If insects hatch at a particular time, how does that affect the timing of bird migration, fish movements, or the flowering cycles of plants?

Jack Turner writes in *The Abstract Wild*, "Phenology requires a complete immersion in place over time so that the attention, the senses, and the mind can scrutinize and discern widely – the dates of arrivals and departures, the births, the flourishings, the decays, and the deaths of wild things, their successions, synchronicities, dependencies, reciprocities, and cycles – the lived life of the earth. To be absorbed in this life is to merge with larger patterns. Here ecology is not studied but felt."

For me, to study "the lived life of the earth" is to leave no stone unturned, to see no life as less important than another, to respect and revere the diversity and complexity of human and non-human life.

Some folks have a hard time slowing down long enough to look at where they are. Constantly in search of new experiences in new places, they may be heard repeatedly reciting the slogan, "Been there, done that." They're missing something much deeper by looking for what amounts to a one-night stand. While such brief intersections in time and space can be scintillating, what every place on earth needs is people interested in a life-long love affair.

Immersing oneself in a place over many years doesn't drain away the fascination for it. Rather, repeated contact creates an intimacy that broadens one's view and appreciation, much like looking over many years into your spouse's eyes, touching her lips, noticing the curve of her cheeks, and valuing every one of the changes. A deep experience and understanding of beauty requires the perception and contemplation of different light and shadow over periods of time and varying distances. It's a stepping out of oneself and into something else, a spilling over of attention and concern. It's the maturity of phrasing life in the plural "we" and caring as much for the other as one does for the self.

It's also about getting small and seeing the details. The attraction to charismatic megafauna – the eagles, loons, black bears, and wolves of the world – is a starting point, but is ultimately as shallow as seeing beauty only in photo-shoot models and dismissing the rest of humanity. The trick is always to understand something better without losing touch with its magic. In large part, we need merely to go much slower, breathe more deeply, look all around, look again, and allow contemplation to dawn.

I must give some credit to the "Been there, done that" types. At least they are out there experiencing the natural world, looking for adventures, and hopefully not messing anything up too much along the way. It may be that the most endangered thing in this country right now is real experience in wild places.

But I also think that experience in the wild is an exceptional and fleeting experience for most individuals living on a planet housing nearly seven billion people. Finding the miraculous in the common is more what we need, and it's closer at hand. Because it is a state of mind, the study of phenology opens an accessible gateway, or at least puts down the first footbridge, that leads to an understanding of the wild. In many ways it may be more difficult to see the miraculous in the common, and to retain that feeling. Charismatic mountains and wilderness rivers offer instant access to a profound sense of awe, appreciation, and even divinity. But they are too separate from the lives of most people. It is into the common that we need to go to find deep connections to the natural world, and phenology offers one path to get there.

• • •

Historically, phenology had far greater local application than it does now. Farmers everywhere used phenology to dictate planting and harvesting decisions, while gatherers knew when to look for the ripening of fruits, grains, mushrooms, and nuts.

Many people I talk to have a sense that seasonal events "are different" in the Northwoods than when they were younger, but they're unable to provide evidence for their intuitions. A many-year comparison of the timing of events that occur on the same site could offer the details necessary to prove or disprove such beliefs.

I'd love to see people everywhere start charting when particular events take place near them. These events could be simply what takes place in their backyards, or they might include events in a larger area, but what's most important is to make the chronicling manageable, to start out small enough that the effort is easy to accomplish. For instance, you might choose to record the return date for four birds that are readily observable such as robins in your back yard, loons on your lake, and hummingbirds and orioles at your feeders.

Next, you might choose flowers in your yard (record a specific event like bud burst, first full leaf, or first flower), as well as flowers in a nearby woods that are easy to identify and to find. Among these might be lilacs, dandelions, trailing arbutus, hepatica, marsh marigold, or Canada mayflower.

Many other biological and physical events are also easily observed, among them the date that spring peepers are first heard, the first chipmunk is seen, the first fireflies flash, and the ice-off and ice-on dates on your lake.

The options are endless. What you choose can depend solely on what you most enjoy, or reflect your desire to add your observations to an existing database. For instance, the Wisconsin Phenological Society has a list of species it is keeping track of statewide. Perhaps you'd like to be involved in charting a few of the species.

Or maybe the only database you're interested in is the one your family will consult for decades to come. I like to think that our great-grandchildren, or whoever may live in our home in the future, will look at our writings and greatly appreciate the record of this area's natural history. Wouldn't it also be a delight to buy a home and receive not only the title, but a record of observations made in that place before you became the owner?

For further information on phenology, try these Websites:

www.naturenet.com/alnc/wps (Wisconsin Phenological Society)

www.attra.org/attra-pub/phenology.html (National Sustainable Agriculture Information)

www.emannorth.ca/plantwatch/main.cfm (Plantwatch North Program)

• • •

One last thing: Most of this book is drawn from columns I've written for the *Lakeland Times* in Minocqua, Wisconsin, during the period from 1997 to early 2006. I frequently list dates for when particular natural events occurred. Some dates go back 10 years, which could lead some readers to object that this is "old" news and not worth reading. Indeed, the events are old, but I include them because they may shed light on the future. Given the potentially profound impacts of global warming, it's essential that we have place and time markers established for what life looked like at the beginning of this century.

The dates given are a form of citizen science. When I write that the first robin was reported to me on a particular date, clearly that doesn't mean other robins may not have been here earlier. Obviously, not everyone in the Northwoods reports their sightings to me. (Thank goodness, or I'd never get off the phone!) This compendium of personal observations gives us a general picture of north central Wisconsin's Lakeland area at the turn of the 20th and 21st centuries. The data doesn't fit the model of a scientifically controlled experiment or survey, but that was never the intention. Each story is a piece of the larger story of what it is like to live in the Northwoods at this time in history. Each embodies a moment in this wonderfully rich and complex natural world that those of us who live here call home.

March

The word "miracle," the word "resurrection," and the word "revolution," are written with caution; with full knowledge of their overworked lives in clichéd times. But five months of ice washing away in the floodwaters, the launching of millions of birds with the deepest of Faiths, the Green-Up to come on the heels of the sodden gray heaps of snow that melt, saturating winter into fog, into puddles, into mud, and eventually into the first trailing arbutus, the tiny scarlet female flowers of hazelnuts, and the purple-pink-white unable-to-decide hepaticas; that is a miracle. It is glory.

Moats form around the lake edges, the ice like a pancake in a skillet, and one day the wind rushes from the South and ripples the ice sheet, driving it onto shorelines to slice trees off and buckle the piers of people who didn't know ice was like slow dynamite—a tornado reduced to a crawl—but a tornado, by God.

And then the ice is gone, leaving intensely blue waters; a blue that we'll never appreciate as much as we do now in its first cold blush, the sun playing on it like it never does in August, dazzling its millions of rays of light onto ev-

ery inch of water starved for months under the ice that muted its life into a semi-darkness. If fish could sing, the lakes would resound. And if the moribund, patient lilies could smile in the sediments knowing of their resurrection to come in July—ah, the waters would be warm in a week.

— John Bates, "If Fish Could Sing," *Seasons of the North*

Two things are required to truly see: knowledge and love. Without love, we don't look. Without knowledge, we don't know what it is we are seeing.

—Chet Raymo, *Natural Prayers*

Flowing Water Again

Spring brings many resurrections, and near the top of the list is the transformation of ice and snow into flowing water. Captive for five months, the water begins to drip, then trickle, then gently flow, then rush, carrying with it anything soluble, along with countless insoluble items. The thaw serves as a giant broom sweeping the landscape, loading up soil and the products of decay and hauling them down into ditches, streams, rivers, lakes, and eventually oceans.

When the thaw begins, the water has nowhere to go and stands adrift on top of the frozen soil. We haul our rubber boots from the depths of closets to navigate this new terrain.

Then the frost goes out of the soil. The meltwaters seep in and saturate every pore until there's nowhere for the water to go, and again pools appear on top of the land. But now we have mud underfoot. Our dirt roads and driveways turn to Silly Putty, and every geologic depression in the woods turns into a vernal pond, a temporary oasis where frogs and salamanders breed and raise young.

The Manitowish River almost always opens in the marshlands below our house sometime in March, and though the ice flows away, another surge comes toward us—thousands of birds. Waterfowl rest blithely on waters that were ice just a few days before. Goldeneye, trumpeter swans, mallards, Canada geese, and common and hooded mergansers all glide in as if they'd been hanging around just over the hill all winter. In the next few weeks, nearly 30 species of waterfowl may pass through or take up residence in these cold waters. When the rivers open, so do the floodgates of spring.

Here are 18 years of records for the opening of the Manitowish River just below our house (five other years are lost somewhere in the chaos of file cabinets):

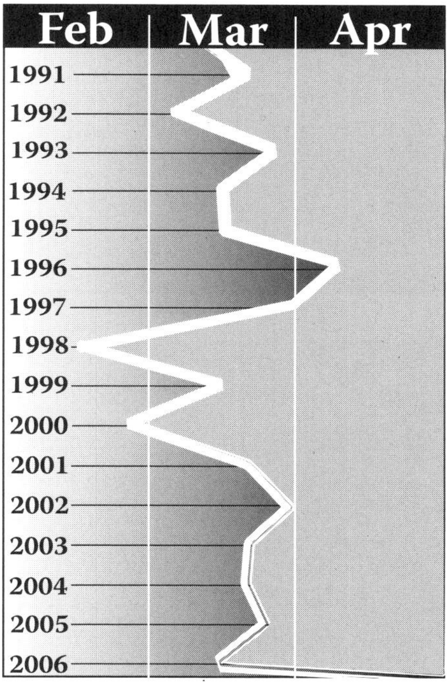

March 30, 1984
March 7, 1985
March 20, 1991
March 4, 1992
March 26, 1993
March 14, 1994
March 15, 1995
April 9, 1996
March 30, 1997
February 16, 1998
March 14, 1999
February 28, 2000
March 21, 2001
March 30, 2002
(The river opened on 2/19, but iced back over on 3/3.)
March 22, 2003
March 21, 2004
March 25, 2005

March 14, 2006 (The river opened up on 12/30, but iced-over again in late January.)

The 18-year average is March 18th.

Teetering on the Brink

March can be a cruel month for wildlife. In his book *Winter: An Ecological Handbook,* James Halfpenny talks of six selective winter forces that determine survival. I've taken four of the six that I consider most important and created the acronym TDER to help me remember them. I pronounce the acronym "teeder," and find the term is most easily remembered by thinking of winter forces as a teeter-totter, a balancing act with life and death consequences. The "T" stands for timing, the "D" for duration, the "E" for extremes, the "R" for repeatability.

The timing of the occurrence of intense cold or heavy snow is crucial. For example, the arrival of extreme cold in late fall before the snow has come to insulate the ground can kill many small mammals and plants. In late winter/early spring, a snowstorm can kill animals that have depleted their winter store of fat.

Duration of an event is also critical. For instance, the length of time the snowpack remains can impact survival. If the snow lasts into late April or early May, some animals and plants won't make it. Consider the duration of a storm or cold snap. A day or two of –30°F is one thing, but a week of it is another beast altogether.

Extremes in cold, ice, or snow can be the straw that breaks the camel's back. An organism may be able to withstand –20°F, but –40°F may be too much. Getting around in two feet of snow may be difficult for deer, but three feet may utterly exhaust their energy reserves.

Repeatability refers to the frequency of an event. One blizzard may be survivable, but a second one close on the heels of the first may cause death. Or two periods of extreme cold may overwhelm energy reserves and lead to mortality, although one period is survivable.

The onset of spring is an event humans watch carefully. We bemoan the ups and downs of March and April when we're teased with warm temperatures one day, only to be clobbered the next day with a winter storm. For animals long stressed by winter and hanging on until spring truly arrives, the story isn't about personal comfort or inconvenience. It's about teetering on the brink.

Chickadee Survival at –25°F

On early March nights, the temperature can plummet wickedly, dipping on occasion to –25°F. On nights like that, I get to thinking about chickadees, which regularly have to contend with these deadly temperatures. How chickadees, weighing less than an ounce, survived such intense adversity wasn't known until the 1970s when Susan Budd Chaplin investigated them at Cornell University. Chaplin began by determining the energy expenditures of the birds at a variety of controlled temperatures in a sealed chamber of her lab. As expected, metabolic rates increased at low air temperatures to compensate for the increased rate of heat loss. Knowing the hours of darkness per night, Chaplin could then calculate how many calories of stored energy a chickadee would require in order to see the sun rise in the morning.

Next, she compared the number of calories needed to survive at various temperatures over various lengths of nights to the calories a chickadee actually stored in its fat reserves. (She did this by shooting and killing chickadees in the woods in the early evening and at daybreak, and measuring the difference in fat stores.)

Chaplin found that chickadees began the evening with seven percent body fat, but had only three percent by the morning. Fundamentally, the birds ate like little pigs all day to build up fat, then burned it off at night to stay warm.

Her lab results, however, told her that if chickadees maintained their daytime body temperatures, they would not have enough energy reserves to make it through a night even at 32°F, which is hardly a cold night in the Northwoods. She found instead that chickadees stretched their fat reserves by lowering their body temperatures some 20°F at night, going into a condition of controlled hypothermia. By lowering their thermostat, and by shivering all night despite being sound asleep, they could make their fat reserves last the night.

Still, the chickadees were cutting it close, and their fat reserves were insufficient to last through another day and night if a blizzard prevented them from foraging for food. The only way they could survive was to utilize shelter at night to further reduce heat loss. While chickadees don't build winter shelters, they were found to sleep in almost any tight cranny or cavity, or in dense vegetation or conifers. As proof of how tight their evening chambers may be, look for a chickadee at your feeders to have a bent tail in the morning, a likely indicator that it jammed itself into a tiny cavity the night before.

Barred Owls Starving in March

Susanne Brown reported the following: "Spring is a while off yet for us. About 10 days ago [3/2/06], the most recent good snowfall put our snow depth in northern Iron County over 25 inches and over 31 in the western Upper Peninsula. We've had about 185 inches so far this season [in the Bessemer, Michigan, area].

"I found a dead barred owl just after the last good snowfall, on the Little Turtle Flowage, west of Mercer. The bird had succumbed not more than a couple of hours before I found it. It had fallen, cleanly and neatly, face down into the snow, as if it had literally just tipped over from its perch in the white pine above it. The bird was freshly dead when I found it about 10 a.m. When I called the local wildlife biologist [Bruce Bacon], he said he had just returned from checking the sighting of another barred owl, dead under another tree, tipped over and succumbed to starvation. He told me the same phenomenon occurs this time of year, nearly every year. It's surprising, but true apparently, that even for a bird native to the region, our winters can be just too much."

Attack of the Flying Squirrels

Every winter, Al Denninger feeds corn and a variety of grains to a herd of deer. One evening in March of 2004, he got home late and had to fill the feeder when it was pitch black. He opened up the top of the feeder and suddenly something leaped onto his throat. Al, a Vietnam vet, said he screamed "like a little girl," and was more terrified at that moment than at any time in his tour of Vietnam.

This was his introduction to a clan of flying squirrels that spends most of its time living in his deer feeder. He's since grown accustomed to them, and he now approaches the feeder, taps on the sides to let the squirrels know it's him, and the squirrels then simply watch as he pours in the food. A few squirrels now know him so well that they crawl up his arms and perch on his shoulders while he works. Al says they often huddle together for warmth and look like a "big ball of eyes."

Aurora Alert

The northern lights can appear at any time of the year, so how does one know when to look for them? Just sign up on this Website list-serve to be alerted when you're most likely to see northern lights: http://www.gi.alaska.edu/mailman/listinfo/gse-aa. Whenever activity on the sun reaches the necessary threshold to produce an auroral display, you will be notified when to go out and look for it.

Remember that northern lights often come and go during an evening display, so if at first you don't see them, keep checking—they will likely appear at some point that evening.

Banding Great Gray Owls

Bruce Bacon, DNR wildlife manager in Mercer, Wisconsin, banded 46 great gray owls in northwestern Wisconsin during the winter of 2004-05, many of them in March. Surprisingly, all but a few of those were robustly healthy. That was remarkably good news given that biologists feared the enormous influx of great grays was a likely indicator they were starving.

How does one trap and then band a great gray? Here is Bruce's description:

"A lab mouse is gently tossed into the snow about 4-5 feet in front of the bander, who is holding a large musky landing net. I usually hide the net behind me or off to one side. Mouse movement and noise is what triggers the owl's hunting instincts. If your mouse doesn't move (snow, cold, etc.), you nudge it with the net, or pick it up and toss it closer to the owl. As you can see, there is a fair amount of movement by the bander, and the owls certainly see the net. If I have a mouse who's on a lunch break, I put it back in the bucket and try a different mouse. Movement by the mouse is the key.

"Black mice work best on winter owls. Once the owl decides it's lunchtime, you can tell from their behavior. You then wait for the owl to plunge onto the mouse, at the same time tossing the net over the owl.

"For the mouse lovers out there, I have yet to have an owl talon the mouse as the owl's attention is diverted to the net at the last split second, and the mouse just gets pushed into the snow. For those who feel the owl deserves a mouse dinner after being once handled and banded, the owls will not take a mouse as you release them. They drop the mouse, just as some birds defecate on release 'to lighten the load' on escape. Often upon release the great grays fly back to the same perch."

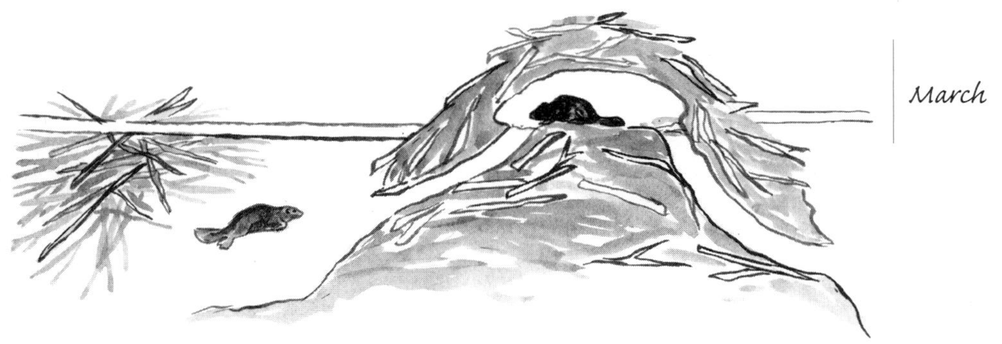

Beaver Lodging

March beavers finally emerge from their winter lodge and can be seen foraging along open river shorelines. They've spent five months or more together in family units within the lodges, which would give the average human family an out-of-control case of cabin fever (or inspire homicide ...). But beavers appear to get along famously within the lodge, even at times accepting the presence of other mammals like otters and muskrats.

Why leave the lodge? This communal nest is the largest constructed by any animal, and it's warm and clean by most any standards. From all outward appearances, the lodge looks to be little more than a pile of mud, sticks, and debris, but the inside floor is smooth and silky, the walls trimmed evenly so not a nub protrudes, and the chambers devoid of any trace of food, fecal material, or odor. It appears that beavers rate the Good Housekeeping Seal of Approval.

Inside temperatures on a 0°F day may reach 60°F. Much like cows in a barn, a family of beavers packed into a small space can generate a lot of heat. But the scientific literature says that swimming in icy waters to the food cache in front of the lodge can induce hypothermia within 30 minutes, despite the beaver's renowned insulated pelage. Warming up is little problem if the beavers can return to a heated lodge. However, if the lodge is allowed to cool during swimming forays, the beavers could be in trouble.

Scientists have found that unlike most animals, beavers forage without attachment to a biological clock. Thus in winter, they don't feed during certain predictable activity periods throughout the day and night. Biologists speculate that feeding must be staggered, leaving several beavers in the lodge at any given time, to ensure that the lodge is kept warm. Beavers apparently understand that it's difficult to warm up a cold, empty house with body heat alone. It's quite possible that beavers have adapted their foraging behavior in order to meet their household temperature needs.

The Miracle of Buds

Pussy willows typically break their buds and start to billow out in March. They're the first buds to break, the official harbingers of a spring that is usually still some time away, even though the pussy willows tempt us to think otherwise.

Buds wait all winter, surviving the harshest weather nature can throw at them and opening at just the right moment. They are packages that contain different contents: Some buds harbor new leaves (like a butternut or hickory); some contain flowers (like alder, hazelnut, and birch); some encase both the flower and the leaves (like cherry, juneberry, and apple). Since all are packed with nutrients, they are prized as winter food by many mammals and birds. Some trees (balsam popular and mountain ash) enclose their buds with sticky resin to deter predators. Some (like white birch) can add chemicals to make their buds unsavory. However, most trees depend on the combination of producing an extensive number of buds and the harshness of the winter to win the battle for germination. A simple ratio in which there are more buds existing than there are predators to eat them ensures the growth of new leaves and flowers in the spring.

Those shrubs and trees like willow, aspens, hazelnut, and alder that produce separate buds for their leaves and flowers may open their flowers a month before they open their leaves. Wind pollinators usually open their flowers early in spring, because the formation of leaves would reduce the wind flow through their branches. But trees that rely on insect pollinators may open their leaves as much as five months before their flowers, as with witch hazel. More typically they act like basswoods, which produce their flowers a month or so after they leaf out, just when bee populations are at their peak.

Buds have evolved to apparently judge the best time for flowering and leafing. Even when we get early thaws and warm weather, they are seldom fooled into budding out, using the interplay of temperature, day length, and length of cold exposure to set them into proper motion.

Bud opening is a small miracle that most of us take for granted, except in March when it seems the buds will never break. To get a leg up on spring, cut some small twigs from early bloomers (aspen, willow, alder, red and silver maple for instance) and put them in a jar of water. In a few weeks, they'll flower and then leaf out, giving you a preview of what's to come in April and May.

Daylight and Temperatures Increasing!

- March 6 marks the day when our average high temperature finally gets back up to freezing at 32°F. Our average days from here on should be above freezing.
- On March 8, we receive 11 hours and 30 minutes of daylight.
- March 18 marks the first time since September 26 that our day will be longer than our night.
- By March 27, we will experience 12 hours and 32 minutes of daylight. Get out the sunscreen! Every new day now brings an additional three minutes of daylight.

Crust Snow

Snow conditions can be great for "crust skiing" in March. If the snow pack is compressed and crusted with an inch or two of snow, you may want to put on a pair of skis and explore areas that might be inaccessible during the summer. Mary and I explore some of the huge bog complexes in our area every March, and except for encountering a few more alder swamps than any sane person would want, we've had some wonderful skiing.

While crust snow is revered by skate-skiers, for animals it may present either a great opportunity or a serious problem. Animals with low body weights and big feet see the upside—they can be supported by the crust, giving them an important energy-saving advantage when seeking plant browse or prey animals. However, heavier animals with smaller feet see the downside—they break through the crust, often cutting their legs on the sharp edges, and they must exert much more energy to find food. Deep crust snow can effectively trap animals like deer.

The ability of an animal to move on top of the crust is related to the weight the animal's foot places on the snow, a variable called "foot loading." Those mammals with the lightest foot loads are best adapted to living in deep snow conditions, and are generally least affected by crusted snow. Foot loading is often expressed in grams per square centimeter. The snowshoe hare and red squirrel rank at the head of the class with the lowest average foot loading—about 20 gm/cm2. The lynx exerts 100 gm/cm2; the red fox 180 gm/cm2; bobcat and coyote 330 gm/cm2; and the wolf 500gm/cm2.

Foot load isn't the whole story though in coping with deep snow. Two researchers added the factor of chest height to create a morphological index for snow-coping animals. A higher chest height makes for much easier movement through deep snow. Thus, a white-tailed deer and a moose both have relatively small feet, but compensate in deep snow by having a high chest—a moose's chest is typically 42 inches off the ground. Topping the morphological index for large North American mammals are caribou, followed well back by moose, which are followed closely by the wolf, wolverine, and coyote.

How Birds Play

When ravens perform acrobatically in flight for hours at a time, is it possible they are "playing" on the air currents? We readily accept that mammals play—we all have seen domestic puppies and kittens play, and scientists acknowledge that young wild otters, raccoons, foxes, and others play as well. We humans, mammals that we are, clearly play, too.

We have greater difficulty, however, calling certain bird behaviors a form of play, though scientific studies have documented many behaviors that don't appear to fit into any other category.

Researchers have found that play is most sophisticated in birds that have a well-developed forebrain, the part of the brain most important to learning. Those birds that rely most on learning for their development are those that play the most. The corvids—crows, ravens, jays, and related species—are considered the most intelligent family of birds, and by correlation, the most playful. Ravens and crows have often been observed utilizing air currents, swooping down to the earth and back up again over and over. They are thought to clearly be playing.

The most common form of play is termed "object play," where birds manipulate nonedible objects like stones, leaves, feathers, and twigs by tossing them into the air and catching them, or dropping them and catching them from midair, or shaking them and tossing them hither and yon.

Another form of play is called "locomotor play." Examples include captive ravens repeatedly sliding down a smooth piece of wood in their cage, wild ravens repeatedly sliding feet first down a snow bank on their tails, or common eiders riding down tidal rapids, only to walk back up the shoreline to the head of the rapids and shoot the rapids over and over.

Social play is less common than the other types, and corvids exhibit more complex forms than all other birds. A common raven was once observed playing a game with a dog in which each animal took turns chasing the other around a tree. Corvids also have been observed playing what appear to be versions of "keep-away," "follow-the-leader," and "king-of-the-mountain." Captive ravens play balancing games, such as trying to stand on a stick or a bone held in their feet while balancing it on top of a wooden perch. Some have been seen walking slowly to the end of a small branch until it bends downward, turning the birds upside down. Other captives act like gymnasts by falling forward from their perch while holding on with their feet, hanging upside down with wings outstretched, and then letting go with one foot.

Researchers speculate that their playful inventiveness allows them to adapt to so many diverse nesting habitats around the world. Corvid chicks are quite slow to mature as well—they take more than 40 days to fledge from the nest—extending the learning period they have with their parents, and probably enhancing their adaptability.

Separating playing from behaviors designed to increase survivability is a difficult call to make. Do the forms of play humans engage in also often teach us things, therefore becoming functional as well as fun? Is fun an end unto itself or just one of several reinforcing outcomes attached to a behavior that is intended to enhance survival?

We'll never know, of course. I'm reminded of a quote that has always struck me when we try to categorize animal behaviors:

"We need another and a wiser and perhaps a more mystical concept of animals ... For the animal shall not be measured by man. In a world older and more complete than ours they move finished and complete, gifted with extensions of the senses we have lost or never attained, living by voices we shall never hear. They are not brethren, they are not underlings; they are other nations, caught with ourselves in the net of life and time, fellow prisoners of the splendor and travail of the earth." —Henry Beston, *Outermost House*

Bucking the Trend

On March 12, 2002, Penny and Mike McCormick in St. Germain reported 13 deer at their deer feeder, five of which were bucks still carrying their full racks. Given that deer are supposed to shed their racks in December and January, they wondered how the bucks could still be antlered, and asked if the mild winter might be the primary factor.

I called Bruce Bacon, DNR wildlife manager in Mercer, to get his thoughts on the matter. Bruce said that game farm bucks that receive supplemental nutrition often carry their racks into March. Wild bucks that are fed throughout a mild winter will sometimes carry their racks into March as well. Bruce knows of one buck that maintained its rack all the way into April of 2001. In hard winters, white-tailed deer with restricted diets often cast their antlers early.

Antlers are the only regenerating living tissue in the entire mammal kingdom. The bond between the antler and the pedicel degenerates very rapidly—a buck can be picked up by its antlers one day and cast them the next.

Migration Roadblocks

By the end of March, nearly every native species of waterfowl can be found on open water here in northern Wisconsin, tundra swan flocks are in the air, sandhill cranes are in the fields, raptors (kestrels, harriers, turkey vultures, et al) are reappearing, killdeer and great blue herons are arriving, saw-whet owls are singing, and the truly hardy songbirds (robins, red-winged blackbirds, tree sparrows) are drifting in. It's a magic time when the weather is right.

But at least once in their lives, most of those birds have been stopped in their northward surge by the climatic roadblock called "The Northwoods." In a cold March, the birds may see little sign of the ice going off our waters, and two feet of snow may still blanket the woods. That makes for slim pickings to fill an avian stomach, so early migrants often are backed up for a while well south of here.

Nevertheless, keep an eye peeled. Some waterfowl, like trumpeter swans, geese, and goldeneyes, always manage to find whatever open water is available.

Usually by spring equinox, our first robins, starlings, and red-winged blackbirds will have returned. We always gnash our teeth when they return, because we know the hardships the weather will likely put them through, but most seem to take it all in stride. All three birds are fine singers. Even in harsh weather, the robin usually sings just before first light to welcome the morning. A late March day with a light snowfall accompanied by the singing of robins and red-winged blackbirds is an anticipated annual treat.

If you look at a range map of all three species, they breed throughout North America, as well as south to Mexico. They winter only as far south as is necessary, which means they are often present in southern Wisconsin throughout the winter. So, they're only a hop, skip, and a jump from our area to begin with. A break in the weather can jump-start the optimists (or lunatics) among them, and send them winging north. Even though I hate to see them arrive because I'm concerned about their survival, I also can't wait to have them back (maybe even the starlings).

Fire Escapes, Convenience Stores, and Full-Service Hotels

Numerous reports in March often stream in from southern Wisconsin celebrating the migratory return of sandhill cranes, meadowlarks, killdeers, red-winged blackbirds, and most species of waterfowl.

In the Northwoods, our first spring bird migrants typically don't return until mid-March. Their journey is fraught with many difficulties, but one of the most significant is finding a safe place at night to rest and find adequate food.

To put a migratory bird's needs into a frame of reference, think where you stay at night when you are traveling. Do you sleep in the car, camp, stay at a Motel 6, or bask in luxury at a top-end hotel? Do you bring your own food, buy a sandwich at a fast-food store, or look for an opulent meal at a classy restaurant?

Certainly, there are differences between the way we select our level of comfort at our stopover sites and the survival needs of a long-distance migratory bird, but the analogy has some merit. Birds select their stopover sites based on a variety of factors:

- What is the resource availability (food and water)?
- Does the site provide cover from weather?
- Does the site provide protection from predators?
- Does the site contain too many competitors?

Sometimes the site selects itself because the weather becomes extreme and the birds are forced to land. Sometimes the birds' physical condition deteriorates to the point where they have no choice but to land, or an ecological barrier presents itself that can't be crossed without stopping to refuel. High-quality stopover sites are essential because this is a period of vulnerability for birds. It's also a period when many birds must build up their strength in order to arrive on their nesting grounds in the best condition for breeding. Weakened birds are less successful in finding mates and ultimately in raising young.

Of course, not all stopover sites are created equal. Dave Ewert, who has worked on the stopover ecology of birds for 15 years in the Great Lakes region, the Bahamas, and the U.S. Virgin Islands, says there are three types of stopover sites for migrants: fire escapes, convenience stores, and full-service hotels.

The fire escapes are the lowest quality sites, and receive infrequent use, but they are vital when they are needed. Birds need to bail out when the winds change, a storm hits, or they simply become exhausted and have to land immediately. Islands in oceans or large lakes are great examples of important fire escapes. Sometimes these "islands" are freighters or sailing ships. Many ship captains can tell stories of exhausted birds landing on their ships unable to fly another mile.

The convenience store sites offer some food and cover, but they're limited. These sites are used frequently but don't provide optimum conditions for building fitness.

The full-service hotels are used most often, and provide the highest quality food and cover. These are sites where food resources abound, and thousands of birds can land, stay for several days or weeks to rebuild strength, and then make the jump to another stopover site or fly all the way to their breeding grounds.

Birds need all three types of stopover sites, not just the best ones. They still need convenience stores and fires escapes, which are typically isolated stretches of woods or beach or quiet open water, because so much of our landscape is fragmented. Once a bird reaches the Northwoods, the forest habitat is nearly contiguous, but south of here, the patchwork of farms, towns and cities, and industry often makes for limited stopover habitat.

The best stopover sites have:

- High insect productivity in the spring
- High insect and fruit productivity in the fall
- Structurally complex plant communities with water available

Migration often coincides with, and depends on, the hatching of insects. Thus, the Great Lakes shorelines are exceptionally important sites for migrating birds. Coastal areas along Lake Michigan can produce millions of early-hatching midges that emerge just in time to feed hordes of hungry migrants. Birds focus their migration paths on where the food is, and the aquatic insect hatch has proven to be a reliable predictor of their migration patterns.

The problem along coastlines is that people want to live there. According to demographers, three out of four Americans will live within 50 miles of a coastline by the year 2010. That's not a good scenario for the millions of birds that depend on coastlines for wild fruits and insects.

The field of stopover ecology is relatively new, and scientists are in a race to learn as much as they can before critical stopover sites are lost or dramatically degraded. Some sites are extraordinarily important, like the 300-mile-long coastal area between Lake Charles, Louisiana, and Corpus Christi, Texas, where songbirds arrive from Central America after flying 600 miles over the Gulf of Mexico. In one day, 150,000 birds per mile can arrive along that 300-mile front. This amounts to a total of 45 million birds that have flown all night, and, if luck has been with them, have arrived exhausted in the U.S. and looking desperately for food.

What can individuals do? Each of us can provide excellent habitat on our property, which means providing food, water, and cover in as many natural forms as possible. It's impossible for any one of us to provide for all the needs of the more than 150 nesting birds that are returning to the Northwoods. I don't know that any of us really knows what all those needs are anyway. Maybe the most important thing to do is to remember that we are members of a biological community, and when we sign our names on our properties with chainsaws, lawnmowers, and the like, we are demonstrating what that membership means to us. Of all the membership cards we carry in our wallet, possibly none is more important than our God-given membership in the natural world.

Maple Sugar Moon

The full moon in March is called the "Maple Sugar Moon," according to the Anishinabe. This moon carries great meaning for Mary and me, because we are often out of maple syrup by March, a near catastrophe in our household. We always watch to see when the first taps appear on the maple trees and try to buy local syrup at the earliest opportunity.

Gawk and Awe With the Ravens

As tourists, Mary and I invaded Arizona for a week in March 2005, and, after viewing one stunning vista after another, Mary appropriately dubbed our expedition "Gawk and Awe." We split most of our time between hiking around the red-rock spires in Sedona and traversing the south rim of the Grand Canyon. As first-time visitors, we gawked continuously in the finest of tourist traditions at the jaw-dropping landscapes. And despite the presence of thousands of visitors, we found numerous places to enjoy the views in near solitude, a necessary condition for us to relax and feel at ease in a place.

I bring up a trip to the Southwest in a book about the Northwoods because the most memorable bird of the trip was, surprisingly, the common raven. Ravens dominated the skies over the Grand Canyon, wheeling, barrel-rolling, tumbling, and endlessly gliding in what certainly appeared to be sheer pleasure. They may well have been engaged in various pair bonding and territorial defense maneuvers, but with all that vast expanse and rising warmth under them, they seemed to enjoy just using the wind to cavort over one of the most beautiful places on Earth.

These ravens were quite tame, too, permitting us very close views through our binoculars. As intelligent as they are reputed to be, I'm sure the ravens have learned they are protected within the boundaries of the national park. Their sense of safety gave us ample opportunity to observe their wingspread of nearly 4.5 feet, which makes them the world's largest passerine, or songbird. That's a pretty impressive title given that passerines make up the largest order of birds in the world—some 59 families and about 5,100 species of the world's 8,650 bird species.

Ravens nest from beyond the tree line in the Arctic south to Nicaragua (though not in the southern Midwest or the southeastern U.S.), from western Alaska to the far eastern coast of Maine, and also in Iceland, Europe and Asia, and Africa.

Here in the Northwoods, ravens should be sitting on nests in March—some have been observed nesting as early as late February.

Life Down Under—Otters

One March day in 1997, two friends and I hiked along Moose Lake and Moose Creek north of Mercer in search of wolf tracks. We didn't find any wolves, but we did find numerous otter scat sites along the creek shoreline where small patches of water were open.

I see numerous otter trails every winter, often back in the woods away from water, and I frequently observe a few holes in lake ice that appear to be maintained by otters. I wonder how the otters find these holes since they really can't cut a hole in thick ice on their own. I once watched otters break very thin ice on the Manitowish River with their heads, then bite the ice to enlarge the holes, so possibly they establish some holes as the ice forms, and keep the holes open throughout the winter.

I've wondered too how once they dive under the ice, they find their way back to the hole. Wouldn't it be extremely easy to chase a fish, get turned around under the ice, and not know where the hole was?

Otters are obviously a lot smarter than me, because I would drown on my first foray. A study in Alberta, Canada, found that otters almost invariably used old beaver lodges to enter the water. Sometimes, the otters even ripped apart beaver dams in order to lower the water level beneath the ice and create a corridor of travel to food resources. The researchers found that otters were so dependent on beaver that their northern limit coincided with that of the beavers, even though good habitat was available further north.

I hadn't considered abandoned beaver lodges as otter entrance points, but it certainly makes sense. I wonder if otters enter active beaver lodges and try to force the residents out so they can gain access to the lake waters.

We did see an active beaver lodge on Little Moose Lake, which is connected to Moose Lake by Moose Creek. We had some fairly easy walking along the creek banks, a favor we suspected to be courtesy of a beaver dam that had likely inundated the area in previous years, making a meadow out of what should have been tag alder heaven.

March Madness

In 1998, the warm weather proved January and February to be impostors, while March wore its same old clothes, meaning a change of clothes virtually every day. One Friday I was out mountain biking, on Saturday canoeing, on Sunday cross-country skiing, and on Monday, I stayed inside to keep warm!

March is defined by its lack of definition. In human terms, it might be seen as having a bipolar disorder, manically gorgeous one day, depressively gray the next, and utterly unpredictable in its timing.

Merlins Returning

On March 29, 2002, we had a pair of merlins visit our feeders in Manitowish. Since merlins eat songbirds, the feeders were instantly evacuated, and there wasn't a songbird visible out any window! One of the merlins, an adult female, gave us long, close-up looks, so much so that we were able to read the band numbers on her left leg. I called Bruce Bacon, wildlife manager and bird bander at the Mercer DNR, and he told us she had been banded in 2000 in Mercer. At the time, her nest was high up in a pine tree in an old crow's nest on the edge of a field. In 2001, she moved her nest to just south of Mercer, near our new cell tower. Again, the nest was high in a pine in a confiscated crow's nest.

Bruce estimates there may be 40 or more pairs in Wisconsin now, and merlins appear to be increasing every year throughout the northern lake country. They typically nest high in pines in a commandeered crow's nest on the edge of a lake. The male is smaller than the female, has a higher-pitched voice, and is grayer overall.

Monarchs' Inexplicable Recovery, or Hello, I'm a Recovering Butterfly

In early 2002, the first reports of a massive monarch butterfly die-off came trickling in from their wintering grounds in Mexico.

Eventually, researchers estimated as many as 500 million monarchs died in January 2002, by far the largest die-off ever observed. Fears were rampant that monarchs would have a tough time recuperating, and in fact, monarch numbers in the summer of 2003 appeared quite spotty in the U.S. and Canada. Some areas experienced abundant numbers while others reported virtually none. Anecdotal reports from people around the Northwoods indicated smaller numbers of monarchs were being seen. The fall migration was also reported as scant at many monarch watch locations.

But in the winter of 2002-03, researchers found that the monarch roosts in the mountains of Mexico were covered with close to the average number of monarchs that have been seen over the last decade.

The scientists happily scratched their heads, amazed and perplexed at the monarchs' recovery. They had no concise explanations, only the puzzled pleasure of reporting that somehow the monarchs repopulated and found their way to their mountainside roosting sites.

Birds on the Big Screen

I can't recall ever recommending movies in my books, but I'm compelled to suggest several movies about birds that are must-sees. *Fly Away Home* is a movie made in 1996 about a 13-year-old girl and her father, who teach an orphaned flock of Canada geese to fly and then in their ultralight airplanes lead the geese on a 500-mile migration flight south. The footage of the geese flying beside the ultralights is inspiring and beautiful, particularly given that geese will soon be on the wing and entering our air space.

Then came *Winged Migration*, made in 2003, a film that is cinematically astounding. Its beauty literally takes your breath away at times. At our house, there is a rating scale for movies called the "How did they do that?" scale, which simply totals the number of times one of us sputters out that phrase. We easily hit double figures in the first half hour of this movie.

Finally, rent *The March of the Penguins*, which came out in 2005 and was an amazing commercial success. The adaptation of emperor penguins to the Antarctic region borders is utterly remarkable. Despite being part of the National Geographic Specials series, which are typically relegated to the non-commercial public TV stations, this film made it to movie theaters and competed admirably with the likes of Harry Potter.

Moths in March

Lee Nielsen e-mailed me one early spring day, marveling that moths were flying on March 19, 2003, near his home in Arbor Vitae. Lee wondered how they could survive the winter, and what their life cycle is.

mourning cloak butterfly

I'm no expert on moths, so I consulted Bernd Heinrich's marvelous book *Winter World.* Heinrich has one chapter specific to wintering insects, and he notes that many insects, such as female ichneumon wasps, mourning cloak butterflies, some of the sphinx moths, and owlet moths, overwinter as adults. The wintering moths live what Heinrich refers to as a "reversed life cycle." By this he means that they prosper and mate as adults in winter, lay eggs in early spring, and then watch their larvae and pupae grow in late spring and summer. These moths shiver in the winter to generate enough heat to fly, needing to bring their body temperature up to 30°C before their short wings can gain enough power to get them off the ground.

Heinrich writes at length about the freeze tolerance abilities of these overwintering adult insects, and notes that insects in general "have collectively pushed the limits of things possible, in terms of diversity, beauty, noxiousness, social organization, architecture, powers of flight, sensory capability, and the ability to survive extremes of climate."

I don't know what species of moth Lee Nielsen saw at his home, but I, too, marvel at what seems impossible. While we marvel, the first mourning cloak butterflies should be appearing anytime. Larry Weber, a teacher, naturalist, and author from the Duluth area (see his excellent book *Butterflies of the North Woods*), reports that his earliest sighting on mourning cloaks occurred on March 7th, and his average first sighting is April 8th. He notes that Compton tortoiseshells emerge from hibernation around the same time, and April 8th is also their average date of first appearance. Both butterflies eat tree sap in the early spring, which is really the only food that's available while the snow is still on the ground.

Mountain Biking and Hiking in March

What good is a snowmobile trail when we have an early snowmelt in March? Well, they're great for mountain biking on cold mornings. Mary and I often mountain bike snowmobile trails in March (February 19 is the earliest date we've ever been out biking these trails). Even with an early melt, we're usually in for a long two months until our real spring actually shows up, so if you're looking for an interesting recreational diversion, try exploring by bike the hundreds of miles of frozen snowmobile trails. It beats staying indoors.

If biking doesn't trip your trigger, hiking might. One March, Mary, Callie, and I traveled up to the Porcupine Mountains for a little snowshoe adventure, but there wasn't enough snow to warrant the use of anything other than our boots! So we hiked down to Lake Superior along one side of the Presque Isle River and came back on the other side. Our biggest problem was our footing on some of the icy hillsides. Other than that, hiking was good! The lack of snow presented a great opportunity for extensive hiking into areas we might not reach in the summer.

We northerners spend a fair amount of time complaining about March, but I believe in accepting what you're given in this life. If Mother Nature provides us something other than what the seasons usually offers, then so be it. Just as adaptability is a desirable characteristic for any plant or animal in nature, so it is for humans. One of our tasks in life, it seems to me, is to simply enjoy whatever opportunities life offers.

Mute Swans

Mary, Callie, and I observed two mute swans on the Manitowish River on March 20, 2005. They were probably migrating through to another location further north. We haven't seen mutes on the Manitowish in many years, so we were quite surprised and a little disturbed to see them.

While beautiful, mute swans are exotic, non-native birds that compete with trumpeter swans for similar breeding and feeding sites. The presence of mute swans in the wild could potentially interfere with the very successful but still tenuous trumpeter swan recovery effort. Mute swans also compete for resources with other waterfowl such as loons and ducks, and colonial waterbirds like black terns, tundra swans, and geese. Mutes will sometimes completely displace or even kill native waterfowl. While trumpeter swans may also compete with other waterfowl, this is a natural occurrence because it occurs between native species.

The mute swan population is exploding along the Atlantic Coast from Massachusetts to Virginia and is expanding rapidly in the Midwest. Many state natural resource agencies have enacted mute swan control policies that include egg addling (which kills embryos), the removal of problem birds, and prohibitions against the import, export, possession, release, or sale of these birds and their eggs.

In Wisconsin, the DNR solicited input from the public during five meetings in 1995-96. The department proposed a policy to prevent further expansion of mute swans in the wild and control the swan population by sterilizing adult swans and addling eggs. Citizens voiced strong support and very little opposition to this proposed policy. The Wisconsin Society for Ornithology, the Wisconsin Audubon Council, and the Chequamegon Audubon Society endorsed the need for control.

In 1997, the DNR established a policy with a long-term objective of achieving zero mute swan young production in the wild by the year 2005. A Mute Swan Population Control Program was initiated and egg addling was done each spring from 1997 to 2000. During the 2000 control season, some negative public sentiment arose. New strategies were drafted through an extensive public input process and new policy was created in 2002 to remove all free-flying mute swans from Wisconsin, except for a two-township study area in northwest Racine County.

I've seen mutes on Chequamegon Bay near Ashland, and I suspect these two were from that population. I strongly support the DNR's position on mutes, particularly given the highly successful efforts that have been made to reestablish trumpeter swans on our lakes and rivers. It's a hard call that the DNR made, but given all the other invasive, non-native species in Wisconsin, it's one that I hope the public recognizes as wise.

Phenology and Global Warming

Phenology, the study of the timing of natural events, leads many of us to record the dates of the first robin, ice-up and ice-out, the first hepatica, the first skein of geese, and so forth. Aldo Leopold, author of *A Sand County Almanac,* also studied phenology, recording the spring arrival of birds and the blossoming of plants at his famous "shack" in southern Wisconsin from 1936 to 1947.

His daughter, Nina Leopold Bradley, an excellent plant ecologist in her own right, moved back to the Leopold Preserve in 1976 and began keeping similar records. During this time, she tracked 300 different natural events and found that one-third of them are now happening earlier than they once did. She and several other researchers then focused on 55 specific spring events, and found one-third of those to also be occurring earlier. The Eastern phoebe, for instance, is returning about 20 days earlier in spring than it used to.

The Leopolds' data was collected over a long enough period of time to arguably show that there's an overall trend. Other scientists are finding similar trends around the globe. It appears that global warming may be changing the actual unveiling and appearance of spring.

I see indisputable evidence that global warming is occurring, but some question either the data or the conclusions drawn from the data. I encourage you to keep your own accurate records, over the course of decades if possible. Only then will you be able to say for yourself that temperatures are clearly going up or down, and that wildlife and wild plants are being affected.

Questionable Behavior by Question Marks

On March 6, 2005, when temperatures hit 50°F in the sun, Michael Mitchell in Arbor Vitae noticed a movement on his deck rail: "It was a butterfly in full regalia. It took flight and I followed it to my truck bed where it stayed and dined on salt from my rock salt bags. I retrieved my field guide and matched it to the name 'question mark.' "

Question marks (*Polygonia interrogationis*) are identified by the silver "?" on the underside of their hindwings. They hibernate over the winter as adults, so a warm sunny day might entice one to become active. I don't know how easy it is for a question mark to enter and exit a state of hibernation, so I'm unable to comment on whether this is a risky behavior or just normal spring procedure. In *Butterflies of the North Woods,* Larry Weber writes that the earliest he has seen one in the Duluth area is April 19th.

Radar Ornithology

From the Wisconsin BirdNet on March 16, 1999, came the following posting from Florida:

"Readers from the more northerly latitudes of eastern North America can rest assured that passerine migrants are on the move and headed your way. Last night I captured a series of images from the Key West, Florida Nexrad radar between 7 and 11:30 p.m. There was a moderate volume of migration that is probably typical at this time of year on a night with favorable weather conditions. These images show birds beginning to depart Cuba between 7:30 and 8 p.m.. By around 10 p.m. birds have begun to arrive over the Keys. Since conditions were favorable most of the birds passed over the Keys and continued to fly over the Gulf, Florida Bay, and southern Florida, as shown in the last image at 11:26 p.m."

Most people these days use the Internet for up-to-the-minute weather forecasts, but it's now equally possible to find up-to-the-minute pictures of how bird migration is progressing.

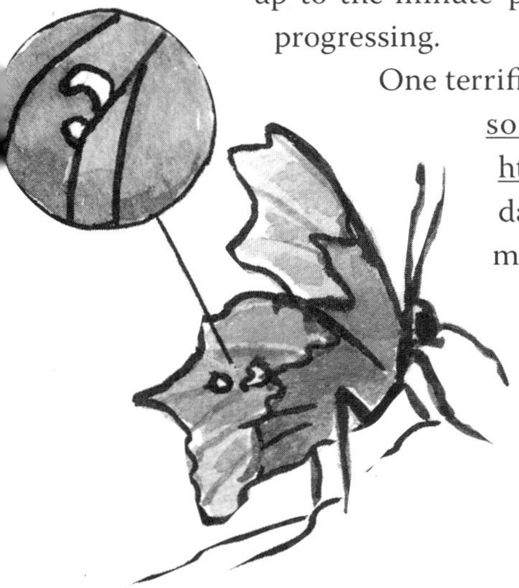

One terrific Internet site, http://virtual.clemson.edu/groups/birdrad/comment.htm, gives a complete tutorial on radar ornithology, and I highly recommend visiting it. As the site explains, "NEXRAD is a Doppler radar, and it can track . . . aerial biota such as insects, birds and bats . . .

"After sunset the surface of the earth cools, and columns

> of warm, rising air dissipate. As a result turbulence aloft decreases and the atmosphere becomes increasingly more stable. Many species of birds migrate at night to reap these energy-saving benefits.
>
> "On a typical evening during spring and fall migration, birds often depart 30 to 45 minutes after sunset . . . Birds migrating at night are typically most dense around 1,500 feet above the ground."

The tutorial shows how to interpret radar images and determine the density of the migration on any given night. There's a bit of an art to it, but what an amazing tool!

Recreation in the Northwoods

A 1999 DNR publication, "Preserving Wisconsin's Outdoor Legacy" (#WM-273), is an attempt to collect the existing data on the economic value of fish- and wildlife-based outdoor recreation in Wisconsin and put it all in one source. This document provides a compelling case for the importance of outdoor recreation in Wisconsin, and as such should be required reading for all chambers of commerce, media, resource managers, and associated private businesses.

Looking at the big picture, the annual economic impact of the fish and wildlife recreation industry in Wisconsin is over six billion dollars, and the industry employs nearly 86,000 people. Over 1.7 million state residents participate in fish- and wildlife-associated recreation. Non-residents flock to our state too, for wildlife-related recreation. Four hundred thousand come just to watch wildlife, and Wisconsin sells the second highest number of non-resident fishing licenses in the nation.

The question is what do people do when they are "recreating" in Wisconsin? The answers should guide us in management of our resources, as well as in the development of our businesses and services. The extensive scope of the publication allows me to only quote a few of the statistics:

More than 1.6 million Wisconsin residents 16 years and older actively participated in wildlife watching activities—more than any other outdoor activity.

Wisconsinite participation in outdoor recreation activities breaks down as follows:

- 71% WALKING FOR PLEASURE
- 58% PICNICKING
- 52% BICYCLING
- 45% FISHING
- 42% MOTORBOATING
- 41% DAY HIKING
- 38% BIRDWATCHING/NATURE STUDY
- 24% TENT CAMPING
- 22% HUNTING
- 17% CANOEING
- 15% SNOWMOBILING
- 14% CROSS-COUNTRY SKIING
- 13% ATV RIDING
- 7% JET SKIING

Closer to home, a survey of northern state forest use found that the most common activities of visitors included:

- 81% HIKING
- 59% FISHING
- 58% CAMPING
- 54% BOATING
- 35% BIKING
- 20% HUNTING
- 14% SNOWMOBILING
- 13% CROSS-COUNTRY SKIING
- 8% ATV RIDING
- 1% JET SKIING

Red Squirrels Budding

Ada Karow from Lac du Flambeau called me one mid-March to ask if I had ever watched red squirrels eat the buds on maple trees, as she had done that afternoon. I hadn't, though I knew red squirrels pierce the bark of maples with their teeth and then drink the sap. I was curious whether the literature said anything about squirrels eating buds, so I turned to Hartley Jackson's *Mammals of Wisconsin* and learned that red squirrels consume the "soft inner bark and buds, blossoms, and tender leaves of several kinds of trees, particularly maples, aspens, willows, and birches."

Most of us tend to think of squirrels as seed eaters, but given that seeds aren't available year 'round, it only makes sense that they would eat other things. In fact, their menu may include some animals such as the young of birds and rabbits! Given the wide array of foods that they eat, the red squirrel can't be limited to the seed eater category, but falls instead into the category of an "opportunistic feeder."

Snow Depth, Rough-legged Hawks, and Arctic Owls

In March of 1999, I drove a crew of birders from our area up to Duluth to find Arctic owls. There we met Laura Erickson, an author, broadcaster, and ornithologist from Duluth, whose knowledge of northeastern Minnesota we hoped would lead us to the owls. Unfortunately, very few Arctic owls (snowy, great gray, boreal, and hawk owls) had been seen that winter, and we were unable to locate any. Much of Canada had experienced a relatively mild winter like ours, offering little incentive for the owls to move south in search of prey.

Instead, we found rough-legged hawks in all the traditional places that the Arctic owls are typically found. Along one five-mile stretch of road, we saw 13 rough-legs hunting the nearly snowless fields along the highway. Usually, these arctic tundra nesters winter in southern Wisconsin, but in light snowfall years, they often remain further north in significant numbers.

Rough-legs eat rodents in open grasslands and croplands, so we very seldom see them in the forested areas of the Northwoods. Snowy, hawk, and great gray owls occupy the same general open habitat, but they can capture rodents within a snowpack. Great grays can hear and locate a mouse through 18 inches of snow and plunge through the snow for the capture. Little snow yields few owls, but as is the case with the natural world, one species' loss is another's gain, and in this particular year the snowless habitat niche was filled by rough-legs.

As hawks go, rough-legs are easily identified. The tail is mostly white with a broad black band or bands toward the tip. Overhead, look for a dark patch at the bend of their wings, or "elbows," and a black belly-band. Like many hawks, they have different color phases. The dark color phase shows less white on the tail and a much darker overall body.

Our journey also netted us boreal chickadees, a northern shrike, gray jays, common redpolls, bald eagle, and what we think were lynx tracks along a back road we were scouting.

Salmonella Outbreak

In 2000, redpolls were found dead or dying in some northern Wisconsin counties, and state wildlife health officials were urging people to clean their feeders in order to prevent disease from spreading among birds. Dead redpolls also were discovered in Alaska, North Dakota, Minnesota, Quebec, New York, Virginia, and North Carolina. Locally, Marge Gibson at the Raptor Education Group in Antigo received calls for several weeks concerning dying siskins and redpolls.

In 2006, our area was hit again by salmonella poisoning, though this time in the months of January and February.

The disease was likely spread by contact between birds, especially where they were concentrated at feeders. Disease can also be transmitted through droppings onto birdseed that is eaten by birds using the same feeders.

Feeders should be cleaned with a solution of one part bleach to 10 parts water. The entire surface of the feeder should be scrubbed or brushed. Additionally, accumulations of discarded seed and droppings under feeders should be removed.

If people see dead or sick redpolls, they should keep their cats and dogs indoors, since with certain strains of salmonella the animals could become infected through eating affected birds.

Dead birds should be removed from feeder areas. People can pick the birds up by using a plastic bag to avoid direct contact with the bird; it's important to wash carefully after handling potentially diseased birds.

March is a good time to get out and clean those feeders!

Saw-Whet Owls

Over the years, I've received many phone calls in early March from people seeking help in identifying an incessant soft "beeping" they hear at night, a sound many liken to the slow-ringing, bell-like alarm that's rigged up to dump trucks to warn people when they back up. The sound is the male saw-whet owl's territorial and mating song, which has been variously likened to bells, whistles, metallic sounds, or to a UFO landing in your backyard. The saw-whet's name comes from a part of its song that I've never heard: rasping notes that come usually in threes, and apparently sound like a saw being filed—*Skreigh-aw, skreigh-aw, skreigh-aw.*

I've never tried whistling back to them, but the literature says they will often respond by flying right to you, by tooting back, or by making an array of sounds not found on any recordings. They may produce sounds like the wail of a screech owl, or catlike whines or yelps, or even notes like those of a barred owl.

Most saw-whets migrate, unlike barred and great horned owls, which stay the winter. The male saw-whets return in March and try to lay claim to territories through their songs. I suppose whoever drones on the longest wins. The females may not return until much later, but their reappearance and acceptance of mates brings all the tooting to a rapid end. Soon they're setting up households in tree cavities, often in the old nesting holes of a flicker.

Saw-whets typically roost at night in dense conifers, low and deep in the branches. If approached, they are reputed to be as calm as little Buddhas, watching your advance with little fear.

Science and Spirit

Judging by all the political controversy over the teaching of evolution in schools, it certainly seems that science and spirit are in conflict. But to my mind they aren't at all. Both scientific study and spiritual endeavor seek the same things—answers to how and why life exists, and how we are to lead our lives in the greatest balance. I find them to be supportive of one another, rather than antagonistic. I want science to explain as much as it can, so I can better understand how humankind and Earth's incredible array of life work together. Science has swept away a tremendous amount of fear and myth over the last few centuries, so we no longer beat drums to scare away the dragon devouring the sun when an eclipse occurs, like the Chinese once did. Science enlightens us, as does faith. They meld together like the mind and heart, each needing the other.

gray jay

Both science and spirit allow me to experience my life as a joyful seeking, as an extraordinary mystery, and both provide me with revelations now and again to light the way among a host of small understandings.

So often in life we seem to need to push something down in order to raise something else up. I strongly believe that we don't need to put science down in order to feel a deep spirituality, nor do we need to dismiss faith in order to look at the world scientifically. I may well be wrong, as I often am, but I firmly believe we need to honor both science and spirit, and be deeply grateful for both.

In his book *Skeptics and True Believers*, physicist Chet Raymo writes, "It seems to me that science is part of the traditional religious quest for the God of creation … We are at our human best as creatures of the shore, with one foot on the hard ground of fact and one foot in the sea of mystery."

For Raymo, and for me, science is not spiritually destructive. It illuminates the world and inspires awe, praise, and reverence. It seeks truths and changes as knowledge and insight expand, much as we all do in our daily lives and in our spiritual quests. When asked if he was religious, Albert Einstein once replied, "Try and penetrate with our limited means the secrets of nature and you will find that, behind all the discernible concatenations, there remains something subtle, intangible, and inexplicable. Veneration for this force beyond anything that we can comprehend is my religion."

Changes in North American Spring

Green-up begins in late March, when the world seems to burst out in every shade of green imaginable. Numerous regional studies have shown that many spring events like plant leafing and blooming, arrival of migrating birds, and insect hatching are occurring earlier in response to warming temperatures, especially since the mid-1950s. But since regional studies present an uneven picture of events on a hemispheric scale, we need studies that can evaluate changes on the largest stage possible.

Mark Schwartz, a professor of geography at UW Milwaukee, published a paper in 2006 in the journal *Global Change Biology* entitled, "Onset of spring starting earlier across the Northern Hemisphere." Results of his research confirmed a nearly universal earlier onset of spring warmth, as well as earlier last spring-freeze dates across most of the temperate Northern Hemisphere. His data showed that first leaf dates (measured by the time of shrub budburst and the first greening of lawns) are getting earlier in nearly all parts of the Northern Hemisphere. The average rate of change from 1955-

2002 was about 1.2 days per decade, or nearly a week earlier since 1955.

The length of the freeze period—the number of days between the first autumn freeze and the last spring freeze—also decreased at a rate of 1.5 days per decade, amounting to over a week since 1955.

The agricultural implications are many, in particular for farmers who must contend with a changing growing season length, as well as earlier dates for planting and harvesting.

The implications for the Northwoods are also many. If plants are budding and blooming earlier, it creates a ripple effect through the ecosystem, as insects adjust their life cycles to earlier plant growth, and concurrent adjustments are made up the food web. Some species will respond favorably and prosper, while others will respond poorly and be at a competitive disadvantage.

So, spring is coming earlier. Given most people's cabin fever in March, I suspect that sounds pretty good, as long as we don't consider the ecological implications.

Snow Fleas

Every March, warm weather brings millions of barely visible snow fleas to the top of the snowpack, where they pepper the snow in such numbers that it boggles the mind. It's as if the waiter at a fancy restaurant, the one who comes by with the pepper grinder, went mad—"You want pepper?! I'll give you pepper!!!!!"

Less than an eighth-inch long, with six legs and no wings, snow fleas have nothing whatsoever to do with flea-dom, though they hop around a bit like fleas. They actually belong to a group of arthropods called springtails, their distinguishing feature being a springing organ on their hind end that is folded up and held by a hook mechanism. When the hook releases, the spring propels them upward and outward away from danger, though I'm not quite sure what dangers lurk in the minds of springtails. Given that they can't control the distance of their flight or the direction, they may fling themselves just as likely into greater danger as find an escape route.

Snow fleas play a beneficial role in recycling organic matter and building soil, and they aren't harmful in any manner to people or pets. They live in the soil, in decaying leaves, under bark, and in decaying logs, and feed on microscopic algae, fungi, and decaying plant matter. They seem to like maple sugar, and often are found swarming around sap buckets.

Native to every continent in the world, snow fleas have been found on Alaskan glaciers half a mile from the edge of the ice and ground where they feed on the pollen of trees and the spores of ferns. You can find springtails on top of pond ice and even on icicles. One source I have says that springtails often migrate over several days on top of the snow, moving a short distance en masse to a better feeding area. Hard to band them though, so I'm not sure how you tell if the one you saw yesterday is the same one you're seeing today.

What motivates them to leap, and what purpose it serves, remain a mystery. Some believe that since they feed in wet areas, the springing helps them escape the trap that water represents. Equally mysterious are their appearances and disappearances in these isolated patches. They appear to burrow directly through the snow, and often radiate out from tree trunks. Why they hang out on the surface of the snow and how they keep from freezing are also mysteries.

Snow fleas would appear to make a good meal for something, and in fact, gray jays have been observed scooping up snow laden with snow fleas, presumably eating them. But whether other species make use of this bounty is unknown.

Earliest Nesters

As cold as it can be in March, great horned owls are currently sitting on nests. One is tempted to classify them as crazy fools, but after 10,000 years or so of adapting to northern winters, I suspect they know what they're doing. Wisconsin has three verified reports of great horned owls laying eggs before the end of January, but mid-February is more common. Gray jays are next in the nesting line. These birds have been seen building nests as early as late February.

Mary and I often watch eagles carrying sticks to their nest across the river from our house as early as mid-February. So eagles are at work, too, and egg incubation may occur as early as March 15, though typically they won't be sitting on eggs until April 1.

The Eyes Have It

Owls see differently than most birds. Most predators, and in particular owls, have large eyes that are set in front of their skull, unlike smaller prey species like songbirds, whose eyes are located on each side of their head. Side-mounted eyes give songbirds greater peripheral vision, a necessary life-saving function with predators around.

Because each eye's field of view overlaps that of the other eye, an owl's forward-facing eyes give it binocular vision and greater depth perception at the expense of seeing to the sides. In this respect, its eyes are much like ours. However, an owl's eyes are fixed and immovable in their sockets, and thus owls can only see a 70-degree field of view. They compensate by swiveling their head to see from side to side, a function they have evolved by growing extra vertebrae in their neck. These vertebrae allow them to rapidly rotate their heads a full 270 degrees.

Woodcocks occupy the opposite end of the spectrum. Their eyes are set high and back on their head, in the best position for watching for aerial predators while they are head down probing the mud for insects. Woodcocks actually have better binocular vision to their rear than to the front.

An American bittern has eyes set so low on the sides of its head that it can stretch its neck straight up in a defensive posture and still see directly ahead.

Birds like pigeons and coots walk or swim with their heads moving back and forth. Shorebirds often bob their heads up and down or teeter back and forth while standing. Still other birds stretch up and down while perched on a branch. All of these behaviors are aimed at improving their vision. These birds all have minimal binocular vision, and their movements provide them with different views that increase their depth perception and aid them in estimating distance. A robin cocking its head at different angles before grasping a worm is simply trying to get the exact three-dimensional position of the worm.

Tundra Swans

Tundra swans typically migrate through our area in mid-March. Although most tundras typically fly over our area without stopping, a number of flocks do stop over on the Wisconsin River just south of McNaughton.

They typically fly high in a V-shaped formation, calling while beating their wings slowly and shallowly. Listen for their high-pitched, quavering, somewhat goose-like notes. One ornithologist says, "The talkativeness of these birds is one of their most striking traits—on water and also flying. A large flock up high sounds to me like a mob approaching the city gates or the castle."

Turtles on Ice

Around spring equinox, I often wonder what might be stirring in the minds of hibernating animals. I remember one early winter day seeing two large snapping turtles through the clear ice of the Turtle-Flambeau Flowage. They were close to shore and lying in the sediment in about a foot of water. I marveled then at the way air-breathing reptiles can lie buried in mud for six months of the year and still emerge hale and hearty after ice-out.

Even more intriguing are the hatchlings, which emerge in September only to head for water and burial in mud for the first half-year of their lives. Bernd Heinrich, a well-known naturalist and author, relates how one September he gathered three snapper hatchlings as they popped out of their nest in his neighbor's gravel driveway. He placed them in an outdoor aquarium along with an array of minnows, various aquatic insects, and tadpoles. By early December, the aquarium had iced over, and the little snappers had still never eaten.

The turtles appeared dead, but when in late December he brought the aquarium inside and scooped the ice off the top, the turtles became lively and fed voraciously. Presumably, if he hadn't brought the hatchlings inside, they would have remained inactive until the spring, and emerged even more voracious.

Every other newborn animal I know keeps its parents incessantly busy feeding it. But snappers apparently can begin life by fasting for nearly eight months.

Even more remarkably, in early life they're on an oxygen-fast. All turtles must breathe air, but Northwoods snappers go through the entire winter without taking a single breath.

Two recent studies offer some insight into the hibernation physiology of turtles. One was a study of map turtles in Vermont's Lake Champlain. The researchers equipped the map turtles with radio transmitters and found that in autumn they moved three miles up into the Lamoille River. They then piled on top of one another in a deep depression in the river bottom, apparently to escape the current.

The biologists returned monthly to the communal site and using a chain saw, cut through the ice and dove into the water to bring the turtles back to the surface. They took blood samples to measure concentrations of oxygen and carbon dioxide, acidity, and lactate, and basically found that the turtles somehow breathed oxygen all winter despite the fact they were unable to use their lungs. The researchers were not able to determine how they accomplished any oxygen intake, but they did observe that the turtles all rested with their heads and legs fully extended, presumably exposing as much of their skin as possible to take up dissolved oxygen from the water. The turtles remained in their communal hibernaculum for five months until the ice melted, then returned to Lake Champlain to spend the summer.

Another study brought painted turtles into a laboratory, sealed them into an aquarium, and then bubbled the water with nitrogen gas to drive off all the dissolved oxygen. These turtles still survived for nearly four months.

The story gets even more complicated. To add to their winter oxygen stress, painted and snapping turtles typically bury themselves in mud, thus depriving themselves of the dissolved oxygen that is present in the water, but found in very limited concentrations in the mud. The researchers speculate that they bury themselves to reduce predation by raccoons and others as the ice goes off.

As far as I can determine, no one really knows how wintering turtles survive and why they act as they do. Heinrich asks the question, "What is death to a turtle?" For half their lives, turtles live under ice, buried in mud, not breathing, not moving, and likely living without any heart activity. In the spring, they rise to the surface, presumably take a few breaths, and swim away, as turtles have done for millions of years. Spring brings many resurrections, but the rebirth of turtles may be one of the most remarkable.

Vernal Equinox

The official fanfare for spring begins around March 20. The equinox marks the day when the sun sails along the equator and thus rises in the due east while setting in the due west. This is one of the first times since September 26 that our day will be longer than our night, which is worthy of a deep sigh and enthusiastic applause.

The equinox doesn't mean spring is around the corner. The equinox just means we can see the snow that remains for longer periods every day. As in many inaugurations, the new office holder takes a month or more to figure out what he or she is supposed to be doing. Still, the first robins and red-winged blackbirds commonly appear on the equinox, so keep an eye out for these most welcome harbingers.

Sandhill Surprise

Rolf Ethun watched a sandhill crane flying across Hiawatha Lake near Boulder Junction on March 23, 1997. The crane was heading south at the time, possibly having seen that fierce weather was in store for it if it remained. Sandhills do return when the snow is still on the ground, often in the first week of April, but Rolf's sighting is the earliest I have ever heard of for this area.

Observing cranes is a time-honored activity. Our daughter Callie loves Greek history and pulled this quote from Aristotle in his *History of Animals*, written nearly 2,400 years ago: "Many indications of intelligence are given by cranes. They will fly to a great distance and high up in the air, to command an extensive view; if they see clouds and signs of bad weather they fly down again and remain still. They, furthermore, have a leader in their flight, and patrols that scream on the confines of the flock so as to be heard by all. When they settle down, the main body go to sleep with their heads under their wings, standing first on one leg and then on the other, while their leader, with his head uncovered, keeps a sharp look out, and when he sees anything of importance signals it with a cry."

Many sandhills return to southern and central Wisconsin in early March. In 2002, I read a wonderful crane-related e-mail from a birder driving through Chicago in mid-March. He wrote: "While traveling home from Jamestown, NY, today, I thought the road miles were getting to me when I saw huge flocks of sandhill cranes kettling over the city of Chicago. My first thought was that these birds were looking for the marshes that used to be there. At any rate, it was an incredible sight and I could actually see some of the crazy drivers looking up at the swarming cranes!"

Home Is Where the Nest Is

"Location, location, location," goes the cry of realtors everywhere, particularly in our lake-rich area. But migrating birds understood this concept long before humans put property up for sale. Most birds have been proponents of private property for eons, though a number of species have also advanced the radical agenda of communal living. Whether private or communal, property values will dramatically escalate for the avian population in the next two months. Winter property that wasn't worth a song will now be worth a choir.

Where a bird constructs its nest depends on available building materials, whether the site can be heated by the sun or cooled by winds and shade, how defensible the site is, and its accessibility. For example, eagles build their nests typically in a crotch of a tall pine tree about a quarter of the way down from the top, presumably because they want the following:

- Some cooling shade on their chicks to prevent overheating
- Branches strong enough to hold a nest that can weigh a ton
- Clear access for landing and take-off
- Enough height to get immediate lift without flapping
- A site well off the ground to limit mammalian predators

Every bird has its own "dream" house site and construction. Loons prefer islands to lessen predation, and they must nest right on the edge of water, in part because they walk so poorly. Their no-setback rule also permits them immediate escape into the water in case of attack. Raven nests typically contain deer, bear, hare, or moose hair to cushion and insulate the eggs since the female is often incubating in subzero temperatures in March. Cliff swallows need a continuous source of mud during their nesting season in order to build and repair their precipice-hugging structures.

Winter wrens must love a good windstorm, because they need a site with blown-down old trees in order to build their nests deep in the tipped-up root mass. Their nests are beautifully camouflaged with moss and evergreen twigs, and have only a quarter-inch opening for access, so the winter wren seldom has to fear predation. The male does all the building of the nest, and often builds several others in different sites, all of which are used to attract a female. She chooses the best nest, signifying her choice by adding some nest lining to her new home.

Brown creepers choose one of the more remarkable but practical kinds of nesting sites. They build under the loose flaking bark of dead trees—most often balsam firs. The outside bark must keep the nests dry while hiding the nests from sight.

Birds nest in a host of different sites and build a broad variety of structures because diversity increases the chances of survival. If birds chose similar nesting sites, then predators would have little trouble finding them. As it is, chipmunks and red squirrels are estimated to raid more than 60 percent of songbird nests in many locations. Ingenuity in design and placement are at a premium if birds don't want their chicks to become breakfast for another animal.

So returning birds lead a precarious life. As "your" birds return, give some thought to what each species requires for nesting, and see if your property provides these essentials.

Skunk Cabbage

Sometime in March, our first spring flower blooms—the homely but remarkable skunk cabbage, a common resident of rich wetlands throughout the state. Its rank, unpleasant odor doesn't lend itself to poetry, but its ability to generate its own heat and melt the snow around it always sparks scientific interest. The skunk cabbage is one of the few plants in the world to utilize cellular respiration to generate heat, making it possible for the plant to be as much as 30°F warmer than the ground and air around it. When the temperatures warm to above freezing, the flower can produce enough heat to keep the enclosed and insulated flower near 72°F.

The "skunky" smell and mottled red exterior of the skunk cabbage gives it the appearance of rotting meat, which is attractive to early pollinating flies, beetles, and even mosquitoes, all of which inadvertently transfer pollen from plant to plant. Some researchers believe the insects may be attracted to the warmth of the flower as much as the carrion mimicry.

All of the super-early flowers, birds, and insects gain a competitive edge over their cronies by being the first residents of the spring, but the risk is great. March will always be the siren singing, the master beguiler, the seductress. The survivors of her lure will be those with adaptations to cold or those with an escape clause in their spring contract.

Window Treatments

Migrating birds are returning, and one of the issues that always comes up is how to prevent birds from knocking themselves silly or killing themselves when they fly into windows. The number of birds that die by flying into buildings and/or windows is estimated in the hundreds of millions nationwide, so this is not a small problem!

What to do? The Wisconsin Humane Society offers a number of anti-bird-collision window treatments that appear very promising. One product is called "CollidEscape," an easy-to-apply window film that saves birds' lives by reducing reflections on the outside of the glass. The film can be cut with scissors, is easily removed, lasts for years, and is transparent so you can still see out your window. You may have seen this material on the outside of buses with images printed on it.

Another option is an easily mounted temporary black fiberglass bird screen. These screens come with a black plastic top and bottom frame that mount to the outside of your window with suction cups. The birds simply bounce off the screen or avoid it altogether.

Two other products may help as well. You can purchase static cling window appliqués that simply attach to your window. They come in various images like chickadees and hummingbirds. Another product is a holographic plastic film strip that flutters and shimmers in the wind to repel birds.

Check the Humane Society's Website: www.wihumane.org. Click on "wildlife," then "bird collision prevention."

Another solution is to utilize white or light-colored window shades, blinds, or drapes. When these are drawn, they eliminate much of the mirror effect or transparency of windows. The downside, of course, is that you have windows so you can look outside. When you're at work or on vacation, however, drawing the curtains is an excellent practice.

The last option is to tilt your windows down when installing them. Tilting the glass in a window causes them to reflect the ground rather than possible shelter and escape routes for fleeing birds.

Rather than altering your windows, you could instead consider altering the placement of your bird feeders. Bird feeders placed closer than three feet to windows can reduce fatal collisions, because birds don't have an adequate distance in which to reach high flight velocity. On the other hand, placing the feeders more than 30 feet from a window will also reduce window collision risk because, at that distance, birds are more likely to recognize that the reflected image is part of a house and are less likely to fly toward it for safety.

If you do have a bird bop itself on your window, and the bird is living but lying dazed, you can protect it by placing it in a cardboard shoebox with ventilation holes until it has a chance to get its wits back. In a few minutes, open the lid outside and release the bird. Otherwise, birds left to recover lying below your feeders are often the targets of local predators. That's not all bad—predators have young to feed, too—but sometimes it's quite satisfying to be able to briefly hold a bird and examine its markings, as well as give it a chance to live.

Nest Sites of Wintering Birds

Not many bird species are foolhardy enough to spend the winter months in northern Wisconsin. The question often comes up: Among the species that most of us see at our feeders during the winter, which ones are permanent residents that nest here, and which are visitors from the far northern boreal forest or tundra of Canada?

Let's just look at the finch family. Often the most numerous birds at our feeders—pine grosbeaks and common redpolls—will return to Canada sometime in March, or perhaps April. Pine grosbeaks, despite their name, nest in the spruce and fir boreal forests of Canada, and do not usually nest in pines. Only two records of pine grosbeaks nesting in Wisconsin exist, one from 1890 and the other from 1940.

Common redpolls are anything but common in Wisconsin during the summer. They breed very far north in the arctic tundra scrub, nesting in dense low shrubs. Redpolls at our feeders in March may travel 1,000 miles north of our area before settling down for the breeding season. Their winter invasions suggest they follow an every-other-year cycle.

Crossbills, both red and white-winged, rarely remain in Wisconsin. Crossbills are nomads of the spruce woods, wandering in large flocks throughout the boreal forests of North America. Nesting can occur in any season, even winter, and just about anywhere in conifers, depending on the abundance of seed cones.

The breeding range of purple finches extends northward to central Canada and as far south as central Wisconsin. So some purple finches will migrate through, while others will stay and raise young.

The house finch, native to the Southwest, now nests throughout the United States, refusing to breed only in southern Florida and along the coast of Texas. Some may migrate to areas just a little north of us, but most house finches at your feeders are likely permanent residents. The first nesting record of house finches in Wisconsin occurred in 1986, so they are truly newcomers to our area. They may be competing with purple finches and reducing their presence.

Evening grosbeaks nest mostly in Canada, but do reach the southernmost edge of their breeding range in northern Wisconsin. Not until 1964 was a nest actually located in Wisconsin, but summer records are now relatively common. We've had a pair nesting somewhere nearby and bringing their young to our feeders for many summers. Evening grosbeaks were originally known only in the western states, and were virtually unknown east of the Great Lakes before the 1890s. They now breed throughout New England and Quebec.

Pine siskins are relatively similar in their nesting pattern to evening grosbeaks, reaching their southernmost breeding range in northern Wisconsin. The first known active nest wasn't found until 1948 in Iron County. Siskins remain uncommon breeders in the Northwoods, nesting most commonly in conifers and mixed woods. However, we have them nesting around us, as evidenced by their presence throughout the summer. Like redpolls, they seem to irrupt in large winter numbers on an every-other-year basis.

American goldfinches nest into southern Canada, as far south as Georgia, and as far west as California. We may have some goldfinches migrate through in the spring, but many are permanent residents. Their winter numbers seem to be the inverse of the redpolls. Whenever we have good redpoll years, the goldfinches are down, and vice versa. Why this relationship exists is a good question with no answers that have been discovered.

Rapturous Contemplation

On the first day of my astronomy classes, I tell my students, 'This course will not help you make a buck.' Few students run for the door. What draws them to astronomy is not greed but a longing of the soul to know its place in the universe. Nothing practical, nothing that will help pay the bills. Just a long interval of rapturous contemplation of the objects of the soul's longing.

—Chet Raymo, *Natural Prayers*

Bird Divorce

Given the flow of bird migration, pair bonding, and territorial establishment that begins in March, it's important to note that there is divorce in the bird world. Actually, only a few animals divorce, because only a few form pair bonds in the first place. Only around five percent of mammals, for instance, establish pair bonds, including a few species of mice. The human divorce rate is somewhere between 40 and 50 percent, so we're no model of perfect pair bonding.

Among those animals that do form pair bonds, most experience some divorce. In the bird world, even swans divorce, though only at a 10 percent rate for mute swans, while Berwick's swans almost never split apart. The masked booby, on the other hand, has a divorce rate of nearly 50 percent, much like humans. However, if you see masked boobies in the Northwoods, you better check the octane in what you're drinking.

Some scientists object to the anthropomorphic term "divorce," preferring synonyms such as "breakage," "dissolution," or my favorite, "nonretainment." While these terms offer a certain academic ring, I'm not sure saying that my first wife and I nonretained each other accurately describes the event. Or saying that today I'm happily retained by Mary does justice to the commitment.

Some bird divorces get nasty, but spotted sandpipers put a unique twist on the "other woman" theme. The female keeps a harem of males in her territory, the males being objects of desire to other females who try to take over the stable of males. Researchers have watched the ensuing fights between the females result in broken legs and pecked-out eyes. The males sit by and watch the females battle each other without raising a wing to help, apparently because they realize it's in their best interest to belong to the strongest female.

Ornithologists have described at least 11 hypotheses explaining why birds divorce. One theory makes particular sense to me—the "keeping company" hypothesis. The idea is that if a bird couple keeps each other company all year long, the birds are more likely to stay together for life. Those species that stay together for only a brief courtship find it much easier to dispense with loyalty, and typically seek new horizons.

The moral to the story? Spend time with your mate, keep one another company, and you'll outlast the average masked booby.

Solar Eclipse

Solar eclipses occur when the moon comes in direct alignment between the earth and the sun, but since the moon is a relatively small sphere, it casts a shadow only 100 miles wide on the earth. Only those observers along this very narrow track are able to view a total solar eclipse.

A total solar eclipse took place on March 29, 2006, but wasn't visible in North America. Totality began at sunrise over eastern Brazil, headed northeast over the Atlantic Ocean, hit land in western Africa, swept over Ghana, Togo, Benin, Nigeria, Niger, Chad, and

Libya, leapt over the Mediterranean, then tracked through central Turkey, northwestern Georgia, and across Kazakhstan and Mongolia before sunset called a halt to the whole shebang.

On average, any specific spot on Earth is treated to a total solar eclipse only once in 360 years, and the phenomenon lasts only seven minutes! The entire United States and Canada won't experience a total solar eclipse again until 2017. The last time the moon's shadow fell upon us was in 1979.

The earliest recorded solar eclipse probably occurred on October 22, 2137 B.C. The event was recorded in the ancient Chinese chronicle Shu Ching some 2,000 years before the Greeks learned to predict eclipses. The story goes that two royal Chinese astronomers, Hsi and Ho, were so drunk that they failed to warn the people of the eclipse, and the people rioted, beating drums to frighten away the dragon that was devouring the sun.

Ancient Chinese law didn't look kindly upon such irresponsibility, and apparently the two happy astronomers were hung, not just hung over.

Lunar Eclipse

A full eclipse of the moon can only occur when the earth drifts to a spot exactly between the sun and the full moon, and casts its large shadow onto the moon, a phenomenon that usually occurs twice a year. During a total lunar eclipse, the full moon's glow can decline to one ten-thousandth of its normal brightness, depending on the amount of atmospheric dust, clouds, and pollution impeding the view from the earth at that moment. A Mexican volcanic eruption in 1982 bathed the atmosphere in so much dust that the moon became hard to find.

Eclipse dates have been predictable for many centuries. Columbus and his crew were stranded on the island of Jamaica in 1503, his ships damaged beyond repair. The situation was grave because the native Arawak Indians had finally wised up and declared they would no longer trade their food for useless trinkets. Columbus knew that a lunar eclipse was going to occur on February 29, 1504, so he scavenged food for his crew until that day and announced that God was so angry with the Arawaks for the treatment of his crew that he was removing the moon as a sign of his wrath. According to Columbus's diary, the Arawaks fell for the ruse, promising to provide all the food the sailors needed if God would return the moon to them. Thus the sailors' starvation was prevented, buying them enough time to be rescued and taken back to Europe.

History might well have been written differently if the Arawaks had understood the timing and nature of eclipses.

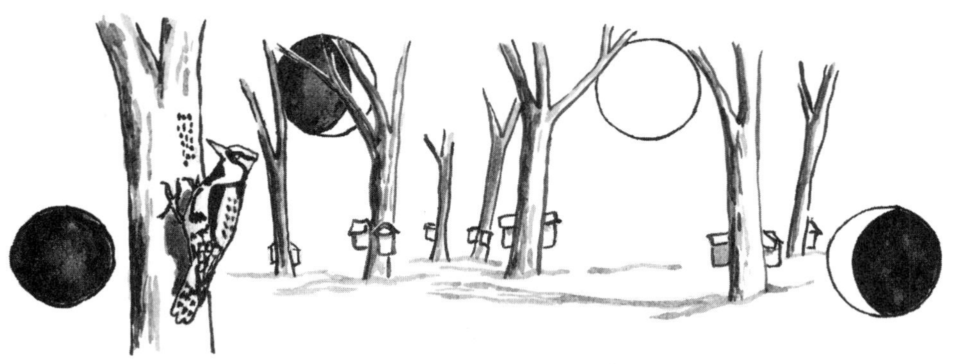

April

April may be the most under-appreciated month in the Northwoods. Many folks close down their businesses and take off for points south, expressing great glee in missing the mud season. But spring often arrives at warp speed, and the vacationers miss its resurrection. From a birder's perspective, April is glorious. One nesting species after another returns and sings its heart out. The more northern nesting species pass through too, often stopping to visit awhile and grace us with their presence.

In 2002, April threw just about every kind of weather punch at us that it could muster. Mary and I were crust skiing on two feet of snow in the Powell Marsh on April 6, and a week later we were walking the snowless dikes counting birds. In what seemed a blink of the eye, winter passed into spring, with temperatures reaching 80°F on April 15 and 16. What an incredible transition!

The rapid snowmelt led to intense flooding in the U.P. of Michigan and some of the northern counties of Wisconsin. The ice went off many lakes around April 17. We had tornadoes touch down in the Lakeland area the next day.

By April 21, it was snowing again with 3 to 4 inches of accumulation! On April 23 and 24, we had lows of 24°F and 21°F respectively. The next day it snowed, as it did on April 27, 28, and 29. It seems April got its role reversed with January and February in 2002.

Crazy stuff for humans to experience, but doubly crazy for plants and animals that can't hide behind windows and sit beside wood stoves.

The Pleasures of Counting Cranes

The annual Midwest Sandhill Crane Count takes place in mid-April. I have coordinated the count for Iron and Vilas Counties for over a decade, and the process is simple. Every counter is assigned an area to observe from sun-up until about 7:30 a.m. Counting is done visually or by listening for the unmistakably loud, rattling calls.

Why bother to count cranes? Aldo Leopold, as usual, said it best: "The ultimate value in these marshes is wildness, and the crane is wildness incarnate."

The enjoyment of the count stems as much from hearing and seeing a host of other birds and mammals, as it does from finding cranes. Anything can happen on an early April morning in Wisconsin, and often it does. Being in a wild marsh, river, or lake before daylight is a multi-faceted gift. Leopold wrote: "It is a fact, patent both to my dog and myself, that at daybreak I am the sole owner of all the acres I can walk over. It is not only boundaries that disappear, but also the thought of being bounded. Expanses unknown to deed or map are known to every dawn, and solitude, supposed no longer to exist in my county, extends on every hand as far as the dew can reach."

In 2000, our crane counters saw and heard a delightful array of creatures, despite the freezing rain and high winds. Suzanne Brown observed a kestrel, shovelers, scaup, trumpeter swans, a snipe, and a snow bunting, among others, on the Little Turtle Flowage.

In their canoe, Rolf and Winnie Ethun fought the winds on the Turtle-Flambeau Flowage and saw sturgeon jump on three different occasions.

Jim and Karen Cramer scoped the farm fields near Eagle River and found two cranes feeding in the grass among a herd of six deer. They also saw a hen pheasant, a rarity up here, and a herd of 30 domestic buffalo in a field, a rather startling sight in the uncertrain light of a Northwoods dawn. I asked, but they denied having any high-octane substances in their thermos.

Mary and I observed a flock of golden-crowned kinglets, several rough-legged hawks, and a hen turkey on the south end of the Powell Marsh, while Glenn LeFeber and Gail and Jean Wolf took the north end of the Powell and spotted at least 10 cranes, or as many as 20 if their counts weren't duplicates.

The weather was terrible, but, as always on a crane count day, it was a great morning to be out.

Crane Hunting

Countywide meetings of the Wisconsin Conservation Congress take place in April, and one of the many items under consideration in 1998 was a resolution to create a limited hunting season on sandhill cranes. The rationale for hunting sandhills was based on crop damage concerns.

The International Crane Foundation in Baraboo prepared an excellent summary of the issue, suggesting that a limited crane hunt will not solve crop damage problems, and that alternative options exist. To get a copy of this summary, call the ICF at (608) 356-9462, or go to their Website—www.savingcranes.org.

As of 2006, the issue has not rematerialized, but proposals to hunt cranes will likely resurface in the future. Whatever decision is made, it must be biologically based. The International Crane Foundation is an excellent source of the baseline information that will be required in the decision-making process.

Incompetent Bald Eagle Parents

For many years a pair of eagles has nested in the tall red pines on Bob and Carolyn Kovar's property in Manitowish Waters. In the spring of 1997 one of the eagles failed to return, and a new mate filled in the gap. No young, however, were produced that spring. In 1998, Bob watched the eagles frequently leave the nest for up to 10 minutes. Bob wondered two things: How long does it take for an egg to cool and become infertile, and secondly, are some eagles incompetent parents?

I called Bruce Bacon, wildlife manager at the Mercer DNR. Bruce said that early in the incubation period, the eggs can tolerate cold very well, but as incubation progresses and the embryos develop, the eggs become more susceptible to chilling. Short trips off the nest during the day usually don't pose a significant problem because daytime temperatures are usually warm. But leaving the nest at night when the temperature frequently drops below freezing is usually deadly.

Bruce added that there are incompetent parents in the animal world just as there are in the human world. Younger birds tend to be less experienced and do a poorer job, but the good news is that the incompetent parents don't pass on their genes. Bruce noted that if a bird is neglecting its incubation chores, it may be because the eggs have broken due to contaminant loading, predators getting the eggs, or a host of other possibilities. There's really no way to know unless one climbs the nest, and that's verboten at this time of year.

Bald Eagle Weight Lifting

The question often arises as to how much an eagle can carry. Eagles have historically been accused of carrying away everything from sheep to babies. Two studies on the lifting capacity of bald and golden eagles should scientifically put to rest such stories. A golden eagle was launched from a 15-foot high platform with a 10-mph wind blowing. The eagle was put through six flights, each time with a different amount of weight strapped to its legs. With two one-pound weights attached to its legs, the golden flew 162 yards easily. When the weights totaled four pounds, it flew 64 and 58 yards with significant straining. When carrying a total of eight pounds, the eagle "flapped its wings wildly and managed to fly only 10 and 14 yards."

Since eagles only weigh eight to fourteen pounds, with much of their bulk deployed in feathers, it's little wonder that they would have great difficulty carrying anything more than four pounds.

One Skein of Geese

The first flights of geese come through the Northwoods during the last week of March, but most appear in April and are soon sitting on nests. Aldo Leopold wrote, "One swallow does not make a summer, but one skein of geese, clearing the murk of a March thaw, is the spring." Thoreau perceived Canada geese as "the grenadiers of the air ... coming to unlock the fetters of the northern rivers."

Biologist Frank Bellrose summarized the aesthetic implications of the first flight of March geese this way: "For the farmer, the rancher, the city dweller, and the Cree Indian, the northward flight of Canada geese symbolizes spring."

Geese are among the very first nesting birds of the spring, and usually by the first week of May, we begin seeing goslings. In early springs, we sometimes see goslings in the last week of April!

At this time of year, people often see geese lying flat, while thrusting their necks and heads far out in front of them. We've seen this display many times near nest sites. This is a display posture the geese employ to indicate threat or possible aggression if you dare come nearer to the nest. If you see a goose doing this, it's time to move away.

The female does all the incubating of the eggs, while the male stands guard nearby. If she leaves the nest to feed, he'll accompany her to the site and then back to the nest. Once the eggs hatch, the territorial boundaries immediately dissolve. The goslings leave the nest within a day, and the family begins moving together in what becomes a mobile territory.

Geese often build their nests on high ground within 50 yards of water in order to give them a view of the neighborhood. Typical sites include marsh hummocks, beaver lodges, muskrat huts, dikes, and small islands.

It's difficult today to remember that back in 1920 the giant Canada goose was thought to be close to extinction. Extensive management efforts were undertaken to bring Canada geese back by building a system of wildlife refuges and enacting hunting laws. Today, this success story has turned into a contentious issue as populations of geese continue to increase in urban and suburban environments.

It's exceptionally sad that such a beautiful bird has become literally despised by so many people. We're quite fortunate in the Northwoods that geese remain relatively uncommon, though their numbers are increasing. I hope we never lose the feeling of magic when a "V" of geese first reappears in the spring.

Endangered Dancing?

In 2004, I led a short trip to the Crex Meadows Wildlife Area near Grantsburg, Wisconsin, specifically to see the dancing of sharp-tailed grouse. The grouse, unfortunately, were only somewhat cooperative, the males displaying little of their usual testosterone-driven behavioral frenzy. Still, we had some opportunities to observe the males engage in their fascinating array of behaviors such as spinning liking a little wind-up toy, stamping their feet, flutter-jumping, and inflating a violet sac on the sides of their neck while bowing and uttering deep-throated cooing sounds.

Sharp-tails are barely hanging on in Wisconsin. On the nine tracts of land managed for sharpies in the state, the total number of dancing males in 2005 was 114, down from 148 males in 2004. Another 215 dancing males were found by the Sharp-tailed Grouse Society in unmanaged habitats, again a decline from the 243 found in 2004. The overall population has shown a general decline in numbers since 1999.

Only 50,000 acres of Wisconsin's former millions of acres of barrens remain, most in isolated pockets too small for breeding success. When habitat shrinks below a certain critical minimum—believed by biologists to be 10,000 acres—the sharp-tails fail to reproduce.

If you have time in April to see dancing sharp-tails, six of the nine DNR-managed sites offer observation blinds to the public. Contact the DNR for more information.

Celestial Events

- By April 5, we will have 13 hours of daylight; by April 14, 13½ hours; by April 24, 14 hours.
- On April 12, 1961, Uri Gagarin became the first human to travel in space.
- On April 13, 2029, Asteroid 2004-NM4, estimated to be 1,300 feet wide, is expected to sail within 22,600 miles of the earth.
- On April 20, our average low temperature will have climbed back up to 32°F.
- The Lyrid meteor shower occurs around April 22. The meteors emanate from the vicinity of the star Vega almost directly overhead, at a rate of about 10-15 per hour. While this rate is less than overwhelming, the meteors are usually very bright.

Deer Resistant Trees, Shrubs, and Perennials

Deer eat about five pounds of woody browse a day during the winter, prompting one biologist to observe that deer eat cereal four months of the year and the box the other eight. Think how many buds that represents! However, not all trees, shrubs, and perennials on the landscape menu are equally appealing to deer. If you're landscaping and want a plant or two to survive, here's a sample list of native plants that deer typically find less tempting to browse into oblivion. However I must add a disclaimer—a hungry deer is likely to eat just about anything:

Trees

Balsam fir (*Abies balsamea*)
Tamarack (*Larix laricina*)
White spruce (*Picea glauca*)
Black spruce (*Picea mariana*)
Jack pine (*Pinus banksiana*)
Red pine (*Pinus resinosa*)

Shrubs

Winterberry (*Ilex verticillata*)
Juniper (*Juniperus* sp.)
Virginia creeper (*Parthenocissus quinquefiolia*)
Sumac (*Rhus* sp.)
Ninebark (*Physocarpus*)
Spirea sp.
Bunchberry (*Cornus canadensis*)

Perennials

Baneberry, white (*Actaea pachypoda*)
Columbine (*Aquilegia* sp.)
Jack-in-the-pulpit (*Arisaema triphyllum*)
Wild ginger (*Asarum canadense*)
Milkweed (*Asclepias* sp.)
Starflower (*Trientalis borealis*)
Marsh marigold (*Caltha palustris*)

Check with a Northwoods nursery to get a complete list of native plants and advice on repelling deer. Ten-foot-high fences work the best, but then you feel like you're living in a prison camp.

The Early Bird Gets the ...

One of the many species of birds that will soon be returning to its breeding territories in northern Wisconsin is the spotted sandpiper, one of only two shorebirds to nest in our area. The spotted sandpiper has a relatively unique breeding arrangement that would effectively eliminate it from running for political office. Spotted sandpipers engage in complete sex-role reversal, utilizing a mating system referred to as "serial polyandry," or "many males." The females select and defend territories, initiate courtship, and mate with two or more males. The males do most of the nest building, and handle most of the incubation of eggs and brooding of chicks. Once egg-laying occurs, the female abandons the nest and her mate, and begins courtship of another male, a process she may repeat up to four times in a breeding season.

One interesting twist to the tale is that researchers have found that the female can store sperm from a previous mate for up to a month, so she need not mate with a new male in order to lay succeeding clutches of eggs. Thus, the ensuing males may incubate eggs and raise chicks that are not their own. This practice led John Eastman, author of *Birds of Field and Shore*, to observe that, at least for spotted sandpipers, "the early bird gets the sperm."

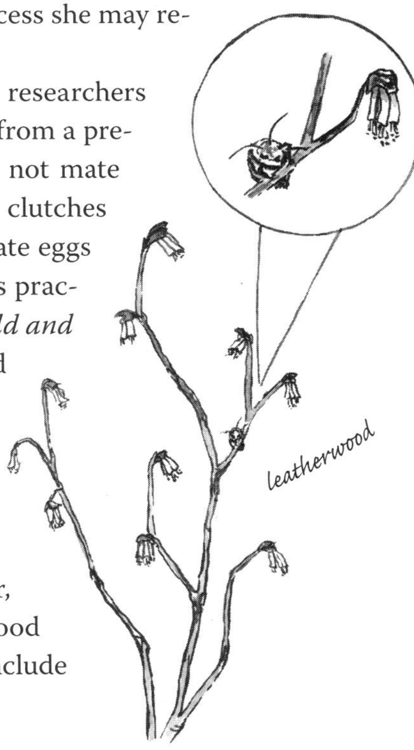

leatherwood

First Flowering Shrubs

The first flowering shrubs of spring typically bloom in early April—tag alder, hazelnut, and pussy willow, with leatherwood hot on their heels. Early flowering trees include aspens, red maple, and silver maple.

One of the earliest small shrubs to flower is leatherwood (*Dirca palustris*). Leatherwood is likely the prettiest of these early flowering shrubs and trees. Its dangling yellow flowers look like tiny hanging lanterns on an oriental shrub.

Leatherwood grows in damp, rich woods, unlike our impoverished pine woods, so one usually needs to locate a good hardwood stand in order to find leatherwood.

Leatherwood's bark is extremely tough and pliable. It was twisted into cordage and baskets by many American Indian tribes—the Iroquois, Menominee, Potawatomi, and Ojibwe among others. Simply strip the bark off with a knife for immediate use as twine, or for an even stronger use, braid it for rope that is as tough as many modern-day materials.

Owl Count

Concern over possible changes in the distribution, population status, and habitat for many species of owls has initiated a new volunteer owl-monitoring project in Minnesota and Wisconsin. This is a collaborative effort involving the Hawk Ridge Bird Observatory in Duluth, the Natural Resources Research Institute, and the Minnesota and Wisconsin DNR. The main owl survey period takes place in March and April along randomly located routes. Volunteers travel the routes at night, stopping and listening for two minutes at 10 sites spaced a mile apart along the route. Each route is run on two different nights to account for variation in how owls might be calling on a given night.

2005 was the first year of the count, and the results were very encouraging. Roger Yaeger and Jim Baughman ran two routes in eastern Vilas County, one near Land O'Lakes and the other near Conover, and the variety in the numbers they found says a lot about the vicissitudes of doing bird surveys. On April 4, they ran the Land O'Lakes route and heard one barred owl. On April 6, they ran the Conover route and heard 7 saw-whet owls and one barred. On April 13, they repeated the Land O'Lakes route and had one barred and 2 saw-whets. All these are respectable numbers, but they hit the jackpot on April 17 when they repeated the Conover route, and heard 6 saw-whets, 2 barreds, 2 great horneds, and one long-eared owl. They also heard one additional saw-whet, one barred, and two more long-eareds, but couldn't add them to the count because they heard the additional birds outside of the prescribed time limits.

What's in a Flood?

Mary and I paddled a section of the flooded Manitowish River on April 13, 2001, thoroughly enjoying the temporary "lakescape." The floodplains were filled with water. We could cut across the ox-bow curves and paddle over the marsh grass to save time, although saving time isn't why either of us paddles rivers. We sighted king-fishers, eagles, common loons, mallards, blue-winged teals, common mergansers, hooded mergansers, ospreys, buffleheads, golden-eyes, black ducks, wood ducks, and heard our first phoebes all along the river. Song sparrows had already taken up residence along many of the shrubby shorelines and were singing in full voice.

Every year, we look forward to the annual spring floods along the Manitowish, knowing that they provide habitat for migrating birds, as well as a host of ecological benefits.

Floods are in the state and national news every spring. Their damage to property can be extensive, and their power is truly awe-some. I don't wish to minimize anyone's personal loss due to floods, but we often think of floods as terrible natural disasters, when it's essential to remember that floods have always existed and actually provide very positive ecological advantages. The difference today is that floods do far more damage than they did historically, and we often have brought the damage on ourselves. When we build on floodplains, drain wetlands, channelize waterways, farm up to the edges of rivers, and pave thousands of acres of land with asphalt, the ensuing result is that we see more floods and experience greater destruction.

Rivers exist primarily to do one thing—drain water to the next lowest point. We run into problems when people don't have enough personal experience with a place to know what to expect from a river's drainage, or they don't pay enough attention to the river until it flows into their basement. Sometimes people want to think that flooding problems have been obviated through technology, but this is not generally the case.

Floods will always be with us. We literally have no choices relative to their existence. Instead of trying to prevent them, we must learn to understand and respect the processes that lead to flooding in order to minimize the economic damage to human society.

So, what do we need to know? Let's start with terminology. Luna Leopold, former chief hydrologist for the U.S. Geological Survey, referred to discharges large enough to overtop riverbanks and flow into the floodplain as "overbank flows." Now I doubt "overbank flow" will soon become part of our everyday lexicon, but what Leopold was trying to point out was the relative frequency of such flows without invoking a word like "flood," which conjures up raging calamity.

Leopold stated that a river channel will have only a moderate or small amount of water flowing in it on most days. Several days in any given year, rain or snowmelt will fill a channel to its peak, but not over its banks. And only approximately twice a year will heavy rains or snowmelt produce enough surface runoff to fill a channel and overflow onto its floodplain.

A great, catastrophic flood typically occurs only once every 50 years. During the enormous floods in the Upper Mississippi River Valley in 1993, the rainfall that fell was so extraordinary that the event will not likely be repeated for another 1,000 years.

The intensity of a rainfall also helps determine peak runoff. An inch of rain over 24 hours is a very different animal than an inch of rain in one hour.

So, "overbank flows" occur every year on rivers. On a river like the Manitowish, which has nearly 90 percent of its shoreline still intact and natural, an overbank flow is seldom a major issue, because the Manitowish still has most of its flood plains intact. These wetlands soak up the flows when the natural capacity of the drainage basin soil is overwhelmed.

The river floods nearly every spring after snowmelt. The difference is that no one has built on the floodplains along the Manitowish. We gaze on the overbank flows with curiosity, wondering where the ducks and geese are, rather than wondering if we will survive the flood.

Bonaparte's Gulls

On a trip I led to Crex Meadows Wildlife Area in April 2004, we spotted 57 total species, one of which was a small flock of Bonaparte's gulls feeding on one of the many flowages. Bonaparte's gulls historically numbered up to 25,000 along the western shore of Lake Michigan in late April, but they now arrive in smaller flocks of a few thousand. In March of 2004, a Milwaukee birder reported more than 1,500 visible from shore on Lake Michigan. On April 29, 2006, an Ashland birder reported more than 2,900 had poured in overnight onto Chequamegon Bay in Lake Superior.

Bonaparte's gulls are easily identified by their completely black head and a long wedge of white on the outside edge of their wings. Several other gulls have black hoods, but only the Bonaparte's and Franklin's gulls are regularly seen passing through the Midwest, and the Bonaparte's are by far the most common.

In the late 1800s, these handsome gulls were shot by the thousands in southeastern Wisconsin for the millinery trade. The slaughter of egrets, herons, and other birds by plume hunters was finally ended with the signing of the Lacey Act in 1900, making it illegal to transport birds between states. The Migratory Bird Treaty in 1918 was the real turning point, permanently closing hunting seasons on insectivorous birds and non-game birds, except for scientific or propagating purposes under permits. The taking of nests and eggs of all migratory birds was also prohibited, and seasons were set on migratory game birds.

Nature's Gliders

Over the years, numerous people have told me about their interactions with flying squirrels. Here's a brief sampling:

Linda and Joe Mastalski have observed flying squirrels year 'round for the last 20 years at their home south of Minocqua, often seeing up to seven at a time gliding in and taking suet or seeds. Gordon Hasse, a Woodruff native, has flying squirrels gliding from a pine tree to his feeder and back every night, never leaving a track in the snow. Jack and Barbara Bull from Winchester watch flying squirrels all winter long. When their cat sits staring out the window at night, that's the signal that the squirrels have arrived at the feeder. Jodi and Bill Scheels, who live north of Mercer, have flying squirrels zoom in from their apparent dens in dead elm trees to the Scheels' sunflower seed feeder every night during the winter.

And finally, Woody and Inga Hagge have attracted flying squirrels to their feeders for more than 20 years. Woody has even "petted" the tails of several while they clung head down at their feeder tree. Woody and Inga have learned the specific fly-ways used by the squirrels and position themselves on their deck during the summer so they can feel the movement of air as the squirrels fly just overhead. They've had up to 16 flyers at their feeder at one time!

Gone Frogging

I've been a volunteer frog counter for the DNR for more than a decade, and I've found that every year is different, due primarily to varying air and water temperatures. In 1999 I did the first of my three frog surveys for the year on April 29, and found most wood frogs had already stopped calling, while spring peepers appeared to be significantly lower in number than a few weeks earlier. No doubt our drought that spring caused reduced water flows in the bogs and vernal pools that serve as the mating sites for our early spring frogs. A few weeks later, a good dose of rain did wonders to bring the chorus back up to its more typical full-throated orchestration.

Four years later, during a warmer and wetter spring, the breeding frogs suddenly burst into activity around Manitowish on April 23. Spring peepers, wood frogs, and chorus frogs sang at the top of their lungs, and even our sub-freezing nights didn't seem to moderate their ardor. We heard leopard frogs less than a week later at Powell Marsh.

The Wisconsin Frog and Toad Survey (WFTS) was initiated in 1984 in response to concerns that anuran (frog and toad) species were declining. Nearly 120 roadside routes are now sampled throughout the state, each route consisting of 10 listening sites. Frogs are counted by first listening for and identifying their calls, then rating their frequency on a 1 to 3 index, one meaning that individuals can be counted with space between their calls, and three meaning the frogs are in full chorus, their calls constant and overlapping.

Each route is run three times: once in early spring (April 8-30), once in late spring (May 20-June 5), and once in summer (July 1-15). I often have to run my early spring route right at the end of April, or into May, if the cold weather hasn't abated enough to get the frogs excited.

Twenty-one years of data collection across the state show varying population trends for each species. Eastern gray treefrogs, bullfrogs, and northern spring peepers show an increase in abundance; American toads and wood frogs appear relatively stable; and Western chorus frogs, northern leopard frogs, pickerel frogs, and mink frogs show a decline.

Volunteers are still needed for a number of routes throughout the state. When asked what you're doing tonight, how many people get to reply, "I'm going out counting frogs." For more information on WFTS, go to: www.mbr-pwrc.usgs.gov/wifrog/frog.htm.

Global Warming Facts

The National Oceanic and Atmospheric Administration (NOAA) reported that the winter of 1999-2000 was the warmest on record for the United States. The previous record was set in 1998. Every state in the continental U.S. experienced a warmer-than-average winter. Global land and ocean temperatures were also the sixth warmest on record worldwide.

In 2006, at least nine cities in Wisconsin set records for the warmest January ever recorded. Milwaukee averaged 34°F, exceeding the normal average temperature by 13.3 degrees.

It was exceptionally warm in many other places, too, For instance, in Saskatchewan, Canada, many towns broke their records for average mean temperature in January. One city, Nipawin, was nearly 10°C warmer than normal, though for them that meant they averaged –9.2°C.

This wasn't a new trend for Nipawin. Temperatures were first recorded in the area in 1927, and 18 of the 20 warmest Januaries have occurred since 1980.

Of course, records for any given locality are insufficient to give us the big picture of global warming. We need to access NOAA's database, the world's largest statistical weather database that incorporates 105 years of record keeping.

To see the long-term details and draw your own conclusions, visit the NOAA Website at www.ncdc.noaa.gov/oa/climate/climate-extremes.html. Or visit the EPA's global warming Website at www.epa.gov/globalwarming, or the Intergovernmental Panel on Climate Change (IPCC) at www.ipcc.ch/.

If you're not familiar with the IPCC, the World Meteorological Organization (WMO) and the United Nations Environment Program (UNEP) established the Intergovernmental Panel on Climate Change in 1988. The role of the IPCC is to assess on a comprehensive, objective, open and transparent basis the scientific, technical and socio-economic information relevant to understanding the scientific basis of risk of human-induced climate change, its potential impacts and options for adaptation and mitigation. The IPCC does not carry out research nor does it monitor climate related data or other relevant parameters. It bases its assessment mainly on peer reviewed and published scientific/technical literature.

Northward Ho

Expect yellow-rumped warblers to arrive around April 20. Killdeer, harriers, bitterns, loons, phoebes, flickers, tree swallows—you just about name it—they're all coming now. Any warm day with a south wind is your calling card to be outside, binoculars in hand, pocket notebook ready to record sightings.

Hawk Phenology

Mary and I observed some of our first migrating hawks of 2004 in this sequence: a northern harrier on March 27, a sharp-shinned hawk on April 3, and a kestrel and turkey vulture on April 5. (We saw many eagles too, but since many eagles remain all winter, the date of the first migrants is hard to determine.)

When should we expect migrating hawks to arrive in Wisconsin? An article in the fall 2003 issue of *The Passenger Pigeon,* the journal of the Wisconsin Society of Ornithology, provides some insight. The researchers observed migrating hawks over a nearly 20-year span at the Cedar Grove Ornithological Station on the western shore of Lake Michigan about 40 miles north of Milwaukee. They recorded earliest dates of observation, latest dates, and all sightings in-between, then calculated the median date of observation for Cedar Grove. The median dates are as follows:

Species	Median date
• Bald eagle	4/4
• Red-shouldered hawk	4/9
• Rough-legged hawk	4/12
• Northern harrier	4/18
• American kestrel	4/18
• Cooper's hawk	4/21
• Red-tailed hawk	4/22
• Merlin	4/22
• Sharp-shinned hawk	4/23
• Turkey vulture	4/23

- Osprey 4/28
- Peregrine falcon 4/28
- Broad-winged hawk 4/29

Median dates, however, only provide an average. The range from earliest to latest sightings for a species can be very broad. For example, northern harriers in this study fell between March 14 and May 26; rough-legged hawks from March 16 to May 30; sharp-shinned hawks from March 19 to May 30. The median dates give us a good sense of the progression of species passing through during spring migration, but there's lots of room for individual variability within a species.

The Ins and Outs of Ice

The ice went out on the Manitowish River below our house on March 30, 2002. The river had opened on February 19, but iced back over on March 3. That was an odd year—seldom does the ice open and then close back over.

Everyone up here watches for ice-out. Cabin fever is usually raging in April if the winter just won't give up, and our state of mental health gets dicey when the ice just stays and stays.

When can we genuinely expect ice-out? Woody Hagge's 30-year average date for ice-out on Foster Lake in Hazelhurst is April 17, leaving an average of 222 days of the year without lake ice. At only 39 acres, the ice on Foster Lake typically goes out sooner than the ice on larger lakes, but that's not always the case. Other factors, such as ice thickness, the rate of spring runoff, snow depth, wind exposure, water color, tree cover, the presence of springs, and the shape of the lake, influence ice-out dates.

The UW Trout Lake Limnology Station has kept records since 1981 on the average date for the first day of open water on seven lakes, including Trout. They are as follows:

- Allequash (426 acres) 4/20
- Big Muskellunge (930 acres) 4/23

- Crystal Bog (1 acre) 4/19
- Crystal (88 acres) 4/21
- Little Rock (45 acres) 4/18
- Sparkling (127 acres) 4/22
- Trout Bog (1 acre) 4/22
- Trout Lake (3,816 acres total) 4/26 (South Basin)

Ice-out is occurring earlier than it has historically, while ice-up is occurring later. John Magnuson, UW Madison professor emeritus and lead author in an article published in *Science* in September of 2000, statistically demonstrated that ice is going out earlier in the entire northern hemisphere. The article, "Historical Trends in Lake and River Ice Cover in the Northern Hemisphere," analyzed information on 39 sites in the northern hemisphere where ice records were collected for the 150-year period from 1846 to 1995. Over this period, the data shows that breakup dates occurred an average of 6.5 days earlier per 100 years, and freeze-up dates occurred an average of 5.8 days later per 100 years. This corresponds to an increase in air temperatures of about 1.2°C per 100 years.

In 1998-99, the ice went out on Foster Lake in Hazelhurst on April 9, an early date but five days off the record of April 4. However, the lake didn't ice-up until December 16, so the ice lasted only 114 days, compared to the average length of 146 days. Ice cover during the winter of 1995-96 lasted 178 days, so we had 64 fewer days, over two months, of ice in 1998-99 than we experienced in 1995-96.

The records for Foster Lake represent, of course, only one lake in the Northwoods. Tim Kratz, senior researcher and director of the Trout Lake Station, would appreciate seeing other long-term ice data on northern lakes. If you've kept accurate records on your lake over the years, please contact Tim at the Station. He can be reached at (715) 356-9494.

Ice-Out—Loons-In

In mid-April 2004, warm temperatures, torrential rains, and high winds caused a rapid ice-out on quite a number of area lakes.

Loons arrived with the open water, and sometimes before. Here are the reports I received:

4/10 - Ken Boivin watched a loon just offshore from his home on Little Rice Lake in Mercer. The Turtle River enters there, and apparently opened just enough of the lake for a loon to drop in. That same day, Claudia Meinnert also spotted a loon on South Turtle Lake where the Turtle River originates.

4/15 - Ron Hine observed a loon on Lake Towanda in Minocqua, even though the water was only partially open.

4/16 - Linda Thomas sighted a pair of loons on Little Arbor Vitae Lake. Mary and I also observed a pair of loons on the main pool of Powell Marsh on the same day.

4/18 - Jim Sommerfeldt reported that a pair of loons returned to Middle Sugarbush Lake in Lac du Flambeau.

Contrary to popular belief, loons can take off from relatively small bodies of water. Mike Meyer, a DNR scientist out of Rhinelander who has conducted loon research for many years in our area, has personally observed a loon get airborne from a 10-acre lake. The loon used the longest fetch across the lake, then corkscrewed around the periphery of the lake, continually gaining elevation until it rose above the trees rimming the lake. Thus, very small lakes can provide sufficient space for loon landings and take-offs.

Wing Icing in Loons

Loons have little choice but to bide their time until northern lake ice disappears, often gathering in large flocks on open waters just south of us during the interim period. In Wausau, an observer in mid-April, 2003, reported 114 loons congregated on Lake Wausau. Another observer reported more than 25 loons on one bay of the Big Eau Pleine Reservoir, while another birder counted 37 loons on the Stevens Point Flowage of the Wisconsin River.

With all these loons gathered and waiting, we had the very unfortunate timing of an ice storm on April 17. Reports of loons landing on roads during the storm were numerous. But those loons only represented the ones that were found. When this many loons are reported, one can only speculate how many more came down and weren't discovered.

Why loons often ditch their flight onto man-made surfaces remains a point of conjecture. One explanation has held that the reflection of lights makes an iced road surface at night look like a water surface to loons, and they try to land as they would on any lake.

Another theory, called "looming," holds that loons flying during the day (loons are thought to make short "scouting" flights to check out lake ice) may see a mirage-like distortion on roadways due to uneven heating and convection, and as a result may believe the road is water. The weave-like air patterns coming off the roadway gave rise to the term "looming."

A third explanation is that loons ditch onto roads much like a pilot would in an emergency landing. The scenario goes like this: During a heavy migration begun in favorable conditions, the weather changes. The birds find themselves faced with strong headwinds and icing. It's possible that their wings literally ice-up despite their oiled flight feathers, forcing them to bail out wherever they can land. Given how heavy these birds are to begin with, and how they operate within a narrow margin of weight-to-lift ratio, the added weight from ice could either exhaust them quickly or make it impossible for them to fly at all.

The ice storm didn't hit the Lakeland area as hard as it hit counties to the south of us. Mark Naniot, wildlife rehabilitator at the Northwoods Wildlife Center in Minocqua, had only one call from Price County for a stranded loon that was picked up and later released. But three days after the storm hit, Marge Gibson at the Raptor Education Group in Antigo had picked up and released 21 stranded loons. The next day, she had another 3 loons in her care and was looking for a fourth that had just been reported. The loons had all been grounded since the ice storm, and those found on April 21 presumably hadn't eaten for four days. Marge said that after similar "loon-downings" in previous years, she has received calls for a week afterward as people find loons stranded in fields and along roads.

Loons can't walk at all, though they can scoot on their abdomens. Thus, after ditching onto land they're highly limited in their ability to travel to water. Sometimes when they find water, the water surface area is so small that they don't have enough runway to get airborne.

Marge described one woman who had found a loon earlier that day and had taken it home with the intention of putting it on her farm pond. Her good intentions not only put herself at risk due to the loon's spear-like bill, but would also have put the loon into certain jeopardy if Marge hadn't intervened. Loons have never been kept alive in captivity, and a tiny farm pond would effectively serve as a captive site.

When Marge gets a loon into her facility, she checks it over for abrasions on its feet and its keel-like abdomen. If there's a breach in the feathers on the abdomen, the loon won't be able to insulate itself once back on water, so it will become hypothermic and die. Remarkably, none of the loons that Marge treated that week were significantly injured, and all were safely released on Moose Lake near Antigo.

Marge also released a tundra swan that she had treated on April 21. The swan had been shot a few weeks earlier in southern Wisconsin. What induces an idiot to shoot a protected migrating swan is well beyond my ken, but we should all be quite thankful for individuals like Marge Gibson and Mark Naniot, who have dedicated their lives to healing wildlife from the many abuses of humans and the numerous hazards of the natural world.

Lapland Longspurs

On April 28, 1997, I observed a flock of a dozen Lapland longspurs on Powell Marsh. They were feeding on the edge of some upland grasses and stayed put for as long as I wanted to watch them. During their spring migration, Laplands appear most often in large open fields with patchy snow cover. They often congregate in large flocks. Up to 9,000 have been reported in southern Wisconsin farmland counties. To spot them at this time of year, watch any large open grasslands or plowed fields that you can find in the Northwoods. You may see one of our more beautiful and unusual migrating birds. Lapland longspurs nest in the far Arctic tundra region around Hudson Bay and north.

Maple Sugar

I visited the maple sugaring operation of David and Sharon Lintereur in Lake Tomahawk in 2004, and as always when I visit a sugar shack, I came away shaking my head at how much work goes into producing a gallon of syrup. Making syrup is clearly a labor of love, given that the price of a gallon of syrup is much the same as it was 30 years ago. Only the huge operations, or those with a unique marketing niche, can expect a profit—the rest of the operations dream of just breaking even.

Mary and I remain firmly addicted to the real stuff, and easily eat or give away a couple gallons of syrup a year. While our use may seem excessive to some, it's a pittance compared to the importance of maple sugar in traditional native cultures.

Alexander Henry was a well-known fur trader of the late eighteenth century, and his travels and adventures were first published in 1809. In the spring of 1763, Henry accompanied an Ojibwe family of seven, four men and three women, to their sugaring site. He described the operation as follows:

> "The next day was employed in gathering the bark of white birch-trees, with which to make vessels to catch the wine or sap. The trees were now cut or tapped, and spouts or ducts introduced into the wound. The bark vessels were placed under the ducts; and, as they filled, the liquor was taken out in buckets, and conveyed into reservoirs or vats of moose-skin, each vat containing a hundred gallons. From these, we supplied the boilers, of which we had twelve, of from twelve to twenty gallons each, with fires constantly under them, day and night.

> While the women collected the sap, boiled it, and completed the sugar, the men were not less busy in cutting wood, making fires, hunting and fishing.
>
> " ... On the twenty-fifth of April, our labor ended, and we returned to the [trading post], carrying with us ... sixteen hundred [pounds] weight of sugar. We had besides, thirty-six gallons of syrup; and during our stay in the woods, we certainly consumed three hundred weight [of maple sugar]. Though, as I have said, we hunted and fished, yet sugar was our principal food, during the whole month of April ... I have known Indians to live wholly upon the same [maple sugar], and become fat."

And I thought I had a sweet tooth! The work to make this amount of sugar and syrup would have been staggering. It takes 40 to 50 gallons of sap to make one gallon of syrup, and about 50 gallons of sap to make 8 pounds of sugar. Do the math, and the 1,900 pounds of sugar represents some 11,875 gallons of sap, while the 36 gallons of syrup required another 1,800 gallons of sap. Thus, the Ojibwe women gathered about 13,675 gallons of sap in the spring of 1763, and likely had to tap at least 700 maple trees to collect that much.

It also takes one cord of wood to produce about 8-10 gallons of syrup in a modern evaporator, so the men must have had to cut at least 30 full cords of wood for their 12 boilers that had fires under them day and night.

Then they had to transport all of this to their summer village or to the trading post. A gallon of syrup of weighs about 11 pounds, so the 36 gallons weighed nearly 400 pounds. Added to the 1,600 pounds of sugar, the total weight was nearly a ton, divided between eight people.

Historians calculate that the sugar and syrup produced by the Ojibwe in the second half of the eighteenth century probably constituted about one-twelfth of the annual diet of many Ojibwe Indians. Surplus sugar was bartered frequently at trading posts for products like corn or manufactured goods from the French and English.

The Midas Touch

In early April, male goldfinches are easily observable in the midst of their "prenuptial" feather molt. Their patchy appearance will continue to golden-up until, by late April, the males will achieve their full spring plumage.

Typically, the prenuptial molt immediately precedes the nesting season, just before the birds arrive on the nesting grounds. The molt usually involves the loss or change of just a few feathers.

Some species change their winter plumage without molting by simply wearing down their feathers to reveal the brighter breeding colors. Male bobolinks change from a drab winter gray to their attractive black-and-white breeding plumage by a wearing-away of the yellowish tips of feathers that hide the black.

The prenuptial plumage change physically prepares the males for a variety of behaviors. The brilliant red shoulder patches on the red-winged blackbird are exaggerated in their labored flight displays. The male yellow-headed blackbird does its courtship flight with its head cocked upward to fully reveal its coloration.

Sometimes colors have nothing to do with breeding or establishing territories. Dark feathers resist wear better than white ones. Thus, the wing tips of many flying birds are black, since they are often in contact with abrasive ground, tree branches, or coarse grasses.

Some male birds don't rely on color to attract the ladies, but instead try to impress them with their skills. Male terns display fresh-caught fish to females as part of their courtship, while many songbirds appear to be showing off their hunting skills by lowering their bills and pecking at an imagined quarry below them.

Migrations of Another Order

When we think of migration, we usually think of birds, but many other animals migrate in the spring. I had the opportunity at the Wisconsin Association of Lakes Convention in 2003 to listen to a talk by Bob DuBois, a river ecologist for the DNR in Superior. Bob confirmed something I'd heard for a number of years—that a small number of species of dragonfly migrates in the fall and return in the spring.

To the general public, the green darner may be the most familiar of the migratory dragonflies, and it is typically the first dragonfly seen in the spring. Green darners have been recorded in every state in the U.S., as well as southern Canada and south to Honduras. The average return date for green darners to northern Wisconsin is April 25, but where they go for the winter is unknown, as are all the other questions that usually surround a species' migration, such as length of migration, stopover sites along the way, wintering habitat, migration triggers, methods of navigation, and so forth. All we know is that one day very soon swarms of green darners will suddenly appear as if by magic around marshy, still-water habitats.

Our other migratory dragonflies include three species of saddlebags, the variegated meadowhawk, and the wandering glider. A few dragonfly species south of us are even known to cross the Gulf of Mexico in migration!

To identify a male green darner, look for a three-inch-long dragonfly with an all-green thorax and a bulls-eye-like mark on its forehead. Look also for wide blue stripes that run laterally on its abdomen. I recommend purchasing one or all of three books if you want to pursue learning dragonfly identification: *Guide to Common Dragonflies of Wisconsin* by Karl and Dorothy Legler, *Dragonflies of the North Woods* by Kurt Mead, and *Dragonflies through Binoculars: A Field Guide to Dragonflies of North America* by Sidney Dunkle.

While enjoyment of dragonflies may be an acquired taste, everyone can appreciate the fact that medium-sized dragonflies like a green darner eat an average of 400 prey items per day, many of which are mosquitoes. Vive la dragonflies!

Other non-avian migrations occur in April. Early-emerging amphibians like the blue-spotted, spotted, and tiger salamanders often engage in mass migrations from their overwintering sites to their breeding wetlands. The same is true of wood, chorus, and leopard frogs, as well as spring peepers. On rainy nights just after frost-out in northern Wisconsin, amphibians may be seen crawling over snow and ice to get to their breeding ponds. Sometimes the number killed crossing roads to get to their breeding sites is remarkably, and depressingly, large.

Monarch Butterflies on the Way

We generally don't see our first monarch butterflies until late May at the earliest—it's a long flight from central Mexico. Monarchs begin their migration the second week of March and should be in Texas in early April, laying eggs on flowering milkweed plants. The caterpillars will hatch out, eat, pupate, and metamorphose into adults, and these will be the ones we see coming into our state in late May.

Three or four generations of monarchs may prosper during the summer, so the great-grandchildren of the spring migrators are the ones that migrate several thousand miles back to Mexico in the fall, to the same winter roost sites that monarchs have claimed for as long as anyone knows. How their homing system works is unknown. Since no teaching of routes can ever take place, their arrival in our woods around Memorial Day should be filed in everyone's "miracles of nature" folder.

To follow the migration of monarch butterflies, log on to www.learner.org/jnorth.

Mourning Dove Hunt Results and the Conservation Congress

The 2000 advisory vote on hunting mourning doves conducted by Conservation Congress meetings across the state was more revealing for the failure of the process than for its tallied results. Many people came out of those county meetings saying there must be a better way for all of the citizens of this state to advise the DNR on critical wildlife issues than the current Conservation Congress.

This was no "victory" for hunters. The Conservation Congress, a group historically created for the specific purpose of giving hunters and anglers a voice in advising the DNR on hunting and fishing issues, does not speak for all of the residents of this state on environmental issues, any more than the Audubon Society or the Sierra Club does.

Democracy requires inclusion of all voices, and democracy was off the CC agenda in many areas of the state. Proposals were made in numerous county meetings that no one should be permitted to vote on issues or run for office if they didn't hold a hunting license. Some proposed that attendees should hold a hunting license for a minimum of 10 years before being permitted to vote. The additional reports from many county meetings of the disrespect and scorn heaped upon anyone who attempted to speak against dove hunting indicated an effort to intimidate dissenting voices. Clearly, many hunters felt they were the only ones who should have the right to vote on wildlife issues. They apparently saw exclusion of other viewpoints as democracy in action.

This would be like letting only canoeists vote on how rivers are managed. Or only permitting loggers to vote on how forests are managed. Or only allowing ATVers, or hikers, or any other one-issue group the exclusive right to vote on how trails should be utilized.

The entire Congress organization and process needs rethinking if it is to be used as the one means by which the overall public can vote statewide on conservation issues. The Conservation Congress fails the important test of representing an accurate cross-section of the public and of providing an objective analysis of conservation issues.

As for the mourning dove issue, unfortunately, many hunters perceived the vote as a referendum on hunting, rather than regarding it as a specific vote on the hunting of a specific species. The hunting public was continuously rallied under the banner of standing up to the tree-hugging anti-hunter who wants to take all their hunting privileges away. What an unfortunate excess of fear.

It's not only possible, but also necessary, to understand that many, many people who choose not to hunt aren't anti-hunting. Nor are they "The Enemy." Because I choose not to scuba dive, not to run marathons, not to read ancient Greek poetry, doesn't mean I am anti-scuba, anti-running, or anti-Greek.

Similarly, it is not only possible, but equally necessary, for non-hunters to understand that many hunters do not desire to hunt all species, aren't bloodthirsty savages, and do work hard on many valuable conservation efforts. Like the non-hunters, they are not "The Enemy."

It is also equally possible, and necessary, to recognize that the wild plants and animals of Wisconsin don't "belong" to any group or anyone. Most of us, hunters and non-hunters, have long recognized that simply because a species can be hunted without biological harm to the overall population is not sufficient reason to hunt it. Otherwise, all species, with the exception of those protected under the Endangered Species Act, should be immediately opened to the hunt. To argue that the mourning dove was plentiful, manageable, and good to eat was not sufficient to justify its hunt. If that was sufficient, then robins, song sparrows, and the 150 or so nesting songbirds of this area better head for cover.

I believe most of us understand that we need to bring a higher standard to bear on natural resource use and protection in this state. What few of us understand is what that higher standard is, and what forum is the most conducive to the airing of representative public opinion.

Nebraska's Sandhill Crane Migration

In April 2003, Mary, Callie, and I traveled to Nebraska's Platte River to try to catch the tail end of the sandhill crane migration. The peak of the migration occurs from March 20 through April 5, when nearly half a million cranes can be seen. The vast majority of the birds were gone by the time we arrived on April 14, but we still saw at least a thousand in one field alone, and a flock of 200 or more wheeling overhead a few minutes later.

Three subspecies of cranes utilize the Platte—the greater, the

Canadian or intermediate, and the lesser sandhill crane. The lessers are significantly smaller than the four-foot-tall greaters, while the intermediate are in the middle in terms of weight, height, and bill length. In one field, we were able to see several lessers standing next to a greater, and the size difference was very evident. Lessers make up at least 80 percent of Nebraska's population, while the greaters comprise only about 5 percent. The lessers nest in central, western, and northern Canada, so we don't see them in Wisconsin. "Our" cranes are the greaters.

As impressive as the cranes are, the waterfowl are certainly their equal. More than 10 million ducks and geese stage along the Platte, utilizing the host of rainwater basins in south-central Nebraska that lie amidst endless fields of corn.

The Platte River connects the coniferous forests of the Rocky Mountains to the eastern deciduous forests of the Missouri Valley, and lies in the heart of the Central Flyway near the center of the North American continent. Thus it serves as a biological crossroads where east meets west and south meets north.

The river itself is remarkable for its braided, shallow character. It was once called "the river with no banks" because it pours through an extraordinarily broad, flat valley. Seldom does the river compress into one channel. Instead, it often spreads itself into a dozen ribbons of water that flow over its sandy bottom. The river's width makes it ideal for cranes to utilize at night for safe roosting.

The river's flow has been reduced to one-quarter of its historic flow due to irrigation and hydropower diversions, and the rainwater basins have been drained from 100,000 acres to only 21,000 acres. Still, the cranes and waterfowl come in prodigious numbers, having no alternative stopover sites that could begin to provide what the Platte and the nearby wetlands offer.

Nest Boxes

The Cornell Lab of Ornithology is looking for help in learning more about cavity-nesting birds. The success of bluebird boxes has demonstrated that people can have a very positive impact on cavity-nesting birds. As a result, the Cornell Lab has started "The Birdhouse Network," a fun, hands-on study of birds that you can do at home. The lab provides all the information you need to build or purchase a nest box and place it in a good spot. Then you share your observations with them by using their software or data forms.

Since 1999, The Birdhouse Network has provided live images of cavity-nesting birds to viewers around the world. Using a system of Nest Box Cams—small cameras placed inside nest boxes—Internet viewers can follow species such as bluebirds, swallows, barn owls, American kestrels, and chickadees as they build their nest, lay eggs, hatch, feed the young, and much more.

To learn more about the The Birdhouse Network, call (800) 843-BIRD, or visit their Website at: http://www.birds.cornell.edu/birdhouse/.

Taking to the Slopes

As our snow melts, what's left is typically concentrated in shaded woods and on north-facing slopes. I'm sure many of you have noticed in March and April how snow can be absent on the south side of a road, but still deep on the north side. The obvious reason for such a difference has to do with the angle of the sun—south- and west-facing slopes receive the lion's share of direct sunlight, while east- and north-facing slopes enjoy life in a nearly perpetual shade.

Temperatures can be 60°F higher on south-facing slopes, while evaporation rates are typically 50 percent greater. If you enjoy studying plants, take the time to compare the plant communities on north- and south-facing slopes. They can be quite different due to the significant differences in soil moisture and shading.

First Warblers to Return

Yellow-rumped warblers usually arrive in the Northwoods around April 15, the first in the vanguard of warblers to come. I suspect they're our earliest warbler because many winter in the southern states and don't have that far to come. Still, warblers are insect eaters, and a short flight doesn't make life any easier if there's no food when you arrive. The key to their early arrival is likely the fact they consume fruit and berries as a primary part of their diet. Yellow-rumps are also known as "myrtle" warblers for their fondness for waxmyrtle berries in the winter. They also are fond of poison sumac and poison ivy berries, and often overwinter in areas where these are readily available.

Yellow-rumps are considered the most abundant of all warbler species, and are often given short shrift by birders who find them too common. I find them very beautiful birds, and I look forward to their return as much as I do the first robin or the first waterfowl. When yellow-rumps appear, they signal that spring is shifting into a higher gear, and now the incredible waves of migrating songbirds are only a few weeks off.

Peanut Butter, Jelly, and Birds

If you're burned out on P-B-and-J sandwiches, consider feeding the ingredients to your backyard birds.

According to author George Harrison, feeding peanut butter to birds works fine, contrary to myths that the peanut butter can get stuck in a bird's mouth and cause it to choke.

As for jelly, a dish of generic grape jelly works well for attracting orioles.

Cranes, Owls, and Pelicans, Oh My!

Mary and I go birding on the Powell Marsh Wildlife Area in Manitowish Waters as often as we can in April, and we see something interesting nearly every time. In 2004, we hiked areas of the marsh six times in fourteen days. Here are the highlights for each day:

On April 4, sandhill cranes had returned to the marsh.

On April 7, hundreds of ring-necked ducks dominated the open water of the main pool, with small numbers of buffleheads, goldeneyes, mallards, and common mergansers mixed in.

On April 9, we observed 17 hawks in the air simultaneously, all of which were rough-legs or northern harriers.

On April 13, wood frogs began singing on Powell, four days earlier than they started up in the woodland vernal ponds around the marsh.

On April 14, I was watching what I thought were northern harriers sailing low over the marsh, when another "hawk" flushed from the dike just ahead of me. Its tail was banded unlike any harrier I'd ever seen, and it lacked the white rump that is the easy identifying characteristic for harriers. I kept watching, and after it flew directly away from me for a long ways, it eventually turned and I could see that its face seemed to be pushed in. I then looked more closely at one of the other harriers sailing well out over the marsh and noticed the same lack of a white rump, and the same small head. It eventually dawned on me that I was watching short-eared owls, a species I had never seen on the marsh in the 20 years I had been birding there.

On April 18, nine white pelicans were hanging out with the geese and ring-necks on the main pool. That wasn't the first flock of pelicans on Powell that year. A week earlier, Todd Dalle Ave and Kay Krans sighted a small flock of four.

Booming Birds

A number of Northwoods residents and I traveled on April 27, 1997, to the Buena Vista Marsh just east of Wisconsin Rapids to watch the dawn ritual of prairie chicken dancing.

The whole process existed outside of our normal experience, from the early morning rising, to the dark hike into the viewing blinds and the sudden appearance at first light of the male prairie chickens. The males swooped in as a flock (18 total) and immediately began their ritualistic posturing, displaying, and "booming" to attract the females they hoped were waiting in the wings.

Booming is a bit of a misnomer. The males inflate brilliant orange sacs on both sides of their neck and when they release the air they make a low deep sound that is somewhat like blowing across the neck of a large bottle. It's a three note call, the second note falling, and the third note rising back up to the first note's pitch. They seem to be saying, "Who are you," or "Old mul-dooon." A chorus of booming prairie chickens is unlike any other avian music most of us will hear.

The DNR estimates that we have fewer than 1,000 prairie chickens left in the state. Their population appears relatively stable in the Buena Vista Marsh at least, but small flocks in other less extensive grasslands appear to be declining.

Ebb, Flow, and Flood

Spring floods should be regarded as normal and essential disturbances. Like fires, windstorms, ice-push, intense cold, insect outbreaks, disease—the whole laundry list of possible disturbances in the Northwoods—floods are part of our ecological context. Our river communities, plant and animal, adapt to this disturbance, or cease to exist in that area.

What occurs to a river during a flood? A healthy river will usually absorb all but the most catastrophic floods. The riparian plant life holds the shoreline soil in place with its network of roots, while the leaves of shrubs and trees further protect the groundlayer from the pounding and erosive forces of heavy rainfall.

Sometimes a flood scrubs an area clean of vegetation, but most vegetation has adapted to regenerate quickly. For instance, silver maples and willows blossom and go to seed immediately in spring, so the seeds are ready to drop on exposed riverbanks when the traditional spring floodwaters recede.

Floods often improve a river's complexity. Logjams serve to slow and redirect surging currents, causing the river to dig out pools and flow into side channels and sloughs. Floods carry wood and rock debris that drops out of the flow along the way and provides new structure within the river. Since different fish need different habitat structure for spawning, feeding, and resting, floods are actually key events in shaping and maintaining high-quality fish habitat. Recent studies on rivers have concluded that a river needs to mobilize its channel bed every other year on average in order to provide ideal spawning habitat.

During floods, rivers cut new channels, resculpt older ones, clean silt out of spawning gravels, and flush accumulated leaves and woody debris into the water from the floodplain. Floodplains work simultaneously to soak up the high water and then release it slowly, keeping the river flowing in drier months.

Floods carry older organic materials like dead plants from the floodplain into the river, and replace them with newer materials. The floodwater also scours the long strings of filamentous algae, as well as other plants, off the riverbed. Afterward, plant populations often explode due to the nutrient-rich organic debris, fueling a growth spurt all the way up the food chain.

Though some fish and other animals die in floods, most survive by resting in side channels, sloughs, and logjams. When the waters have receded, they multiply due to the abundance of food and new spawning habitat.

Rivers, and the life within them, survive through resilience. A healthy river is self-sustaining and self-healing. Destruction of one life leads to new life in a dynamic ebb, flow, and flood.

World-Class Wanderers

Redpolls, often still lingering at many area feeders in April, should be leaving soon for their breeding grounds throughout northern Canada and Alaska. Band returns on redpolls reveal that they are exceptional wanderers. One redpoll banded in Fairbanks, Alaska, was found two years later near Montreal, nearly 3,000 miles to the southeast. Another bird banded in Quebec City was caught in a bander's trap in Fairbanks. The Fairbanks bander has banded more than 20,000 redpolls, but has only had two to three returns for every 1,000 redpolls he has banded, indicating that they have short life spans and wander far and wide.

More on Skunk Cabbage

Skunk cabbage is considered the earliest spring flower to emerge from the ground, sometimes poking through the snow in March despite sub-freezing temperatures. The fleshy flower cluster hides inside a purple-mottled hood called a spathe. The spathe is gapped on one side to allow pollinating insects to enter, but Thoreau noted that its opening is "lapped like tent doors," sheltering and insulating the flower cluster. Air pockets in the flesh of the spathe help insulate the plant, acting like Styrofoam. The opening deflects and circulates air around the flower, helping to keep the temperature stable. One observer notes that the spathes "create their own near-tropical microclimate in a north temperate spring."

The odor of skunk cabbage is so bad that one writer has likened it to a combination of "skunk, putrid meat, and garlic," which is about as odoriferous as anything on the planet. Any plant which has *foetidus* as its species name is not one to be picked for the dinner table.

On the upside, skunk cabbage probably offers the first pollen and warmth of the spring to honeybees that are struggling to fly in the weather that is typical of March and early April in the Northwoods. And despite the smell, a few species consume the early leaves, including ring-necked pheasants and black bears, though black bears emerging from hibernation have not one whit of selectivity in their feeding. The hollows of the huge leaves are also used by common yellowthroats for nest sites.

Look for skunk cabbage in the mud of rich marshlands and stream edges. The leaves emerge after the flowers, often growing by early summer into massive greenery more than two feet long. Thoreau,

woodland deer mouse

practical woodsman that he was, believed the skunk cabbage leaf to be "the best vessel to drink out of at a spring … It does not flavor the water and is not perceived in drinking." For all we know, Thoreau may have been prone to spring colds and couldn't smell a thing. But next time you're in a pinch and need a drinking cup, you now know the humble skunk cabbage could be your vessel of choice.

Small Mammal ID

Small mammal identification can get mighty confusing. I got a call once about ground squirrels and whether we really have them. Well, here's where common names cause a problem. A lot of folks call a variety of different small mammals "ground squirrels." We do have one ground squirrel—the thirteen-lined ground squirrel, a species often mistaken for and called a chipmunk.

Here's the scoop on the rodents (order *Rodentia*) in north-central Wisconsin. You may see:

- 2 species of chipmunks—least and Eastern
- woodchuck
- thirteen-lined ground squirrel
- 5 species of squirrels—gray, red, fox, northern flying, and southern flying
- beaver
- 4 species of mice—white-footed, deer, meadow, and woodland jumping
- 2 species of voles—

woodland jumping mouse

southern red-backed and meadow

- southern bog lemming
- muskrat
- porcupine

We also have five species of shrews (arctic, masked, pygmy, water, and northern short-tailed) and the star-nosed mole, which are all in the order *Insectivora*.

The thirteen-lined ground squirrel has 13 stripes from the nape of its neck to its tail, seven of which are narrow yellow stripes, while the other six are broader brown stripes with dash lines of yellow down their center. The thirteen-lined ground squirrel runs with its tail held out behind it, while chipmunks hold their tails straight up. Chipmunks have two pale and three dark stripes on the sides of their face. The stripes on the back of the Eastern chipmunk end before reaching the base of the tail and the chestnut-colored rump. The least chipmunk's stripes extend all the way to base of the tail. The Eastern is usually around 10 inches long, while the least is only about 8 inches long.

Telling the difference between the "mousy-looking" guys is another matter altogether. I can at least help you differentiate the groups from one another:

- Mice have large ears and long tails
- Voles have large ears and short tails
- Shrews' ears are not visible, and they have pointy noses
- The star-nosed mole has pink "tentacles" on its nose, and looks rather like an alien creature.

bog lemming

Sparrows—American Tree, Fox, and Song

For most of April 2000, a dozen or more American tree sparrows were competing for sunflower seeds under our feeders. They're easily identified by their rusty cap, the "stickpin" black dot on their chest, and their lack of striping. They're just passing through en route to their far-northern Canada nesting grounds. It's rare to see a tree sparrow past mid-May. The state record for latest observation is May 25, 1970. Typically, they arrive in Iron County around mid-April, but in 2000, they arrived on March 3!

Fox sparrows appeared early that year, too, on March 24 in Manitowish. Our largest sparrow, their rufous tail, rusty streaked breast, gray markings around the neck, and their behavioral habit of "hop-kicking" with their feet to uncover seeds make them easily identifiable. Like tree sparrows, fox sparrows nest from Hudson Bay north, so they're just stopping over and tanking up for the bigger flight ahead. They usually pack their bags and move on by early May at the very latest.

Song sparrows arrived on March 28, and unlike the tree and fox sparrows, they remain to nest. However, this first vanguard was likely heading farther north, because their nesting range extends up to the base of Hudson Bay. Song sparrows live "on the edge," avoiding deep woods and open fields, while prospering in the shrubs and hedgerows of farmlots and suburbia. They seem particularly suited to nesting in the long grasses and bushes bordering lakes and rivers. A spring canoe trip down the Manitowish yields a continual succession of singing males from the willows and alders lining the banks. Nests are generally concealed on the ground within tufts of grass on the banks of streams, though they may nest far from the water as well.

Amorous Frogs

Despite the cold temperatures of the last two weeks in April of 2002, male spring peepers, wood frogs, and chorus frogs were singing with great gusto in hopes of drawing a female close enough to mate. Even on cold nights you have to get out to listen. Wood frogs, for instance, only sing for a few weeks, so their spring choral debut is brief and often missed by listeners who wait for warmer evening temperatures before venturing forth.

Courtship is a word wasted on most frogs. There is no fancy dancing, no color displays, no passing food to one another, no brilliantly choreographed flights, dives, or swims. Romance, with all that it entails, doesn't appear to be in the frog's lexicon. If a gravid female shows up at the pond near the calling male, she will be clasped immediately from on top and behind her forelegs, a position called amplexus. If she is stimulated by this coupling, she will lay her eggs. The male will follow her lead by releasing sperm onto the eggs, fertilizing them externally. For spring peepers, amplexus continues until the female has laid nearly 1,000 eggs.

These eggs will hatch in two to three days, and the young tadpoles will grow rapidly, transforming into adults in six to eight weeks. They will then leave the ephemeral pond for the woods.

It's a race against evaporation for the earliest breeding frogs. They usually breed in temporary woodland ponds that dry up as summer progresses. The evolutionary advantage is that these tiny ponds are fishless, and thus there's much less danger of predation.

Therefore, speed is of the essence for the frogs. There's no time for courtship when the survival of your young depends in large part on how fast they can hatch from their eggs. So the males sing with urgency. A nearby full chorus of spring peepers can just about make you deaf.

Like spring wildflowers, vernal ponds disappear from the landscape by July. They'll refill with waters from the spring snowmelt next April, but their desiccation for most of the year creates significant confusion concerning how to classify them. Are they wetlands and therefore protected, or are they just temporary puddles and therefore something less valued and more easily destroyed?

The frogs don't care to ponder such socio-scientific babble. Instinct calls. It's now or never.

Collared Swans

I did my first paddle of the year on the Manitowish River on April 1, 2005, and I kicked up a number of waterfowl, including wood ducks, hooded mergansers, mallards, common goldeneye, and Canada geese. The best sighting of the day was a group of seven trumpeter swans, two of which were neck-collared. The numbers were E53 and E77, identifying them as a pair of trumpeters that have nested locally for several years.

I'm always conflicted about seeing the neck collars. They take away the "wild" appearance of the birds, but they provide very useful information about the swans' continued use of breeding territories, their migratory movements and wintering habitat, and their length of life.

Patricia Manthey, an avian ecologist for the Bureau of Endangered Resources, keeps track of the trumpeters. She writes: "The USGS Bird Banding Laboratory protocols specify the collar colors and codes for each species of swan. Trumpeter swans in the Midwest may have red, yellow, or green collars. All yellow collared birds come from Wisconsin. Red collared trumpeters seen in Wisconsin are usually from Iowa. Green collared ones are likely to be from Iowa or Michigan, but a few are Wisconsin's. All trumpeter collars have three-character codes containing one letter and two numbers."

She asks that all trumpeter collars be reported to her, and in exchange, she'll send you back some information about the history of the bird(s), such as how old they are, where they were raised, and where they currently nest.

E-mail Pat at manthp@dnr.state.wi.us.

For a fact sheet on Wisconsin's Trumpeter Swan reintroduction program, log on to:

www.dnr.state.wi.us/org/land/er/factsheets/birds/SWAN.HTM.

V-Formations in Migratory Birds

Why do geese, some ducks, cranes, pelicans, and others fly in Vs? The answer is—drumroll, please—no one really knows. What's known is that migrating flocks are generally made up of family groups, which include the young-of-the-year that remain with the adults for the first year of life. The flocks also typically contain some paired birds that have failed to breed and some loners that join the flock in long migration. To confuse the issue, different groups of birds may join together for short flights to feeding areas.

Flying in Vs appears to reduce wind resistance and keeps the families and pairs close together. There is little objective proof for the notions that the flock has a specific leader, or the flock changes leaders every few minutes. The birds all know their individual migration routes, and may be together for no other reason than they're all going the same direction, much like humans heading the same direction on a freeway.

The problem in determining what really occurs within a migratory flock is that researchers would have to be able to fly along at 50 to 60 mph with the flock and watch for interactions among the birds, and this simply hasn't been done.

If V-formation flying is so aerodynamic, wouldn't all birds employ the formation? Most birds don't migrate in V-formations. Night-migrating songbirds (warblers, vireos, thrushes, sparrows, grosbeaks, flycatchers, tanagers, and others) usually migrate alone.

Songbirds that migrate during the day (crows, finches, blackbirds, robins, and others) migrate in flocks more often than night-migrators, but their flocks usually form three-dimensional clusters that offer no apparent aerodynamic advantage. Broad-winged hawks, turkey vultures, Swainson's hawks, and Mississippi kites migrate in two basic configurations. One is a swirling columnar cluster that may include a thousand or more individuals riding a thermal together. The second is an extended cluster that is usually several times longer than its width. Loons fly in loose, poorly organized flocks over water, but come together in closer flocks over land.

The bottom line is that flocks form in a manner that varies greatly among species. No single explanation for why flocking occurs is correct for all birds. Flocking may be utilized to improve navigational orientation, to gain aerodynamic advantage, to aid in finding the best food supply, to aid in preventing predation, or to help locate the best thermals.

West Meets Midwest

We spent a week in April of 1999 in San Diego visiting our oldest daughter. None of us had significant prior experience with western birds, so we were thrilled to see so many new birds, many of which we were only vaguely aware existed. I added 33 new birds to my life list (clapper rails, avocets, western grebes, surf scoters, Anna's, black-chinned and Costa's hummingbirds, phainopeplas to name a few), and watched at length a host of others that I had previously only glimpsed (like brown pelicans).

I was surprised to see a number of birds that I have considered strictly Easterners. For instance, we had white-crowned sparrows in the feeder at our B & B. We caught yellow-rumped warblers in migration. In fact, I saw dozens in one spot in Balboa Park. Robins were coming through, as were dark-eyed juncos. Common ravens were surprisingly common, as were American crows.

Winter Wrens

I suspect few songbirds exist that pound for pound (or ounce for ounce) deliver such an intricate, beautiful, lengthy, and loud song as a winter wren. Sam Robbins, author of *Wisconsin Birdlife,* writes that the winter wren is his favorite bird: "It is sheer bliss for me to drift down the Bois Brule River on a June morning and listen to the endless rollicking trills of this coloratura soprano." Most bird songs last only a second or two, but the song of winter wrens often lasts for seven seconds or more, and contains 108 to 113 separate notes. It's difficult to imagine that the tiny lung power of a four-inch-long bird would be sufficient to sustain such capacity and complexity.

These northern nesters have recently migrated back from our southern states, and will soon be laying their eggs, typically under rotted stumps, in the root balls of recently fallen trees, or in tree roots on the ground. They're singing in full voice right now. Listen for them in conifer swamps and deep woodlands.

winter wren and nest

Northern Wisconsin's Pre-History

Mary, Callie, and I attended a class on Wisconsin's pre-history taught by Katie Eagan-Bruhy, an archaeologist and paleoethnobotanist who teaches at Nicolet College and who also leads digs and surveys for the Chequamegon/Nicolet National Forest.

Katie guided us through the time period from the retreat of the glaciers up to European contact, a period we tend to overlook because it has no written history. But European contact and the fur trade represented only a brief moment in the history of our area.

What did occur here prior to that time? The answers are well beyond the scope of this entry, but people have lived in this area for at least 8,000 years. An archaeological survey of the Manitowish Chain undertaken in 1992-93 by the Nicolet National Forest and the State Region 2 Archaeology Center attempted to quantify the post-glacial history of the area. The survey was conducted in three parts: an archaeological survey in eight of the 14 lakes in the chain; a preliminary geomorphological survey to reconstruct original lakeshores as they existed before the historic logging era; and an underwater survey around Fox Island in Rest Lake in an attempt to relocate any mounds that may have existed on the island. Researchers surveyed more than 29,000 feet of shoreline.

Twenty-six sites were newly discovered and seven previously reported sites were revisited during the field survey. Sixteen of these 33 sites were on Island Lake alone. From prehistory times, the period when no written records exist, one Paleo Period (roughly 8,000-10,000 years before the present) site was found on Spider Lake. Four sites indicated occupation during the Archaic Period (roughly 2,000 to 8,000 years before present). Twelve sites were dated to the Woodland Period, running generally from 500 to 2,000 years ago. Another 15 sites could only be described as "unknown prehistoric" sites.

Seven sites were found from historic times, roughly 100-400 years ago, represented by written records from both Indian and European-American cultures.

If you add these sites together, they total 39. Five sites showed occupation spanning several of the periods, and one spanned all three prehistoric periods.

Nearly all sites are now located on private lands, and property owners have been made aware of the legacy involved. Sites include prehistoric mounds and burials, prehistoric campsites, historic Indian burials, historic sugaring camps, historic logging and boom camps, one historic canal, one historic pitch-making site, and one historic resort.

Unfortunately, archaeological sites in the Manitowish Waters area, like those in most areas, have long been looted. Discretion and respect for private property owners prevent a detailed listing of site locations. However, the report on the survey is a public document available through the Chequamegon/Nicolet National Forest Office in Rhinelander, Wisconsin. Copies may be found in local libraries as well.

Short-Eared Owls

In April, 2004, at Powell Marsh, I watched three different short-eared owls do their best impersonation of a northern harrier, gliding low over the marsh grasses, frequently dipping and turning in their visual probing for voles hidden in the matted vegetation. Harriers and short-ears must put the fear of God in the poor voles, because they comprise nearly 90 percent of the birds' diets.

I was thrilled by this sighting of the short-ears, because confirmed short-eared owl nests are quite uncommon in Wisconsin. The Wisconsin Breeding Bird Survey shows only eight breeding sites in Wisconsin, and only one in the Northwoods near Three Lakes.

I'd love to hear a short-ear calling. Their regular call is described as a series of low hoots, often repeated in sets of up to 20 notes at a time. One source says they sound like an old steam engine. But they also produce a variety of barking, squawking, and hissing notes, as well as engaging in frequent loud "wing-clapping," especially during acrobatic courtship displays. The literature indicates the male employs exaggerated wing beats to rise quickly up to altitudes of

600 to 1,300 feet above the ground. It often hovers, and then glides down while producing wing-claps in bursts of two to six per second. The courtship flight often concludes with the male descending in a spectacular dive with his wings held aloft and shimmying rapidly as he reaches the ground. Wow!

Powell Marsh is ideal habitat for short-ears. They inhabit wide-open spaces like grasslands, prairies, salt marshes, estuaries, mountain meadows, and Arctic tundra, building their nests on the ground like harriers.

Drumming for a Mate

Not all male birds sing or engage in physical displays to establish a territory or to entice a female into mating. To assert their virility, woodpeckers often drum on sides of houses, telephone poles, or any other resonating object. One early May, Mary and I hopped out of our car at Powell Marsh to do a little birdwatching, and immediately heard a loud hammering on metal just up the road. We walked to the end of the parking lot, and there was a male yellow-bellied sapsucker hammering on a yellow "Curve Ahead" road sign. If he wanted to draw maximum attention to his drumming, he succeeded.

Woodpeckers frequently establish "signal trees," using particularly resonant objects to get out the word. For a male, the drumming signals to local constituents that the bird is on its territory, that a no-trespassing sign has been posted for other males, and that he is available for courting.

Interestingly, females may drum just as much as males, especially before pairing off with a male. Just about anything that will make a racket will do for the drumming of either gender—from metal roof gutters, to garbage can lids, tin roofs, and hollow trees.

I receive calls every spring asking how to dissuade woodpeckers from drumming on house siding. Woodpeckers may drum on siding typically for two reasons: one, to dig for insects that are within the siding, and two, to call attention to themselves for mating and territorial purposes.

If you may have insects in your siding, you can apply a wood preservative to halt the insects, and in turn halt the woodpeckers. Or you can cover the area with window screen, heavy plastic, or a tarp to prevent access. If the food incentive is removed, the birds will usually remove themselves as well.

If you have woodpeckers seeking love or territory, they have found that your siding, or your metal chimney, resonates quite nicely and amplifies their drumming for neighborhood birds. If you can insulate or tighten down the material that is resonating, thus dampening the sound, the woodpeckers will usually choose another site.

May

Gratitude is a kind of seeing, an awareness of the magnitude of the gift of this earth. To see the world gratefully is to be endlessly surprised by the bare fact of it, its beauty and power and everlastingness.

—Kathleen Dean Moore, *Pine Island Paradox*

The ancient Celts celebrated May 1 as Beltane, a cross-quarter day marking the midpoint between spring and summer solstice. Beltane meant "bright fire." Bonfires were lit on the hills to herald in the summer and bring prosperity to all. The Druids would rush their cattle through the fires to purify them and to bring luck. Festivals were held to celebrate the fertility and flowering of life. The celebration of Beltane expressed gratitude for the re-creation of the living world.

While we have no parallel to Beltane today, the month of May still stirs the same excitement and joy in our souls. If there's a more intensely vibrant month than May, I don't know of it. Green-up, when the world turns from brown to green, occurs in May. Birds return—we go from some 30 wintering species to our full complement of 150 or more nesting species. Most mammals have given birth to their young by the end of May. Many species of birds have already nested and produced hatchlings by the end of May.

Altogether, life just explodes in this month. I wish I could bottle May for later sipping. Don't let any of it pass you by.

Mayday! Mayday!

"Mayday" is the international distress signal used by airplanes and ships, and it also represents the first day of May, a day traditionally celebrated with activities like dancing around the Maypole. It's also a day that has often been marked by chaotic political demonstrations.

On May 1, 2005, I watched squalls of snow hit the Northwoods throughout the day, at times falling so heavily that the trees across the river were obscured. I thought of how three weeks prior, we had hit 80°F, the ice had gone off our lakes, the birds had been coming in waves, flowers were starting to bloom, the frogs were chorusing at top of their lungs, we were thinking of planting gardens, and we were riding bikes. Spring had sprung, or so we assumed.

The next day, May 2, I looked out my window and saw snow covering the landscape. I wanted to yell "MAYDAY! MAYDAY!" Spring had crashed and burned, emotional chaos was upon us, and we were back to winter.

Of course, all that early April warmth was the most exquisite of teases. We all knew it, but as in all passions and loves, we were quick to lose sight of the rational and instead fell head over heels into the bright light.

It wasn't all a hallucination. The period from March 29 to April 6 was quite warm, and produced perfect southerly winds that carried many early migrating birds to the Northwoods. During those nine days, seven nights produced peak migrations, according to John Idzikowski, a professor and ace birder in Milwaukee who follows migration movements by interpreting radar screens. From April 6 to May 1, a 25-day period, only two other nights produced peak migration. The other 23 days produced very low migration movements or none at all.

The birds were in a holding pattern, stuck on runways south of us, waiting for the dominant weather system over Canada, and its strong northerly headwinds, to leave. Wildflowers had been suppressed as well. Many were "in bloom," but the petals wouldn't open because it was too darn cold. I think I know how they felt.

A River of Birds

Despite the exceptionally warm weather in early May of 1998, very few warblers had returned to Wisconsin. Only a smattering of yellow-rumped, palm, and pine warblers were being seen even in southern Wisconsin. Apparently the neotropical warblers had not been receiving our warm weather reports, and instead were relying on their instincts to tell them when to leave their wintering grounds and how fast to proceed to their nesting territories in the north country. History was certainly on their side. We all know how we can get whomped with a cold spell in May. But the marvelous spring of 1998 lulled us all into believing that summer was right around the corner. And with that belief came the expectation that migrating birds should have been here, regardless of what the calendar said to the contrary.

So where were they? A remarkable e-mail dated April 30, 1998, written by John Arvin, a highly regarded ornithologist from Louisiana, told us they were on their way. Arvin was counting migrating birds from a platform 80 feet off the water on the coast of the Gulf of Mexico near New Orleans, Louisiana. His e-mail reported the following:

> "Up nearly all night marveling. The river of birds continued unabated (ranging from 30-50 birds passing my position per second in the illuminated air space I could see that extends

> maybe 100 m. out from the platform from within a few feet of the water up to about 200 m.). Birds higher than that I could not see but there seemed to be far fewer very far overhead. By 05:00 the rate had fallen off to about 10-15 birds/second ... The sheer numbers of thrushes was staggering ...
>
> "It is now just daylight and the flow seems to have stopped or to have gained enough altitude that I can no longer see them with the unaided eye though there are birds flying around the platform in random directions that had evidently put down during the night and now are being stirred up by human activity ...
>
> "This has been the ornithological spectacle of my entire life. Intellectually I knew that this sort of thing had to happen, at least occasionally, but to actually stand in one place for hour after hour and watch a steady flow pass just a few feet from you is like watching a major river. And attempting to quantify the flow is about like trying to count water in a river. I'm a little rocky from no sleep but I have never been remotely struck by any other ornithological event like I have been by this. I suspect that very few people on this planet have seen what I have seen in the last 12 hours. It is a spellbinding feeling I will carry to my grave."

Seeing 30 to 50 birds per second for hours on end is extraordinary, yet enormous pulses of migrating birds occur with regularity. They often take place along a point of a coastline where birds can make their first landing after a 500-mile crossing. Birds that must fly long distances over water follow the winds—in the spring, the passage of a warm front from the south, and in the fall, a cold front passing from the north. Radar studies have counted up to a million songbirds passing at night during a five-hour period through a mile-wide corridor!

So keep the feeders full, the binoculars handy, and make a point of walking every day you can in May. Major migrations will typically only occur for the next three weeks.

night migrating birds

Avian River, Part Two

Lee Snow from Harshaw visited a bird-banding group on the Gulf of Mexico, and wrote: "The many warblers and vireos, etc., were coming through—species like blue bunting, indigo bunting, worm-eating warbler, prothonotary warbler, painted buntings, white-eyed vireos, and too many to mention—but they seemed to arrive in groups. It was a real thrill to see and view these tiny birds close up that the bander examined, banded, and released. Some had to be fed sugar water as the winds hadn't been favorable for the long flight over the Gulf. Many no doubt didn't make it over."

A Texas Hooker

I realize this is a family book, but we have sightings of a Texas Hooker in our area every May. Tom Nichols, a bird researcher from the Fifield area, wrote: "I am told by a retired airline pilot who is also a birder that for a good migration to occur, a Texas Hooker has to be in place. This means that the jet stream has to swing up from the southwest, eventually turning north towards the Lake States."

When a Hooker arrives, the birds begin to stream in.

American Redstart

Throughout May, Mary and I awaken to wonderful bird choirs, but one May morning a particular songster sang just outside our window and seemed even more insistent than the others. "See-see-see-SEE-oh" it kept saying, or I suppose if you want to be patriotic, you could imagine it singing "Oh-can-you-SEE-oh." Whatever mnemonic trips your trigger, one morning we headed out the door and spent a good 10 minutes getting wonderful views of this black and orange warbler, the American redstart, which obligingly flitted from branch to branch, coming ever closer to us.

Redstarts commonly nest in the Northwoods, usually in deciduous woods near wetlands, lakes, and streams. Look for them in low to medium-height vegetation, and try pishing or squeaking to bring them in. Most warblers do a great job of ignoring pishing, but redstarts often respond favorably.

Backyard Wildlife Habitat

Are you interested in making your property more attractive for a variety of birds, butterflies, and other wildlife? The National Wildlife Federation has put together an excellent packet of information on creating backyard wildlife habitat. See their Website at www.nwf.org/backyardwildlifehabitat/.

Spring Migration at Whitefish Point Bird Observatory

On May 4, 2001, eight local birders and I drove to Whitefish Point Bird Observatory just northeast of Sault Ste. Marie to witness the spring hawk and waterfowl migration. Migrating birds congregate here as they are funneled east along the south shore of Lake Superior while looking for a narrow spot to cross the water. Whitefish Point is only 17 miles from Canada, and hawks are quite tempted to take a shortcut across Lake Superior from the tip of the peninsula. We watched as many hawks started across and then turned around, either heading south toward the Sault, or actually heading back west along the Superior shore.

Crossing big water is very difficult for hawks that depend on rising thermals to buoy their flight. Starting across Lake Superior must be like opening the refrigerator, the cold blast of air above the frigid lake eliminating the thermal lifting power that the warm land so readily provides.

We had hawks in the air virtually every minute we were on the hawk-watch platform. Eight species of raptors soared by us, including sharp-shins, red-tails, rough-legs, broad-wings, merlins, turkey vultures, osprey, and even a golden eagle. Some kettles of broad-wings contained well over 100 birds. I was surprised that we missed bald eagles and kestrels, and we could easily have had red-shoulders and goshawks if we had stayed longer.

We counted 52 species of birds over the weekend, an excellent number given that the major songbird migration had yet to reach so far north. Common loons were, well, common. Whitefish Point averages some 9,000 loons in the spring, an extraordinary number. They were flying overhead, or in front of us off the point and became so ordinary that we easily bored humans soon failed to take notice as they passed by.

Whitefish Point is known for serving up records. One was set while we were there—the first Wilson's plover ever seen in Michigan. Several members of our group viewed the bird closely and were able to add it to their life lists.

In early May 2003, I led another group of birders to the Whitefish Point Bird Observatory, and we hit it! By late morning, the hawks began streaming in, and at one point, the official counter on the hawk platform could see four separate kettles of hawks in the air, totaling more than 400 individuals. Most were broad-winged hawks, but one kettle held at least 60 red-tailed hawks as well. By "kettle," birders mean a whirl of hawks soaring upward like steam from a kettle. The birds gather together to catch a spiraling thermal updraft, and seem to hang in the air.

By 3 p.m., we had seen 10 species of raptors sail by.

All told, we compiled 70 species, including some unexpected ones like a flock of snow buntings on the sandy shoreline of Lake Superior, a Lapland longspur on the rocky shoreline of Lake Michigan near Manistique, and our best non-bird—a cow moose walking out of a bog and across the road in front of us.

Woodcock Courtship Dance

While Callie and I were cruising with our windows open listening for frogs in 2004, we heard a woodcock "peenting" in a cutover area next to the road. We stopped to listen, and I discovered that I'd never taken Callie out to experience the utterly unique courtship flight of the male woodcock.

I suspect that in mid-May, just as dark descends, most open fields in the Northwoods have a male woodcock advertising his availability to any hen willing to listen. The performance is given as punctually as the curtain-rising time for any Broadway play, except for one major difference. The male woodcock begins his dance based on a rather precise measure of available light, and given that sunsets occur progressively later throughout the spring, the male woodcock's dance accordingly starts a minute or two later every night. Males perform on "singing sites" or "breeding fields" that they occupy every spring.

The male begins by uttering a monotonous, nasal, one-note "peent" every few seconds for maybe a minute. Next he leaps off the ground, rising in widening circles to as high as 300 feet while his wings "twitter," then hovering and pouring out a song of liquid chirps. He drops suddenly while still chirping, descending like a maple leaf on a zigzag path to the ground, alights, and immediately begins to "peent" again. If a female has ventured onto his singing ground, he'll walk over to her stiff-legged, and they'll copulate. Being polygynous, no pair-bond is made, and the male goes back to his peenting and dancing with no strings attached. The male gives no parental care, nor does he guard any mate.

The female lays her eggs on the ground in little more than a scrape of leaves, perfect for camouflage given that her coloring is a patterned dead-leaf brown. If all goes well, the usual clutch of four eggs will hatch in 21 days, then within a few hours the young and mother leave the nest together and move to the best site they can find for feeding on earthworms. Worms comprise 50 to 90 percent of their diet.

Sometime in the first weeks of May, take a walk near some open habitat at dusk or just before dawn, and listen for the woodcock courtship flight. It's a one-of-a-kind show.

Bears at Bird Feeders

Every May I get numerous phone calls from people whose bird feeders have been ripped to shreds by hungry bears. Bob and Nancy Hackworthy on Island Lake reported the first black bear mauling of a bird feeder I'd heard of in the spring of 1997. Both of their bird feeders were knocked over, and the bear gobbled all the sunflower seeds.

On May 14, 2001, Andrew Teichmiller woke up to find garbage strewn all over his front yard. The night before Andy had packed his car with all his household recyclable materials, plus the non-recyclable garbage, that he was taking to the recycling station the next morning. He had cracked open one of his windows to keep the smell down a bit overnight, a practical thought, at least on the surface.

The next morning he found the garbage and the remains of his window scattered about, courtesy of a black bear, which certainly found it kind of Andy to provide dinner for him.

A participant in one of my May wildflower hikes told me that a bear had come right through the screen door of the cabin next door to drag out a 50-pound bag of sunflower seeds. Fortunately, no one was home at the time. The bear ate about half the bag, apparently feeling satiated after 25 pounds of seeds.

The pillaging and destruction of bird feeders by bears is a relatively common experience in the early spring when six months of hibernation and hunger coincide with free food on a pole. Bears are hungry in early spring, and the menu items served at a backyard bird feeder are much more easily obtained and far more plentiful than the natural world is often dishing up in early May.

What can you do to avoid the problem? About the only "remedy" is to take your feeders in for several weeks if a bear is in the neighborhood. Bears run regular feeding routes, and if you fail to produce any food, a bear will typically cross you off its itinerary.

The problem with this is that spring is when you want to have your feeders up! To get the best of both worlds, you may be able to bring your feeders in at night and put them out during the day. But bears do feed during the day, so this remedy may be short-lived.

Creating a bear-proof feeder is another idea people have tried, but bear-proof is darn close to being an oxymoron. Bears, like squirrels, usually find ways to overcome the barriers we create for them. And with bears, it can be costly when they find the solution to your bear-proof design, because they use brute strength as their equalizer, which often translates into total destruction of your feeders.

Along with just about everything else in the Northwoods, the real solution is simply learning to live with nature. We should want nature to win most of these conflicts. When we start winning them all, then we will no longer live in a natural world.

Santa Wood Duck

Around Mother's Day 2000, Alvena Kaczmarek reported hearing a thumping around her house on three different occasions. She thought maybe the local bear had returned to knock over her bird feeder again, but no, the feeder was intact. Then she thought maybe it was a deer outside stomping or snorting, but there was no sign of a deer anywhere. Finally, she walked into her living room and saw a female wood duck silhouetted against the glass door, but not outside—it was in the room! Apparently, the wood duck had fallen down the chimney and was flinging itself against the glass door trying to get out of the house.

Woodies nest in tree cavities, so maybe the chimney looked inviting. I wondered whether the duck would return in December with a red suit on, but Alvena never said.

Bird Bands—What to Do If You Find One

One early May, Don Rasmussen in Springstead watched an immature sharp-shinned hawk slam into his window and then fall onto the ground. Don approached it, picked it up, and noticed a band on its leg. He wrote down the number, and laid the bird back down. The bird soon regained consciousness, and flew up into a tree.

Don called me with the number to find out what the protocol was for turning in band numbers. The procedure is to call the Patuxent Wildlife Research Center near Washington, D.C., with the location, circumstances, and date of your find. The toll free number is (800) 327-2263, or you can enter the information on their Website: www.pwrc.usgs.gov/bbl/homepage/call800.htm. Typically, the center will immediately give the date and general region where the bird was banded, and will send a card with more detailed information on who banded the bird, its age and gender, and the specific location where it was banded.

For songbirds, the rate of return on bands is only one in 1,000 (0.1 percent), so songbird bands are a real find. Raptor bands are returned at a 5 to 10 percent rate, while waterfowl average about a 15 percent return.

Band returns provide the raw data for understanding migration routes and timing, home ranges, and a host of other important behavioral characteristics. By calling the above number, you provide the necessary missing link in the efforts of bird banders around the country to add to our understanding of birds.

Beaking of Birds

Most birds have black beaks, but beaks come in all colors, from the brilliant blue of the ruddy duck, to the bright red of the common merganser, and the multi-colored palette of the Atlantic puffins. We often have evening grosbeaks coming to our feeders in May, and I've always found it interesting how their beak changes color from an olive-yellow in the fall to a bright apple green in the spring. The color change occurs as the outer layer (the rhamphotheca) of the beak wears away and reveals new, brighter colors on the growing skin below.

Other birds change their beak colors in the spring, too. Robins and starlings have dark brown bills in the fall, but they both turn yellow in the spring. Some birds' bills go from brighter to darker in the spring. For example, the male bobolink and house sparrow wear black bills while breeding, but yellowish-brown bills in the fall.

Bill coloration has functional purposes. Adult herring gulls have a red mark on their lower beak, which serves as a target for nestlings to peck at and trigger a disgorgement of food. Nestling songbirds are born with a temporary colorful flange at the sides of their mouth, which provides an easy target for the parents transporting food. But just why a snowy egret has a black beak, a great egret a yellow beak, and a toucan has an oversized colorful beak isn't really known.

Blizzard of Aspen Seeds

It snowed aspen seeds over Mother's Day weekend in 1999. The air was literally thick with them at times, and the surface of some area lakes could hardly be seen due to the carpet of white "cotton."

I put a female aspen catkin under a microscope to see just how many seeds one tree might produce. The catkin was covered with about 100 capsule-like structures, each containing the silky white parachutes and seeds that would be distributed to the four corners of the earth on the next big wind. Each capsule contained about 10 seeds, so one catkin produced around 1,000 seeds, at least on this tree. I tried to count how many catkins were on the tree itself and gave up after estimating at least 1,000.

By my math, then, each female tree may produce about one million seeds. Consider that aspens are by far the most numerous trees in the Northwoods, representing 20 to 28 percent of the trees in our northern forests (45 to 50 percent of the upland Northern Highlands State Forest). Add the fact that the seeds are extremely light, averaging about three million to the pound. Then toss in a dry and windy spell to permit the seeds to remain airborne for a long time.

Now you have the makings of the 1999 aspen blizzard.

Aspen seeds remain viable only for a short time and require moist, bare soils and full sun in order to germinate. Abundant seed crops occur on average every four years, so 1999 must have been the BIG year.

The new seedlings may grow two feet by the end of their first autumn, with roots extending 5 to 10 inches down and 16 inches laterally. Their exceptional growth is just one of the reasons foresters love aspen so much.

Aspen buds and catkins are a favorite food of ruffed grouse, but we'd need a grouse in nearly every tree to consume this extravagance.

Celestial Events

- Comet Hale-Bopp left us in May 1997, and won't return until the year 4377. Imagine what the earth, if it's still here, will look like then.
- May 4 brings us 14 1/2 hours of daylight. By May 17, we will be enjoying 15 hours of daylight. Fifteen and a half hours of daylight come our way on June 1. Think of those long December nights and enjoy!
- Look for the peak of the Eta Aquarid meteor shower in the first week of May.
- May 5, 1961, marks the day that Alan Shepard became the first American in space.

Raptor Rapture

Taking groups to an area to witness a hawk migration is a hit-or-miss proposition, and I've missed my fair share of times. On May 9, 1998, a group of 10 of us traveled up the Keweenaw Peninsula to Brockway Mountain Drive, near Copper Harbor. Our intent was to try to catch the annual spring hawk migration. We were blessed with a beautiful day and a moderate east wind that, while not ideal for migration (we were hoping for southwesterly), didn't prevent a steady number of raptors from soaring by. Highlights of the day for me included a low-flying merlin skimming over our heads, a kettle of 27 broad-winged hawks that seemed to stop near us and simply enjoy soaring in the thermals, and numerous sharp-shinned and broad-winged hawks that flew below us in the valley between the ridge where we were standing and another to our south. Looking down on migrating hawks is a rather remarkable experience! I estimate that we saw more than 100 raptors of five different species in 2 1/2 hours, a moderate day by Brockway Mountain standards.

On May 13, 2000, a constant hard rain and 37°F temperatures completely grounded the hawks. Our raptor count for the day was one osprey!

On May 4, 2002, we gave Copper Harbor another shot and hit the jackpot. For the two hours we stood on Brockway Mountain Drive, hawks were always in the air, sometimes 30 or 40 right overhead. Overall, we saw 12 species of raptors, and though we didn't keep count, our count had to easily eclipse 1,000 or more individuals. Our guide, Jim Rooks of Copper Harbor, said the day ranked right at the top of his 30 years of hawk-watching on the mountain,

That day a strong southerly wind pushed the birds up the Keweenaw Peninsula after nearly two weeks of cold and rainy weather out of the north that had grounded most of the migration. The hawks must have been lined up on their migratory runways waiting for the right wind. Broad-winged hawks dominated the sky, accounting for about 90 percent of the flight. But we were also treated to excellent numbers of sharp-shinned hawks, and smaller numbers of rough-legged, red-tailed, and marsh hawks, bald eagles, ospreys, kestrels, merlins, turkey vultures, and an individual Swainson's hawk and one peregrine falcon. The only raptors we missed that we had a reasonable expectation of seeing were goshawks, Cooper's hawks, and red-shouldered hawks.

Not only was the quantity of birds never-ending, the quality of our sightings was exceptional. Brockway Mountain rises abruptly just a short distance away from the Lake Superior coastline. A valley falls away to the south along the ridge, while the lake lies way down below the rock-face to the north. So, the hawks often fly below the ridge, or begin below the ridge and then soar over the edge of the rock-face and right above the heads of observers. More often than not, the birds were so low that Saturday (20 to 50 feet overhead) that binoculars weren't necessary at all. The greatest problem we had was not getting sore necks! What a day!

Economy and Ecology

At the 2003 master plan meeting for the Northern Highlands-American Legion State Forest, many people shared comments on activities they felt would bring the greatest economic inflow to our area. Their ideas included the conversion of public forest lands to a golf course, ATV tourism, more logging, and more old-growth forests to draw hikers and others seeking more quiet experiences.

The multiple-use concept of forest management—the notion we can fundamentally pursue all uses on the land and do so harmoniously—is certainly put to the test within such a planning process. The DNR planners must feel like they've been put on a stretching rack with their limbs pulled in every conceivable direction, while they try to somehow keep the body of their mission intact. Their stated mission is to "assure the practice of sustainable forestry ... that the management of state forests is consistent with the ecological capability of the state forest land ... [and to provide] benefits including soil protection, public hunting, protection of water quality, production of recurring forest products, outdoor recreation, native biological diversity, aquatic and terrestrial wildlife, and aesthetics (Wisconsin Statutes 28.04)."

The attempt to introduce local economics as a major determining factor in management of a state-held resource certainly muddies the waters, particularly when little clear statistical evidence exists to demonstrate what might be gained or lost by one activity. Some activities lend themselves to economic bean counting—how many cords of wood we actually sell or how many golf course passes we issue, for example. Other activities, like how many people come here to watch a sunset at the end of a dock or how many look for wildflowers in their local forest, are simply uncountable.

"One basic weakness in a conservation system based wholly on economic motives is that most members of the land community have no economic value. Wildflowers and songbirds are examples. Of the 22,000 higher plants and animals native to Wisconsin, it is doubtful whether more than 5 per cent can be sold, fed, eaten, or otherwise put to economic use. Yet these creatures are members of the biotic community, and if its stability depends on its integrity, they are entitled to continuance." So wrote Aldo Leopold in his essay "The Land Ethic," which appeared in *A Sand County Almanac.*

I suspect that ecotourism was unknown in 1949 when Leopold wrote this famous essay. Though it's still difficult to quantify the economic reach of non-regulated recreation, today we can more readily put an economic value on the non-consumable plants and non-game animals that don't get measured and sold for direct profit. The measure most commonly used is wildlife-watching, and the document that gives us the most detailed information is the most recent (2001) "National Survey of Fishing, Hunting, and Wildlife-Associated Recreation," put together by the U.S. Fish and Wildlife Service. A booklet offering a breakdown of these statistics in Wisconsin was published in April of 2003, and I'd recommend it to all of you seeking long-term statistics on what types of recreation occur in our state and how much money is spent on them.

Wisconsin's survey revealed that nearly 3.2 million Wisconsin residents and non-residents 16 years and older fished, hunted, or wildlife-watched in Wisconsin. Of this total number:

- 660,000 hunted
- 1,400,000 fished
- 2,400,000 watched wildlife

Expenditures in 2001 in Wisconsin totaled:

- $801 million for hunters
- $1.0 billion for fishing
- $1.3 billion for wildlife-watchers

To be counted as a wildlife-watcher, one either had to take a "special interest" in wildlife around their homes or take a trip for the "primary purpose" of wildlife-watching. Secondary wildlife-watching activities such as incidentally observing wildlife while pleasure driving, trips to fish, hunt, or scout, and trips to zoos, circuses, aquariums, or museums were not considered wildlife-watching activities.

So an argument can easily be made that the activity offering the greatest economic benefit to northern Wisconsin is wildlife-watching.

But I'm uncomfortable using any economic arguments as a basis for how we should manage our forests. I don't think we'll ever be able to accurately assess how everyone recreates and how our dollars are parceled out to each activity, so our statistics will always be suspect. The larger issue is how much economics should enter into the discussion at all. Leopold railed against economic determinism, and repeatedly wrote of his contempt for an economic system that could never fully take into account the value of "things natural, wild, and free." Rather than basing our conservation on economics, he believed we needed to value nature based on the principles of quality—the understanding that we are better off in the long run with wildness left intact. And Leopold argued that while conservation is usually good economics, particularly in the long run, "that ecology, and not economics, is the final arbiter of success in land management."

Put Up Your Hummingbird Feeders

If hummers hold true to form, they should arrive in our area around Mother's Day weekend. Be sure to have your feeders up and ready for them, given that they've just completed a 1,500-mile migration from Central America all the way to your backyard. Remember to use a nectar solution (3 to 4 parts water to 1 part sugar) that has no artificial dyes or sweeteners in it. Clean your feeders at least once a week and more often in hot weather. Hummers drink their weight in nectar every day, feeding at least once every 10 minutes, or visiting more than 1,000 flowers a day.

If you wish to attract more than one pair, put more than one feeder up, widely spaced in different parts of your yard. Hummers are highly territorial and usually won't tolerate intruders at "their" feeder.

A Personal-Space Probe

Ruby-throated hummingbirds returned to our property on Mother's Day, May 9, 2004. Over the years I've heard numerous wonderful stories of hummers landing on people's red hats and clothing, but here's a story that tops them all. Andrea Feener was out working in her yard in Irma. She was bundled up against the cold, wearing a fluorescent orange hooded sweatshirt with the hood tied tightly. A hummingbird suddenly appeared in front of Andrea, hovered close to her face, then stuck its tongue up her nose, apparently believing it had found the mother of all orange flowers. Andrea stood stock-still, though the hummer's tongue "tickled," and the hummer, upon discovering this flower to be nectarless, flew away.

How Andrea managed to stand still for this probing, I'll never know, but it affords her a unique distinction. Not many folks can say they've had a hummingbird seek nectar in their nose.

Hummers have a long, extendable forked tongue that is folded along the edges to act like a tiny channel for delivery of nectar. The hummers actually use their tongues like a straw, sucking nectar from within tubed flowers.

The only other birds that can extend their tongues well beyond their bill are the woodpeckers. Given its name, one would assume that the yellow-bellied sapsucker also draws sap from a tree by sucking, but in fact the tongue on a sapsucker is covered with forward-pointing hairs that act like a brush, collecting sap from the holes they drill in trees. Sapsuckers really ought to be named "sapbrushers."

Our other woodpeckers have backward-pointing barbs on their tongues for latching onto insects when they probe into a hole. Their feeding process is a bit like going fishing with a series of tiny fishhooks.

hepatica

First Woodland Flowers in Pine Forests

The Northwoods finally regains most of its many colors and scents in May. Leading the parade of the first spring wildflowers are hepatica and trailing arbutus. John Burroughs called hepatica "the gem of the woods," its value deriving as much from its early appearance as its array of colors, which include white, pink, lavender, and blue. Hepatica's three-lobed evergreen leaves last all winter, usually turning a rusty purple. New leaves won't appear until after the flowers have gone by. The flowers may be closed during a cloudy day and closed at night, perhaps in order to save heat. Dense hairs clothe the stems, presumably to also conserve heat, but who knows? One author suggests that the hairs serve to prevent ants from climbing the stems and drinking the flowers' nectar without pollinating the flowers.

Hepatica may or may not be scented, though I've never found one to offer a fragrance. Trailing arbutus, on the other hand, seems dipped in the sweetest of perfumes. The delicate flowers often remain hidden under the plant's leathery leaves or beneath the leaf litter. A little sorting and scratching in the dirt usually reveals the flowers, and kneeling to get your nose right down to the ground is the only way to reveal the condensed fragrance of spring that these little flowers hold.

The prostrate stems and leaves creep beneath the pines and are lightly rooted in the dry, acidic soils. Arbutus and pines go together like trilliums and maples do in better soils. Nova Scotia chose the trailing arbutus as its floral emblem, and it is the state flower of Massachusetts. Mary and I would vote to put it on our Northwoods flag if someone ever designed one, along with the white pine and the loon.

Arbutus is in the Heath family, which includes other pine community species like wintergreen and bearberry, and bog plants like wild cranberry, bog laurel, bog rosemary, Labrador tea, and leatherleaf. The word "heathen" supposedly derives from the bog lands, or heaths, that prevented missionaries from gaining access to pagans living on the other side. The non-believers were called "heathens" by dint of the heath plants that separated them from God's true followers.

Giving Birds the Berries

Mary and I continue to plant native berry-producing trees and shrubs to attract more birds to our property. In 2003, we already had high-bush cranberry, black cherry, chokecherry, red-osier dogwood, crabapple, blackberries, gooseberry, and honeysuckles providing birds with a meal, but we knew we could do a lot better. For one, we wanted more native dogwoods, because more than 90 species of birds reportedly feed on the fruit of dogwoods. Round-leafed dogwood (*Cornus rugosa*), panicled dogwood (*Cornus racemosa*), and alternate-leafed dogwood (*Cornus alternifolia*) all are native to the Northwoods and grow abundantly.

Along our wetlands, we wanted to plant winter holly (*Nemopanthus mucronata*) and winterberry (*Ilex verticillata*), both of which produce red berries that attract thrushes, waxwings, and thrashers.

In the dry uplands, we hoped to add more wild roses and various brambles like blackberries, raspberries, and gooseberries. When planted close together, these thorny tangles provide a dense foliage that protects the nests of birds like gray catbirds while providing wonderful fruits. Blackberries alone are utilized by more than 90 species of birds and mammals.

I really wanted serviceberries, or what we call Juneberries (*Amelanchier* sp.), which are easy to plant and produce a purple fruit that is great on pancakes if you can beat the orioles, catbirds, hermit thrushes, veeries, cedar waxwings, and grouse to them.

We also wanted native mountain ash (*Sorbus americana*), which produces bright red berries that last well into the winter, a feature true also of maple-leafed viburnum's (*Viburnum acerifolium*) purple-black berries.

And if we could get thimbleberries (*Rubus parviflorus*) or elderberries (*Sambucus canadensis*) to grow, we could make fine jams, if we could harvest them before they were eaten by the thrushes, scarlet tanagers, red-eyed vireos, and brown thrashers.

By 2006, we had planted nearly all of these, as well as many perennial flowers that produce seeds in the fall and also feed the birds.

We love the idea of perennial fresh fruits and perennial good birdwatching. Why not consider using the lawn mower less and your binoculars more this summer?

Ground Nesters

Many people like to "clean up" the woods around their place and make it look "neat." I do much the opposite, either from a very lazy streak or from what I hope is an understanding of bird nesting sites. It's a surprise to some to learn that a host of birds nest on the ground, utilizing cover of various types to remain hidden. Some birds like killdeer utilize no cover whatsoever except for their cryptic coloration. The bird species that nest on the ground in our area include spruce grouse, ruffed grouse, sharp-tailed grouse, wild turkey, American woodcock, whip-poor-will, yellow-bellied flycatcher, winter and sedge wren, veery, hermit thrush, dark-eyed junco, bobolink, as well as the following warblers: blue-winged, golden-winged, Tennessee, Nashville, palm, black-and-white, ovenbird, northern waterthrush, Connecticut, mourning, Wilson's, and Canada. Numerous sparrows nest on the ground too, including savannah, Le Conte's, song, Lincoln's, and white-throated.

Of course, even if you keep your forest floor natural, you can't expect to have all of these birds nesting, but you may get a few. Thus, I advocate for some random chaos in the woods. Dead trees should be left standing or lying, leaves should be left on the forest floor, shrubs should be encouraged. All of these provide cover, food, and nesting habitat. Walking may be less easy in such a woods, but the life within the woods will be much richer.

Dutchman's Breeches

On May 15, 1997, I led a "spring flora" hike (the quotation marks tell you where I'm going with this) on the beautiful Franklin Lake Interpretive Trail in the Nicolet National Forest. We were bundled in our winter jackets, and a number of snow squalls blew in during

Dutchman's breeches

our hike to help emphasize the theme of spring hardiness in our northern flora and fauna. We had a wonderful time, though we saw really only one species in flower—Dutchman's breeches. Despite the cold, it was growing profusely.

The double-spurred flowers of this species hang like upside-down leggings and are unique except for their likeness to squirrel corn, which often grows among the Dutchman's breeches. The presence of this flower is a good indicator of a humus-rich, neutral soil. Typical community members in a maple woods like the one we visited include trillium, trout lily, spring beauty, and bellworts, though all of these were closed up against the cold.

I suspected then that when some honest spring heat arrived, our flowers would appear in a twinkling, and many would disappear nearly as fast. The blossoms of bloodroot, for instance, usually last just two days, while spring beauties only bloom for three days. Many of these flowers go by very quickly, passing even before it seems that spring has truly arrived.

Hummingbird Behavior

Many people are puzzled by the aggressive behavior of male hummingbirds at their feeder. Typically, the male relentlessly chases off other males from his feeding territory, often doing so for hours at a time. This is common behavior. I have always wondered if the male is chasing the same rival male who is absolutely single-minded in his attempt to usurp the feeder, or whether other males are intruding on the territory. What is clear is that the territorial male has endless energy to chase and chase and chase.

Here's a technical description of this behavior [from *The Birds of North America*, monograph 204, Ruby-throated Hummingbird, by T. R. Robinson, R. R. Sargent, and M. B. Sargent]:

"[The] male [is] intensely territorial during breeding season ... Male's territory [is] centered on food source when sufficient cover available, with mating territory a secondary function. If food source [is] inadequate to attract females, male may move during the breeding season and set up territory elsewhere, sometimes as far as 3

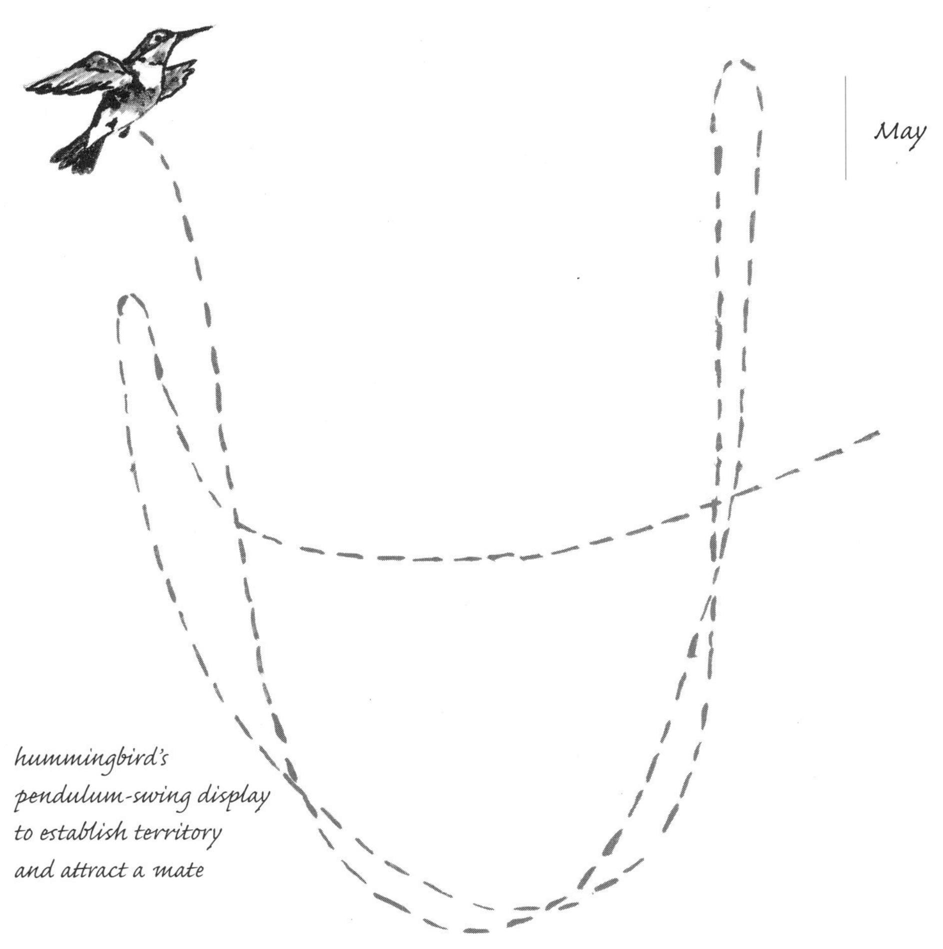

hummingbird's pendulum-swing display to establish territory and attract a mate

km away. Conspecific territorial intruders [are] commonly chased throughout the breeding season, especially by adult males."

A Hummingbird in the Hair Is Worth ...

We had some fascinating hummingbird sightings in May of 1997. On May 26, Tom and Pat Klein were visiting us to pick up some sea kayaks when a female hummingbird flew in through the open passenger door of their car, and klonked herself against the windshield. She sat for a minute between the dashboard and the glass as if dazed, then I picked her up and held her in my hand, the first living hummingbird I have ever held. We could see her heart pounding rapid fire, almost in a perpetual quiver. At rest, a hummer's heart beats 500 times per minute, and when active, 1,000 times per minute. I'm sure this little gal's heart was hammering somewhere in that range, but who can count that fast? I put her in Mary's hand so she could hold her, but the hummer soon flew up into the air.

Then it did the most amazing thing. It landed in Mary's hair, looking for all the world like a shimmering green barrette. I ran into the house to get the camera, ran back out, and was just about to push the shutter button when the hummer flew. Mary said afterward the hummer was so light that she could barely feel it in her hair.

Well, we thought that was it for hummingbird marvels, but half an hour later a male hummer flew in the open driver's side door. I didn't see whether he also klonked himself, but he sat on the floor mat and didn't move. I ran again into the house to get the camera (I'd put it away figuring we had lost our one big Kodak moment for the day), and this time the male remained still while I snapped several pictures. I then picked him up as I had the female, but he was less docile and struggled a bit. I handed him to Mary, and he flew immediately from her hand.

Investing in the Wind

By early May, alders, hazelnuts, and willows have unfurled their catkins, which hang in long, soft tassels. Red, silver, and sugar maples follow these shrubs in the blooming sequence, and the oaks, birches, and ashes come next.

Many folks never even notice these shrubs and trees flowering, and for good reason—the plants don't invest any energy in trying to attract notice. Most are wind-pollinated, gambling that the wind will blow at the right time in the right direction to bring about cross-pollination. These trees and shrubs hedge their bets by producing prodigious amounts of pollen—one catkin on a birch tree may release more than five million pollen grains! Multiply those grains by the number of catkins on an average tree, and the figure quickly becomes astronomical.

Wind-pollinated trees flower early, well before their leaves unfurl, recognizing the value of having an open canopy for the winds to flow through. The female flowers of these trees have enlarged, sticky stigmatic surfaces that help them to grab and hold the tiny floating pollen grains. When a pollen grain sticks to the stigma of a female flower, it sends out a rapidly growing tube that reaches into the plant's ovary. Then the sperm descends from the pollen into the ovary to fertilize the eggs and ultimately form a fruit or nut. The female flowers have evolved to chemically recognize only their own species' pollen and reject all others, even to reject their own pollen, at least until there's no other choice but to self-pollinate.

Later in spring and into summer, other trees and shrubs that produce colorful and scented flowers will put on their show, investing in beauty rather than wind in order to entice insects to do their pollinating.

The trick for all of them is to cross-pollinate, scrambling their particular genes with as many other genes as possible to create new genetic combinations and thus increase the odds of adaptive survival.

Ivory-Billed Woodpecker Lives in 2005!

If you missed the most stunning bird story of the century, an ivory-billed woodpecker, a species presumed extinct in the U.S. since the 1940s, was sighted and confirmed living in the Big Woods region of eastern Arkansas. Tim Gallagher, editor of the Cornell Lab of Ornithology's Living Bird magazine, and one of more than 50 researchers who spent every day for 14 months working to confirm the ivory bill's existence, wrote, "Just to think that this bird made it into the twenty-first century gives me chills. It's like a funeral shroud has been pulled back, giving us a brief glimpse of a living bird, rising Lazarus."

Indeed, extinction is not only the end of life for an individual, but for an entire species. It's the loss of a gift of God and/or evolution, the obliteration of a particular magic unique unto itself. For the ivory-billed, the magic has been rekindled—a species has risen from the ashes after 60 years.

What an extraordinary blessing!

The ivory-billed was once common in the old-growth swamp forests of the southeastern United States. John James Audubon shot and collected numerous ivory-bills along the Ohio, Arkansas, and Mississippi rivers in the 1820s. He wrote that the calls of the ivory-bill "are heard so frequently that ... the bird spends few minutes a day without uttering them."

In 1837, Audubon "found [ivory-bills] very abundant along the finely wooded margins of that singular stream called the 'Buffalo Bayou' in ... Texas, where we procured several specimens."

In the 1870s, timber companies gained access to most of the southern bottomland forests, and began to clear-cut critical ivory-billed habitat.

Theodore Roosevelt saw three ivory-billed woodpeckers on a hunting trip in northeastern Louisiana, and wrote, "They were noisy but wary, and they seemed to me to set off the wildness of the swamp as much as any of the beasts of the chase." Roosevelt was also awestruck by the old trees of the region: "In stature, in towering majesty, they are unsurpassed by any trees of our eastern forests; lordlier kings of the green-leaved world are not to be found until we reach the sequoias and redwoods of the Sierras."

By 1924, though a pair of ivory-bills were found that year near the Taylor River in Florida, many ornithologists considered the species extinct due to loss of habitat and collecting. Two local taxidermists, hearing of the discovery of the pair on the Taylor River, shot both of the ivory-bills—legally!

By 1935 three ivory-bill nests, the last known nests, were located in the Singer Tract in Louisiana. Researchers produced the first motion pictures and sound recordings ever obtained of the species. The Singer Tract was owned by the Singer Sewing Machine Company, and its oak trees were reserved for making sewing-machine cabinets. But the Singer Company soon sold the land to a Chicago-based lumber company, and as World War II commenced, wood that had sheltered the last ivory-billed woodpeckers was made into ammunition boxes and caskets.

In 1941, the National Audubon Society launched a campaign to preserve the Singer Tract as the last reserve for ivory-bills. The campaign failed, and the tract was cut.

In 1944, the Audubon Society sent artist Don Eckelberry to the Singer Tract to sketch the one ivory-bill left. This was the last time an ivory-bill was ever seen in the United States during the twentieth century.

In 1948, three ivory-bills, a subspecies of the birds found in the U.S., were found in the eastern mountains of Cuba.

By 1987, the last sighting of an ivory-bill was made in Cuba. None has been made there since.

On February 11, 2004, a kayaker named Gene Sparling spotted a male ivory-bill while paddling through the Cache River National Wildlife Refuge, and soon one of the most intensive searches ever undertaken for a bird commenced.

The cautionary note in all this was that only one male was known to exist at that time, despite 14 months of continuous field-work over 41-square kilometers of forest. The fact that the ivory-bill was seen only seven more times during this period indicates that the bird was very likely not at the center of its territory, and if it was nesting, was likely somewhere distant from the area where the sightings have occurred.

The good news is that despite the fact that no evidence of a mated pair has been found, the researchers have covered only a small portion of the available potential habitat. The Big Woods extends over 543,000 acres, the second-largest contiguous area of bottomland forest in the Mississippi River basin, which includes 20 distinct types of swamp and bottomland hardwood forests.

The Big Woods isn't ideal habitat at this point because it consists of patches of mature forest among a larger quiltwork of younger forests and regenerating fields. As the forest continues to mature, the very old trees and substantial standing dead and dying trees that are required by the ivory-bills will again dominate. Ivory-bills primarily eat beetle larvae that have bored through the bark of dead and dying trees to feed on the sap wood beneath.

The Nature Conservancy and various partners have safeguarded more than 120,000 acres within the Big Woods, in addition to the specific location of the one known ivory-bill. The bird's discovery was initially kept secret in large part to purchase the necessary additional land to protect the species.

Let's give the last word (for the moment anyway) to Alexander Wilson, a pioneer ornithologist, who wrote of ivory-bills in 1809: "A majestic and formidable species ... his eye is brilliant and daring, and his whole frame so admirably adapted for his mode of life and method of procuring subsistence, as to impress on the mind of the examiner the most reverential ideas of the Creator."

Jeepers-Peepers!

Our youngest daughter Callie has helped me many times to conduct the frog count that I do in Vilas County every year for the DNR, so she's used to the din of chorusing spring peepers. Still, we went out for our first count one year, and at a count site, she looked at me and said, "They're deafening—they're making my eardrums hurt." We had a great night with high numbers of frogs. The wetlands were full of water, as were the vernal woodland ponds, so life was good if you were a frog.

Whence and why all the noise? Male peepers defend a tiny breeding territory, just 4 to 16 inches in diameter, uttering a single-note, high-pitched whistle that slurs upward as an advertisement for females. Males may repeat the note nearly every second during full chorusing events. Researchers report that a single male averages about 4,500 "peeps" a night. Multiply that frequency times a peeper for every square foot or so of a pond, and the racket sounds to some like heavy-metal sleigh bells, or as Chet Raymo writes, "like a zillion wedding guests clanking on glassware with spoons."

When a male enters another male's territory or gets too close, males may also give an aggressive call that is a longer trill of variable duration, but it is usually about a second long.

I've always wondered how females choose males in the midst of this pandemonium, but apparently they are able to distinguish individual males. One thought is that older males tend to call at a much faster rate, and some researchers have found that females are attracted to faster-calling males. Apparently no one has told frog females what every human female knows—beware of fast-talkers.

The relatively sudden chorusing of frogs in the early spring was a mystery to early societies. Pliny the Elder, the Roman naturalist, wondered about all those frogs coming out of nowhere in the spring with their outrageous racket, and could only attribute it to an "occult operation" of nature. When for several weeks an entire marsh becomes a riot of sound, magic seems as good an explanation as any.

Neither Toiling Nor Spinning

Consider the lilies, how they grow; they neither toil nor spin; yet I tell you even Solomon in all his glory was not arrayed like one of these. (Luke 12:22)

I'm not sure which lily this Biblical reference is alluding to, but the Northwoods offers a beautiful array of woodland lilies to enjoy.

In the poor sandy soils so common to the Lakeland area, the first lily to bloom is wild lily-of-the-valley, or Canada mayflower (*Maianthemum canadense*). Canada mayflower grows low to the ground, and blooms from early May into June in a cluster of small, four-pointed white flowers. Two to three shiny leaves usually unfurl in early May, each one heart-shaped at the base and pointed at the tip, with veins all emanating from the base and arching to the tip in typical lily fashion. Sometimes only one long-stemmed leaf will appear, usually indicating a sterile plant, and no flower will appear.

Canada mayflower qualifies as a ubiquitous Northwoods wildflower. It grows in a variety of habitats from sands to cedar swamps, and may even deserve the title of "most common wildflower." Its threadlike horizontal rhizomes create clonal colonies of flowers that profusely dot the groundlayer, making it difficult to walk without crushing a few.

Canada mayflower also goes by "wild lily-of-the-valley" because of the resemblance of its leaves to the domestic variety and the similar scent of both flowers, though the wild variety is much more modest in its scent. *Maianthemum* comes from the Greek for "Mayflower." *Maios* means "May," and *anthemon* translates into "blossom."

Other members of the lily family soon to bloom include bluebead lily, bellwort, twisted stalk, Solomon's seal, and false Solomon's seal. If by some mistake of the glacier you are blessed with better soils, trout lily and trillium, two more lilies, will soon be blooming in your woods.

How High Is High

Jack Bull of Winchester called with the story of an airplane pilot he knew who hit a migrating Canada goose at 20,000 feet. Jack wondered how migrating birds could breathe at that height. After all, humans often need supplemental oxygen at elevations greater than 10,000 feet if we're exercising. Not so for birds. Birds have air sacs that allow for comfortable flight at 20,000 feet. A study done in a wind tunnel that could simulate altitudinal pressure showed that common house sparrows were perfectly capable of flying at altitudes over 18,000 feet.

Most birds don't bother to fly this high however, because they choose the best altitude based on the atmospheric structure that best serves their purposes. If they're a soaring bird, where can they find the best thermals? If the bird is a powered migrant (a bird that has to power its way by flapping its wings almost continuously), where can it find the best tailwind? The fewest buffeting air currents? The coolest air? To climb to 20,000 feet is an enormous energy drain if there's no advantage in doing so.

As for how high birds can fly when they migrate, there's a report of a vulture that collided with a jet at 37,000 feet above Africa, and hawks commonly pass over Panama at altitudes above 20,000 feet.

But then again, some birds like loons, scoters, and pelicans often migrate at water level, their wings sometimes touching the waves.

Many studies have shown that the bulk of songbirds migrate at night, flying no more than 2,000 feet above the ground. Shorebirds and ducks tend to fly somewhat higher, often above 3,000 feet. Migrating waterfowl vary considerably in their altitude. Near shore they tend to fly within 100 to 200 feet of the waves. A study of migrating waterfowl along the Atlantic coast showed that 90 percent of thousands of scoters, mergansers, black ducks, loons, gannets, and other birds flew at less than 200 feet above the waves.

Why fly so low? Low altitude flights help avoid headwinds and lateral winds. Winds aren't as strong near the water because of friction created by the water's surface. The low fliers also achieve reduced drag from vortices formed as their wings move through the air, a process called using "ground effect." Birds often fly as low as possible and into the trough of a wave where wind is virtually nil, then barely gain enough altitude to graze the crest of the next oncoming wave before gliding down into its trough.

Whatever is most cost-effective, that is what a bird will do. If tailwinds are good up high, they'll go there. If a headwind is hammering them, they may stay put, or fly low to the ground. Birds clearly make decisions and adapt their behaviors to weather conditions; this flexibility allows for survival in the varying conditions that spring inevitably brings.

More Aspen?

I read with interest an article in the May 16, 1997, Lakeland Times newspaper concerning the push by the Ruffed Grouse Society for more aspen in the Northern Highlands-American Legion State Forest. At the time, the NH-AL was beginning the rewrite of its master plan, a revision finally concluded in 2005. One of the most controversial questions addressed in the plan was how to manage the forest communities within the NH-AL, a question that will never generate a "right" answer since all answers will be biased according to which value systems are given the highest priority.

The Ruffed Grouse Society rightly stated that our aspen forest community is being lost to some degree. What they failed to note was that the pre-settlement forest of northern Wisconsin was estimated to have only about a 2 percent aspen component, a number that leaped to around 50 percent after the clear-cutting in the early part of the twentieth century. Aspen grows in full sun after major forest disturbance like fire, windstorm, or in our modern era, clear-cutting, so aspen leaped to unprecedented abundance.

Today around 21 percent of the entire Northwoods landscape and about 45 to 50 percent of the forested uplands of the NH-AL are dominated by aspen forest, a decline that has occurred because a portion of these young forests has been allowed to begin the process of succession to other species.

How does one determine what the "right" percentages should be in a large and diverse forest like the NH-AL? Should we try to re-create what was here at the time of settlement? Was that particular moment in forest history the best model? Since forests are dynamic systems that are perpetually changing, is it even possible to manage a forest to maintain a particular complex of communities?

I don't pretend to have answers to these questions or a host of others that could be asked, but I do know that we have an artificially and aggressively maintained abundance of aspen that is still 10 to 20 times as dominant as it was a century ago. What the percentage of aspen should be is open to debate, but I'm absolutely unconvinced that we need more, and I believe strongly that the forest community structure of the NH-AL is artificially skewed toward aspen.

I like grouse, but no more than I like a host of other birds that don't fare well in young regenerating stands of aspen.

[The final plan approved in 2005 called for an increase in the older age classes of forest stands. However, the plan stated, "The composition of the forest would likely change very little over the next 50 years. Aspen stands are projected to decline by two percent ..."]

Painted Bunting in the Northwoods

The most remarkable sighting in May of 2002 was a painted bunting spotted on May 18 in the town of Powell, five miles south of Manitowish. Nancy and Jim Skowlund had the good fortune of hosting this very lost bird at their feeder for nearly a week. I posted their sighting on the Wisconsin BirdNet, and birders from all over the state came up to see the bird and receive the gracious hospitality of Nancy and Jim.

Their sighting is only the ninth recorded painted bunting ever seen in Wisconsin. Painted buntings belong in the American South, usually nesting in states like Texas, Louisiana, and Oklahoma. Peterson refers to painted buntings as the "most gaudily colored North American songbird." There certainly is no mistaking the male. His blue-violet head, red chest and rump, and green on the back give him the appearance of a bird right out of kindergarten coloring class.

Perfect Versus Imperfect Flowers

Every May, Mary and I are excited to see our first hepatica of the year. The cupped flower has six white petals (actually sepals) and many stamens rising around the flower's pistil. The sepals often range in color from purple to rose to white, and after a long winter, they are an absolute delight to see.

Hepaticas are preceded by a number of trees and shrubs that bloom in April, including aspens, or what many folks call popple. The male flowers of quaking aspens come into blossom only on male trees and soon fall onto the ground. However, the female flowers on female aspen trees remain on the trees after their fertilization by the pollen of the male flowers. These flowers change into "fruits" and will soon burst open into cottony, filamentous masses that will carry tiny seeds on the lightest of winds.

The difference in the flowering strategies of these two species is that hepaticas have perfect flowers, while aspens have imperfect flowers. By this I mean if a flower possesses both stamens (male organs) and pistils (female organs), it is termed a perfect flower, or bisexual. If it lacks either, it's is an imperfect flower, or unisexual.

To make the matter a bit more complex, some imperfect flowers are monoecious, meaning they have the sexes in separate flowers but on the same individual, kind of like a coed college dorm. Good examples are the oaks, birches, ragweed, and corn. Other imperfect flowers are dioecious. They practice sexual segregation by having the sexes on separate plants, like separate dorms for the two genders. Good examples are willows and aspens.

I bring this difference up because it's easy to be confused by a plant with two different flowering structures. Take the time to note the different monoecious flowers on common Northwoods trees and shrubs like alders, sweet gale, hazelnut, and birches. The male flowers are typically long catkins that will dispense a cloud of pollen when tapped lightly, while the female flowers are much smaller, discrete structures that often look conelike.

Brilliant Indigo

With a brilliant blue flourish in May 2003, indigo buntings seemed to arrive all at once in the Lakeland area. I received calls for first sightings of indigos from Jack Bull in Winchester, Kay Maki in McNaughton, and Janeen Clark in Lac du Flambeau on May 20; Erick Stark in Manitowish Waters and Marylyne Haag in Boulder Junction on May 21; and Linda Mastalski in Hazelhurst and Jean Long in Arbor Vitae on May 22. Jane Lueneburg in Woodboro even had an indigo bunting drinking from her hummingbird feeder on May 23!

Hard as it may be to believe, the brilliant blue coloration of the indigos actually occurs due to light diffraction through the feathers. Male indigo buntings have no blue pigment in their feathers whatsoever, and if seen in the shade or in silhouette, or even in your hand, the feathers appear solid black.

In direct contrast to the fabulous blue of the male, the female is dull brown. She takes care of all the nest building and incubation in June, while the male spends most of the breeding season perched at the tip of a branch proclaiming his territorial song, which consists of a short series of high-pitched notes usually grouped in double phrases—*"sweet-sweet, where-where, here-here, see-it, see-it."* While males follow a general song pattern, individual birds phrase their songs quite distinctively, so much so that a careful listener can distinguish different males by their songs.

The song phrases of all males in a given area are typically quite similar, a phenomenon explained by the fact that male indigos learn songs by imitating the songs sung around them. Thus, neighborhood dialects arise and are maintained over many years. The males possess strong site-fidelity, meaning they return in spring to their previous nesting locale, which helps the local dialect remain consistent over time.

Indigos live on the "edge," nesting in brush and overgrown fields, clear-cuts, forest margins, and even open swamps. Thus their numbers are much higher than they were before settlement. Their nests are seldom placed higher than three feet, and are almost always built in a brushy tangle with a canopy of leaves overhead. They seem to particularly like blackberries, staghorn sumac, dogwoods, and, if producing a second nest later in the summer, bracken ferns, thistles, nettles, and even purple loosestrife. Indigos forage mostly on the ground, eating equal portions of insects, seeds, and fruits.

Given how low they place their nests, ground predators like raccoons, red foxes, and feral cats take the eggs and chicks, though blue jays may be the major nest predator. Brown-headed cowbirds also parasitize the nests, laying their eggs in nearly 20 percent of indigo nests.

Much as we would all love to have indigos frequent our feeders all summer, they seem to briefly stop by upon their spring arrival, tank-up for a few days, and then head off to nest. I've heard of some folks who do succeed in keeping them around with a mixture of seeds, millet, and peanuts, but we're not so fortunate in Manitowish.

Pine Snakes

Pine snakes are the colloquial term for Western fox snakes, presumably called "pine" snakes because they are often seen in pine woods. They commonly grow from 3 to 4 ½ feet long. Fox snakes look somewhat like copperheads, but we have no poisonous snakes in northern Wisconsin, so there's no need to fear any snake that you see. Beware of picking snakes up, however—many species will bite you simply out of self-defense. While not poisonous, the bites can hurt.

Pine Warblers

Pine warblers typically return in late April, and are usually all back by early May. Their evenly trilled song is one of the first songs that can be heard in pine woods throughout the area.

We have very few bird species that are found almost exclusively in one habitat, but pine warblers are one of the handful. As their name suggests, they are obligates of mature red or white pine forests.

I doubt that many people even know when pine warblers are nesting in the pines on their property. They tend to stay up high in the pines, and their song isn't particularly pretty. Their coloration, too, is a rather demure olive and yellow.

Most of our warblers are still on their way here by early May, and will be arriving in the next weeks. In the meantime, see if you can identify the song of the pine warbler before the bird song level escalates to a crescendo.

Planet Train in 2002

Five planets were gathered close together at twilight in the western sky in May of 2002, and all could be seen with the naked eye. Bright Jupiter was the highest up, while the other four clustered together to Jupiter's lower right nearer the horizon. The five moved around, grouping into new patterns every night. On May 5, Mars, Saturn, and Venus formed a nearly equilateral triangle. On May

10, Mars and Venus were only 1/3 degree apart (less than a finger's width at arm's length). On May 14, the crescent moon nearly joined brilliant Venus, forming a beautiful pairing after sunset.

The last time a widely visible line-up event like this occurred was in February 1940. Astronomers predict that the next visible five-planet array won't occur until September 8, 2040.

The Dunking Raven

Cora Mollen told me the following story of a raven she and her husband Roy observed on their St. Germain property in 2001: "We had thrown old bread out for the blue jays, but a week ago a raven came in for some. He is smart enough to make the trip worthwhile by gathering several pieces in a pile and then flying off with a huge mouthful. The other day, I had a loaf of very hard bread that I broke up and threw out for the birds. I noticed when the raven came he was not happy with the hard pieces. He'd gather them in piles but couldn't carry a bunch of them off … too hard. Yesterday, Roy looked out and there was the raven at the birdbath in the backyard, dunking the pieces of bread in the water. Once they were softened to his liking, the raven gathered a huge mouthful and flew off. This now happens again and again. Smartie!!!!!!!"

The Wing-Droop-Fluff Display

Male birds may wear the showiest feathers and sing the most melodic songs in the spring, but the females nearly always hold the ultimate mating cards. After due consideration of the displays and songs of as many as dozens of courting males, it is typically the females who choose which male they will mate with and when. I'm not sure where the rejected bachelors all repair to when their number hasn't been drawn, but after all their unrewarded testosterone has been exercised, I wouldn't be surprised to find them swapping sad stories at some avian equivalent to a smoky, dark tavern.

One courting activity we watch daily in May is the "wing-droop-fluff display," performed regularly by numerous male evening grosbeaks around our feeders. The males first droop their wings, then raise and spread their tails, then fluff up the feathers on top of their head, and finally begin quivering their wings at a high rate of speed while often rotating their body from side to side. This visual display is performed right in front of the female during courtship, and sometimes prior to copulation. In every situation we've watched, however, the females have either simply ignored the males or flown to another tree, blunting their advances with total disinterest.

But the males appear undaunted, soon displaying their passion again in hopes that maybe this time their performance will overcome the female's indifference.

It must work eventually, because nearly every year by mid-July we have some young fledgling evening grosbeaks visiting our feeders.

Shorebirds

One mid-May the Horicon Marsh Bird Club Hotline Report listed 11 species of shorebirds passing through Horicon, including black-bellied plovers, golden plovers, dowitchers, dunlins, Wilson's phalaropes, and five species of sandpipers. I watch for these reports because they tell me when I should be on the lookout for shorebirds migrating through the Northwoods. Marshes and mud flats along rivers and lakes are ideal habitat in which to look for shorebirds, as are flooded fields and pastures.

Some 47 species of shorebirds exist in the Western Hemisphere, most of which travel extraordinary distances from their wintering grounds to their nesting sites. Red knots are one example, traveling from Tierra del Fuego at the southern tip of South America to the Canadian Arctic, a round trip every year of 20,000 miles.

Most shorebirds migrate late in spring because arrival on frozen Arctic tundra does little for the mating urge and cold weather suppresses the insect population that provides the meals. When the shorebirds do make up their mind to head north, they often engage in non-stop marathon flights of more than 2,000 miles over two to three days. To fuel such flights, several species like red knots and white-rumped sandpipers double their weight.

Consider this in human terms. Let's say you are the average adult male, and you want to travel as fast as you can to the Arctic this spring. So you double your weight to increase your endurance. At 175 pounds, this would mean you increase your weight to 350 so you won't have to eat for a long period, then you lumber off down the trail on a non-stop hike to the Arctic.

Somehow I don't think you would make it.

Major wetlands spaced along each species' migratory route are critical steppingstones for "refueling" the shorebirds. The loss of a major wetland can literally affect millions of birds, so scientists have worked at length to identify the wetlands that sustain the greatest number of shorebirds. The Western Hemisphere Shorebird Reserve Network, established by 120 organizations, has identified 34 wetlands in seven countries that are critical links in the chain upon which shorebirds depend. Coastal sites like Delaware Bay, Gray's Harbor in Washington, San Francisco Bay, and the Copper River Delta in Alaska host more than 500,000 shorebirds, or more than 30 percent of a flyway population! Shorebirds gather in such numbers that the beaches literally disappear under their masses.

The best mid-America stopover site is, strangely, in Kansas at Cheyenne Bottoms. More than 100,000 white-rumped sandpipers alone land and stay there for several weeks before heading to their breeding grounds.

Our area is not on a major flyway, nor is it a major stopover site for shorebirds, but we still see our fair share. Powell Marsh and the Rainbow Flowage are usually the best sites to view shorebirds in our area.

Never Say Never

The most remarkable sighting in our area for the month of May 2005 had to be a snowy owl that spent over a week hunting the Little Turtle Flowage just northwest of Mercer. Mary and I first spotted the snowy on May 17. We drove into the parking lot to go for a walk. Before we even got out of the car, we could see a large white object on the osprey platform about 100 yards away. We were both completely baffled by what it could be. A snowy owl wasn't even a possibility in our mind. So, from inside our car—expert birders that we are—our first appraisal was that someone had put a white plastic bag on the platform. We were very puzzled as to why someone would do that!

When we got out of the car and looked at it through our binoculars, it took the shape of a large bird. Even then, because snowies are nearly unheard of in mid-May in Wisconsin, we simply couldn't bring ourselves to consider identifying the bird as a snowy owl. As we walked closer and closer though, the conversation went something like this:

"That can't be a snowy owl, can it?"

"No, it can't be ... can it?"

"No, that's impossible."

"I think it is!"

"No, it has to be an albino hawk or something."

"No!"

"Yes!"

"No!"

You get the general confused drift. As many times as Mary and I have seen rare birds, and have repeated the cliché, "Never say never," we just couldn't bring ourselves to positively identify the bird as a snowy. Snowy owls just don't sit on osprey platforms on warm nights in May in Mercer. Nor do birds that nest in the far northern tundra nest on Wisconsin flowages.

Eventually, when it swiveled its head toward us and we could look right into its yellow eyes, we had no choice but to accept it for what it was.

Many people got to see the snowy over the next week, including participants attending the North Lakeland Discovery Center's Birding Festival on May 21. It was certainly a highlight for many of the nearly 80 attendees.

The snowy was last seen on May 24, but who knows, it may have stayed far back in the inaccessible portions of the marsh. Never say never.

WHAT A DIFFERENCE DIRT MAKES

I led a wildflower trip on May 15, 2005, hiking into two sites just seven miles apart. The contrast, however, between the flower communities was amazing. I purposely chose these two spots to show just how different our woodlands can look due to the soil composition. The first site was Memorial Grove State Natural Area, an old-growth hemlock-hardwood forest with soil that is intermediate between sand and loam. We could hardly find a flower in bloom at this site, partly because it was barely 40°F and raining and snowing off and on. If conditions had been better, we would probably have found wood anemones, Canada mayflowers, hepaticas, a few jack-in-the-pulpits, and likewise a few barren strawberries, but none in large numbers.

The second site was seven miles south on Sheep Ranch Road where the soil becomes loamy and supports a lush array of rich woodland flowers like bloodroot, trillium, spring beauty, toothwort, wild leek, and rue anemone. Here we had trouble not trampling numerous leaves or flowers with every step we took.

If we'd had the time, we should have started near Minocqua where the soil is very sandy and supports a flower community characterized by species like trailing arbutus and barren strawberry.

The difference in the composition of species and the number of individuals is striking between rich and poor soils. You rarely will find a trailing arbutus or barren strawberry in the rich soil communities, or a trillium, bloodroot, or wild leek in the sandy soil communities.

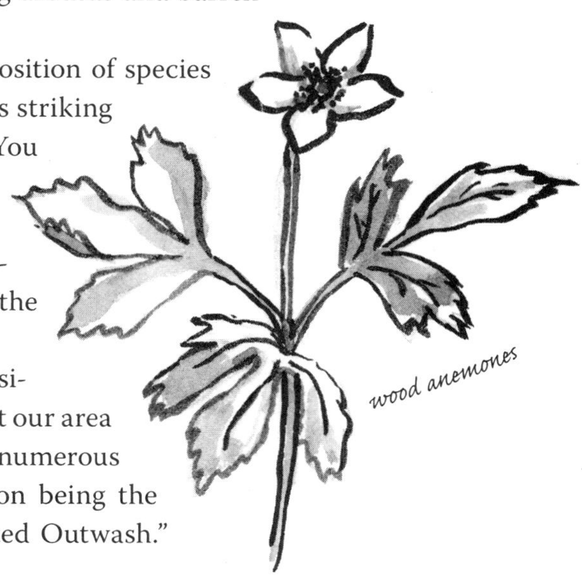

wood anemones

Our general region is classified as the Laurentian Forest, but our area is further broken down into numerous ecoregions, the largest ecoregion being the sandy "Northern Highland Pitted Outwash."

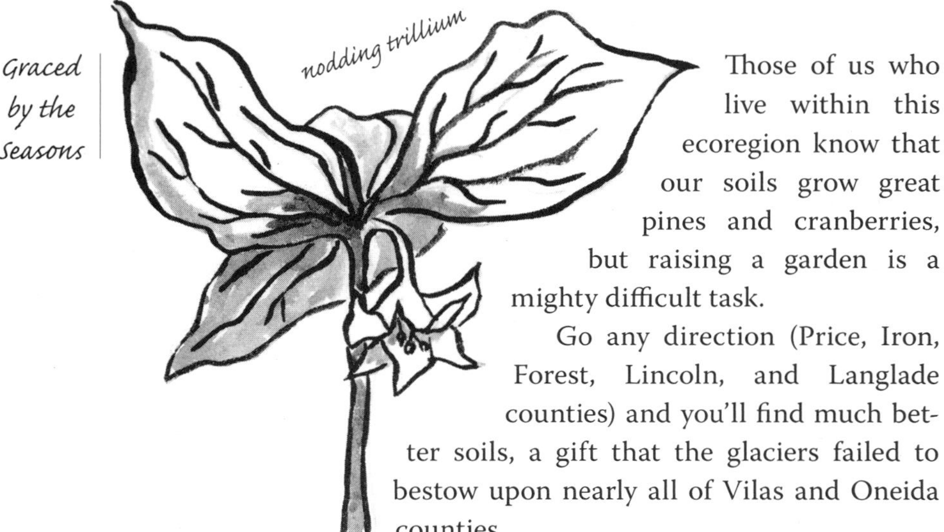

Those of us who live within this ecoregion know that our soils grow great pines and cranberries, but raising a garden is a mighty difficult task.

Go any direction (Price, Iron, Forest, Lincoln, and Langlade counties) and you'll find much better soils, a gift that the glaciers failed to bestow upon nearly all of Vilas and Oneida counties.

If you're looking for the showiest ephemeral spring wildflowers, you have to first find sites with good soils, and that usually requires a road trip outside of Vilas and Oneida counties.

Height of the Concert Season

At no time of the year will bird song usually be more alive than it is in the last two weeks of May. Nearly all migrating birds have passed through or have put down their summer roots here by the end of May. Only half of the known bird species actually sing, utilizing a double voicebox at the base of their windpipe to produce songs. Two sets of membranes and muscles vibrate at high frequencies, permitting some species like the veery to sing in harmony with itself.

Male birds sing in large part to reflect their vigor and quality. The closer to Pavarotti, the greater the bird's vigor, and vigor translates into the ability to attract a female who is looking to produce the healthiest young.

The number of song types in an individual bird's repertoire varies from species to species. Song sparrows produce an average of eight different songs; a starling's repertoire encompasses 67 song types; a mockingbird's includes 150; and a brown thrasher sings more than 2,000. It's doubtful that any human entertainer could master such a broad selection.

Enjoy this most vocally vibrant of times while you can. Leave the window wide open and drink it in. It won't be long until July when the quiet times descend.

Sora Rail

On May 15, 2002, I led a kayak group onto the Little Turtle Flowage just northwest of Mercer, and as hoped, we saw a wide array of marvelous birds. Four trumpeter swans greeted us as we put-in, frequently giving us the privilege of hearing their bellicose trumpeting. An eagle nest facing an osprey nest, a rarity in the Hatfield and McCoy relationship of these species, gave us good views of two of Wisconsin's largest raptors. Sandhill cranes performed their duet songs in the distance. We observed a black tern sitting tight just 20 feet from our boats, and a yellow-headed blackbird provided us close-up looks. Buffleheads, ring-necked ducks, hooded mergansers, pied-billed grebes, Canada geese, snipe, and mallards offered either easy viewing or wonderful calls.

sora rail

But most interesting for the group was our observation of a sora rail. The sora made the mistake of giving its characteristic descending "whinny," or we would never have found it. It was hidden in an area of dead cattail stalks and blended right in. We surrounded the site in our kayaks, and before long all of us got a good look at the secretive rail as it scurried around on top of the vegetation that was lying on the water.

Soras are small, plump, gray-brown, chicken-like birds with a short, bright yellow bill and long yellowish legs. They spend most of their time hidden in dense marsh growth, particularly in large stands of cattails. Their toes are so long that they are easily supported on top of lily pads and floating vegetation. When alarmed, they'll run into the dense vegetation and hide. There are even reports of soras running on the bottom of a stream a foot deep. Though the bird books say soras are quite abundant, they are seldom seen. Sitting quietly at the edge of a marsh opening is the best way to get a peek at one, and we were very lucky this day.

Summer Tanager

In the spring of 2003, the big news at our feeders in Manitowish was that an immature male summer tanager had appeared, a very rare species for the Northwoods. It arrived on May 4, and sat calmly in our platform feeder, sharing sunflower seeds with a flock of evening grosbeaks and holding its ground whenever a grosbeak made a threatening gesture toward it. Our honored guest's colors were extraordinary—a jumble of patchy reds and yellow-greens utterly unlike any other bird that we've had at our feeders.

Few records exist of summer tanagers nesting in Wisconsin in the last century. Summer tanagers nest as far north as central Illinois and all the way down into Mexico. Spring reports in southern Wisconsin have increased in the last few years, but the bird remains quite rare. Only 17 observations of summer tanagers were made in Wisconsin in the 1970s, and 16 in the 1980s.

Natural Population Control

A friend took me on May 24, 2004, to see a sandhill crane nest on his property near the Manitowish River. When we arrived, the adult was sitting on the large mounded nest that protruded just above the wetland vegetation. Unfortunately, our presence disturbed it, and when it got up, it exposed a tiny chick that it was undoubtedly brooding. The adult walked slowly from the nest into the marsh grasses, and the chick followed dutifully along behind it. The gender of the adult was impossible to determine since both adults incubate the eggs and typically change places on the nest four times a day.

Chicks only spend a few hours huddling under the adult before starting to walk, so the chick was probably newly hatched. My friend had observed the nest just two days prior, and the adult was still incubating eggs. Sandhills usually lay two eggs, two to three days apart, so another egg may have been in the nest.

The chicks can swim in two days. Sandhill chicks are called "nidifugous" (nest-fleeing) birds. They must be able to walk, run, and swim almost immediately. Their wings develop slowly while their legs develop quickly. Their legs are essentially fully grown at 32 days, while their first flight won't occur until 10 weeks have passed.

The asynchronous hatching leaves the second chick at a distinct disadvantage to its older sibling. Fratricide is relatively common, with the older chick pecking and fighting the younger at feeding times during the first few weeks of life. The youngest often finally succumbs to the bullying and runs away from the family to die. This doesn't always happen, but only one in five families head south in the winter with two chicks.

Given that sandhills are a long-lived species whose habitat is limited, the survival of only one chick is probably exactly what needs to occur to prevent overpopulation, but it's tough for humans to accept. The sandhills practice an active, if cruel, population control that they have evolved over many thousands of years. They appear to understand that overpopulation is ultimately even crueler than fratricide.

A Fluke of Nature

[Reprinted from an article I wrote for the University of Wisconsin Center for Limnology in May, 2004.]

Pieter Johnson, a doctoral candidate at the Center for Limnology at the University of Wisconsin-Madison, and already a recognized world expert on amphibian deformities, pulls on his rubber boots and leads me into an open field dotted with fifty 300-gallon tanks of water. The tanks contain varying amounts of nutrients, snails, and a parasitic flatworm, or fluke, called *Ribeiroia ondatrae*, all waiting for the mid-July introduction of the key component, frog eggs. Here is where Johnson hopes to demonstrate the link between the extraordinary increase in reports of frog deformities and the numbers of a particular snail, the Rams Horn snail or *Planorbella tenuis*. "The snails are the key to everything. They are the only species that serve as hosts for the parasites," Johnson says. "The more snails that are infected with parasites, the more deformities in frogs."

Nearly a decade has passed since eight middle school children in Minnesota discovered a pond full of severely deformed leopard frogs, triggering a media firestorm. Grotesque pictures of abnormal frogs with missing limbs, extra limbs, limbs jutting in odd directions, or webbing between their limbs briefly dominated the news, but the story quickly dropped out of the public eye.

While media attention disappeared, the issue piqued dozens of scientific studies, all demonstrating that the number of deformities continues to grow. Dozens of researchers have found high frequencies of amphibian deformities in at least 60 different species in 46 U.S. states and parts of Canada, Japan, Australia, and several European nations. Johnson's 2002 broad-scale survey of more than 12,000 amphibians, representing 11 species from 101 sites in five western U.S. states, recorded severe malformations at up to 90 percent rates.

The issue isn't just one of non-Midwestern species in far away places. It hits close to home—deformities are found throughout Wisconsin. The most adversely affected areas include the Midwest, along with the western U.S. and southeastern Canada.

The first questions that arose were whether these abnormalities were normal. Johnson and others exhaustively studied historic records and found that while observations of amphibian deformities were documented for over two centuries, the proportion of abnormalities typically was under 5 percent in any population, and most often involved only a missing digit or part of a limb, not the bizarre spectrum of abnormalities reported in the last decade. Scientists normally expect that a few individuals in any healthy population of amphibians will exhibit aberrations, but nothing of the order and magnitude that researchers were finding around the world.

Dozens of studies since 1995 have narrowed the causes of the deformities down to three major sources:

1. Increased exposure to ultraviolet radiation
2. Pesticide and herbicide runoff
3. The parasitic fluke *Ribeiroia ondatrae*

All three have been shown to act in concert in a dynamic and complex process that contributes to amphibian deformities. But in laboratory and field experiments, ultraviolet radiation and chemical contamination proved not to be the smoking guns that many thought they were. Still, the data clearly implicates them as part of a cocktail of stressors that enable infection by *Ribeiroia* flukes to occur more easily.

Instead, the research consistently has pointed strongly to the flukes as the major causative factor, and to over-fertilized waters as the hotspot sources for the flukes. In his 2002 study, Johnson reported that several geographical regions which were associated with high numbers of deformed amphibians and the flukes were in habitats with a great excess of nutrients, such as farm ponds situated near large quantities of cattle manure and fields with heavy fertilizer use. The excessive nutrients produced masses of algae, which in turn produced higher growth rates and numbers of the snails needed by the flukes.

Early on, researchers realized they needed to know how the flukes spread into other waters, and they found the flukes have a highly complex life cycle requiring multiple hosts to support them from the egg stage to larvae to adults. The *Planorbid* snails function as the first intermediate hosts of the flukes. Here the flukes reproduce asexually within the snail, cloning themselves in high enough numbers that 40-1,000 larvae are released every night per snail. The larvae swim out and look immediately for their next host, the tadpole of a frog, toad, or salamander.

The flukes target the tadpoles' limbs, burrowing into their skin and often forming hundreds of cysts. The cysts appear to obstruct the growth of the tadpole's limbs, causing in particular their hind legs to stop growing altogether, to split into two, or to jut off at an abnormal angle.

Eastern gray tree frog

The tadpoles, if they survive the infection—and many don't—eventually morph into adult frogs. But the adult frogs are dramatically malformed, and thus far more susceptible to predators because they can no longer swim or hop at normal speeds.

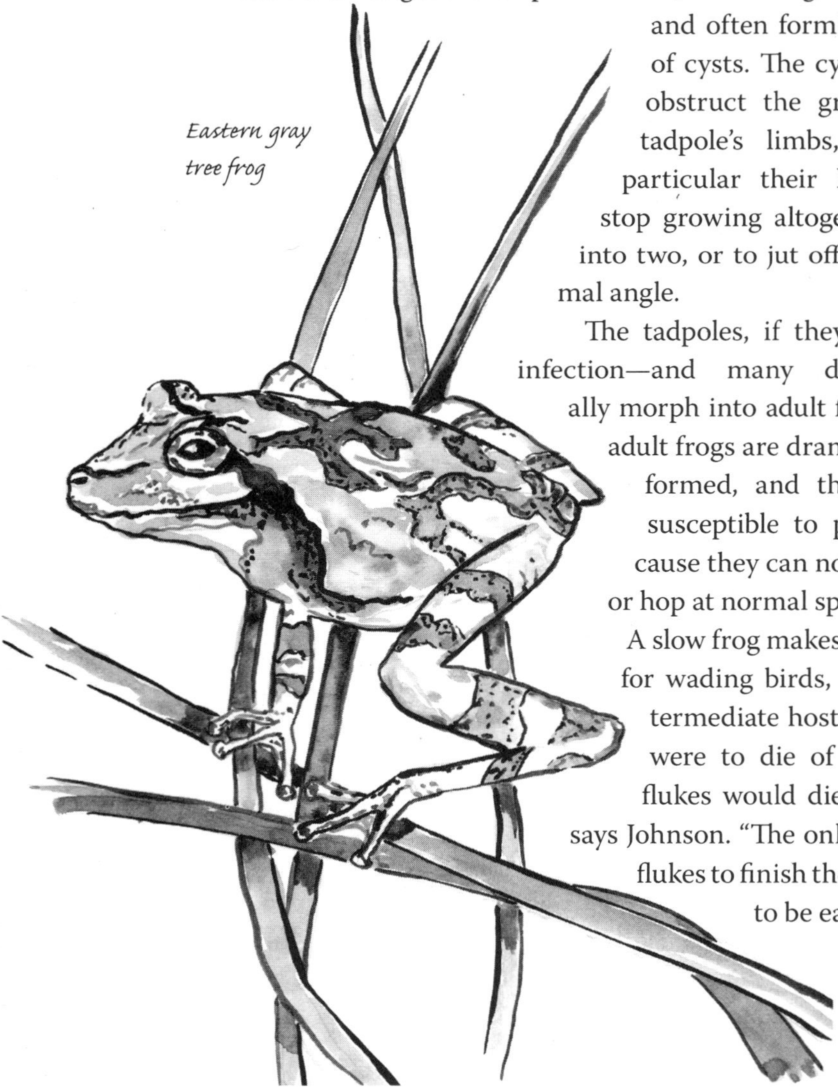

A slow frog makes an easy meal for wading birds, the third intermediate host. "If the frogs were to die of old age, the flukes would die with them," says Johnson. "The only way for the flukes to finish their life cycle is to be eaten by a bird, primarily by herons, though nearly 50 bird species are known to eat frogs."

The flukes lodge in the bird's esophagus, mature, and then reproduce sexually, producing eggs that flow out in the bird's feces. If the feces land on the ground, the flukes die. If the feces land on water, however, the eggs can hatch and re-infect the snails by burrowing under their shells and through their skin.

Nobody knows how long the flukes live in the esophagus of birds, so there appears to be a constant source of new eggs coming into water systems. Johnson notes that, "Birds are vectors as they fly between lakes and rivers. No one knows if the birds are harmed by the flukes. We're currently doing research in Madison to understand more about the role birds play in this cycle."

Frogs, toads, and salamanders are considered "bioindicaters" of environmental health, the proverbial canaries in the coalmine. Since amphibians have permeable skin and shell-less eggs, they are highly sensitive to changes in their environment. Amphibians provide the function of biological monitors of local conditions because they don't wander far from where they were hatched. Deformities in frogs, and their continually decreasing numbers, serve as clear warnings of serious environmental degradation.

Johnson's current study asks the critical question of why the frequency and geographical range of malformed amphibians has apparently increased. He's hoping to discover the secondary factors that are responsible for the increased number of flukes, or the increased susceptibility of the snails. Johnson hypothesizes that habitat alteration, specifically an increase in highly eutrophic waters, lies at the heart of the matter. Higher plant growth increases the snail's growth rates, its survivorship, and its number of generations per season. Is it a clear equation of more algae blooms equals more parasitized snails, which equals more deformed amphibians?

Johnson strongly believes we need to know the impact on amphibians as a species conservation issue. "What will be the impacts if amphibian populations continue to decline?" he asks.

He also notes that amphibians play a key role in how ecosystems function. "The adults help regulate insects. The tadpoles help regulate algal growth. And they all provide food for birds and other predators."

He wonders too if understanding what causes this parasitic infection "might shed light on the mechanisms of other emerging diseases. If we can account for the environmental conditions that drive frog deformities, maybe we can shed some light on the pathways of other new infectious diseases."

Johnson also knows that kids are connected to frogs. "They are our eyes and ears out there," he says. "Kids love frogs. They're the ones who usually find the deformed populations. Kids growing up without frogs would be a very sad loss."

[For more information on Pieter Johnson's work, go to his page on the Trout Lake Station's Website: www.limnology.wisc.edu/Pieter.]

Northern Goshawk

In late May of 2004, Mary, Callie, and I were walking in the Star Lake State Natural Area when a large bird came flying up behind us and landed in a nearby tree, all the time crying a very loud and deep *kak, kak, kak, kak.* Once I got it focused in my binoculars, I clearly saw the characteristic black line through the eye and white line above the eye, and realized it was a northern goshawk, a bird I've only seen on a few other occasions during all my wanderings in the Northwoods. I've heard from researchers how the female goshawk will fiercely defend her nesting territory, and will knock the hat off your head if you get too close to the nest. Given its persistent and highly aggravated calling, I suspected we were on the edge of its nesting territory.

Goshawks are "a shadow cast in gray, with piercing red eyes that radiate malevolence," says one account. They're known for their incredible speed in flight and their single-mindedness in either outflying prey or actually running it down on the ground. One story related by Arthur Bent, in his *Life Histories of North American Birds of Prey,* tells of a goshawk that chased a chicken through a farmyard and ultimately under the skirts of a farm wife, who used a broom to fend the bird off.

The size of the nesting population of goshawks in Wisconsin remains open to debate. Many believe the bird's scarcity indicates that it should qualify for listing as a threatened or endangered species.

Romancing the Runway

In 1999, a trumpeter swan took a shine to the planes at the Manitowish Waters airport and repeatedly landed and took off in concert with them. The trumpeter became so territorial around his new winged friends that he would often become aggressive when a pilot or mechanic approached a plane. The bird was subsequently removed and used as part of a captive breeding program.

Imprinting on planes has been used to teach birds new migration routes, so there is a positive spin to romancing an airplane. Nevertheless, the trumpeter story illustrates the negatives of habituating wild animals to humans. Swans are all too often fed by people, thus decreasing their fear of humans. When territorial issues arise or the free lunch is withheld, swans can get very aggressive. While it may be difficult to resist the desire to attract such beautiful birds, we do them a significant disservice by domesticating their behavior. We owe it to the swans to respect their wildness.

May Wild Strawberries?

Wild strawberries are usually a treasure we enjoy from mid- to late June, but on May 29, 1998, we were eating handfuls, the earliest we can ever recall savoring the sweetness of these tiny strawberries.

There are berries, and then there are wild strawberries. Izaak Walton said all that ever needs to be said about them: "Doubtless God could have made a better berry, but doubtless God never did."

Bugs and Birds

The Manitowish was still in flood in mid-May 2002, with water filling the floodplains. The sedge meadow below our house was under water, giving us lakefront property without the high taxes for several weeks. The woodlands were saturated, too, providing enough vernal ponds to satisfy any number of frogs.

Paddling was good, but the bad news was that the cold, rainy weather slowed wildflower blossoming and canopy leaf-out. The cold also slowed the prodigious hatch of insects that so much water normally produces. That would seem like good news to humans, and it was in terms of our outdoor comfort, but it clearly stressed the insectivorous birds. Numerous people from around the state reported that insect-eating songbirds, usually difficult to see because they feed in the leaf-canopy, were being seen near the ground or at feeders, and were acting positively tame in comparison to their normal behavior. Many woodland warblers were observed feeding in farm fields, particularly in manured fields where insects could be found in higher numbers.

Warblers were also seen kicking through the leaf litter like sparrows and thrushes, a very unwarblerlike behavior. I loved every minute of the no insect state, but for the sake of the birds, I was happy to see the insects finally hatch.

Aerial Spraying for Forest Tent Caterpillars

I received numerous phone calls in 2002 from people in lake associations who wanted to know if the aerial spraying of their lakeshores for forest tent caterpillars was a good idea. I said no, and the reason is simple. No insecticide is specific to only forest tent caterpillars. Even using the least harmful insecticide available (Btk—*bacillus thuringiensis var. kurstaki*), other caterpillars of moths and butterflies would also be killed. Even worse, use of less specific insecticides like malathion would kill insect families like bees and other beneficial insects.

From my standpoint, the potential negatives simply outweigh the positives. Questions of this kind are a value judgment based on personal pros and cons, like so much of ecosystem management. The forest tent caterpillars were nearing the end of their three- to five-year-cycle, and as we had seen for the last three years, the vast majority of trees rebounded from their defoliation and grew new leaves several weeks later. Some trees did die, but dead and dying trees provide habitat for a host of birds. Some 30 species nest in tree cavities, and many more use the bare branches for perching (eagles and osprey for instance) or displaying during courtship.

By all means, if you ever have particular favorite trees that should be protected, then take cautious steps to do that. But spraying hundreds of acres along lake shorelines opens up a potential Pandora's box. We need to find a way to live with insect cycles, rather than trying to control them with a solution that has the potential to be far worse than the original problem.

Principle of Highest Use

The master plan for the Northern Highlands-American Legion State Forest came out in 2005 after a long process of public review and comment. The depth of the document is a profound improvement upon the 1982 plan, providing careful readers with a great deal of detail upon which to understand our biotic communities and then make educated responses to management proposals.

I've read the 240-page plan, and I'm reminded of Leopold's definition of a conservationist, and his understanding of the biases inherent in managing land. He wrote, "I have read many definitions of what is a conservationist, and written not a few myself, but I suspect that the best one is written not with a pen, but with an axe. It is a matter of what a man thinks about while chopping, or while deciding what to chop. A conservationist is one who is humbly aware that with each stroke he is writing his signature on the face of his land. Signatures, of course differ, whether written with axe or pen, and this is as it should be."

The complex NH-AL master plan is the signature of the DNR for this property, and their signature will, of course, vary in some details for nearly everyone who reads the document. That's expected. Leopold wrote that "the wielder of an axe has as many biases as there are species of trees on his farm," and noted that "there is skill in the exercise of bias."

The master plan is an exercise in bias, or, if you prefer, in values. Given the same set of baseline statistics of how much forest we had before settlement and what plant communities they represented, and considering what we have now and what we could work toward having in the future, literally everyone in the state will have a different vision of what the definition of "should" ought to be, given their biases.

How then can the DNR, or the citizens of the state, come to agreement on what set of values/biases we will choose to guide us, on what signature we should agree to write? Leopold offered this: "The technical education of the American forester aims principally to teach him how to raise and use timber... But when the forester begins actual work on a forest, he is called upon to solve a much broader problem. He is charged with the duty of putting land to its highest use."

Highest use is, of course, another value-laden term. But the DNR has a guiding principle that I find most helpful. Their bottom-line goal given by statute is to "protect and enhance" the state's lands and waters. Everything that is done should meet this criterion first and foremost. Has the land and water been protected and enhanced by a given management action?

The final draft makes many very positive changes (by my set of biases, of course) to current forest management—see the inclusion of numerous new state natural areas, the designation of the Bittersweet Lake Recreation Area, the long-awaited commitment to at least minimal old-growth forest management, the establishment of ecological reference areas, the expansion of the boundaries, and many others.

However, the action I find most objectionable, and by far the most biased, is the continued management of nearly 50 percent of the upland forests as aspen forest, and the doubling of current harvesting levels. This despite the fact that Wisconsin Statute 28:04(2) clearly states that "the range of benefits provided by the department in each state forest shall reflect its unique character and position in the regional landscape." The draft property goals list as the number one goal to "provide a diversity of terrestrial and aquatic biological communities, including a range of forest types and age classes, with emphasis on communities that are special to the NH-AL State Forest."

So, what is the unique character and position of the NH-AL State Forest? What communities are special to the area? The master plan divides the property into 22 management areas, of which six are called forest production areas. The pre-settlement description of each area given in the master plan tells us explicitly what the area once supported, which without question is the unique character of each.

- **Winegar Moraines**—"At European settlement, the uplands were mostly covered with hemlock/yellow birch, with maple as a secondary species." It's now 46 percent aspen.
- **Manitowish Peatlands**—"At European settlement, the vast majority of the area was dominated by swamp conifers, and open wetlands, with the northern portion of uplands associated with hemlock, white birch, and white pine, while the southern areas had more red pine, white pine, and aspen." Of the upland forest, over 50 percent is now aspen.
- **Vilas Sandy Plains North**—"At European settlement, this area was mostly covered with white and red pine." The area is now 43 percent aspen and 16 percent red and white pine.
- **Vilas Sandy Plains Central**—"At European settlement, this area was mostly covered with white and red pine." The area is now 39 percent aspen and 13 percent red and white pine.
- **Big Arbor Vitae Loamy Hills**—"At European settlement, the upland areas contained several different forest types including white and red pine, northern hardwoods, hemlock-hardwoods, and even some jack pine/scrub oak." The area is now 50 percent aspen.
- **Oneida Sandy Plains**—"At European settlement, this area was mostly covered with white and red pine." The area is now 45 percent aspen.
-

Overall, aspen was originally found on less than 5 percent of the lands that comprise the NH-AL. The vast majority of the NH-AL was white and red pine. We profoundly increased the aspen community by a more than tenfold leap through clear-cutting and burning at the turn of the century. Why do we continue to maintain this vastly disproportionate aspen acreage today? The plan offers no explanation as to why, but simply says that it will.

As for providing diversity, would anyone, forester or non-forester, contend that managing nearly one-half of the upland NH-AL as aspen meets the definition of providing a diversity of terrestrial communities?

What the actual percentages for each forest community should be is open to debate, and the exercise of our biases. But there are biases, and then there is blindness. The continued management for so much aspen, despite all the chapter and verse in the master plan calling for diversity and management that reflects the unique character of the NH-AL, is a purposeful turning of a blind eye to the real calling of the NH-AL's varied forest communities. A forest made up of half aspen miserably fails Leopold's test of "highest use."

Principle of Highest Use Relative to ATVs

I have one other objection to a very small part of the plan that would set a dangerous precedent. This is the potential inclusion of an ATV trail.

I fully understand that the pressure on the DNR to include the trail has been unremitting, but their guiding principle is to "protect and enhance." Can anyone possibly suggest that the placement of an ATV trail will protect and enhance our public lands? The cry for access to public lands by ATV users simply because they are taxpayers has no basis. Use of public lands must be restricted to those who have demonstrated stewardship over time, something the ATV community has, without hyperbole, utterly failed to do. There's no constitutional right to utilize public lands when the use will clearly have significant negative impacts.

We hire people based on their resume and their references. Nevertheless, ATV riders demand to be "given a chance." They have been afforded past opportunities, and their abysmal resume and references tell us to steer a very wide berth. Let them return in 20 years with references saying what good stewards they have been, and let someplace other than the NH-AL be the experimental ground for their exoneration.

Role Reversal

Deer typically drop their fawns over Memorial Day weekend, which leads to two stories I heard in May of 2000. One concerned a person who was walking on Powell Marsh Road when a red fox ran full speed across the road in front of him, followed closely by a deer. Upon seeing the person, the deer reversed its direction and went back into the woods, only to stop and snort continually for several minutes.

The other story took place near Madeline Lake Trail in Woodruff. A motorist and a bicyclist both watched a coyote tear across the road in front of them with a deer close on its heels.

What to make of what appears to be predators chased by prey? It seems reasonable that in both cases a doe was protecting her fawn(s) from a predator who came too close for comfort. Rather than flight, it chose fight, and apparently in both cases the deer was winning the fight!

Memorial Day—Hold the Firecrackers Please!

The end of May signals that nearly all of our 150 or more nesting bird species are sitting on eggs or are already raising young. I mention this in hopes that residents and visitors alike, who often shoot off firecrackers around this time, will refrain from doing so.

I frankly don't have any data suggesting how most nesting birds or denning mammals respond to firecrackers. One loon researcher

I know has observed that a number of people come to landings and start shooting off firecrackers on Memorial Day. She has seen loons abandon their nests during the noise.

I also know that one of our dogs hides and shakes like a leaf when she hears firecrackers. One of our earlier dogs used to jump through screen doors in fear. If you want wildlife around your place, it seems prudent to reduce startling noises. No other month resonates with as much new life as May. And no other month deserves our attention and respect more.

June

You must have the bird in your heart, before you can find it in the bush.

—John Burroughs, 1908, *Art of Seeing Things*

For me, June's keynote is the cornucopia of bird song that occurs at dawn. First light comes at 4 a.m., but if you can pull yourself out of bed, there's no better time to hear birds in their full voice. Most birds sing with much more energy at first light, singing both more songs and a greater array of songs. In fact, some birds sound almost frenetic in their delivery, producing songs at a more rapid speed and with much shorter pauses between songs. A number of birds even sing entirely different songs at dawn from those they sing during the day. For instance, a male yellow warbler may sing 12 different types of songs during his dawn chorus, before reverting back to the single song type that he will sing for the rest of the day.

Different species join the dawn choir at varying times, each apparently responding to a different internal light meter. American robins, perhaps our greatest avian insomniacs, typically lead the way, often singing a full hour before sunrise.

Some birds have dawn song repertoires that seem endless, while others just play the same old record over and over. Brown thrashers put nearly all other birds to shame with more than 2,000 song types. They're the superstars. But those that are merely stars in the avian song world include American robins with 70 songs, red-eyed vireos with 50, song sparrows and northern cardinals with nine, and red-winged blackbirds with six. Uncreative by comparison are eastern wood-pewees with three songs, eastern phoebes with two songs, and least flycatchers with but one song. *Che-beck!* they say, over and over again.

Mary and I try to awaken every June morning near first light, because amazingly and sadly, bird songs begin waning by mid-June. Once the period of caring for the young begins, singing inevitably declines and often stops altogether. So take the time now to listen to birdsong, because you won't hear such extraordinary vitality again until next year.

Why Sing at Dawn?

Why birds sing with such enthusiastic energy at dawn will likely always be a mystery, but that doesn't mean we lack for theories. Dawn obviously follows night, a time when most birds remain quiet and inactive, and when many birds are preyed upon. Vocalizing loud and clear at dawn may signal to any non-breeding birds on the perimeter of a territory that "I am still here, still healthy, and this territory is still mine!" It may be that singing right away in the morning is the best time to attract females, since most songbirds migrate and arrive on their territories at night. (This theory explains spring, but not early summer after migration has ended). It may be that since dawn is typically the calmest period of the day, singing simply carries farther than it does at other times. It's also possible that singing before first light may be the most efficient use of energy at a time when the light is too poor to forage for insects.

The amount of light rather than the time of day determines the onset of singing in the morning. If it's cloudy, singing may be delayed in the morning, and clouds may hasten the end of singing at dusk.

A morning solar eclipse dramatically illustrates this process. As totality nears and dusk descends, the diurnal (active during the day) birds gradually stop singing, while the nocturnal and crepuscular (dawn and dusk) species begin singing. Once totality has passed and the morning begins to brighten, the diurnal species chime in again, while the others fade out.

If avian music is what you want to hear, dawn is when the action is. Social dominance, pair bonds, and territorial defense all get pronounced anew, and in no uncertain terms.

Adoption Without All the Legal Hassles

On June 20, 2005, Gray Rusch reported observing a female hooded merganser herding 16 chicks behind her on a quiet bay in the Rainbow Flowage.

Anyone who lives on water has at one time or another seen a single adult or pair of waterfowl with an abnormally large family of chicks trailing behind them, sometimes as many as thirty or more. The term for this process is "post-hatch brood amalgamation," and the combining of families can occur through a number of methods. Chicks can be adopted, they can be aggressively kidnapped, or several broods may simply combine to form what's called a "crèche," with one or more of the adults acting as the day care teacher(s).

The adults attending to the chicks perform only two real functions—they guard the young, and they guide them to good foraging areas and safe resting sites. Waterfowl chicks are highly "precocial," meaning they're born mobile and able to feed themselves. Thus, the adult parental duties for waterfowl are significantly less complicated than if their chicks were born immobile, with their eyes closed, and totally dependent on food provided by the parents, as is the case for all songbirds.

Diving ducks like mergansers employ brood amalgamation most commonly, but Canada geese do so as well. Why brood amalgamation occurs remains unclear. Broods may be combined as a result of competition between females for brood-rearing areas, as a means of competing more successfully for food resources, as a means of reducing predation, or because birds with poor parenting skills or who are in poor condition simply give up their young to adults more capable of parenting them.

Canada geese pairs are known to use different chick-rearing methods in different years, and although Canada geese are frequently studied birds, researchers still don't know why. All that can be said for sure is that waterfowl nurseries occur and that they usually lead to greater survival of the young.

To know if you're looking at a brood nursery or possibly a single family unit, you need to know the average size of broods. Here's a listing of nesting waterfowl in our area with the average brood size and the minimum and maximum ranges in parentheses:

Species	Avg. brood	(min-max)
Common loon	2	(1-2)
Pied-billed grebe	5-7	(3-10)
Trumpeter swan	4-6	(2-9)
Canada goose	4-7	(4-10)
Mallard	7-10	(6-15)
Blue-winged teal	8-11	(6-15)
Wood duck	10-15	(6-15)
Ring-necked duck	8-10	(6-14)
Hooded merganser	10-12	(7-13)
Common merganser	8-11	(6-13)
Red-breasted merganser	8-10	(5-11)

Bluffed by Badgers

In June of 2000, Terry Daulton and Llona Clausen drove down a dirt lane near Presque Isle Lake and came upon three badgers eating turtle eggs in the middle of the road. So intent were the badgers upon their meal, growling continuously as they fed, that they never noticed the approach of Terry and Llona, who ended up standing no more than 10 feet away, watching and listening to their gluttony.

Finally, one badger looked up amidst its growling pleasure and recognized humans nearby! Its hair stood straight out. Given the badger's squat shape, this means the hair actually stood horizontal rather than vertical. Then the badger backed up and charged at the two women. Fortunately for Terry and Llona, who have little practice in fighting hand-to-claw with badgers, it was a bluff, and the badgers soon beat a retreat down the road and into the woods.

Berry Good

Strawberries, blueberries, dwarf raspberries, and occasionally Juneberries come ripe in June. We actually ate some ripe Juneberries on June 28, 1998, a first for us for as long as we can remember in the Northwoods. Up here Juneberries generally deserve the name "Julyberries."

Birds of the Clear-Cut

One pre-dawn in late June 1999, I tagged along on a bird survey with Amber Roth, then a UW graduate student researching bird populations in clear-cuts. We began our walk at 5 a.m. on a site that had been clear-cut three years earlier, and which was dominated by 6- to 8-foot-tall aspens, or what's better known as a "dog-hair stand" of popple. Mixed in were some choke cherries, Juneberries, red oak, and red maple.

A hike in a young aspen stand is not a walk in the park. It's very dense, it's wet, it's tangly, and you can't see 20 feet in front of you. In other words, it's a jungle. Nevertheless, young clear-cuts can be excellent sites for birds that are adapted to brushy habitats.

We saw and heard a bevy of birds, including alder flycatcher, American goldfinch, American redstart, American robin, black-and-white warbler, blue jay, brown-headed cowbird, cedar waxwing, chestnut-sided warbler, common yellowthroat, golden-winged warbler, gray catbird, hairy woodpecker, house wren, indigo bunting, mourning warbler, Nashville warbler, northern flicker, Baltimore oriole, red-eyed vireo, rose-breasted grosbeak, ruffed grouse, song sparrow, veery, and yellow warbler, for a total of 25 species in three hours.

Amber later sent me a list of other species she had spotted on past visits to this particular site. It included among others: American woodcock, black-billed cuckoo, Cape May warbler, chipping sparrow, common raven, common snipe, sandhill crane, tree swallow, white-throated sparrow, and numerous others.

An impressive list. There are, of course, other issues relative to clear-cuts, such as forest fragmentation, soil erosion, creation of monotypes by planting red pine, and others that will always make the subject of clear-cuts controversial. I am not suggesting that clear-cutting is inherently "good" because of the number of birds that utilize these sites, but I was surprised to see the level of bird activity present in the clear-cut. We often forget that many birds evolved to utilize open grasslands, shrublands, and young forests.

Some folks suggest that clear-cuts replicate the habitats we lost when we became so proficient at preventing and controlling wildfires. They don't. Fires typically left vast stands of residual trees in the form of standing dead trees, some live trees, and some unburned patches. Clear-cut practices that leave residual trees and patches of live vegetation better approximate the conditions left by historic fires, but don't replicate burned areas by any stretch of the imagination.

We certainly saw the value of leaving some standing trees during our walk. Some large standing oaks were absolute magnets for birds that used them for singing perches. Males need to be seen and heard in the spring, after all, and one needs a high perch to serve as the stage.

Black Flies

Black flies (Family *Simuliidae* or "little snub-nosed beings") usually hatch out in mid- to late May and are still happily biting into mid-June. One June, I received five black fly bites on the back of my neck, and they swelled and itched for a week. Unfortunately, that's a rather normal response to the virulent bite of black flies. When they bite, one often doesn't feel the bite, but a few minutes later, the swelling and itching begins. Some folks are highly sensitive to their bites. One person told me that his wife was bitten around the eye, and as a result her eye swelled shut for several days.

Though rather minute (less than 1/8-inch long), and not possessed of the annoying whine or buzz of mosquitoes, these little humpbacked assassins can hatch in prodigious numbers from clear, fast-moving streams, and make life absolutely miserable. Fortunately, their life cycle is rather short. The adults usually last only into mid-June in our area before laying eggs and dying.

Of 1,554 species (!) described worldwide, at least 61 identified species exist in the Great Lakes region and New England, though only a relatively small number of species suck blood, and only the female of those species requires the blood meal. In fact, males don't even have mouths capable of biting. One species, *Simulium euryadminiculum,* specializes only in taking the blood of loons.

The females that do bite are unrelenting in their efforts. They utilize serrated, overlapping mandibles that act like a pair of scissors to snip a hole in the skin of their prey. Stewart Edward White, a Northwoods writer who penned *The Forest* in 1903, preferred black flies to mosquitoes, though in a manner that suggests the psychological strain that black flies induce: "[Black flies] hold still to be killed. No frantic slaps, no waving of arms, no muffled curses. You just place your finger calmly and firmly on the spot. You get him every time. In this is great, heart-lifting joy. It may be unholy joy, perhaps even vengeful, but it leaves the spirit ecstatic."

Mr. White sounds a bit over the edge, but black flies can do that to you. Many people dream of an insect-free world. Some believe we have a right to live in one, and thus advocate the use of chemical sprays on everything everywhere. But since the fossil record shows that black flies have been on Earth for an estimated 180 million years, I doubt our chances for success. What to do? Adapt. Wear long-sleeve shirts, a head scarf or a head net if you must, utilize some DEET or Skin-So-Soft as a repellant, and get on with your life.

Black Fly Bites—De-Itching

How does one go about treating the incredible itch and swelling of black fly bites? Jack Bull suggested using Chapstick on the bites, which I tried, and it worked! I have no idea why, but with black flies, who cares?

Helen Williams on Crab Lake makes a solution of Adolph's unflavored meat tenderizer and slathers it on. She follows it up with a 1 percent hydrocortisone cream. Helen says she even used this remedy for a scorpion bite that a man suffered in Africa, and it brought the swelling down very quickly.

Black-Winged Redbird

I seldom see scarlet tanagers, but now and again I get lucky. I led a hike in June 1999 on the Raven Trail, and our group not only got superb close-up views of two scarlet tanagers, but we also were able to watch the male feeding a female.

This was a treat. The male's jet-black wings and tail contrasted beautifully with its brilliant red body. In fact, once you spot a scarlet tanager, it seems impossible to believe that you once had to search for it.

Thoreau wrote, "It flies through the green foliage as if it would ignite the leaves."

The female, on the other hand, blends in well with sunlit leaves, her greenish back and yellowish underside camouflaging her presence.

Scarlet tanagers nest predominantly in oaks, usually well out on the branches, and up 10 to 15 feet. One ornithologist calls them "the appointed guardian of the oaks ... drawn to these trees as if they were magnets." Not only do they prefer oaks, they appear to require extensive stands of mature trees. A pair requires a minimum of about four acres of woodland, with eight acres being optimal. However, even in optimal habitat, their numbers are precious few compared to species like red-eyed vireos and Eastern wood-pewees.

Primarily insect eaters, scarlet tanagers also feed on wild fruits like blackberries, sumac, and elderberries. I'd love to see a picture of a scarlet tanager foraging on a crimson plume of sumac.

California Meets Wisconsin

Mary, Callie, and I spent late May and early June 2003 in Redwood National Park and Sequoia National Park. We were on a mission to hike among the biggest trees on earth, and so we did. The trees were so big, and so remarkable in so many ways, that Mary and I had a hard time not continually exclaiming things like "Oh my God!" and "Unbelievable!" We finally settled down at Callie's prompting to merely gasping when we would come upon yet another redwood or sequoia 20 feet or more in diameter and 300 feet tall.

I did have one complaint—the birds were singing so far up in the foliage that there was no way I could see them, and they would have nothing to do with my "pishing." I guess California birds don't like Wisconsin accents.

One interesting Wisconsin connection was the number of bird and plant species that were common to both California and northern Wisconsin. At one point I was completely perplexed by a rather large songbird that was sitting high up in a sequoia. The bird had an orange breast and a white lower belly with spots. We were in the Muir Grove of sequoias, several miles back from any roads. What could it be? I kept asking myself as I thumbed furiously through my bird book. Eventually it flew low enough that we could clearly identify it as ... a juvenile American robin!

But in a sequoia grove? Yep. Robins turned out to be the most common bird we saw in the sequoias, along with a few other old friends like golden-crowned kinglets, red-breasted nuthatches, winter wrens, dark-eyed juncos, and hermit thrushes. Song sparrows were common in the roadside shrubs, but they sang a different song than our northern Wisconsin birds.

In the redwoods, we saw near carbon copies of our thimbleberry, Canada mayflower, wild ginger, wood strawberry, Dutchman's breeches, starflower, and large-flowered trillium.

Then again, we saw birds we'd never seen before, like common murres, black guillemots, black oystercatchers, Allen's hummingbirds, and white-headed woodpeckers. Among the unfamiliar plants were manzanita, incense cedar, snowplant, rhododendrons, California poppies, and on and on. And ... nary a mosquito!

Maybe the most remarkable thing of all was how equally happy we were to come home. We were visiting some of the most beautiful places the earth has to offer, and yet we were glad to return, unlike numerous others we overheard who were depressed about going home and "returning to reality." How fortunate we are to live in this reality of freshwater lakes and rivers, extensive forests, and wildness.

Waterspouts

One early June, Dean Acheson called with a sighting of a waterspout. This was a very unusual sighting, particularly since it happened during the early evening of a rather normal day with no storm clouds in view. Dean said that the spout developed near their fishing boat and lifted 2 to 3 feet off the water, like a vacuum sucking up water. It lasted for possibly 10 seconds, moved a little ways from the boat, and then was gone. His son Scott was in the bow of the boat and the spout actually hit him. Scott could feel the wind pushing him!

Now assuming Dean's sobriety at the time, the question is what caused the waterspout to occur? I have no experience with waterspouts, so I referred to the book *It's Raining Frogs and Fishes: Four Seasons of Natural Phenomena and Oddities of the Sky* by Jerry Dennis. Dennis writes that waterspouts occur frequently over inland lakes and large rivers. They can be devasting tornado-like structures, or they can be made up of gentle winds that barely lift a spray off the surface.

Dennis actually derived the title of his book from the phenomenon of waterspouts. An article by an ichthyologist that appeared in the journal *Natural History* in 1921 presented 44 accounts of people who witnessed rains of fish. One account of a "boisterous" rain of herring in Scotland in 1821 described fish so abundant that the land tenants had to turn over all the fish they picked up to the landlord. A more modern account in 1931 by the *New York Times* described a rain of perch so heavy that traffic was forced to stop.

The craziest account was from another article that appeared in *Science* magazine in 1947, written by a biologist for the Department of Wildlife and Fisheries in Louisiana. On October 23, 1947, a morning rain on the town of Marksville, Louisiana, dropped fish ranging from 2 to 9 inches long. The author was in a restaurant at the time when the waitress informed him that fish were falling from the sky. Two merchants were reportedly hit by falling fish as they walked to their businesses. Main Street had areas that averaged one fish per square yard. The biologist collected many of the fallen and identified them as locally native fish—large-mouth black bass and hickory shad in particular. Most likely, the article said, waterspouts were the cause of the redistribution of the fishery.

Dean failed to mention whether the waterspout that visited him dropped any fish into his boat. I suspect that if it did, he kept that part of the story to himself.

Cavity-Nesting Birds

Why should we maintain old trees and standing dead trees? Here are 32 reasons:

1. American kestrel
2. Barred owl
3. Black-backed woodpecker
4. Black-capped chickadee
5. Boreal chickadee
6. Boreal owl
7. Brown creeper

8. Bufflehead
9. Chimney swift
10. Common goldeneye
11. Common merganser
12. Downy woodpecker
13. Eastern bluebird
14. Eastern screech-owl
15. European starling
16. Great-crested flycatcher
17. Hairy woodpecker
18. Hooded merganser
19. House wren
20. Northern flicker
21. Northern saw-whet owl
22. Pileated woodpecker
23. Prothonotary warbler
24. Red-bellied woodpecker
25. Red-breasted nuthatch
26. Red-headed woodpecker
27. Three-toed woodpecker
28. Tree swallow
29. Tufted titmouse
30. White-breasted nuthatch
31. Wood duck
32. Yellow-bellied sapsucker

chickadee

Celestial Events

- The Seneca Indians called June's full moon the "Strawberry Moon," in reference to the profusion of wild strawberries in flower at the beginning of the month, and the fruits that usually appear before the end of the month.
- The moon often appears a honey-orange color as it travels across the night sky in June. The moon is at its greatest distance south during June, and appears to track quite low across the sky. The moon's path during this month actually mirrors the low trajectory of the daytime sun during December. The honey-orange color is created because light must pass through the thick lower atmosphere. Most of the blue light is absorbed and scattered by the atmosphere, leaving the red spectrum to dominate the moonlight.
- By June 1, we will be recipients of 15 1/2 hours of daylight—65 percent or more of every day for the next month will be light. From June 11 to 20, we'll have the earliest sunrises of the year, all commencing at 5:08 a.m. The longest periods of daylight during the year will occur from June 17 to 24, which will provide us with 15 hours and 44 minutes.

Wild Calla

Wetland areas are often graced by blossoming wild calla lilies in June. Wild calla appears to be a single club-like flower sheathed by a soft white petal, but actually the white "petal" is a modified leaf (spathe) that acts as a hood for dozens of tiny flowers that are crowded onto the vertical "club." In late summer, the cluster of flowers turns into a cluster of bright red berries.

Calla flowers share a similar flowering process with bunchberries, which are also profusely in flower this time of year, mainly along the edges of wetlands and moist woods. Bunchberries appear to have four white petals, but those petals are also actually modified leaves. The interior of the flower actually contains a dozen or more tiny flowers that will become a bunch of red berries in August.

Historical uses of plants always fascinate me. Wild calla had a purpose that I would never have dreamed of—it apparently provided the source of white starch for stiffening the huge ruffled collars seen in Elizabethan portraits. Closer to home, I have found no specific use of the plant by the Ojibwe, but neighboring tribes like the Potawatomi made a poultice of the roots to reduce swelling.

Condors!

No, not in Wisconsin.

Mary, Callie, and I journeyed to the Four Corners area of the Southwest in 2005, and in the course of our travels we spotted six condors. Given that the total wild population in the world as of January 2004 was 89, this means we saw around 7 percent of all the wild condors in the world! We watched an adult and an immature bird flying above the Colorado River near the Vermillion Cliffs National Monument, and later that day watched a flock of four adult condors sailing and circling on the thermals along the North Rim of the Grand Canyon.

Even over the Grand Canyon, which diminishes anything one compares it to, the condors looked big. The California condor is the largest bird in North America, with a wingspan of 9½ feet, and a weight of 17 to 25 pounds. By comparison, bald eagles have wingspans up to 7 feet and weigh from 10 to 14 pounds.

The story of the rescue of the California condor is really quite remarkable. A healthy population of condors once ranged throughout the coastal region of America from British Columbia to Baja California, east to Florida and north to New York. But by 1965, only an estimated 60 condors existed. They were included on the first federal list of endangered species in 1967. By 1982, only 21 to 24 were estimated to remain in the wild, and extinction was considered a certainty. A very controversial captive breeding program was begun, and all the remaining wild birds were eventually trapped. By 1987, for the first time since the Pleistocene era, condors no longer soared over North America.

The next year, 1988, the first successful captive breeding among California condors occurred at the San Diego Wild Animal Park. In 1990, two pairs "double-clutched," and two other pairs "triple-clutched." (When eggs are removed from the nest, the female will promptly lay a replacement clutch, a process called double-clutching.) By the end of 1990, 40 birds existed in captivity.

In 1992, the first California condors were released back into the wild, and although two men were caught later that year trying to shoot them, the condors survived that attempt on their lives. In October, though, one was found dead from poisoning. The source of the poisoning remains unknown to this day.

In 1996, six juvenile condors were set free atop the Vermillion Cliffs in Arizona, marking the first time in 70 years that condors flew over Arizona.

More releases occurred over the next six years, and in 2003 a wild condor chick hatched, survived, and fledged, the first wild condor chick to fly since 1983.

Lead poisoning, shootings, and collisions with power lines continue to take their toll, but by the end of 2005, nearly 100 wild condors were alive in the American West, an extraordinary tale of restoration that is still unfolding.

Small Is Also Beautiful

On that same Western trip, we took a hike in the Colorado Rockies at around 8,000 feet, and were continuously serenaded by ruby-crowned kinglets. I was never really all that clear on the ruby-crown's song before this trip, but after two hours of hearing song after song, I'm darn sure of it now.

I was surprised to hear the ruby-crowns (as I was pine siskins, hermit thrushes, and evening grosbeaks), because I thought their southern range barely extended into the Northwoods and was mostly way up into Canada. Not so. Weather conditions in the American Rockies are cold enough that northern Canadian birds often nest as far south as the Arizona Rockies. Check the range maps for these birds in your bird books, and you'll see a finger of nesting range dipping down and following the Rockies almost to Mexico.

Ruby-crowns are the antithesis of condors. Among northeastern birds, only the ruby-throated hummingbird is smaller. They're hyperactive little things, flitting about incessantly in total contrast to the long soaring flights of the condors. But as small as they are, they are named "kings" because the male can raise the ruby-colored feathers on his crest if he's emotionally charged-up due to a territorial conflict.

Ruby-crowned kinglets and their relatives the golden-crowned kinglets rarely visit backyard bird feeders. They prefer to dine on insects high in conifers, gleaning them from the bark, branches, and foliage. If you want to see them, they will often come down in response to "pishing," but you have to be fast with your binoculars because they don't tend to hang around for long. The ruby-crown's song in particular is quite complex and musical, and worth learning. In fact, these little kings are as fascinating as the king of all our North American birds, the California condor. Small is beautiful, if you take the time to look.

Spawning Redhorse and Hungry Eagles

One early June, Mary and our two daughters canoed the Manitowish River, putting in at the Hwy. 51 landing. From here, one canoes immediately into a short rocky stretch of riffles that curves around a bend into some more rocky riffles. Then the river quiets and flattens, and the substrate reverts back to the normal sandy bottom of the Manitowish. This little run may take all of a minute, but in that time, Mary and crew canoed through spawning redhorse so thick that they were bumping up against the canoe! This was remarkable enough, but when they looked up from the water, they saw numerous eagles in the surrounding trees, all obviously observing the same phenomenon but with a different intent. Eowyn guided the canoe to the shoreline, and soon the eagles flew from the trees, soaring ever upward into a circling kettle of nine birds.

Mary and the girls paddled downstream and continued to kick

up eagles along the way. They ultimately saw 16 adult and immature eagles before they pulled out three hours later at the Hwy. 51 wayside.

They also paddled right up to what must have been a very young fawn, which was standing in marsh grass right on the river's shoreline. The fawn never moved more than a foot or two, and the canoeists sat and admired it from less than 10 feet away for nearly five minutes. The three were convinced they could have gone right up to it and touched it if they so chose. Eventually, Eowyn guided the canoe onward, leaving the fawn right where it had been all along.

Conifer-Nesting Birds

Why maintain or plant conifers on your land? Here are 20 reasons:

1. Bay-breasted warbler
2. Blackburnian warbler
3. Black-throated green warbler
4. Blue jay
5. Cape May warbler
6. Chipping sparrow
7. Evening grosbeak
8. Golden-crowned kinglet
9. Gray jay
10. Magnolia warbler
11. Northern goshawk
12. Pine siskin
13. Pine warbler
14. Purple finch
15. Red crossbill
16. Ruby-crowned kinglet
17. Rusty blackbird
18. Sharp-shinned hawk
19. Solitary vireo
20. Yellow-rumped warbler

Cowbirds

We have our share of cowbirds at our feeders, a scene that, along with starlings, we regret viewing. Cowbirds, as most of you know, lay their eggs in the nests of at least 140 species of birds, which will then raise the cowbird young. Because of their greater size, the cowbird chicks usually get fed first and most, in many cases resulting in the starvation of the host chicks whose nest they have expropriated. Researchers have speculated that cowbird chicks get their head start in part because they prolong the incubation needed by the eggs of the smaller host birds.

A Canadian study confirmed this theory by studying the amount of time the eggs of the yellow warbler (a common nesting species in the Lakeland area) took to hatch in 41 nests containing a cowbird egg and 26 nests without the intruders. As expected, the normal 11-day incubation of the warblers was extended by a day and a half in the nests with the cowbird eggs. The reason for the longer incubation is that the much larger cowbird eggs simply keep the incubating parent from making optimal contact with its own eggs.

The researchers also found the brown-headed cowbirds' eggs develop very quickly for their size, giving them an additional developmental advantage.

A female cowbird routinely removes one host egg for each egg that she lays, and the female may crack an additional host egg when she lays her own because cowbird eggs have unusually tough shells.

The entire process is called "brood parasitism," and it affects smaller birds to a greater extent than larger birds simply because the larger cowbird chicks crowd out and out-compete their much smaller nestmates.

Cowbirds are blamed for the decreasing populations of many species of birds, though historically they appear to have been of little consequence because their habitat was so limited. They reside in fields and farms, along the edges of forests, in residential areas, and in the shrubby habitat along wetlands.

Migrating Geese in June?

Flocks of geese flying in their typical "V-formation" and heading north are sometimes seen into June. The question is, what in the world are they doing, particularly given that geese have been nesting in our area since late April and some broods of goslings are already a month old. Bill Volkert, the resident DNR wildlife manager at Horicon Marsh, resolved the mystery in an e-mail to members of the Wisconsin BirdNet group. I've quoted his response in part:

"The local nesters don't breed until at least 2 or 3 years old and begin to hatch their young around the last week of April or first week of May, so the young are already about one month old at this time [early June]. Some of the young become mixed up with other nearby families (they seem to be imprinted on "geese" but may not recognize their parents) and are often adopted by these parents. That's why we may see families with 10 to 20 young.

"So what we have is not only a lot of young around at this time, but some families ending up with what are called "gang broods." Additionally, you also have a lot of non-breeders (young birds from last year or the year before), plus failed breeders (unsuccessful and destroyed nests), and birds whose young have been adopted by other families.

"The opinion seems to be that these birds gather together to form their own flocks, and in order to reduce competition on the nesting grounds and find an isolated area where they can molt their feathers in mid-summer, they make a "molt migration." Since they won't be able to fly during the molt, they leave in advance so as not to compete for food with the rapidly growing young in the area..."

Common Warblers

Mary, Callie, and I spent late May and early June 2001 driving the circle tour around Lake Superior, and backpacking in Sleeping Giant Provincial Park and Lake Superior Provincial Park. The birds in Lake Superior Provincial Park were in fine voice, particularly American redstarts, which seemed to be singing just about everywhere. Redstarts are physically very distinctive with their black upper body and bright orange patches on their wings and tails. But their songs are so variable that they can make you a bit crazy. Individual males have a repertoire of four or more different songs, and may sing different songs consecutively. The most common song sounds like *see-see-see-see-seeoo.* The good news is that they sing throughout the day, often at mid-day when most warblers have long since quieted down, and that they come in nicely to "pishing."

We have 23 nesting species of warblers in the Northern Highlands-American Legion State Forest. Four of them are rarely seen, while eight species are uncommon, five are fairly common, another five are common, and one is abundant. In trying to learn warblers, start with those you're most likely to see or hear. The ovenbird is our most abundant species, and the Nashville, yellow, chestnut-sided, yellow-rumped, and common yellowthroat are common nesters.

If you know those, then try the fairly common ones—golden-winged, black-throated green, pine, black and white, and mourning warblers.

Dragonfly Territories

Dragonflies hatch out in good numbers in June, and they actively patrol the skies for mosquitoes and other insects. On a bird hike in the Powell Marsh in early June of 2003, our group stopped to listen to some birds singing, and we soon had at least 20 dragonflies zooming amongst us, feeding on all the mosquitoes we had attracted to that spot. Not only did they relieve our immediate situation, but we weren't bothered by mosquitoes for the rest of the hike! This made no sense to me, but I wasn't about to argue.

You might note during your walks or paddles how many dragonflies will follow you a short way, then turn around and head back to the spot where they first began their escort service. They don't continue to follow you because many dragonfly species, like most birds and animals, protect specific territories during the mating season. Only male dragonflies defend a territory, and usually only against other males of its own species. Some perch in the territory, while others fly over it continuously. Male skimmers are known to raise their brightly colored abdomen in a threat display, much like a red-winged blackbird displays its red shoulder patch, or a blue jay raises its crest. Some skimmers try to out-duel intruders with high-speed parallel flights, though it's unclear how the territorial winner is determined.

darner (eyes meet)

head from top

clubtail (eyes separated)

spiketail (eyes meet in point)

You won't always see dragonflies acting territorial. If the male population is too high in an area, it may be impossible for a male to defend a territory, and territoriality simply breaks down. Some species, like spiketails and clubtails, appear to lack the territorial instinct entirely.

Territoriality extends beyond the three-dimensional space to the female herself. Once the male has bred the female, the male will often hover near the female or remain attached to her until she lays her eggs, in effect maintaining his territoriality until the very last moment. The reason for such possessiveness is because the males of most species have an apparatus that, during mating, can remove the stored sperm from the previous mating. So, the last male suitor is the one that fertilizes the eggs; hence the need to guard the female until she lays her eggs.

Non-Native Species

Mary, Callie, and I spent the last week of May and first week of June 2002 in Greece looking primarily at archaeological sites. We also managed to squeeze in some hikes to look for flowers and birds, and I got a kick out of seeing a host of the non-native species common in Wisconsin actually in the habitats and geographical regions where they belong. Species like St. John's-wort, chicory, hawkweed, mallow, pineapple weed, purple vetch, yarrow, mullein, stinging nettle, goatsbeard, forget-me-nots, and others made me feel like I was partially at home.

We also saw hordes of house sparrows and good numbers of European starlings, both of which were introduced into the U.S. with disastrous results. Mute swans, another species whose introduction into the U.S. had negative impacts, were common on Lake Geneva in Switzerland.

We also saw some marvelous native species. Out of the nearly 30 new bird species we saw in Greece, our favorite bird, hands down, was the hoopoe. We've never seen anything remotely like it. It frequented the ancient site where Aristotle taught Alexander the Great when he was a youth, adding an exotic element to a place that already had a bit of an otherworldly air to it.

The tree that amazed us most was the plane tree (*Platanus orientalis*), a relative of sycamores. Plane trees grow to enormous girths. We visited the oldest tree in Greece, a plane tree estimated at more than 1,000 years old, which was some 50 feet in circumference. Several towns built their central squares around these huge trees. We could sit at cafes situated under their enormous branches and wonderful shade, enjoying a cup of tea and rolls. I loved the fact that these towns honor their trees by putting them at the center of their cultural lives.

Emblem Birds

Places become dear to us over time and through experience. Memories, tripped by some sensory trigger, flood back from the richness of having been fully alive in these places. The places may be those of Grand Canyon or Rocky Mountain grandeur, or as simple as a fishing hole on a creek or a grandparent's cabin down an old wagon track. These places are endowed with meaning by a wealth of experiences as diverse as the humans who perceive them.

Wendell Berry wrote a short essay nearly 40 years ago entitled, "Emblem Birds of the Long-legged House." In it, Berry describes how particular birds had become the spirits of where he lived in an old family house along the Kentucky River. From his house, which was perched on stilts to escape the spring floods, he could watch a green heron fishing every day from a branch of an old willow that had fallen into the river. He could also step outside nearly anytime and hear the seven-noted song of the yellow-throated warbler high in the white sycamores, "a voice passing overhead like the sun."

The song eventually came to hold a power over him, and he became dependent on the yellow-throat to greet him every spring, to touch him and reassure him of the continuity of life. The yellow-throated warbler became his "emblem bird," the most characteristic voice of that place.

I'm convinced we all should have these connections to place, these keynotes that we must hear or see or smell in order to feel "placed," to feel at home, to feel that everything is somehow right. Many people developed these connections long ago. In conversations that have ensued over several decades of river tripping and woods walking, I have heard from some that the unearthly nighttime wail of loons over their lake speaks to their spirit more than any other voice. Others speak of the smell of a particular woods or wetland. Some don't feel right until they're adrift in their canoe, in the channel and current of a river that has flowed for 10,000 years or more. One family told me that the pungent smell of sweet ferns was the first thing they experienced when they got out of their car at their cottage, and that fragrance confirmed that they were "Up North."

We humans are particularly drawn to the spectacular and the charismatic. Thus the flight of an eagle, the dive into water of an osprey, the gangly grace of a great blue heron come to mind first for most of us when asked to consider what would be our "emblem" birds. At our home on the Manitowish River, we look out to our south over a large wetland expanse, part of the floodplain of the river and thus an area that breathes of muck and sphagnum, of sedges and willows and alders. To our north lies upland, a mosaic of pines and the cutover forest of aspens and white birch, all densely pockmarked with wetlands.

For Mary and me, the emblem bird of the river floodplain, at least in the early spring, is the red-winged blackbird. We faithfully look for the first flocks every mid-March, waiting anxiously for the males to return and set up their raucous territorializing, their "konk-a-lees" assuring us of the eventual end of a long winter and the wild delight and power of a river that will soon come into flood. The birds flash their red epaulets from their black wings, presaging the extraordinary colors soon to emerge from the dark earth. They are vibrant, squawky, sassy, tough, and prophetic, a balance of energy and vision worthy of March.

We also watch the waters for returning waterfowl, and I take the greatest pleasure in seeing the first male hooded merganser, its white hood raised like the meter flags in old taxis signaling that they are open for business—females take notice! They are spirited little things, diving and popping back up in such quick motion that they seem more fish than bird.

Late in April, we listen for the first hermit thrush in the upland woods, their flutings the necessary orchestral preface to the opening of hepaticas and wood anemones.

Come dusk along the edges of summer wetlands, the downward vibrational spiral of the veery's lament speaks of a beauty that we must revel in, knowing that it will fade soon enough.

Fall's emblem will always be the V-skeins of chorusing geese sailing south on bracing winds, but also the kettles of broad-winged hawks milling and sailing, milling and sailing in funnels on invisible winds high up, like an atmospheric kaleidoscope.

Winter touches the real spirit of this place, as only the most resilient and spirited birds remain. And of those few who choose five months of snow and cold, the black-capped chickadee does so with the greatest apparent spunk, guile, and sheer grit. It belongs most to this place. So common to us all, so small and unassuming, and yet chickadees characterize the pine uplands throughout all seasons of the year. Social enough to share our feeders and eat from our hands, chickadees are yet so wildly tough that we will never fathom the core of their nature. Their call notes in January perk me up, remind me that if a bird weighing only a third of an ounce can survive subzero temperatures and sing about it the next day, so can I.

Emblems help us in our effort to find the spirit of a place. They lead to reverence, to a belief in the soul of a place, which seems to me to be at the heart of why most of us come to live in the Northwoods. Find the emblem of your place this summer. Hold it dear, and share it with those you love. Doing so may be the best conservation practice of all.

Escapees on the Loose

Yellow iris, lupines, and forget-me-nots come beautifully into flower in June, but are only here because they've escaped from people's gardens and become naturalized. On paddles we lead along the Manitowish River from Hwy. H and K to Island Lake, our groups see many forget-me-nots and yellow irises along the wet shorelines.

Lupines flower along dry roadsides throughout the north country, but these aren't wild lupines. Wild lupines don't flower up here, but if they did, one of the ways to tell them apart from the garden variety is through height. The escapees are 2 to 4 feet tall; by comparison, the wild ones are 8 to 24 inches in height. Wild lupines also only have 7 to 11 leaflets, while the garden variety has 12 to 18 leaflets.

False Advertising

Among the many June flowers in bloom are three wildflowers that ought to be charged with making false advertising claims, using unfair trade practices, and conducting illegal interstate commerce. These flowers clearly are in the business of duping insects, and they appear to have no moral qualms about it. They produce showy "fake" flowers to lure unsuspecting insects in, then take advantage of the visitors' innocent natures by using them to transport their product, in this case, pollen, to another flower. High-bush cranberry, bunchberry, and wild calla are the culprits, and if insects had lawyers, these guys would have been put away a long time ago.

Bunchberry and wild calla modify one or more of their leaves to look like flashy flower petals. Then the plants color them white to put on a bright face. In fact, their real flowers are tiny and non-descript, and are all bundled in a small club-like structure that would be very unlikely to catch the attention of a wandering insect looking for a good time.

High-bush cranberry approaches its criminality a bit differently, producing large, bright-white sterile flowers without any male stamens or female pistils to ring their otherwise real, but quite tiny and uninteresting, flowers.

It's a scam, but since adult insects very seldom live from one year to the next, no hue and cry gets transferred between generations, and next year's insects will fall for the same hoax as every generation has before them.

Fledging Into Adulthood

We saw a fledged young purple finch in our yard on June 19, 2003. The purple finch was raising a big ruckus around one of our tube feeders, crying constantly with its mouth open and demanding that one of the adults nearby feed it. It followed an adult male purple finch around the edge of the circular plate on the bottom of our tube feeder, and finally got so frustrated when the male wouldn't feed it that it jumped on top of the male! They both crashed down onto our deck. The male flew into a tree, and the juvenile flew back up onto our tray feeder, still calling piteously for someone to feed it. Eventually it started to work on some sunflower seeds, though it really didn't seem to understand how to eat one.

The nesting process for nearly all of our songbirds passes pretty quickly. Most of our small songbirds incubate their eggs for around

11 to 14 days, and then it's only 8 to 25 days of feeding until the young have grown to full size and take their first flight, or fledge. Here are some examples of fledging periods:

Bird	Fledging period
Eastern phoebe	15-16 days
Wood-pewee	14-18 days
Cliff swallow	21-25 days
Gray jay	15 days
Hermit thrush	12 days
Gray catbird	10-11 days
Indigo bunting	9-10 days
Black-throated green warbler	8-10 days

For larger birds, the process is much longer—a raven fledges in 38 to 44 days, a great blue heron in 56 to 60 days, and a bald eagle in 70 to 98 days. Three months is long, but it's nothing like the 18 years that we humans require.

Fledging doesn't mean the end of parenting; in fact, after fledging, altricial young (born naked, immobile, and unable to feed themselves) may be fed for more than twice as long as they were fed in the nest. So the parents aren't off the hook just because the young can fly. Any human parent who has sent a youngster off to college only to have him or her return home after graduation understands this principle of extended parenting.

Leeches in My Breeches

The classic leech moment was immortalized in the movie *Stand By Me* when the young star of the film crosses a swamp and discovers to his horror that his breeches are filled with leeches. The scene reminds me of a morning when Eowyn, our oldest daughter, then a teenager, rafted a section of the Manitowish with two of her girlfriends. One was a city gal with a great fear of spiders and other crawly critters.

We dropped them off early in the day to float the river. Later, we were driving to Manitowish Waters, when from the distance three young women came running out of the woods toward the road. We quickly reached them, and, to our surprise, there were our daughter and her friends, all in their bathing suits, and all extremely upset.

When we finally got them settled down enough to relate their story, we learned they had been having a wonderful float down the river, hopping on and off their rafts to swim, until ... (drum roll) THE LEECHES! Somehow the girls swam into a weedy section of the river, and when they got back on their dime-store rafts, they discovered dozens of leeches on their legs. Worst off was the city girl who says to this day she had at least a hundred baby leeches on her legs.

I'm sure they screamed loud enough to scare most of the birdlife in the county, then left their rafts to float the river without them, and ran pell-mell to the road, though what they expected to occur there, I'm not sure. Thankfully, and remarkably, we were the first ones to intercept them.

This was all brought to mind a few years ago when we observed two painted turtles laying eggs, both of which had leeches attached to their shells. Being of an inquiring mind, I wondered which end of the leech was which, what did what, and for that matter, how in the world did they mate? After some research, I learned that the sex life of a leech is probably as astonishing as that of any animal in the natural world.

First off, individual leeches bear both sex organs, a condition I think would lead to great confusion when mating time arises. Leeches are hermaphroditic, possessing a pair of ovaries and several pairs of testes. How they decide who gets to be the male and the female is worthy of pondering, but once the gender choice is made, most leeches inseminate one another by "hypodermic impregnation." This delightful method involves the male depositing spermatophores almost anywhere on his partner's body, whereupon the spermatophores secrete enzymes that eat away the partner's flesh. The sperm cells then enter the partner's body cavity where they are either killed by defensive cells or suspended in the blood and pumped to the ovaries where they fertilize the eggs. It takes a good three days for the leech's body to heal from the holes bored in it by its partner's spermatophores.

Just thought you'd like to know.

Flowering Shrubs

Many showy shrubs come into flower by early June, and as a result the Northwoods is at its aromatic peak. Nannyberry, black, pin, and choke cherries, and red-osier dogwood are just a few of the native shrubs you should be seeing and smelling. The non-natives, like lilacs, flowering crabs, and apple trees, are glorious as well, and while I often rail against exotic species, I can't find a bad word in my vocabulary to use regarding these particular immigrants.

Our native cherries (genus *Prunus*) bloom in a succession, beginning with pin cherries, then black cherries, then choke cherries. The flowers of the pin (*Prunus pennsylvanica*) cherry are arranged in an umbel, where each flower radiates from one point like the ribs of an umbrella, while the stalked flowers of the black (*Prunus serotina*) and choke (*Prunus virginiana*) cherries are organized in a plume-like shape called a raceme, each flower borne along a common stem.

The flowers of Juneberries (genus *Amelanchier*) are long gone by June, and are forming fruits. *Amelanchiers* have more than 80 common names, probably more than any other group of plants. Serviceberry or shadbush may be two of the most common. "Service" came into use because the early blooms indicated that the frost had gone out of the ground sufficiently to perform services for those who had died over the winter. "Shad" is so called because the timing of the blooms coincides with the period when shad spawn up the rivers.

Our affection for Juneberries comes not only from the early blooms, which signal spring's arrival, but also from the delicate flavor of the berries. Some American Indians called the plant "Saskatoon," and added the berries liberally to dried meat to form pemmican.

If you're not familiar with Juneberry trees, they typically grow to 10 to 20 feet tall and need sun, so they're usually found along roadsides, forest edges, old railroad tracks, and similar locations. The berries first blaze bright red, but gradually turn purplish. That's when you want to pick them, that is if you've managed to beat all the birds to them. The berries are mildly sweet and firm, much like a blueberry. The simple, alternate, toothed leaves look similar to a choke cherry's.

The wood is heavy, close-grained, and strong, and as a result Juneberry earned the additional name of "lancewood" for its use as arrow shafts, fishing poles, canes, tool handles, and the like.

The value of Juneberries spans the globe. Nearly 25 species are native to North America, Europe, Northern Africa, and Asia.

Fogbow

Mary and I took several early morning walks in mid-June 2001, in part to hear the last lengthy chorusing of birdsong for the year, but also because of the beautiful fogs that settled in on those cold mornings. We wanted open vistas in which we could immerse ourselves in the fog and then see the fog lifting, so we hiked the Powell Marsh one day and the Little Turtle Flowage the next. The Little Turtle offered the largest surprise. A fogbow arched perfectly over the lifting fogbank, weakly colored but clearly a bow.

I can't recall ever seeing a fogbow before. Several weeks earlier, we were treated to a brilliant double rainbow over the marsh below our house. We've seen sun pillars, parhelic circles ("sun dogs"), moon and sun haloes, various arcs and coronas, but never a fogbow. The sum total of what I can learn about them is that they are also known as cloudbows or white rainbows, and that if they have any color at all, the colors are very weak.

We watched the fogbow over the course of 20 minutes, until all that was left was the right side base of the bow, faintly glimmering where it appeared to touch ground on the shoreline. Possibly our ignorance of the meteorological whys and wherefores of fogbows is all for the better. Mysteries allow us to keep our sense of wonder undiminished by the facts.

Forget-Me-Nots

The wet edges between our yard and the lowland woods often support a mass of forget-me-nots (*Myosotis scorpioides*), each flower beautiful with its five pale sky-blue petals and an eye ringed in white and yellow. The ring around the center serves as a guide to lead pollinating insects to the nectar and pollen.

This European immigrant has been naturalized throughout Wisconsin, but had a long lineage before it ever set foot in our state. The flowers have long symbolized friendship and loyalty, if not love, and stories of the name's origin abound in many languages. In his book *Hedgemaids and Fairy Candles,* Jack Sanders writes, "In one widely told tale, a knight was walking with his sweetheart alongside a pond or river when he saw some of these flowers growing on an island in the middle of the water. Foolish with love, he jumped into the water, armor and all, and managed to grab a bunch of flowers, and toss them to his lover before sinking below the surface. His last words were, 'Forget me not!' "

Tennyson wrote of "the sweet forget-me-nots that grow for happy lovers."

Longfellow glowed in his poem "Evangeline":

> *Silently, one by one, in the infinite meadows of heaven,*
> *Blossom the lovely stars, the forget-me-nots of the angels.*

If you're ever in Alaska, impress the locals with your knowledge that the forget-me-not is their state flower.

Foulds Creek

Over the years, I've led a number of groups to a deer exclosure (a cage that keeps deer out) near Foulds Creek. The deer-proof fencing was erected in 1945 and is in rough shape now. The exclosure was built to demonstrate the need for controlling the deer herd and the harvest of does. It was also an attempt to understand the botanical impact of deer on woody browse in deer yards.

Some controversy surrounds the Foulds Creek exclosure because the role of snowshoe hares as equally important browsers has not been acknowledged. Regardless of whether deer and/or hares are the culprits, the visual difference between the flora outside the exclosure and the flora inside is dramatic. Hemlock regeneration is non-existent on one side of the exclosure right up to the fence, while hemlock saplings and seedlings are dense just inside the fence.

The point I always wish to make to my groups is how a forest community can be significantly shaped by the presence or absence of major browsers. I'd like to see deer and hare exclosures put up along some of our local nature trails so that hikers could observe the dramatic effects of browsing on our plant communities.

Frog Counting

On June 2, 2004, I conducted the second run of my annual frog and toad surveys in Vilas County for the Wisconsin DNR, and winners of the highest volume award for the night were Eastern gray treefrogs. It may have been my imagination, but I'm not sure I have ever heard them sing quite so loudly or in so many places. The song, if you can call it that, is a short staccato blast usually issued from shrubs and trees around permanent or semi-permanent wetlands. A chorus of these guys can hurt the ears.

Eastern grays are considered late spring breeders, along with American toads. Both come into peak breeding when water temperatures reach 60°F, so their choraling presence is almost as accurate a measurement of water temperature as a thermometer.

Once water temperatures reach 70°F, the summer breeders come into full song in permanent waterbodies. These species include green frog, mink frog, and bullfrog. Their numbers are seldom as high as the spring breeders (spring peepers, wood frogs, and chorus frogs) simply because fish predation occurs in permanent waters and not in the temporary woodland ponds used by spring breeders.

I heard my first green frogs a few days later on June 6, but they weren't in full voice. We needed a string of warm days and nights to bring lake temperatures up enough to inspire their amour.

Great Blue Heron Population

I occasionally receive calls asking whether great blue herons are declining. The callers are generally not seeing herons in areas in which they were common before, and want to know what happened to them. Unfortunately, Wisconsin does not have a statewide census of herons, so there's little quantitative data on which to base an answer. However, based on 30 years of surveys conducted annually by volunteers, great blue heron numbers in most U.S. states and Canadian provinces appear to be stable or increasing.

While the national great blue heron population may be doing well, it's very common to have local fluctuations. Great blues nest in rookeries, or colonies, typically numbering around 40 nests, but rookeries can be as small as a dozen and as large as a thousand nests. Shifting and relocation of rookeries occur naturally and frequently. Herons sometimes leave a colony site for no apparent reason, but often there is a causative factor like the nest trees falling over in flooded areas, disturbances from humans, or bald eagles preying on heron chicks.

Sometimes herons kill their own nest trees through the accumulation of their excrement, a process called "guanotrophy" by some biologists. An older rookery can smell like a fetid stew and look like a spring snowstorm just blew in.

The colonies are akin to a city tenement building, with some trees supporting four or more nests, and the bottom nests representing the low-rent district. At the same time, a rookery has so many landings, take-offs and glide-overs taking place simultaneously that an O'Hare Airport air traffic controller would be disoriented by the commotion.

Great blues are one of our earliest spring migrants, usually arriving by March 30, well before the ice goes off the lakes. The female lays a clutch of four to five eggs by the first week of May or so, with chicks appearing typically by the first week of June.

Feeding four clamorous chicks is full-time work. Great blues are opportunistic feeders, foraging in fresh and salt water, in uplands and wetlands, in tidal and non-tidal marshes. Their diet is a vast smorgasbord of organisms and includes eating gophers in upland fields, sora rails in marshes, and fish, frogs, and snakes along river and lake shorelines. When the adults return to the nest, the chicks grab their bills, triggering a regurgitation of partially digested food into the mouths of the young.

Adults typically forage 12 or more miles from the rookery. If your home is not within that general radius, you may not see many herons, and you may conclude that they are declining. There is some evidence of a population decline in the southern part of the state, but the jury is out on the population dynamics in our area of the Northwoods.

Great Crested Flycatchers

I received reports from numerous people who saw great crested flycatchers in June of 1998. One caller had them nesting close to his home. The flycatchers were giving him quite a show by hawking insects that were hovering in front of his picture window.

Great crested flycatchers are nearly robin-sized and quite handsome, their yellow belly and cinnamon tail serving as clear identifiers (unlike many of the other flycatchers who fall in the "little brown bird" category). Their song, a simple loudly whistled wheeep, also provides a telltale ID. Great cresteds usually "hawk" for insects, meaning they sally briefly from a tree perch to capture insects in flight, then return to their perch. At least 52 kinds of beetles, along with bees, wasps, sawflies, moths, mosquitoes, houseflies, and spiders, as well as a variety of berries make up their dinner menu.

Great cresteds usually nest in low cavities in open deciduous woods, one of 30 or more species of birds in our area that require cavities. They may also nest close to human habitation in bluebird houses, in town parks, old orchards, and around farms.

Great Gray Owl Update 2005

Remember all the uproar about the once-in-a-lifetime invasion of great gray owls in the winter of 2004-05? Well, in June of 2005, six to 12 great grays were still in northern Wisconsin, most in Bayfield County. One great gray was seen as far south as northern Polk County, while another was spotted near the Crex Meadows Wildlife Area in Burnett County.

"Lots" of great grays were reported still around the Duluth area. I received a picture from a friend in Bayfield who photographed a great gray sitting on a bluebird box.

Whether the great grays that remained in Wisconsin actually nested was never determined. The winter of 2005-06 was the opposite of its predecessor—we were hard-pressed to find even one great gray in the entire state at any given time.

The Jack/Jill-in-the-Pulpit

Jack-in-the-pulpit is a uniquely beautiful woodland flower, but it also has a unique biology. Most often, the flowers are unisexual, meaning the plant is either male or female. To determine the sex, you must gently pry open the "pulpit" to look at the base of the spadix. If the flowers at the bottom of the pulpit are like tiny green berries, the flower is female. If the flowers are like threads, and they shed pollen, the flower is a male.

The truly remarkable aspect of the jack-in-the-pulpit is that a plant may change sexes back and forth over the years. Which sex the plant is depends on how much food has been stored by the corm during the fall. In a good year, a female flower will come up with two leaves. In a marginal year, a male flower with one leaf will arise. During a poor year, only a leaf will emerge. In 1997, Wanda Nelson from Arbor Vitae sent me a photo of a 32-inch-tall jack-in-the-pulpit she discovered near Big Papoose Lake. That's a giant flower, and thus it was very likely a female.

Over a given jack-in-the-pulpit's lifetime, it generally produces a male flower half the time and a female the other half. Humans would have to undergo years of psychoanalysis if this strategy occurred to us, but the "Jacks" or "Jills," as the case may be, seem untroubled by their duality.

"A Dinosaurian Gum-Ball Machine"

Mid-June marks the typical egg-laying time for snapping and painted turtles. Turtles require warm weather in order that the soil will be heated sufficiently for their eggs to incubate and mature. Sunny days also provide necessary basking opportunities. Turtles need vitamin D for the uptake of calcium from their food, which in turn contributes critically to eggshell development, and to shell development in younger turtles.

Eggs typically incubate for 60 to 90 days, but cool weather can lengthen the incubation period, sometimes enough to prevent hatching of the young until the following spring. The incubation temperature also influences the gender of the young snappers and painteds. More females hatch from nests with high incubation temperatures, while more males come from nests with low temperatures.

Watching a turtle laying eggs seems like an invasion of privacy. It also pales in comparison to watching an action film. Egg-laying requires a certain deliberateness, and turtles are certainly masters of that. In his book *Natural Prayers*, Chet Raymo describes an egg-laying snapper as "a dinosaurian gum-ball machine disgorging its contents." Snappers are our biggest gum-ball machines, laying from 30 to 80 round eggs, while a smaller turtle like the painted will typically lay eight to 10 elongated eggs.

All turtles lay their eggs on land, and there's a direct correlation between size and number of eggs—the bigger the turtle, the more eggs. The eggs all seem to taste good, too. Turtle nests apparently contradict the notion that there is no such a thing as a free lunch in the natural world, because just about anything that can dig up the nest does—from crows to skunks to foxes. People have even reported seeing deer digging up the nests!

Still, if only a few young reach the water and survive their perilous first year (largemouth bass, northern pike, and bullfrogs readily snap up the young), turtles can reach prodigious ages. Both snappers and painteds mature in five to seven years, and can live for more than 40 years. Thus they can endure high predation rates and still maintain their populations.

However, predators like raccoons and coyotes have burgeoned in the last century, so turtle populations are already at significant risk in many locations. Toss in the American love affair with cars, the ever-increasing numbers of which kill ever-increasing numbers of turtles, and all species in Wisconsin are considered to have declined in the last century. It's estimated that only 5 percent of the eggs laid statewide survive to hatching. Of those that hatch, only one in a hundred will make it to adulthood.

Five of Wisconsin's 11 turtle species are listed as endangered, threatened, or as species of special concern.

I don't know of a study that gives the specific status of turtles in the Northwoods, but the wood turtle, the only turtle whose range is specific to the Northwoods, is listed as a threatened species. Wood turtles take 10 to 12 years to mature and often nest communally, which permits easier predation. And some people apparently still collect wood turtles for food or for the pet trade, a reprehensible practice for a society that clearly knows what's at stake.

The best help we can give turtles is to keep our shorelines as natural as possible—in particular, by leaving trees that have fallen into the water. Denuded shorelines leave little feeding or basking habitat, while seawalls prevent turtles from accessing uplands for nesting and riprap often traps baby turtles between the rocks as they make their way back to the water after hatching.

I'm an advocate of wild places, places where random and often chaotic natural events are allowed to occur. We all love the water, and the best love we can give back to our lakes and rivers is to let them function naturally.

Ground-Nesting Birds

Why should we avoid disturbing Northwoods forest floors and grasslands? Here are 33 reasons:

1. American woodcock
2. Black-and-white warbler
3. Blue-winged warbler
4. Bobolink
5. Canada warbler
6. Connecticut warbler
7. Dark-eyed junco
8. Golden-winged warbler
9. Hermit thrush
10. Le Conte's sparrow
11. Lincoln's sparrow

12. Louisiana waterthrush
13. Mourning warbler
14. Nashville warbler
15. Northern bobwhite
16. Northern waterthrush
17. Ovenbird
18. Palm warbler
19. Ruffed grouse
20. Rufous-sided towhee
21. Savannah sparrow
22. Sedge wren
23. Sharp-tailed grouse
24. Song sparrow
25. Spruce grouse
26. Tennessee warbler
27. Veery
28. Whip-poor-will
29. White-throated sparrow
30. Wild turkey
31. Wilson's warbler
32. Winter wren
33. Yellow-bellied flycatcher

Mergansers Playing the Stork

On June 8, 2001, Art Bernhardt observed a female hooded merganser leave a nesting box on his property and fly away carrying an egg in its bill. Art keeps track of the comings and goings of the merganser through his window, which looks out on Trout Lake. The merganser flew by "at a distance of about 15 feet with an egg in its bill! It flew out low over the water as it normally does and disappeared against the far shore trees."

Art correctly noted that cliff swallows have been observed carrying their eggs in their beaks to the nests of other individuals and depositing them, a unique form of nest parasitism. Brown-headed cowbirds are well-known brood parasites, laying eggs in the nests of a host of other species. However, they're not known to carry eggs to another nest.

But hooded mergansers? *The Birder's Handbook*, written by Ehrlich, Dobkin, and Wheye, says that hooded merganser "females lay [eggs] in each other's nests resulting in dump nests with up to 36 eggs." In an essay on parasitized ducks, the authors discuss how intraspecific brood parasitism (parasitism within members of the same species) is common among ducks. Ducks seldom defend their nests during the laying period, making it easy for another duck to fly in and lay its eggs in the nests of others. Female ducks often return to nest near the place of their birth, so it's likely that daughters or sisters are often parasitizing one another.

I called wildlife biologist Bruce Bacon, who was involved in several duck studies in the past. Bruce said that dump nests in wood ducks and mergansers are probably more common than non-dump nests. By dump nests, Bruce means nests that have the eggs of more than one female. Bruce once found a hen wood duck incubating 28 eggs, 24 of which hatched. He's seen numerous instances of a female brooding several different species of eggs—for instance, a merganser brooding wood duck eggs in addition to her own. Red-headed ducks also lay their eggs in many other duck species' nests.

However, Bruce said that there is very little documentation of ducks carrying eggs, and very little is subsequently known about this practice. Thus, Art's observation is highly unusual, and whether the merganser was carrying her own egg, the egg of another hoodie, or the egg of another species is impossible to know.

Hummers For Lunch?

A bird-watcher on Witches Lake described to me a distressing scene she witnessed: "A hummingbird was at the window box enjoying the flowers, and right before my eyes a sharp-shinned hawk swooped down and took the hummer. I couldn't believe my eyes. Next morning, another hummer was at a feeder and the sharp-shinned took him also. I 'get it' that the hawks have to eat too, but why a hummer? It hardly seems worth the trouble since they are so small; how much of a meal could that be? I am also astonished that the hawk could actually catch a hummer."

I'm not sure why a sharpie would bother with a hummer, given that a hummer only weighs one-tenth of an ounce, and would hardly provide meat enough for one chew. I watched a sharpie nearly take a hummer from one of our feeders a few years back, so I've seen the astonishing speed of a sharp-shinned hawk. As for why a hawk would eat something that could be used for little more than a toothpick, I'm at a loss.

Loon Drama

Al Toussaint on Alva Lake in Oneida County reported an ongoing story of the loons on his lake. Al has watched loons successfully raise chicks on Alva for many years. Most recently, they had raised their chicks on an artificial platform. In 2005, they nested again on the platform but were driven off by an immature eagle. They re-nested on a hummock in a bay of the lake and were successfully incubating two eggs until June 25. That morning Al heard a frantic calling coming from the loon nest, and when he motored over to it, he found an immature eagle standing on a dead female loon on the nest. Al scared the eagle off the loon and found that the adult loon was still warm, as were the eggs.

The next day the male loon, which was banded and known to be at least 15 years old, was incubating the eggs. He'd been doing most of the incubation anyway, so this wasn't a great change, except now, when he wanted to go feed, there wasn't a mate to take over the incubating chores.

The story grew more complicated as the week progressed. On Monday, June 27, a pair of loons showed up on the lake—an unbanded female and a banded male. Al was now concerned that if the new pair mated on the lake and regarded it as their territory, the new pair would kill any chicks that emerged from the other nest, as loons are known to do.

The first male eventually left the nest on June 30, and abandoned the eggs. In the next few days, six or seven other loons were seen on the lake, indicating that the lake was an open territory for the taking, though for the rest of the summer, no pair claimed it for their own.

The dead female loon had been banded in 1998 on Alva Lake, and had been there ever since with the same male. What will occur in 2006 will be most interesting to watch.

Loon Nurseries

In 1999, Melanie Panush told the story of a pair of loons that nested near her home on Myrtle Lake, a quiet, little 22-acre pothole of a lake. Two chicks hatched out in June, and within a few weeks the adults and the chicks were seen walking across a bog to get to Garth Lake, a 114-acre lake, where they spent the rest of the summer.

Why would they leave, Melanie asked, particularly since Myrtle has lots of fish? She noted that while Myrtle is tiny in surface area, it is 45 feet deep. Garth, on the other hand, is only 22 feet deep.

I suspect the answer had to do with the way adult loons take their chicks from their nest sites to "nursery" sites within a few days of hatching. These are usually shallow, protected coves with lots of small fish and undisturbed shorelines that offer hiding places. Myrtle's size and depth doesn't appear to offer shallow bays for a nursery, but it apparently is ideal for nesting. It sounds like the loons simply adapted, utilizing each site to meet their specific needs at the time.

Loon Phenology

Paul Brenner reported the phenology of loons nesting one year on Maple Lake in Boulder Junction:

> Ice-out on 4/25.
> Loons appeared on the lake on 4/25.
> Loons on top of a raft nest on 4/28.
> Loons mated on the raft on 5/3.
> First egg laid on 5/15.
> Second egg laid on 5/18.

Incubation usually lasts about a month, so Paul's loon chicks should have hatched out around June 15, which is average for our area.

The "Moon" Moth

I stopped at my sister-in-law's home in Manitowish Waters on June 18, 2005, and there clinging to her garage in the late afternoon was a luna moth (*Actias luna*), one of the most beautiful moths in all of the eastern United States. Their 3 to 4½-inch, sea-foam green wings have translucent eyespots on both the fore- and hindwings, while the hindwings are particularly notable because of the long curving tails that look like the tails on a kite or like a pair of legs.

Observing a luna moth during the day is quite unusual given that they only fly at night and typically hide motionless in the tree foliage during the day, where they look exactly like every other leaf on the tree. This luna moth was startlingly apparent against the log siding of the garage, and it didn't fly away when I approached it, a sign of an animal that uses cryptic coloring as its primary defense.

While luna moths are relatively common, they are rarely seen because the adults only live for up to a week, and are usually nocturnal during their short life span. In fact, the adults are unable to feed, lacking the proboscises—the long, slender mouthparts—typically found in other moths and butterflies.

The adult's brief agenda in life is simple—breed, lay eggs, and die. The female emerges from her cocoon, unfurls her wings, and already laden with eggs, is immediately ready to breed, often mating before she even takes her first flight. From a scent gland on the posterior of her abdomen, she emits an airborne chemical pheromone that is sensed by the bushy antennae of the male, and he immediately hones in on her. Scenting, or "calling," typically takes place after midnight, and if the pair is undisturbed, they will remain in copula until the next evening. Once they separate, the female soon begins laying her eggs, often ovipositing them on white birch leaves, one of their favored host plants in the Northwoods.

The eggs incubate for 8 to 13 days, then the caterpillar emerges, lime green in color with a pale yellow horizontal line along each side and reddish-orange spots on each body segment. The caterpillars are herbivores, living a sedentary life munching leaves without doing any significant harm to their host plants. While they prefer white birch trees, the caterpillars also feed in the north on alder, beech, cherries, willow, and hazelnut. The caterpillars are spectacular in their own right, growing to 3½ inches long.

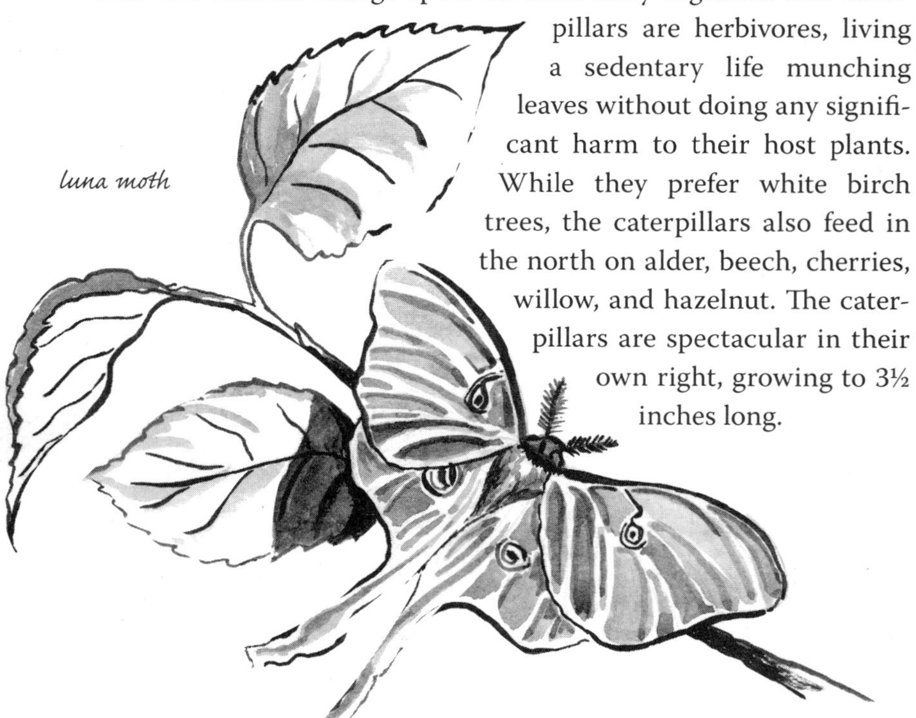
luna moth

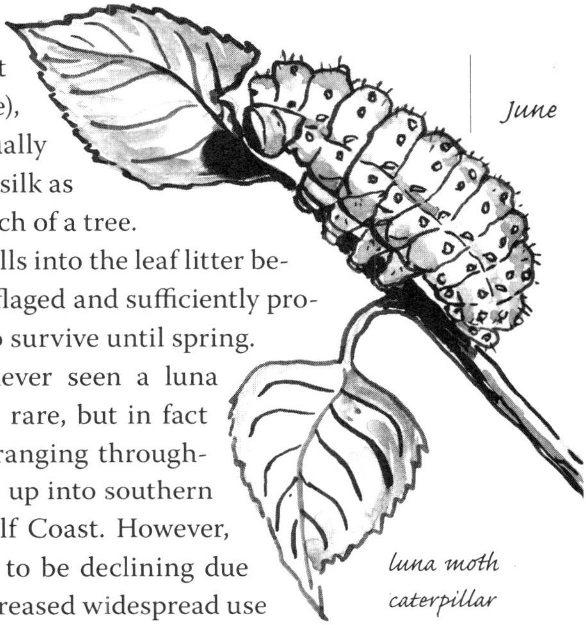

As members of the giant silkworm family (Saturniidae), the caterpillars will eventually spin a papery cocoon made of silk as well as leaf pieces from a branch of a tree. The cocoon then eventually falls into the leaf litter below the tree where it's camouflaged and sufficiently protected from the winter cold to survive until spring.

Since most folks have never seen a luna moth, many assume they are rare, but in fact they are relatively common, ranging throughout the eastern United States, up into southern Canada and down to the Gulf Coast. However, wild silk moths are reported to be declining due to habitat destruction and increased widespread use of vapor lights, which disrupt their mating cycle. As a general rule, unless you have essential reasons for keeping yard lights on at night, both the natural world and your neighbors appreciate the lights being switched off.

luna moth caterpillar

Mallard Nesting in a Tree

Rudy Becker sent me several pictures of a mallard nesting about 30 feet up in a red oak tree on their Big Arbor Vitae Lake property. The nest is a large stick nest like a hawk might use. Rudy wanted to know how the mallards could build such a nest given their difficulty in even getting to the nest, how the chicks would get down, and how common it is to find a mallard nesting in a tree.

The literature says that most mallards nest on the ground within 100 feet of water, and most often in marsh growth. They are also known to nest on muskrat lodges, small islands, dikes, and far from water in hayfields and meadows. Nests have been found in tree hollows, flower boxes, forests, and landscape plantings, too. Arthur Cleveland Bent in his classic 21-volume series *Life Histories of North American Birds* mentions that mallards along the Pacific coast were found nesting in the fork of a large tree, but that's the only record I can find in my library of books. So, it appears Rudy has a very unusual duck on his hands.

As for how the chicks will get down, I would imagine they would jump down like wood duck chicks do.

And as for building the nest, my bet is that they didn't build it, but rather found it deserted. I just can't imagine how a mallard would carry sticks with webbed feet—much less actually weave a nest.

One Ordinary Extraordinary Night

In June of 2000, Linda Thomas of Sayner wrote to tell of the sights and sounds she heard one early evening while sitting on a deck overlooking Plum Lake. She observed little brown bats hawking insects, a flying squirrel working its way through an oak tree, a pair of whip-poor-wills and a pair of nighthawks swooping in search of insects, and a variety of calling frogs.

Her note reminded me of the many frog counts I have done for the DNR over the years, and how half the fun (or more) has been hearing night sounds other than frogs.

I did a count on June 6, 2000, beginning just as dark set in, and finishing in total darkness about 10:30 p.m. At the first site, Jag Lake, a lone spring peeper chimed off and on, but the most remarkable sound was something I'd never heard before—the constant rain of droppings from the forest tent caterpillars that were defoliating the shoreline trees. For a welcome contrast, a loon serenaded me with much prettier music from far out on the lake.

My next stop was at a bog along County H. Here, with our lack of water, the bog was high and dry, and bereft of frogs. But several veeries sang their ethereal descending song from trees around the bog edge, while hermit thrushes gave their flute-like, ascending, and varying song from the upland woods on the other side of the road.

At Nichols Lake on the edge of Boulder Junction, the frog action is always secondary to whether the whip-poor-will that has been there for more than a decade has returned, and he was present again that year. A woodcock also gave its unmelodious and repetitive peent from the upland behind the lake, a rather late presentation for the male who "dances" just about every early evening, but usually only in May.

At Whitney Lake, spring peepers, American toads, and green frogs chorused. Whitney is always rich in singing frogs, but I also look forward to discovering whether the beaver that has been there every year will once again be patrolling the shoreline. It was there on cue, startling me as always with the smack of his tail, even though I'm always ready for the sound. On a quiet night, a beaver tail thwacked on smooth water is like the solid crack of a bat at a ball game. Common snipe winnowed overhead as the beaver whacked the water again and again. During an earlier frog count in May, Mary and I had listened to one of the beavers chewing a nearby tree.

At Rice Creek on Hwy. K, a deer crashed through the marsh and back into the woods when I came down to the creek to listen for frogs. Usually at a bog a quarter mile east of the creek, barred owls do their "southern cooking" call—*Who cooks for you, who cooks for you-all?* Not this year, but I only stayed at the site for five to 10 minutes. Maybe the owls were just quiet during that period.

Eastern gray treefrogs were in full chorus at Whitney Flowage, their short staccato call loud, intense, and constant.

It was really a rather ordinary night as frog survey nights go, but ordinary in the Northwoods is always nothing short of remarkable when you think about it.

Oranges for Birds

Although the orioles have usually departed from our feeders in June, we still often have catbirds coming in to feed on the orange halves that we put out. They vigorously rip out chunks of orange and swallow them with apparent relish. The payoff for us is we get to hear their random and complex singing every morning at dawn.

Jack Bull in Winchester called one mid-June to report that several yellow-bellied sapsuckers were eating his oranges, a behavior I've never heard of from sapsuckers. He also said the sapsuckers hung from his hummingbird feeders and drank sugar water, again a behavior I've never heard of in sapsuckers.

Why not try cutting some oranges in half, impaling them on a nail, and seeing what comes in to feed? You might be in for a surprise or two.

Pizza, Pizza, Pizza, PIZZA!

Jack Bull in Winchester reported that an ovenbird had flown into one of his windows and died. Jack had never seen one before, which I suspect would be the case for most Northwoods residents. Most people have heard them, though, as ovenbirds are very common. Their rising crescendo of *Teacher, Teacher, Teacher, TEACHER!* rings boldly in the spring and nearly all day long in any maturing forest. I prefer to think of the song as *Pizza, Pizza, Pizza, PIZZA!* The pizza, after all, goes in the oven, and I need all the memory devices I can come up with.

To some degree, ovenbirds, with their streaked breast plumage, resemble wood thrushes, but ovenbirds are much smaller and have dull orange crowns and pinkish legs. They're also secretive, and are difficult to spot even when they're singing their hearts out from 30 feet away. I've had some success "pishing" them in closer, but they more often stay close to the ground and don't move.

Ovenbirds may be warblers, but they behave quite unlike most other warblers, which forage and flit quickly in the upper branches of trees. Ovenbirds are a ground-nesting warbler, and they build a unique nest out of dried leaves and other vegetation that is dome-shaped like a Dutch oven. The adults enter from the side and the roof sheds water. I'm surprised that more birds don't utilize this design, but apparently rain doesn't bother most birds. The nest is exceptionally well-camouflaged. I've yet to find one, though I haven't tried very hard out of fear of forcing one to abandon its nest.

Despite its camouflage, the nest is often raided by red and gray squirrels, raccoons, snakes, skunks, weasels, and feral cats and dogs. Cowbirds parasitize at least half of all ovenbird nests by laying one of their eggs in the nest, while removing one of the ovenbird's. But even though the cowbird hatchling is far larger than the ovenbird young, the nestlings apparently compete adequately enough that some survive, and thus researchers estimate that ovenbirds only lose about 15 percent of their eggs to cowbirds every year.

As many times as I've heard ovenbirds sing in the woods, I've never heard the male's courtship flight song, which occurs on overcast days and at dusk. As he flies over his territory, the male apparently sings an exuberant song that is a jumble of musical notes. Thoreau called the ovenbird the "night warbler," and was never able to identify the flight song.

Ovenbirds provide an important ecological service. They love to eat spruce budworms, a major insect pest, and often produce up to three broods of young during outbreaks of the budworm.

A Phenology of Fragrances

The sweet scent of wild roses graces many a riverbank in June. Poet Mary Oliver wrote of roses in her Pulitzer Prize-winning book *American Primitive:*

... day after day
the honey keeps on coming
in the red cups and the bees
like amber drops roll
in the petals ...

The timing of wildflower fragrances can be used as a phenological guide to spring and summer that's almost as reliable as a printed calendar. Here's a sequential guide Mary and I made to the most aromatic northern wildflowers from early spring into summer:

Skunk cabbage (you have to admit it's fragrant!)	early April
Trailing arbutus	late April
Juneberry	early May

Wild cherries—pin, choke, black	mid-May
Wild lily of the valley (Canada mayflower)	mid-May
Sweet fern (the leaves, not the flowers in this case)	late May
Three-leaved false Solomon's seal	late May
Lilac (I know they're not wild, but how can they not be included?)	late May
Apple blossoms (see above)	late May
Dogwoods—gray, red-osier, alternative-leaved, round-leaved	mid-June
Bush honeysuckle	mid-June
Wild rose	mid-June
Spreading dogbane	late June
White water lily	mid-July
Basswood	mid-July
White and yellow sweet clover	late July
Common milkweed	late July
Wild bergamot	late July

I'm sure we missed a few, so feel free to make up a list that fits your area. Most importantly, take the time to smell the wild roses.

Pine Pollen

If the water along your shoreline is yellow, look up to the pines above you and point the finger of blame. Pines produce both male and female cones, and the tiny male cones manufacture prodigious amounts of pollen in mid-June that blows off in sheets in a good wind. The pollen then forms on the water surface and eventually sinks to the bottom.

In the meantime, the scales on the female cones are slightly separated, and a small amount of fluid, secreted by the pine, collects in the crevices between the scales. If a grain of pollen sifts down between the scales and onto the fluid, the cone will absorb the fluid, and the pollen will come to rest on one of the two ovules found at the bottom of each cone-scale. The cone soon closes, grows eventually to full size, and in two years will ripen and drop its winged seeds (except for the jack pine, whose cones must await a fire or extreme heat before they open).

Plague of Forest Tent Caterpillars—2000

I'm looking for synonyms for "outbreak." How about infestation, blight, epidemic, eruption, invasion, siege, plague? Those all work, and they all fit the 2000 outbreak of forest tent caterpillars that were happily munching any local broadleaf tree or shrub they could find. I led a June hike that year at the North Lakeland Discovery Center in Manitowish Waters, and the 20 hikers and I observed the active defoliation of red oak, red maple, quaking aspen, beaked hazelnut, and blueberry by these caterpillars. Many trees were already entirely defoliated, looking like they might on a late October afternoon in preparation for winter.

However, not all plagues really deserve the term, and that is true of the forest tent caterpillars. They're a short-term, cyclical phenomenon, usually lasting for three to five years, and typically reappearing again in explosive numbers 15 years or more later.

They're a native species, and they have attracted attention since colonial times. That's good news, because if they've been here for at least 250 years, the natural system has developed means by which to check their numbers. Various predatory beetles, ants, spiders, birds, and small animals feed on the caterpillars and their pupae. Several species of flies and wasps parasitize the eggs and larvae, and a variety of viral and fungal diseases destroy large numbers of caterpillars.

Still, lots of trees were entirely defoliated despite the efforts of all the caterpillar killers. The good news was that most trees simply grew new leaves later in June, though the leaves were fewer in number and less robust. Those trees that were already under significant stress from some other source (disease, other insects, drought, and so forth) suffered the worst effects, and some died.

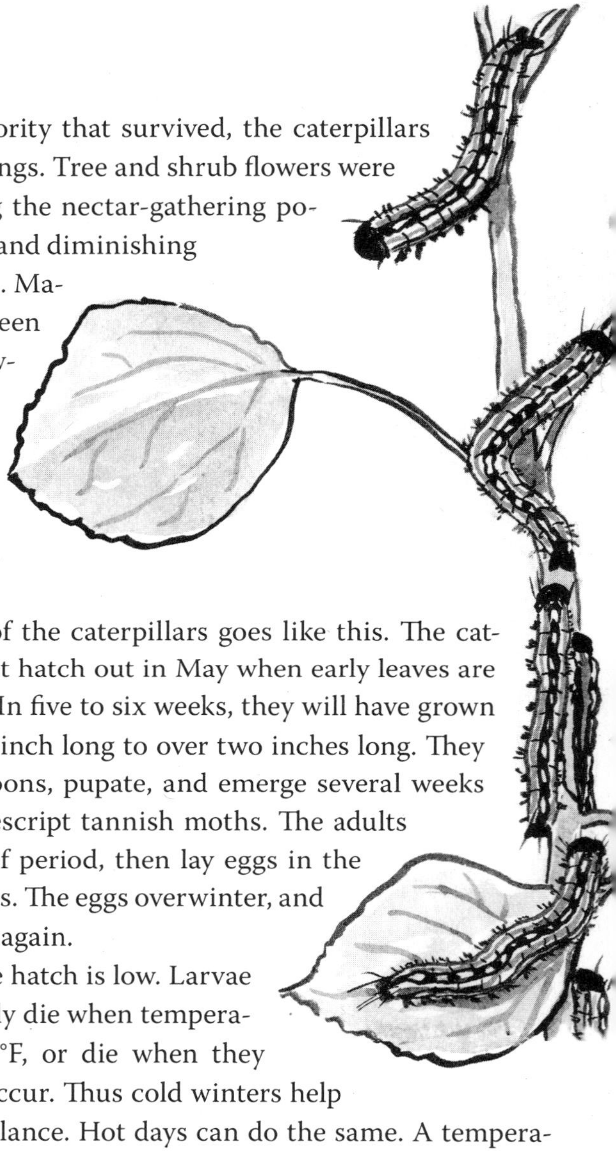

For the vast majority that survived, the caterpillars altered the way of things. Tree and shrub flowers were often eaten, reducing the nectar-gathering potential of honeybees, and diminishing fruit/seed production. Maple sap may have been reduced the following spring because of stress on maple trees. Diameter growth may have been reduced by as much as 90 percent.

The life history of the caterpillars goes like this. The caterpillars typically first hatch out in May when early leaves are beginning to unfold. In five to six weeks, they will have grown from an eighth of an inch long to over two inches long. They then spin silken cocoons, pupate, and emerge several weeks later as adult, non-descript tannish moths. The adults are active only a brief period, then lay eggs in the upper-crown branches. The eggs overwinter, and then we start all over again.

In most years, the hatch is low. Larvae in the eggs will usually die when temperatures fall below –42°F, or die when they hatch if hard frosts occur. Thus cold winters help keep these guys in balance. Hot days can do the same. A temperature of 100°F in the shade can kill the moths during their emergence or contribute to low viability of eggs when they're laid.

Most extension agents recommended no control measures in 2000 since the caterpillars were typically too high up in the tree for spraying to be effective, and there were just too darn many of the caterpillars anyway. It was too late to spray in June, because to be effective, you need to spray the caterpillars shortly after their emergence.

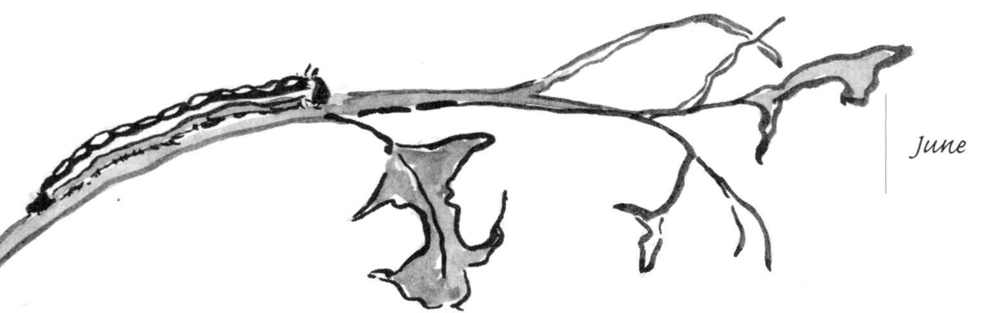

Plague Part Two—2001

In May of 2001, the forest tent caterpillars were again defoliating significant numbers of trees throughout our area, particularly aspens. Many people were in a panic regarding the caterpillars. They wanted to do something, anything to resolve the problem. The first thought of many was to purchase an insecticide, any insecticide, to try to kill the little beasts. However, the cure had the potential to be worse than the illness. No insecticide was specifically targeted for forest tent caterpillars. Some were specifically targeted for caterpillars in general, but most insecticides simply killed most insects. Since 90 percent or more of our insects are beneficial, and because insects are a key food source for higher-level predators in the food chain (from trout to warblers), the indiscriminate killing of insects could do far more harm than good.

I understood the desire people had to protect trees. Many trees on our property were affected, too. What was difficult for all of us to understand was the need to protect the diverse community of other species that utilize the trees. We needed to look at the forest community as a whole rather than the individual trees.

We were told, and I was repeating, that the typical cycle of the forest tent caterpillar lasts three to five years. Most of us were in year three. We were told that a parasitic fly would soon enter upon the stage, parasitizing the pupae of the caterpillars and killing them. Then we would all be complaining of having so many of these non-biting flies hanging around!

All of that came true.

Some trees died. But the trees that died likely became the home-sites for some of the 30 species of cavity-nesting birds we have in northern Wisconsin, like chickadees and red-breasted nuthatches. In death, trees often provide more food and shelter for birds than they did during their lifetimes. That was a difficult lesson for all of us to learn firsthand.

Plague of Caterpillars Stopped by Crisco!

Joanne Reynolds from Hazelhurst observed that the forest tent caterpillars were always crawling up her trees, so she endeavored to put a band around her trees that would stop their upward progress. She tried everything in the house and discovered that a 6-inch-wide band of solid Crisco stopped the little fiends cold in their tracks. They would congregate by the hundreds below the band, and Joanne would then spray them, kill them, and haul them away with a coal scoop. I'm worried about what this means relative to cooking with Crisco, but the good news is that Crisco is a stop sign for forest tent caterpillars.

Joanne said that all the extra sunlight in her yard created from the trees that were defoliated before she discovered the Crisco trick were a boon to her flower gardens and other understory plants. Joanne is a smart lady—she knows enough to look at the bright side, and she understands that in nature something usually benefits at something else's expense. She also noted the presence of a very large beetle that she immediately crushed out of fear, but later read about and found was named "Caterpillar Hunter." Its function was to prey on the caterpillars of gypsy moths and tent caterpillars. She is now encouraging the beetles rather than crushing them.

Friendly Flies

Mary and I hiked and biked quite a bit in early June of 2002, and we found that just about any time we stopped and stood awhile, we became the resting posts for a large contingent of "friendly flies." If you have never met these native flies up close and personal, they're a bit larger than the average housefly, with large red eyes, and a checkerboard black and gray pattern on their back. However, you'll likely notice their namesake behavior long before you'll identify their physical attributes—they are friendly to a fault. Brush them off and they'll come right back. They just won't take "no" for an answer, no matter how many times you try to persuade them. Fortunately, they don't bite. If they did, they could raise some serious Cain.

The good news in 2002, of course, was that their population was way up in response to the forest tent caterpillar outbreak. Historically, 80 percent or more of the control of a forest tent caterpillar outbreak has been attributed to the presence of friendly flies. The female fly lays her living offspring directly on the cocoons of the forest tent caterpillars in late June and early July. The fly maggots bore a hole in the pupae that are inside the cocoon and feed on them, ultimately killing them.

The friendly flies began to decrease in number in mid-July, shortly after what was left of the forest tent caterpillars emerged as moths from their cocoons. The flies soon dropped to the ground, where they spent the winter, and didn't emerge until early the following summer.

Since the population of friendly flies corresponds to the peak of the caterpillar population, the flies can become exceptionally abundant in the final year and the following year of the caterpillar collapse. So, in 2002, we were faced with a year of those chummy fellows to tolerate, but the trade-off was certainly worth it. By 2003, we were hard-pressed to find any forest tent caterpillars in our local area.

The Mosquito Crop

First the good news—virtually no friendly flies or forest tent caterpillars were present in the summer of 2003. The three to five year cycle was completed in most areas, and we knew we wouldn't see those lovely creatures again for a long time to come.

The bad news was that we had an exceptional bounty of mosquitoes. Though much of June had been dry, water remained high in most lakes and rivers, as well as in vernal ponds and swamp woods that are often dried up by June. These made perfect breeding grounds for mosquitoes. I hate to repeat this figure, but it's instructive as well as depressing: one acre of good breeding habitat may produce 1 to 9 million mosquitoes.

Given that the land surface of Vilas County is around 18 percent wetlands, and another 15 percent is lakes and rivers, that's a lot of acres for the production of mosquitoes. We had to make peace with them as best we could. I tried to remind folks that mosquitoes are attracted to heat, carbon dioxide, movement, and lactic acid (a by-product of exercise), so the calmest person tended to be the person least bitten.

Thankfully the males feed on nectar and not on us—life would have been really difficult if both genders saw us as a meal.

Raptor Education Group/ Northwoods Wildlife Center

In 2001, I was part of a group of teachers who visited with Marge Gibson, heart, soul, and main bird rehabilitator for the non-profit Raptor Education Group in Antigo. Wisconsin had been subjected to a series of violent storms during mid-June, and Marge had received seven immature eagles that had been blown out of nests in the course of a few days. She had her hands full to say the least. Marge showed us her indoor flight "cage," a three-story high, several-hundred-foot-long structure that gives raptors like eagles the space to learn to fly or regain flight again after an injury.

We're very fortunate in north-central Wisconsin to have the Raptor Education Group, along with the Northwoods Wildlife Center in Minocqua, performing the dual tasks of rehabilitating wild animals and educating the public to be aware of and understand the natural history and needs of wildlife. Your involvement with and support of both organizations is very important. Call the Raptor

Education Group at (715) 623-4015—www.raptoreducationgroup.org or the Northwoods Wildlife Center at (715) 356-7400—www.northwoodswildlifecenter.com

Shrub-Nesting Birds

Why should we maintain shrub habitat on public and private lands? Here are 18 reasons:

1. Alder flycatcher
2. American goldfinch
3. Bell's vireo
4. Black-throated blue warbler
5. Brown thrasher
6. Chestnut-sided warbler
7. Clay-colored sparrow
8. Common yellowthroat
9. Gray catbird
10. Hooded warbler
11. Indigo bunting
12. Loggerhead shrike
13. Northern cardinal
14. Red-eyed vireo
15. Swainson's thrush
16. Swamp sparrow
17. Willow flycatcher
18. Yellow warbler

Squirrel Mystery

Audrae Kulas on Little Gibson Lake told me of a black squirrel that digs up stones, licks all sides of them while holding them in its paws, then runs off into the woods with them, always in the same direction—a behavior she has witnessed numerous times. My suspicion is that the rocks provide some needed minerals for the squirrel, but why it carries the rocks away, and where it puts them remains a mystery to me.

Summer Solstice

Summer officially begins around June 21. The sun's rays will fall farthest north of the equator, and our day will be the longest and our night the shortest of the year in the Northern Hemisphere. The sun will be traveling its arc at 35° north of the equator, and setting at 8:53, resulting in daylight that lasts past 10:00 p.m.

As impossibly early in the season as it may seem, this day marks the reversal of the sun's slant northward. The days now very gradually become shorter even as the temperatures continue to warm into July. The sun temporarily appears to stall before it begins its plunge back southward. The latest sunsets of the year occur between June 20 and July 1, coming at 8:53 p.m.

After the solstice day, however, sunrises will begin to occur one minute later than the previous day for the first time since December 27.

Summer solstice nights are the ones I remember best as a child, when it seemed like you could play forever before it got dark. I also remember distinctly my anger at my parents for calling me in to go to bed before it was even dark! How could they! Summer solstice is the time when kids get the least amount of sleep—there's just too much light for them to stay in bed very long. We adults should follow their lead.

Two Wonderful Scents

In June, wild roses and spreading dogbane come into fragrant bloom in open areas throughout the Northwoods. Wild roses have been developed into horticultural varieties since earliest recorded times. Remarkably, the word "rose" remains standard in most languages. In English, French, German, Danish, and Norwegian, a rose is a rose. In Italian, Spanish, Portuguese, Latin, and Russian it is rosa. In Dutch it is roos, in Swedish ros, and in Hungarian rozsa. So we needn't worry about whether "a rose by any other name would smell as sweet," because people don't call them by any other name.

Another traditional phrase, "Her life is a bed of roses," or conversely if times are bad, "Her life is no bed of roses," comes from times when people of means actually slept on mattresses filled with roses. Rose flowers have been used as a garnish, while the leaves were sprinkled on meats, and the juice used as a flavoring. Rose tinctures, rose waters, rose sauces, you name it, all have taken their magic from the wondrously fragrant petals of roses.

The fruits, known as rose hips, were eaten raw by American Indians, though they're mighty seedy and dry. They're high in vitamin C, and are commonly made into jellies and used in teas. We're not the only ones who like them. Grouse, bears, coyotes, deer, rabbits, and thrushes are among the many species of animals that eat the fruits, buds, stems, and foliage.

A number of species of wild roses grace our area, but I tend to see the swamp rose most often. It grows abundantly along the shorelines of many of our rivers and in swamps.

Spreading dogbane is less showy, but it packs just as much sweet fragrance as the wild rose in its tiny, bell-like pink flowers. It's found mostly in open upland areas. Identification is easy because of its opposite leaves and the milky latex it exudes when a stem is broken.

bog laurel

Flags, Bladders, and Pitchers

In June, blue flag iris often flowers in profusion in wetlands and roadside ditches, while common bladderwort also comes into flower in wetlands and shallow lake margins. The common bladderwort's yellow flowers are borne above the water, while the rootless stems simply float horizontally under the water. The bladders on the underwater stems capture minute water animals and digest them. A hair-trigger mechanism inflates the bladder, sucking in water and the organism if something touches one of its hairs. It's a remarkable carnivorous plant, worthy of your further investigation

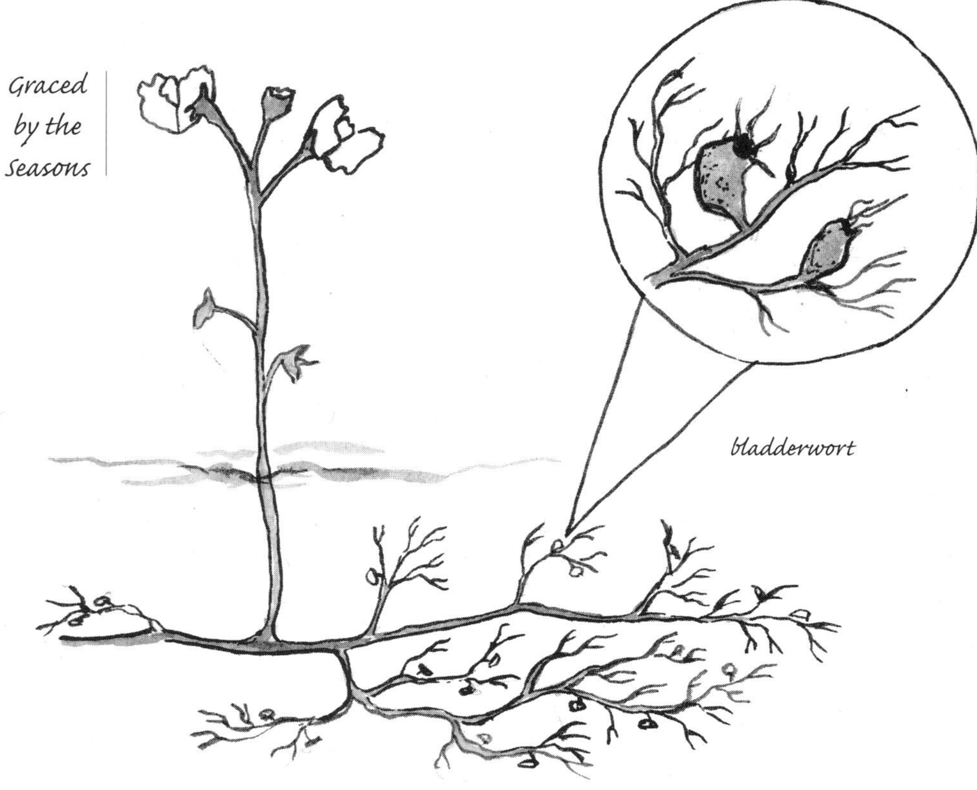

using a hand lens or a compound microscope.

Pitcher plants are also in flower in the bogs in June. The tall burgundy flowers stand a foot above the pitcher-shaped leaves—it wouldn't do for the carnivorous leaves to capture the insects that pollinate the flower. Though pitcher plants capture insects, several species of insects live inside the water-filled pitchers, including the pitcher plant midge and the pitcher plant mosquito.

Whip-Poor-Wills

I'm always amazed at the whip-poor-wills' non-stop repetitive rendition of their name. One wonders when they find time to breathe!

Numerous people have mentioned to me that they used to hear whip-poor-wills but no longer do. Whip-poor-wills are a bit particular in their habitat needs. They don't tolerate populated areas, and are seldom present in coniferous forests. They favor oak woodlands for nesting, though their nest is nothing more than a level spot on the ground. Where oaks aren't present, whip-poor-wills are unlikely to nest. They winter in mature tropical forests south through Central America, and are considered at risk due to the continued destruction of tropical forests.

One ornithologist renders the whip-poor-will's call as *purple-rib, purple-rib, purple-rib,* demonstrating the phonetic flexibility of the English language in interpreting bird songs.

Whip-poor-wills commonly call 50 to 100 times in a row, at a pace of once per second. It's enough to drive a pacifist to the gun shop when the song occurs just outside your window before dawn. Nonetheless, the woods would be greatly impoverished without the whip-poor-will's voice.

Stealing Kisses

A discussion of witches'-brooms sounds like a lead-in to a Halloween story. Likewise, a discussion of mistletoe implies the start of a Christmas story. But this is June, and I have no desire to bring the thoughts of winter holidays upon us any sooner than necessary. The witches'-brooms and mistletoe I wish to discuss are botanical. Most of you have seen witches'-brooms, which appear on a tree as a large clumped growth of stunted twigs and needles so closely packed together that they suggest the straw of a broom. Sometimes, they look like large nests, but they can range in size from small spindly masses to huge clusters larger than an eagle's nest.

The growth is often caused on conifers by dwarf mistletoes, a group of 40 or so species across North and Central America. The stems of the mistletoe parasitize trees, penetrating deep into the host tree's trunk to steal nutrients and water. The tree responds to this "infection" by profusely sprouting new branches and leaves, eventually creating the dense growths that we have figuratively called witches'-brooms.

While the brooms are indeed parasitic and may kill their hosts over time, they also provide considerable benefits. Animals utilize the brooms because they provide nearly impenetrable protection from predators and weather. Red squirrels and flying squirrels frequently nest within the brooms, and even pine martens are known to nest in the brooms. Ten perching birds and eight raptors, including goshawks and long-eared owls, may also nest within these structures. At least a dozen species of birds, including grouse, feed on the shoots and fruits of the mistletoe, while the thicket hairstreak butterfly's larvae feed solely on mistletoe. Porcupines also feed heavily on the nutritious shoots, and sometimes utilize the brooms for shelter.

So, while mistletoe steals for a part of its living, it also is utilized by a host of organisms, offsetting the effects of its amorality. Given that mistletoes "steal" from a tree in order to live, stealing a kiss from someone under the mistletoe at Christmas only makes sense.

Yard Lights

Back in 2000, 2001, and 2002, when we were inundated with forest tent caterpillars, I wrote, "The adult moths of forest tent caterpillars are attracted to lights. Do yourself a favor, and your neighbors a favor, by turning off your yard lights. By doing so, you will very likely reduce the number of egg masses that will be laid by the moths on nearby trees. If you need evidence of their attraction to light, take a drive into Minocqua in early July to one of the gas stations that is lit up like a celestial body, and note the squadrons of moths circling the lights."

But yard lights cause other problems. I understand that people want yard lights primarily for safety reasons, but undirected light is a pollutant. Lighting up your neighbor's property with your lights every night is akin to blasting music or sending smoke into your neighbor's home all night long. I hear more complaints about yard lights than just about anything else during the summer (though nothing compares on the complaint meter to PWCs).

The solution is very simple—either turn out the lights, utilize motion-detection lights, or shade the lights to direct their beam only onto your site. For suggestions on how to do this, and other reasons to control indiscriminate lighting, see the following Websites:

Fatal Light Awareness Program: http://www.flap.org/links.htm

UK Department of the Environment: http://www.detr.gov.uk/planning/litc/

http://www.badlighting.com/

"The Paranoiacs Among Birds"

On June 30, 2003, Mary and I paddled in the cattail and wild rice marsh of the Little Turtle Flowage northwest of Mercer. We were on the marsh by 6:30 a.m., a little late for the best bird chorusing, but early enough to revel in many of the bird songs and behaviors that occur as the rising sun warms a marshland. We were greeted near the landing by a pair of trumpeter swans with three tiny cygnets. We put in quickly and numerous wood ducks lifted from the young wild rice stems and flew to the far side of the marsh. Tree swallows worked the air above us, eating the myriad insects, but never consuming enough mosquitoes.

We worked our way into the tall islands of cattails and soon heard marsh wrens singing from nearly every large clump. Their reedy rattle varied among individuals, as is typical among marsh wrens. In fact, individual western marsh wrens may sing more than 100 song types, so variations on the basic marsh wren theme—a trilling *tek-tek-k-jijijijijijiji-jrr* sort of sound—are the norm.

Marsh wrens sing both day and night, probably in order to deter other male marsh wrens that may invade their territory and try to destroy their eggs. One study found that nearly 10 percent of all marsh wren nests fail due to attacks by other marsh wrens, and many other nests suffer partial losses of eggs or chicks. One writer refers to the marsh wren as "a Nazi among its own kind" and as "the paranoiacs among birds," in reference to their aggressive raiding of other nests and their perception that anything near them is a threat. Another study found that marsh wren eggs have much thicker and stronger shells than most songbird eggs, likely an evolved defense intended to protect them from one another.

Mary and I paddled right up to several nests, each woven globe built amid cattail stems about 3 feet off the water. Interestingly, the entrance to marsh wren nests is located in the side, sort of like a door, which leads to a short tunnel that projects into the nest. The male builds numerous nests—up to 27 according to one source—but usually only five, and all grouped in a central area called a "courting center," where the male does most of his singing. The female ultimately chooses which nest she would like to use, then they add additional layers and lining to make it their own.

Marsh wrens exhibit site fidelity from year to year, returning to the same home marsh to nest. Their fidelity is to the site more than their former mate, however, and even if the female chooses the same mate, biologists believe it's more due to territory attraction than individual attraction, a not-uncommon behavior in many birds.

We left the marsh wrens eventually and had the pleasure of black terns foraging in the air around us for a short spell. We surprised several families of ducks, and watched both a female wood duck and hooded merganser try to lure us away from their chicks with distraction displays that made them appear wounded and unable to fly. We even had brief, furtive views of two sora rails walking amidst the cattails, though they are masters at being secretive. An adult eagle sat next to its nest with a full-grown chick hulking in the nest as it oversaw the morning's activities. I'm sure its presence added an element of fear for the many species of waterfowl present.

The marsh choir will soon come to an end and we'll have to wait until next May for its resumption. If you haven't sat in a marsh just after dawn yet this year, the time to go is now.

Winning One Battle on Exotic Lake Species

[Reprinted from an article I wrote for the University of Wisconsin Center for Limnology in June, 2004.]

From its brilliant surface, no one would imagine that Sparkling Lake in Vilas County has been a lake under siege. But scratch the surface, and two exotic species that have dramatically altered the lake's ecosystem come into view. The invaders—rusty crayfish and rainbow smelt—have pushed the once plentiful yellow perch and cisco to near extinction, prevented walleye from reproducing, and decimated beds of aquatic plants.

Researchers from the University of Wisconsin Trout Lake Station and the Wisconsin DNR have initiated a study to understand the dynamics of lakes like Sparkling, how people influence them, and how exotic invasions can be reversed. Some of the answers, believes University of Wisconsin-Madison graduate student Brian Roth, may be in their latest round of research.

"Rusty crayfish appeared in northern Wisconsin lakes in the late 1950s, and were first seen in Sparkling Lake around 1975," Roth observed. "Rusties" have continued to invade other lakes and streams since 1983 when they were finally banned as bait from all Wisconsin waters, but most of the damage had been done by then."

Studies over the past two decades found that rusty crayfish are bigger, more aggressive, and hatch out earlier than northern Wisconsin's two native crayfish, the benign fantail and blue crayfish. Thus, rusties often become dominant when they are introduced, and with a rapacious appetite for aquatic plants, soon devastate plant beds that historically served as food, cover, and hatching and spawning sites for aquatic insects, invertebrates, and small fish. "In high densities, rusty crayfish can become the equivalent of clear-cutting loggers," noted Roth.

To make matters worse, rusties also eat fish eggs and invertebrates like snails along the lake bottom.

In Sparkling Lake, rusties mowed down the plant beds to the point where small fish like bluegills and pumpkinseed that rely on plants for cover and spawning were almost entirely removed. Their loss caused top predators like bass, walleye, and muskellunge, which strongly prefer a diet of small fish to crayfish, to decline. The end result was radically altered fish populations in Sparkling.

To further complicate matters, rainbow smelt were introduced into Sparkling Lake around 1981, likely from anglers washing their nets out in the lake on their way home from fishing the annual spring spawning run in Lake Superior. "Smelt eggs stick to everything," said

Roth, "and nets full of spawning fish are equally full of eggs."

Smelt dramatically affected yellow perch and walleye in Sparkling, but just how remains a mystery. Roth said there are two hypotheses: "One, smelt hatch before walleye and perch do, and can monopolize zooplankton resources such that juvenile walleye and perch die out. Two, smelt young are simply more effective at preying on zooplankton and are able to out-forage young perch and walleye, causing them to die out."

The bottom line is that both walleyes and perch were nearly extinct in Sparkling prior to the study. "If the DNR or tribes didn't stock walleye on the lakes where smelt have been introduced, anglers wouldn't be able to catch walleyes after ten years, because none would be there," Roth noted.

The smelt's impact on the native cisco in Sparkling was equally great. Smelt directly prey upon cisco, and by 1990, cisco were also nearly extinct in Sparkling.

Surprisingly, smelt have failed to appear on the radar screen of most Northwoods residents who worry more about Eurasian milfoil and other exotics. But anglers realize, said Roth, "If you want a walleye population, keep the smelt out. On nearly all the lakes where we have good records, walleyes have declined after smelt have gotten in, as have yellow perch."

What, then, to do? The key is that adult walleyes eat smelt, while adult bluegills and smallmouth and rock bass eat the smaller, young crayfish. Roth believes that Sparkling Lake can reach a stable state where the predators can control the smelt and crayfish if three things occur:

1. The adult smelt and crayfish populations can be dramatically reduced.
2. The aquatic plant beds can be restored.
3. The predator fish populations—the walleye and bluegills in particular—can be restored.

Enter Steve Gilbert, DNR fisheries biologist for Vilas County. For many years, Gilbert has been doing fall fish surveys of Sparkling

Lake by electroshocking the entire shoreline and islands. "We had excellent young-of-the-year walleye recruitment in the 1970s and early 1980s, but by the 1990s, we found virtually no walleye young except during years where we stocked. In 2003, we found only one individual young-of-the-year."

Gilbert estimates that Sparkling's total smelt population reached 1.2 million in the 1990s, and the walleye young didn't stand a chance. The DNR stocked walleye fingerlings in 1997, 1998, 2001, and 2002, but the survival rate was absolutely dismal—in fact, zero survived in 2002. So, Gilbert began stocking larger walleyes that averaged about 8 inches long, and found that nearly two-thirds survived. He stocked 2,500 of these in 2002, and 3,000 in 2003. Some of the 2002 fish are already sexually mature, and they're all eating juvenile smelt.

But word gets around about bountiful walleyes, so another piece to solving Sparkling's fish puzzle had to be put into place. Gilbert and Roth realized anglers could alter the whole experiment by harvesting the stocked walleye and the repopulating bluegills, so the DNR has placed stringent regulations on the number and size of fish that can be taken, and are encouraging catch-and-release as much as possible for now. "A key issue is that people take out the big walleyes as soon as they reach 15 inches, and it's the big walleyes you have to keep in the system. They're the ones that will eat the most smelt," said Roth.

Roth and Gilbert also realized that without reducing the smelt population, the DNR would have to stock walleye in perpetuity, because none of their young would survive.

Enter Katie Hein, a graduate student at UW-Madison, and undergraduate Stacy Lishcka. Their job has been to capture adult rusty crayfish and smelt in order to "flip" the system into something as close to a crayfish-and-smelt-free environment as possible. The results have been impressive.

In one week in the spring of 2002, they caught 170,000 smelt, a whopping 1.5 metric tons. In 2003, the catch was only 45,000, because most of the smelt spawned before the ice went out. In 2004,

Hein and Lishcka outsmarted the early spawners by chopping through the ice to place their fyke nets, and they hauled in nearly 90,000 smelt. Summer estimates of the total smelt population in the lake have dropped from the original estimate of 1.2 million, to 750,000 in 2001, and to 370,000 in 2003. Roth and company believe with continued netting and the successful stocking of walleye that the smelt are on their way out, but it may take another 10 years.

Summer crayfish trapping yielded 11,000 in 2001, 38,550 in 2002, 22,585 in 2003, and only 9,098 in 2004. Catch rates are clearly declining, as are the size and age of the catch. Hein and Lishcka are gathering many more females and juveniles than in earlier catches, a clear sign that they're making a major dent in the population.

General observations of the aquatic plant beds all indicate that they are regenerating, and if predators can become abundant enough, it's expected that their consumption of young crayfish will keep the rusties under control.

The final problem to face is that research monies run out next year, and Sparkling Lake is only one of a number of lakes with crayfish and smelt invasions. The researchers fervently hope that lake associations or other organizations will take what the study has shown and implement similar harvesting and stocking techniques to bring their lakes back into a natural balance.

Vilas County, with its nearly 1,300 high-quality lakes covering almost 15 percent of its land surface, would seem to be the last place in Wisconsin to have serious fishery issues. But exotic species are equal opportunity invaders.

Roth summed it up: "It's all a matter of perspective. If all people want is some really big walleye for about five years, they can let the smelt go. If people don't care about aquatic plants and bluegills, they can let the rusty crayfish go. But I don't think that's what people want to do if they care about their kids and grandkids catching fish."

July

Pilgrims often journey to the ends of the earth in search of holy ground, only to find that they have walked on nothing else.

—Scott Russell Sanders

In the early morning fog of one Independence Day, Mary and I paddled the Little Turtle Flowage near Mercer. Fog amplifies distance and height because it erases the familiar. But it also swallows and diminishes sound. So, from our kayaks, the small marsh grew large, the cattails rose like forests in the vapory distance, and the sounds we heard seemed close and unusual. Black terns flitted and dove all around us, calling overhead with their squeaky cries, dipping and darting through the mist. A startled pied-billed grebe lit up suddenly with its loud *cow-cow-cow-cow-cow* call, but stopped short, and just as quickly was si-

lent and invisible. We heard grunts and snorts and almost a purring inside one colony of cattails, and soon a family of otters emerged, one of the adults rising up and down out of the water to spy at us like the periscope of a submarine. Whatever otters deem fit to talk about in the early morning, we were privy to the conversation.

Two swan necks appeared out of the fog, still startling white even within the mist. We knew they were probably escorting five cygnets (we had seen them two days before), but the young never appeared out of the curtain of cattails and cloud.

Several times, a hen merganser suddenly came running across the water in front of us, performing a distraction display to draw us away from her chicks. Little did she realize that we would never have seen her or her chicks in the mist if she hadn't given such a theatrical performance.

Bullfrogs bellowed, mink frogs tapped, green frogs twanged. Marsh wrens gurgled, swamp sparrows trilled, common yellowthroats told us of their witchcraft—*witchety, witchety, witchety,* they slowly sang. A catbird sang its jazzy riff. Snipe winnowed overhead, eventually appearing in the sky as the sun gradually burned the fog off.

The sky cleared and the colors of the aquatic flowers came up like little suns.

And still there was only the sound of the marsh, the sights of the marsh, the life of the marsh.

I read a beautiful definition of freedom: "Freedom isn't doing whatever you want—it's knowing who you are, what you're supposed to be doing on this earth, and then doing it."

The marsh was doing exactly what it was meant to do, and we felt that we were doing exactly what we were meant to do. Give me the freedom, harmony, and independence of a wild marsh any day.

No Wake

Most nesting loon pairs typically have chicks by mid-June. However, nesting pairs whose eggs were preyed upon, or whose eggs failed, will often re-nest. Thus some loons may be sitting on eggs during July. Unfortunately, the period around July 4 is a traditional time for massive numbers of speedboats to take to the water. Please respect the no-wake zones. The zones exist not only to prevent shoreline erosion, but to protect incubating shoreline birds that can easily lose their eggs to one unruly wave.

Dawn on the Manitowish

One early July I awoke at 4:15 a.m. and was on the Manitowish River by 4:45 in hopes of catching the dawn chorus. I expected that the chorus would be diminished compared to a month ago, given that virtually every mated pair should have been on nest for weeks, and many young had hatched. Singing declines so dramatically by July that people often wonder if something catastrophic has happened to the birds.

As expected, the choir was muted, but it wasn't quiet either. Hermit thrushes, red-eyed vireos, pine warblers, and black-throated green warblers sang consistently from the uplands. (What song is more beautiful than the hermit thrush's?) The real action, though, came from the willows and alders that line much of the Manitowish. Here, song sparrows, swamp sparrows, alder flycatchers, yellow warblers, and common yellowthroats all chanted robustly, offering musical companionship as a guide and meditation. Mist flowed over the river, and a doe and fawn came down for an early drink, crossing immediately in front of me.

It took a while to settle in to the river's rhythm. One has to breathe slowly, move gently, and bring the mind into the present moment before the life of the river can fully be heard. A small band of mosquitoes also chose to accompany me, and they too chanted their song in my ears. Accepting their presence and not getting worked up about it is a necessary emotional state as well, though not an easy one to attain.

The sunrise came on in a very subtle pink and passed by quickly—there was no charismatic glory on this morning. A family of kingfishers became very agitated at my approach and four leapt from the same branch, all constantly rattling at me like I was an enemy. By 6:00, the sun had been up for nearly half an hour, and the birds had quieted. The slanting light lit up the red pines and the marsh grasses. Certainly the most beautiful light of the day occurs just as the day arrives and just as it departs.

I came under the bridge just before the takeout on Hwy. 47 and was quite surprised to see that barn swallows nesting under the bridge had built their nests vertically on the sides of the huge wooden support beams. They used the ends of the bolts coming through the wood as their base and anchored their mud structures onto them. In past years, they've simply built horizontal nests on the top of the crossbeams under the bridge, seemingly much easier and more stable structures to build.

The books say barn swallows construct bowl-shaped nests from mud pellets, either as adherent structures plastered on a vertical surface, or as statant structures placed on a horizontal surface. Each nest requires from one to 2,000 beak loads of mud.

The next bridge just 50 yards downriver, the Hwy. 47 bridge, is concrete, and for many years, cliff swallows have built their flask-shaped nests on its vertical concrete surfaces. About four out of five nests appeared to have broken off and fallen into the water, so only six active nests remained, all appearing to house chicks.

We watch both species of swallows every year come to a large mud puddle at the end of our driveway, and fly away again and again with mud. I've worried for years that our sandy soils don't have enough clay in them to make solid houses, and judging by the cliff swallow houses, I'm right. But to note that the barn swallows are choosing to build on vertical surfaces makes me wonder if the mud is okay, or if they get mud from along the river that has more clay in it. One way or another, we will never fill in that hole at the end of our gravel driveway. It's not just the mud for the swallows, but killdeer nest in the gravel, and a number of birds work the gravel to obtain grit for their digestive systems.

I pulled off the river at 6:15, the smell of river and wetlands and the song of birds powerfully within me. Aldo Leopold wrote: "It is a fact, patent both to my dog and myself, that at daybreak I am the sole owner of all the acres I can walk over. It is not only boundaries that disappear, but also the thought of being bounded. Expanses unknown to deed or map are known to every dawn, and solitude, supposed no longer to exist in my county, extends on every hand as far as the dew can reach."

Such was true for Leopold back in the 1940s, and such is true today. The bird chorus may be quieting in July, but how enjoyable it is to witness the rest of the world come awake.

The Freshwater Blob?

While paddling on the Turtle-Flambeau Flowage over the years, Mary and I have pulled out of the water large gelatinous "blobs" attached to woody debris. These creatures are a bit hard to describe. They are colonies of "moss animals," *Pectinatella magnifica* to be exact, and are a member of the animal phylum *Ectoprocta* (common name—bryozoans), a group whose fossil record extends back to the Upper Cambrian, 500 million years ago.

They are very strange looking things, rather incomprehensible within the normal scope of the box we put most animals in. They resemble a stiff, clear-gray Jell-O. A fertile imagination could see the colony as a giant brain. The gelatinous colony is 99 percent water, but firm and slimy to the touch. The surface appears divided into tiny rosettes, each with 12 to 18 "zooids." Each microscopic zooid has whorls of delicate feeding tentacles that sway slowly in the water and capture food. Bryozoans feed on small microorganisms, including diatoms and other unicellular algae. In turn, bryozoans are preyed on by grazing organisms such as fish, and are also subject to competition and overgrowth from sponges and algae.

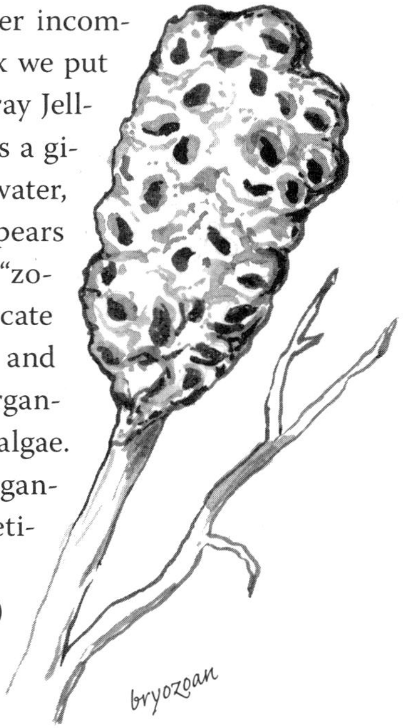

bryozoan

Massive colonies may exceed 2 feet (60 cm) in diameter, although typical sizes are 1 foot or less. The colonies form on submerged logs, twigs, even wooden docks. Bryozoans are all aquatic animals, and most are marine, except for the freshwater forms classified in the Phylactolaemata.

Interestingly, we sometimes find a large mass of freshwater sponge attached to the same underwater branch that holds the largest bryozoan colony. Freshwater sponges are equally difficult to comprehend within our usual definition of "animal."

Researchers at the Trout Lake Limnology Station have studied sponges for many years, but their current study of coarse woody debris in water seems most relevant to our sightings, given that if the fallen trees had been removed from the water, the sponges and bryozoans would probably not exist there. In fact, researchers estimate that the removal of coarse woody debris from the shoreline of one's property, an act that can be done in a weekend's worth of work, would take 150 years to reverse! Whatever you may think of such organisms as sponges and bryozoans, leave that woody debris in the water—it's habitat for a host of common and uncommon organisms.

horsefly

Fourth of July Flies

No Northwoods summer would be complete without the constant circling buzz around one's head of a small army of deerflies and horseflies. Without horseflies, however, many of you would not be up in the Northwoods right now celebrating the Fourth of July. It's said that the Declaration of Independence was signed on July 4, 1776, under duress. The delegates would have preferred to sign the document at a later date after further discussions, but apparently the horseflies were biting so fiercely in Philadelphia at the time that the delegates decided to quickly sign and adjourn in order to get away from them. Without horseflies, we might be celebrating the Eighteenth of August, or some such date, which doesn't quite have the same ring to it. So the next time you have a horsefly in your sights (like when it's biting you right in the middle of your back where you can't possibly reach it unless you're a yoga master), you might hum a brief patriotic tune prior to squashing the little bugger.

deerfly

Moonbow

In June of 2001 Mary and I saw a fogbow, something we had never seen before. Two weeks later in early July, our sighting was eclipsed by several friends sighting a moonbow! Marilyn and Bill Gabert, Bob and Carolyn Kovar, and Tom and Jeanne Joseph were out on the water on the full-moon night of July 4, when near 11:00 p.m. they saw a 180-degree white arc emanating from the horizon. Jeanne described it this way:

"Last night we witnessed the most amazing sight. After the late night fireworks, we were on the water, and we saw what looked like headlights in the sky, but they stayed there and didn't move. After a while we realized that this light went across the entire sky like a rainbow, except it was at night. It had a faint pink/red tinge to it. It was also cloudy and misty at the north end of Rest Lake and across from it was the full moon in a clear sky. It was also misting lightly at the north end. It was so beautiful to watch. I've never heard of a moonbow before but I will never forget this sight."

Well, I'd never heard of a moonbow either, and after being assured by all parties of their relative sobriety, I consulted my trusty *National Audubon Society Field Guide to North American Weather* and learned the following:

"Occasionally, when the moon is bright, its light can be adequately reflected and refracted to produce a colored bow, known as a moonbow, in the nighttime sky. It differs from a rainbow only in that a moonbow's colors are less intense. Moonbows are most frequently sighted around tropical islands (Hawaii and the Caribbean), where nighttime rain showers and partly cloudy skies are more common than at higher latitudes."

It appears that on the night of our July 4 fireworks, the most beautiful fireworks occurred well after the crowds had gone home.

Beavers and Stream Ecology

In mid-July of 2000, Mary, Callie, and I paddled the upper end of the Turtle River from Winchester to Cedar Lake, and the repeating theme was beaver dams. We crossed eight in all. We were fortunate during this paddle to be able to scootch over most of the dams while remaining in our kayaks. Had the water levels been normal, we would have been getting out and pulling the kayaks over the dams, often a tricky proposition.

The upper Turtle flows mostly through lands owned by a paper company and the state, and is generally inaccessible by roads. This makes the upper Turtle difficult for trappers to reach, so the beaver maintain natural population numbers.

Beavers can dominate the ecology of a small river like the Turtle. One Canadian study of the effect of beavers on small- to medium-sized streams found that "where beaver remain largely unexploited, their activities may influence 20 to 40 percent of the total length of 2nd to 5th order streams with the alterations remaining as part of the landscape for centuries."

That's quite a statement! It says that around one-third of the total length of all undisturbed small-to-moderate-sized northern rivers are altered in some manner by beaver dams. The key word in that sentence, however, is "undisturbed." Very few of our rivers are undeveloped, unaltered, or undisturbed, so beavers today are seldom permitted to impact rivers to their full capability.

Beavers built an extraordinary number of dams on the study rivers: Active dam density ranged from 8.6 dams/km to 16 dams/km. The mean was 10.6 dams/km, or about 17 dams per mile.

Beavers remain the object of a love/hate relationship with humans too. Most people enjoy seeing beavers until the beavers' activities begin to alter their personal shoreline. Then a war ensues until the "problem" beavers are trapped out. Given the population changes in the last century, it's remarkable that beaver meadowlands can still be seen today in many areas even after the beaver's removal—a testimony to their landscape influence.

Birds and Insects

Our ordeal from 2001 to 2003 with forest tent caterpillars brought up the topic of which birds eat insects, which kinds they eat, how many, and so forth.

Most birds are opportunists, eating what the table provides, and thus taking advantage of insect outbreaks to gorge themselves. Historical references talk about enormous flocks of California gulls appearing in 1848 to eat the hordes of crickets that were destroying the Mormon fields around Salt Lake City. The Mormons erected a California gull statue in Temple Square in Salt Lake City to honor them.

Grasshoppers swarmed through the Mississippi Valley, destroying farms in the latter part of the nineteenth century. Birds from kinglets to whooping cranes fed on them, including fish-eating birds like great blue herons, flesh-eating birds like hawks and owls, and waterfowl like ducks and geese.

In 1920, clouds of rose beetles invaded the area around Clovis, California, and after eating all the rose flowers, began consuming the foliage in the vineyards, until great flocks of Brewer blackbirds appeared and cleaned the beetles out.

Very interestingly, one reference describes how passenger pigeons ate caterpillars during outbreaks. Maybe their extinction has helped species like the forest tent caterpillar to explode in such high numbers.

These insect outbreaks are rather rare events, however. Most insectivorous birds live ordinary lives as professional insect catchers, experts in their trade. And most eat a wide array of insects. A study of northern cardinals, an omnivore, found that the birds ate 51 species of beetles (including wood borers, fireflies, click beetles, and others), 12 kinds of *Homoptera* (including cicadas, aphids, and leafhoppers), four species of grasshoppers, and a variety of caterpillars, ants, termites, flies, and dragonflies.

The vast majority of birds, even those considered fruit and seed eaters such as grosbeaks, buntings and many sparrows, feed their nestlings the high protein diet of insects. But nearly all birds eat what the habitat provides. One study examined the stomach contents of 2,346 adult grackles (a romantic job if ever there was one), and found their food intake to be 70 percent plants. Another study of grackle nestlings found their intake to be 89 percent animal—mostly insects.

Insect-eating birds can be divided into feeding "guilds," which consist of species that use the same class of resources. There are leaf gleaners, such as warblers, that nab insects from leaves; bark gleaners, like nuthatches and creepers, that hunt the surfaces of bark for insects; wood and bark probers, like woodpeckers, that dig in wood to expose hidden prey; air salliers, such as Eastern kingbirds, various flycatchers, and cedar waxwings, that take off from a perch and snatch insects from the air; and gleaners of aerial plankton, such as swallow, swifts, and nighthawks, that fly continuously and capture insects and other creatures flying or floating in the air.

The problem with the concept of guilds is they over-simplify what most birds actually do. Most birds utilize several methods to capture insects. Yellow-rumped warblers are a good example. They glean leaves, glean bark, feed on the ground, capture flying insects, and in the winter, eat fruit.

Which of all of our nesting birds ate the adult forest tent moths? Darn few, which is part of the story of how this insect population was able to build to such high numbers in such a short time.

Float Like a Butterfly

Every year we look for the buoyant, butterfly-like flight of black terns when we paddle the Little Turtle Flowage. The terns dip and dart sharply, abruptly, hawking insects on the wing or hovering and diving for small fish on the water's surface. They seem to float in the air with the acrobatic skills of butterflies, their continuous sweeping flight over the marshlands appearing effortless.

The terns nest on the LTF because it provides them their favorite habitat—emergent marsh. They use the floating stems of wetland plants, the cattails and bulrush and pickerelweed, to build their nests right on top of the water in a soggy heap that only a marsh dweller could love.

Terns nest in "terneries," large colonies where they typically nest close together and often act in concert to drive away intruders.

One July, Mary and I watched a black tern carry a small fish to a nest site within some vegetation, and obviously begin to feed its young. The excited chattering of the chicks when the adult alighted clearly told the story of a breakfast forthcoming.

I paddled quickly over to see if I could get a glancing look into the nest. I'd never seen a tern chick before, and though it's bad form, I thought I could do it so fast that I wouldn't interfere.

Well, you'd think after so many years of playing naturalist that I'd know better, but sometimes desire clouds both common sense and ethics. I got to the nest and immediately saw a chick swimming frantically from the nest for the deeper cattails nearby. Meanwhile, two adult terns came for me, hovering and darting near my head while screaming their displeasure.

I beat a hasty retreat and got scolded by Mary, too, for such indiscretion. She was right, of course, and for several reasons.

Black terns are a "species of special concern" in Wisconsin, an indication that black tern numbers may be declining and/or that their breeding range is contracting. The special concern designation is one step away from listing the black tern as a threatened species, and in fact, the Wisconsin Bureau of Endangered Resources may soon recommend that black terns be officially placed on the state's threatened species list.

A 2001 study published in *The Passenger Pigeon*, which summarized the numbers and distribution of breeding black terns in five southeastern Wisconsin counties, brought some good news. Black tern numbers were comparable to counts made in a similar survey in 1979. Still, while the population in those five counties appeared stable over the last 20 years, the actual numbers totaled only around 200 adults. Tiny populations of any species on only a few scattered sites inevitably raises legitimate fears regarding the odds of long-term survival. Overall in Wisconsin, black terns have experienced a large population decrease over the past 30 years, and the availability of suitable habitat for breeding is expected to continue to severely deteriorate in the future.

The best data on continent-wide population trends comes from the North American Breeding Bird Survey (BBS), which indicates that black terns declined significantly survey-wide at an average rate of –3.1 percent annually (–61.1 percent overall) between 1966 and 1996.

Habitat loss is considered the major factor in population declines, but terns have plenty of natural enemies looking to raid their nests, too. Raccoons, gulls, and weasels, among others, can cause havoc in a colony.

The young chicks leave the nest a few days after hatching, and are closely guarded by the parents until they fledge about three weeks later. The chicks have no choice but to grow fast, because black terns usually leave for South America by mid- to late August, and that's precious little time to become a long-distance flier.

When feeding, black terns are grabbers, not spearers. They either pluck insects from the surface or plummet headfirst into the water to snatch small fish.

The quickest way to distinguish terns from gulls is by comparing them in flight. Gulls usually fly with their bill directed straight forward, while terns typically point their bill and head downward, seemingly always scanning for food. Terns' wings are typically more slender, pointed, and graceful than gulls. Their sharp-pointed bills are also unlike the hooked bills of gulls, and their notched tails contrast with the wider tails of gulls.

Crazy for Blueberries

Early July is usually blueberry-picking time, and like most berry-producing species in the Northwoods, blueberries are found in open woods and clearings where the sunlight can reach the leaves.

Some 30 species of blueberries live in eastern North America, many dwelling in wetlands and bogs. A smaller number of species grow in drier soils along forest edges and within open woods and fields, the most common of which are velvetleaf blueberry (*Vaccinium myrtilloides*), low-bush blueberry (*V. angustifolium*), and high-bush blueberry (*V. corymbosum*).

I've never been big on differentiating species of plants that bear great-tasting fruits. Who wants to take the time to key them out when there are berries to be picked? After all, there's a time for science and a time for gluttony, and the wise, well-fed person knows the difference.

All blueberries have warty twigs and bear small, whitish, bell-shaped flowers that produce blue-purple-black sweet fruits, and that's probably all any of us really needs to know. You can also pick huckleberries (*Gaylussacia baccata*), which can be differentiated from blueberries by the fact that they don't have warty twigs and only have 10 seeds (blueberries have over a hundred tiny seeds). And you can pick bilberries (various species of *Vaccinium*), which also look and taste an awful lot like blueberries.

Picking blueberries can often be a race with a host of wild birds and mammals that prize them just as much as we do. Some 53 other species of birds and mammals compete with us for the rights to any given blueberry patch. Spruce grouse and rough grouse are particularly gluttonous in their consumption, but a variety of other birds like scarlet tanager, bluebird, catbird, oriole, robin, brown thrasher, and towhee seek them out, too. For that matter, our dogs browse them, though blackberries seem to be their favorite.

Little mammals like white-footed mice, chipmunks, and skunks eat the berries, but the big daddy forager of them all is the black bear, whose delicate foraging technique includes tearing off mouthfuls of twigs along with the berries.

The winter twigs are relished by rabbits and deer, which we can attest to in our garden—the rabbits browsed our cultivated blueberries right down to the ground late one fall.

Blueberries were highly important to Native Americans. They dried the berries and then pounded them together with strips of dried venison to make pemmican, a food renowned for its durability (but not for its taste). In his 1932 book *Ethnobotany of the Ojibwe*, Huron Smith wrote, "Blueberries are a favorite food with the Menomini. They gather them in large quantities and dry them in the sun as raisins or currants are dried for winter use. They are dried on a scaffold thatched with rushes. Dried blueberries and dried sweet corn are eaten together, sweetened with maple sugar, as a special dish."

Smith wrote another book in 1933, *Ethnobotany of the Potawatomi*, and added that the Potawatomi made "a practice of lining their berry pails with the leaves of sweet fern which they claim keeps the berries from spoiling." Current day blueberry pickers might benefit from this advice.

Medical uses for blueberries listed in *Plants Used by the Great Lakes Ojibwa* included an infusion of leaves as a blood purifier. Francis Densmore wrote in 1926 that the Ojibwe placed dried flowers on hot stones as an inhalant to treat "craziness." She added, "This was said to be one of the remedies given by Winabojo," the great Chippewa deity and prankster figure.

I don't know whether blueberries cure craziness, but I know that a person would be crazy not to be out picking blueberries in July.

One-Hundred-Year Storms

Storm winds wreaked havoc on much of the Northwoods in 1999. An early morning storm on July 22, 1999, knocked down a host of trees in the Manitowish Waters area, including a big red pine on Bob and Caroline Kovars' property on Wild Rice Lake. The tree had special significance because it had been the site of a large eagle's nest since the 1950s, and two eaglets were in the nest at the time.

The Kovars lost just two trees to the storm. The eagle tree snapped off halfway up, and when Bob cut it up the next day, he found the wood to be more punk than fiber. Add the enormous weight of an eagle's nest to a tree with heart rot, and the recipe usually yields a blowdown or a snapped tree.

The two eaglets were up and flying soon afterward, and Bob saw the adults feeding them, so apparently they all survived the event, though concern remained about where the adults would nest in the future. Eagles seldom take to platforms, so all the Kovars, and the many other people who had watched the nest for decades, could do was hope the eagles still liked the neighborhood and would rebuild in a nearby pine. And that's exactly what they did in 2000.

A far larger "storm of the century" occurred on July 4, 1999, in the Boundary Waters Canoe Area Wilderness in northeastern Minnesota. Winds blew in excess of 90 miles an hour, cutting a swath 10 to 12 miles wide and 35 miles long from Basswood Lake to the Gunflint Trail. An estimated 380,000 acres of the 1.1 million acre wilderness were affected, creating a forest mosaic ranging from complete and partial blowdowns to areas that were improbably skipped altogether.

Over 200,000 people annually visit the more than 1,000 lakes and streams that comprise the BWCA and the 1,500 miles of canoe routes that link them all together. In fact, this is the nation's most used wilderness area. After the storm, many portage trails were impassable.

A search and rescue operation in the BWCA was completed on July 19. Twenty reported injuries occurred when trees were dropped on campsites and nearly four inches of rain inundated wilderness campers.

Dan Markofski from Manitowish Waters and Kevin Tadych from Minocqua, both experienced, seasoned outdoorsmen, were caught in the storm in Quetico Wilderness Provincial Park in Canada, just across the border from Minnesota. They had spent a week camping and canoeing and were just one lake crossing and a short portage away from their car when the storm hit them. They were midway across their last large lake when they suddenly saw a wall of waves, wind, and rain sweeping toward them. The rain was horizontal, and the waves instantly grew to heights of 3 to 4 feet. The canoeists fought to stay upright for a minute, but quickly capsized. They hung on to the canoe, swallowing water with each wave, unsure if they were going to make it. After 10 minutes in the water, they knew if they kept hold of the canoe, they could ride it out.

Forty minutes later they washed up on an island, canoe paddles still in hand, but all their gear was swept away. They righted the canoe, dumped the water out, and headed for the portage. Remarkably, they found all their gear in the water and on shore. However, the portage, only 60 rods long, was completely blocked by downed trees. They worked for an hour and a half along with three other groups with bow saws to cut their way through, and eventually made it to the parking lot. Many of the cars in the lot were crushed under trees, but theirs was untouched.

Several evacuation helicopters flew over in search of people who were injured or unable to move due to the blowdowns.

Dan heard of a Boy Scout leader who saved his troop by ordering them all into the lake as big pines came toppling down on their campsite. Shallow water was likely the only "safe" place during this once-in-a-century storm.

Blowdowns are nothing new in the Northwoods. J. W. Hoyt described the "forests" of Clark County in 1860:

> "There are ... a great many windfalls, some of which are miles in length. Here can be seen thousands of acres of trees that have been blown down or broken off, the stubs of which are still standing. The fire runs through these windfalls every year or two, and kills all the vegetation."

R. D. Irving, a geologist, wrote in 1880 of a blowdown in the Lake Superior region:

> "The great windfall of September, 1872 ... is as much as forty miles in length, though it is reported to have a greater length than this. It crosses the Chippewa River ... with a width of about one and one-half miles. When last traversed in 1877, this windfall had been partly burned over, but was, for the most part, made more impenetrable than ever on account of the new and dense growth of bushes and small trees. In crossing it on the Penokee Range, it was found necessary to cut the way with an axe for nearly a mile and a half."

A single storm on July 11, 1936, on the Menominee Indian Reservation blew down 30 million board feet of timber. Storms in 1949, 1951, and 1952 blew down 1.5 million board feet of virgin forest, or about 27 percent of the total area, in the one square mile of the Flambeau River Forest State Scientific Area. An extraordinary storm on July 4, 1977, blew down the rest of the scientific area, better known as "The Big Block," a site that was the largest remaining virgin stand of timber in Wisconsin. Mary and I visited the site in 1978, not having heard that the storm had leveled it, and found two-feet tall aspens wherever we looked.

The 1977 storm (what is it about July 4th and storms?) was classified as a downburst, a wind pattern that has had winds clocked at 157 mph. It leveled 850,000 acres of trees along a course 166 miles long and 17 miles wide.

Historically, the downed wood from such storms has provided the fuel for many a large fire years later.

Forests are always changing, either slowly through succession, or rapidly through events like blowdowns and fire. Jack pine and red pine are particularly fire-dependent, so their loss as mature trees is also their gain as seedlings.

Birds like woodpeckers, which thrive on the insects that feed on the downed trees from a blowdown, skyrocketed in numbers, while other birds that utilize old growth had to relocate. And though it was deeply saddening to see so many trees down, it's normal and natural, and should be understood as just that.

Brown Pelican!

I received a call in late July of 2002 from Bob Kelly, who owns a place on Big Sand Lake near Phelps. Bob and many of his neighbors had been observing an adult brown pelican for several days that was lounging around on the lake, sometimes even sitting on people's docks.

The significance of this sighting was that brown pelicans breed either along the Atlantic or Pacific coasts, and in case you haven't looked at a map recently, that's a fair piece away. According to Sam Robbin's *Wisconsin Birdlife* (1991), Wisconsin has only had four documented records of brown pelicans, the last one occurring in 1978 in Door County.

I've seen brown pelicans in southern California. They're beautiful birds, and remarkably graceful flyers. To have one wander into northern Wisconsin will always raise unanswerable questions. Was it lost? What brought it here? What in the world was it thinking? Unless you know someone who speaks pelican, we'll be left to our usual conjectures. In the meantime we can simply marvel that it was here.

Catching a Hummingbird

One July day, Mary, Callie, and I watched a sharp-shinned hawk sit by our bird feeder for about 10 minutes. The sharpie apparently was hoping for an easy meal of songbird, but only the hummingbirds had enough audacity to come close to the hawk and continue sipping sugar water at their feeder. I had no sooner said to Mary and Callie that the sharpie would most likely not bother trying to catch a hummer, when it suddenly leaped from its branch, swooped around the hummingbird feeder, grabbed at the hummer, and high-tailed it away. It flew so fast that we couldn't tell if it had successfully nabbed the hummer or not!

The hummingbird would have provided little more than a bite since it only weighs one-tenth of an ounce. But I suspect the sharpie couldn't tolerate the tiny bird's total indifference to its fearful presence, so it took a swipe at the nearest hummer just out of frustration. We were hoping the sharpie would nab one of the chipmunks or red squirrels that so enjoy our bird feeders, but no such luck.

The fact that the sharpie came as close as it did to the hummingbird says volumes for its ability to successfully feed on woodland songbirds. Remember, hummingbirds are unsurpassed in their aeronautical abilities. They can swoop, roll, tumble, stop on a dime, hover, fly backwards, shift sideways, fly straight up and down, and cruise full speed at 60 miles per hour. The literature says they even fly 47 to 49 miles per hour during courtship chases around the yard! If a sharpie can catch a hummer, it can catch anything it wants.

Cedar Waxwings

In July, we regularly hear and see flocks of cedar waxwings along the Manitowish River. Their lispy, high-pitched "songs" are barely audible, but in a flock, their constant, thin trilling *seee-seee-seee* can be quite noticeable. Certainly their quiet voice is no match for their physical beauty. The silky plumage, crested head, black mask through the eyes, and yellow-tipped tail create an unmistakable identity. Only their close cousin, the Bohemian waxwing, could be confused with them.

Cedar waxwings begin nesting from late June into July. Even when nesting, waxwings continue their amiable manner, socializing freely in flocks of 10 to 100 birds. They defend only a small space right around their nests, which can be as close as 25 feet away from one another. A dozen or more pairs may be nesting within a radius of 150 yards and searching for food as a flock.

The male is courting the female if you see a "side-hop" display. The male sidles up to a perched female, hops sideways, and offers to pass her a berry. If she accepts it, she'll hop away, then hop back and pass him the berry. They may hop and pass that berry for 15 minutes before one eats it. I suppose they are each saying to the other, "No, I insist. After you!" This deference builds the pair bond.

While waxwings eat berries almost exclusively in the winter, insects make up the hatchlings' initial diet. Within a few days, the adults begin feeding the chicks fruit, arriving at the nest with their crops full of berries, and then regurgitating the meal one item at a time into the gaping mouths of the chicks. Cedar waxwings often produce two broods, and may be feeding young into September, well after many birds have migrated south.

We regularly see waxwings flitting out over the river to capture a flying insect, then perching on a branch along the river to enjoy the meal. Many folks don't see waxwings because waxwings don't eat seed or suet, so they don't visit backyard feeders. But they are around in good numbers, and you'll discover their presence if you take the time to listen for their high whistling song.

Celestial Events

- Sunsets at the beginning of July begin occurring one minute earlier than the previous day for the first time since December 6. July 2 marks the mid-point of the year. By July 10, we will have lost 15 minutes of daylight from our solstice peak of 15 hours and 45 minutes. By July 26, we'll have lost 45 minutes, our days shortening to 15 hours.
- The Delta Aquarid meteor showers usually peak between July 27 and July 29. They average about 20 meteors per hour.
- The average warmest days of the year occur between July 17 and August 2, when highs average 80 degrees. Statistically, July 24 is the hottest day of the summer in the U.S.
- Neil Armstrong left the first human footprints on the moon on July 20, 1969.

Twenty Years of Common Loons in Wisconsin

Loon chicks should have hatched on most area lakes by July, and loon watchers are being treated to the sight of the adults ferrying the chicks on their backs. At this time of year, people often wonder if the hatch is a good one or not, and on a larger scale, how loons are doing in general in Wisconsin.

In 1995, LoonWatch conducted its third common loon population survey in a series carried out over five-year intervals since 1985. Survey volunteers counted adult loons and chicks by boat or from shore using binoculars or spotting scopes. The 1995 adult common loon population estimate was 3,017, up from the previous estimates of 2,420 in 1990, and 2,385 in 1985. Loons were present on 55 percent of the lakes surveyed. Chick production in 1995 was estimated at 678, compared to estimates of 608 for 1990 and 516 in 1985.

The 2000 survey was conducted on 151 lakes in 25 counties. The population was estimated at 3,131 adults and 462 chicks. The adult population did not differ statistically from 1995; however, the chick population was the lowest on record.

July 16, 2005, marked Wisconsin's fifth loon population survey, and 253 pre-selected lakes were surveyed, the most ever visited during the survey's 20-year history. The total number of adults, 3,373, and chicks, 805, was also the highest ever reported. Until statistical analyses are complete for the 2005 survey, it's unclear whether this will translate into a statewide population change.

Researchers continue to be deeply concerned about the ongoing development and recreation pressures occurring on moderate to large lakes in the Northwoods. The loon population will remain stable only if we can identify and protect existing loon nesting and rearing habitat. The nesting range of the common loon once reached as far south as Illinois and Iowa, but now lies primarily in the northern third of Wisconsin. Hopefully, we will have the foresight to protect the range that is left.

Conservation Easements

In the last few years, I have been asked to assess the conservation value of lands for people who are trying to receive a conservation easement, and the more I've learned about conservation easements, the more I've become a true believer. Conservation easements are truly win-win deals. When you create and donate a conservation easement to a charitable organization, you still own the land and can continue your current use of it. But by protecting your land from future development, you receive an income tax deduction based on the value of the development rights you give up. In addition, since you are reducing the value of your property, your estate tax drops and your property tax should decrease.

By restricting your right and the right of any future owner to develop the land, your land will remain undivided and undeveloped. The plant and animal communities will remain undisturbed by additional human occupants, and you and all future owners will save very significantly on taxes. What you lose, of course, is the ability to divide the land into small parcels and make more money in your lifetime.

From the standpoint of protecting our lakes from being divided into the tiniest lots allowable by law, conservation easements may protect the very things that brought most of us here in the first place—peace and beauty. By protecting forested uplands from division into lots, natural plant communities will be protected from fragmentation and left intact, providing habitat for the many wildlife species that prefer less disturbed or undisturbed sites. Conservation easements are a very powerful tool in protecting important conservation lands without having to purchase those lands with public funds.

Not all property is eligible. Lands must have significant "conservation values" that meet certain legal standards. For local information on conservation easements, contact the Northwoods Land Trust in Eagle River (715) 479-7530; the Last Wilderness Conservation Association in Presque Isle (715) 686-7441; or the Lakeland Conservancy in Minocqua (715) 356-9591. The statewide organization for land trusts is called the Gathering Waters Conservancy. Call (608) 251-9131, or see their Website: www.gatheringwaters.org.

Courtship Feeding

Now and again we are able to watch female house and purple finches under our feeders fluttering their wings with their mouths wide open while males feed them. At first glance they appear to be fighting, but really they're engaged in courtship feeding in preparation for a second mating and nesting. The female appears to play out the role of a young fledgling being fed. By begging for food, the female apparently helps reestablish and reinforce the pair bond. For his part, the male demonstrates that he is a capable provider, worthy of being accepted as a mate.

Dog Days

We seldom have any true "dog days" here in the Northwoods. Ninety-degree weather with high humidity is a rare visitor. Most of us believe the origin of the term "dog days" rests in the image of an exhausted dog lying in the heat of a summer day with its tongue hanging to one side, panting like a furry locomotive. The explanation seems logical, but it's historically incorrect.

Actually, "dog days" refers to Sirius, the Dog Star, which during July and August in far southern climates rises brilliantly in the east before sunrise. Sirius was blamed by the ancient Egyptians for the heat of the summer; they assumed a star that bright had to be giving off excess heat, and so Sirius became the scapegoat for the droughts and burning heat of their summers. "Dog days" traditionally lasted from July 3 to August 11.

We see Sirius only in our winter sky in the Northwoods. Its –1 magnitude makes it the brightest star in the winter heavens. Sirius is about nine light years away and thus is one of the closest stars visible from Canada and the United States. But it has not one whit of influence on our summer days.

Dog Versus Eagle

Sharon Lintereur in Lake Tomahawk e-mailed this story to me in July 2005: "Wednesday afternoon I let the dogs out and one of our cats got out. I was just going outside to take the dogs for a walk when an eagle came straight down after the cat. Doc, our golden retriever, ran after the eagle and saved the cat's life.

"John, it was probably 3 or 4 inches above the cat, talons down ready to strike. The eagle pulled up and flew down our driveway with Doc chasing it. It was so low that I could have jumped on its back, and the wind from its wings was unbelievable. Doc chased it down the driveway until it flew over the trees.

"Needless to say, Doc is David's dog and my big, brave Irish setter ran in the house right behind the cat and they both hid. Doc stayed outside and paced up and down the driveway just in case the eagle came back. I have never seen anything like this that close up before. I was, needless to say, in awe of this bird. No one was hurt and it took me about half an hour for my heart to stop pounding. This is a story that I will tell for years."

Dwarf Enchanter's Nightshade

On a hike in the Memorial Grove of the Chequamegon National Forest, our group came upon numerous tiny white flowers called dwarf enchanter's nightshade (*Circaea alpina*). The plant only stands 3 to 10 inches tall, and its two-petaled flowers were so inconspicuous as to be barely noticeable, yet I was curious why it has this most interesting name. *Circaea* is in the evening primrose family and not the deadly nightshade family, so why its common name describes it as a nightshade isn't at all clear.

After considerable research, I found the genus name *Circaea* derived from the mythological enchantress Circe, who was reputed to use a poisonous member of this genus in her sorcery. Circe detained Odysseus in his voyage to return home and went so far as to turn his men into pigs. The enchanter referred to in the name of this plant is apparently the clinging enchantress Circe. However, I was unable to find in any of my resources whether this particular plant is poisonous.

As is sometimes the case with plants, the story behind the name may be more interesting than the plant itself.

I do know the story behind Memorial Grove. The 68-acre old-growth hemlock-hardwood stand was dedicated to four Forest Service employees who lost their lives in World War II. The site is one of the finest remnant stands of old-growth hemlock in northern Wisconsin, and it is listed as both a state natural area and a federal research natural area. In Wisconsin, old-growth hemlock forests with very little evidence of human disturbance are rare. The oldest hemlock in Memorial Grove was dated in 1991 at 302 years old.

Fish Wins!

George Nelson was fishing on Presque Isle Lake in July of 2002 when he observed an immature eagle hit the water surface with its talons in hopes of pulling out a meal. Instead, the eagle dropped into the water and began struggling to take off. Soon it was pulled under the water and never resurfaced. Likely the eagle's talons had become embedded in the fish, and the fish was so big and strong that it kept swimming and pulled the eagle under.

I've been told stories by many folks of watching eagles swim a fish ashore that was too large to get airborne, but this is the first time I've ever heard of the fish turning the tables and in effect becoming the predator. If any one catches a musky sometime on Presque Isle Lake and finds an eagle band in its stomach, we'll know the rest of the story.

Fluid Archaeological Trails

I co-led a trip in July of 2001 down the Manitowish River, which is nothing unusual except for the fact that we paddled a 400-pound, 26-foot-long Voyageur canoe. Grant Herman from Northland College brought the college's replica of a North canoe down, and eight of us piled in. Grant steered from the stern, and I worked the bow. The other six provided the oomph to keep us moving at a constant speed downstream.

Remarkably, we never got hung up on rocks or shallow sands, made it around every meander, and never once had to get out and push the canoe for any reason—a better record than I usually have in my kayak! The boat handled beautifully.

The difference between our modern journey and a Voyageur expedition was that we didn't have to carry 3,000 pounds of trade goods. Some folks had a pretty healthy lunch, but not enough to sink the canoe to the point that there was only four inches of freeboard, as was the case for the Voyageurs.

Plus, we paddled at a very modest rate, with lots of stopping to talk about this and that. The Voyageurs kept up a high rate of speed, averaging 40 strokes a minute. They were on a mission, after all, while we were seeking a re-creation without the struggle. Grant led us in singing the French songs of the era, and maybe a few old pines heard something they hadn't heard in 160 years.

The Manitowish is one of many fluid archaeological trails in the Lakeland area, our rivers having once connected the world. We tried to experience a hint of that ancient connection, and likely succeeded as much as we moderns are capable of in a day. The lower Manitowish flows much as it always has, sans houses, pollution, or shoreline usage except for deer trails and beaver cuttings. We tried to honor that, keeping our impact to a minimum, and in doing so, tasted a bit of the flavor of how the Voyageurs lived several centuries ago.

Special Delivery?

Greg Linder from Woodruff reported a remarkable blue heron sighting in July 2002. He was near the Minocqua Public Library on the road that winds along one of the bays of Lake Minocqua when he saw a great blue heron standing smack dab in the middle of the road. That's pretty unusual in itself, but then the heron proceeded to walk over to an open mailbox and repeatedly stick its head inside the box, pull it out, stick it back in, and so on, until it finally found what it wanted or gave up the game. Then it slowly walked back across the road and into the water where it went upon its normal way.

So (and I love these questions) Greg asked, "What do you suppose it was doing?" Well ... maybe there was something making noise in the box like a cricket or grasshopper or something. Or maybe the mailbox owner left something in the box or received something that left a residual smell, or …

The truth is, I don't have a clue. Maybe the bird was just checking the mail. I would have been more concerned if this heron was seen sitting at the library in front of a keyboard and checking its e-mail.

Green Frog Six-Note Chorus

In mid-summer, male green frogs wail away just about every night from the shallow waters of our lakes and rivers, hoping for female companionship. Their call, usually described as something akin to strumming a loose banjo string, wouldn't attract me, but then lots of humans like rap music, leaving one to conclude that music is truly in the ear of the beholder. Using the word "chorus" for the singing of green frogs would indicate some attempt at coordinated notes, but the irregular intervals that occur between twangs suggest something far more random than a musical melody.

Green frogs actually produce six different vocalizations. The first and most commonly heard is known as the "advertisement call." The second, termed a "high-intensity advertisement call," is a faster repetition of the banjo plucking, maybe like an aspiring bluegrass plucker. The third is a "growl," given by wrestling males. The fourth is termed an "aggressive call," a single, very loud and abrupt call that nearly always precedes a physical confrontation between males. The fifth is a "release call," a series of short chirps given by either sex in hopes that the male that has a grip on them will release them. And finally, the sixth is the "alert call," given also by both sexes when something startles them and they typically leap into the water.

Most of the singing will come to a close once the males have had a chance to fertilize a female's eggs. The female chooses her mate, apparently preferring males with territories that include lots of submergent plants like *Elodea,* which provide a mat for her eggs to lie upon. She'll lay some 3,000 to 5,000 eggs, each tiny, black egg embedded with all the others in a filmy foot-wide egg mass that initially floats on the water surface and then settles onto plants below the surface.

Green frogs and bull frogs are usually the last frogs to sing over the course of the summer and will soon grow silent, leaving late July often eerily quiet. Enjoy their music while you can.

Ground-Nesting and Shrub-Nesting Birds

When most people look for bird nests, they peer up into trees, without realizing that many birds nest on the ground or low in shrubs. Nearly 150 species of birds nest in the Northern Highlands State Forest, and of those, nearly one-third nest on the ground and another one-fifth nest in shrubs.

Little is absolute within the bird world, however. Individuals within a species often show significant variation in where they nest, demonstrating how habitats are frequently preferences and not absolute requirements. For example, in a long-term study of New England northern hardwood forests, ovenbird nests were found on the ground 100 percent of the time, but veery nests were found on the ground 36 percent of the time and in shrubs 64 percent of the time.

There's a lot of variation in what comprises a nest, particularly on the ground. Loons build a sodden mass of vegetation on the edge of the shoreline, while pied-billed grebes and black terns build their sodden nests out on the water. Some ground-nesters like bobolinks build in open areas such as grasslands, while others such as ovenbirds utilize cover from understory plants in a forest. Meanwhile, the killdeer and nighthawk nest in gravel and build in the open along highways or on the roofs of buildings.

What brought this to mind is the number of properties I see in my travels that have "clean" forest understories, a sort of park-like effect, as well as large lawns. We mow a small portion of our property right around our house in order to keep mosquitoes down, make a space to hang up laundry, and plant a garden, but otherwise we try to let the natural world run its course, leaving the understory plants alone and letting trees die and fall down. Because of that, I think we're rewarded with a beautiful bird chorus in the morning and a rich array of birds to watch throughout the day. I encourage other homeowners to treat their property as naturally as they can. The reward will be less work and more birds.

Horseflies/Deerflies—Help!

Horseflies and deerflies are always hard at work taking their ounce of flesh. Both are in the family *Tabanidae* and are collectively referred to as "tabanids." The females are the blood feeders, inflicting the bites, while the males drink nectar and other plant substances. Most horse- and deerflies prefer large mammals like deer, cattle, and horses, but are also quite willing to dine on humans when we make ourselves available. Some horseflies are as small as half an inch long, while others are an inch or more in length with a 2-and-a-half-inch-long wingspan!

Horseflies seem to prefer to bite ankles, while deerflies work on the head and neck. They will land on your hair and try to wiggle their way down to your scalp to take a bite. While trying to land in your hair, a dozen or two may cavort at high speeds around your head, circling and circling like jet skiers who don't know what a pain they truly are.

I can't find a figure for how many kinds of tabanids live in Wisconsin, but Illinois boasts 109 species, many of which have never been described beyond their identification. Tabanid larvae live in water or in wet soil, but most of us fail to notice them until they hatch out as adults and race in their version of the Indianapolis 500 around our heads.

I have learned of one possible way to deter the little demons. A product called "Deer fly defense patch" is a double-sided tape that you attach to the back of your hat, making you into a walking flytrap. One fellow I know reported catching 54 deerflies in a few hours on the back of his cap. The only source I've found for the patches is on the Internet from Gardens Alive (www.gardensalive.com). Look for it under pest controls.

Marshan Love

Bob Kovar in Manitowish Waters wrote about a mountain biking journey he and his wife Carolyn "enjoyed" on the Powell Marsh in July of 2005:

"... Away we went down the long gravel dike. It was beautiful, a slight humid breeze in our faces, wildflowers every shade of the rainbow in all their splendor. We came to the crossdike and there were 2 sandhill cranes standing there. We stopped. They stopped. They flew and we turned back towards the cranberry marsh. As soon as we turned, the wind stopped (now at our backs) and within minutes it felt as though we were biking in the sand at Tulum. The going got slower and slower, the alderbrush got taller and taller between the sand islands until we finally had to dismount and break trail. I was amazed how tall and thick it had become between the islands that I rode through seamlessly earlier this spring.

"So, we're stopped, I'm carrying both bikes now by their necks, thrashing through the alderbrush and the first sighting I wanted to tell you about appears. A swarm of deerflies that obviously hadn't eaten in thousands of years descended upon us like the birds in Hitchcock's movie. I, being the one carrying two bikes by their scrawny little necks and sweating profusely under the Mayan sun, was of course mauled by the little beasts as I had nothing to swat at them with except 2 mountain bikes. While the bikes were impressively much heavier than the ordinary deerfly, I lacked a certain finesse at hitting them, and they commenced to chew large chunks of flesh from the small webs between my fingers as well as inside my hairless helmet. Carolyn was just thrashing and swatting—and for the first time in our 25 years of marriage I saw her sweat.

"While that is a sighting in itself, the REAL thing I wanted to tell you is that as we continued the Bataan Death March to the trees that signified the edge of the cranberry marsh, at the bottom of the rise before the trees, the ground exploded with about 12 sharp-tailed grouse. I smiled for a moment, and in between cussing and bleeding, swatting and sweating, and swinging bikes at flies with all the grace of an inmate at Bellevue, I realized why I love it here. We sure do have to work for it sometimes though eh?"

If These Flies Are Our Friends, Who Needs Enemies?

The appearance of literally millions of friendly flies took the definition of "friendly" to new heights in 2002. "Companionable, chummy, neighborly, kindly, amiable, benevolent, helpful, affable, clubby, gregarious, pally, congenial, cordial, genial, jovial," says the thesaurus. Clubby works best for me—I'd have liked to have taken a club to a few million of them.

friendly fly

Rumors flew all that summer about where all these flies were coming from. I'd like to repeat once again that both the caterpillars and the friendly flies are native species. They were absolutely not introduced by some devious government agency that had nothing better to do than to raise billions of these organisms in secret greenhouses and drop them from silent, camouflaged helicopters late at night.

To accuse the DNR of dropping flies on us or, from the large file of local newspaper headlines blasting the DNR, wanting to take away all of our private piers, or our private property, is absurd. I believe in democracy, free speech, and the absolute need for civilian watchdogs of governmental agencies. But as a society, we seem more and more prone to crossing the line from vigilance to paranoia, from a search for facts to a ballooning of rumors, from a discussion of issues to an indiscriminate bashing of individuals and entire agencies. Let's call a halt to this hate-filled institutional bigotry. The DNR has a lot of tough calls to make in their legislated decree to "protect and enhance" our environment. They must enforce the laws our legislators create. The DNR has made its fair share of mistakes in the past and will make its fair share in the future—I disagree with quite a few of its management policies. But on balance, the Northwoods is a far better place due to the DNR's efforts.

North America's Nightingale

Bird song grows sporadic in July, but some birds still sing consistently throughout the day, and loveliest of all to my ear is the hermit thrush. The hermit thrush's reverberating, flute-like song is so beautiful that in the stories of the Mohawk tradition, the hermit thrush outflew all other birds to heaven and there learned its song. The vibrational quality of the song is akin to the sound made by Australian didgeridoos, or the hollow sounds made by kids around the world by blowing into a bottle. The song ascends, often ending in what seems like an impossibly high note, and each song begins in a different key from the preceding song, giving the hermit thrush a variety of tones unlike most avian singers.

To identify the song, listen for how every song opens with a thin, 1/2-second-long whistle, then is followed by a rapid escalating jumble of echoing notes that many people feel rivals the music of the European nightingale. The hermit thrush's song approximates a complete pentatonic scale with all intervals in play. S. P. Cheney, writing in 1891, eloquently described the song: "After striking his first low, long, and firm tone, startling the listener with an electric thrill, [he] bounds upward by thirds, fourths, fifths, and sometimes a whole octave, gurgling out his triplets with every upward movement. Occasionally, on reaching the height, the song bursts like a rocket, and the air is full of silver tones. A second flight, and the key changes with a fresh, wild, and enchanting effect ... it is like listening to the opening of a grand overture."

One researcher slowed the song down, and found that a typical song lasting less than 2 seconds may include 45 to 100 notes and 25 to 50 pitch changes, an effort the researcher called a "musical microcosm ... the highest summit in the evolution of animal music so far known to us."

I wouldn't know a pentatonic scale from a bathroom scale, but I do know beauty when I hear it, and the hermit thrush provides its acoustical definition.

Hermit thrushes sing with grandeur, but try to find one, and you have a search on your hands. Their secretive habits keep them inconspicuous, and their hermit-like nature makes them difficult to approach. Their nests are built on the ground and are well-concealed. Their olive-brown coloration and the brown-and-white spotting on the breast provide them with an invisibility cloak of sorts. When I saw my first hermit thrush nest, canopied by low vegetation, I was within 3 feet of it and I still had to have it pointed out to me.

Hermits sometimes respond to "pishing," but usually in a shy, inconspicuous manner, rather than the bold manner in which many birds simply fly right up to take a look at you.

As a ground nester, hermits are susceptible to the usual host of predators such as raccoons, weasels, skunks, and snakes. If you want to encourage hermits to nest on your property, by all means leave your understory vegetation intact and let chaos reign. Ground-nesting birds need cover, and clean understories are sterile understories.

I find it amazing that John J. Audubon and Alexander Wilson, ordained by everyone in early American ornithology, never heard hermit thrushes sing, and even Thoreau failed to describe them clearly. I can't imagine how they missed the hermit thrush's orchestration, a song as close to sacred as any you're likely to hear.

Hooded Mergansers as Pests?

A local lake association newsletter a few years back recommended that its members try to remove two families of hooded mergansers from the lake because they ate fingerling fish. I was surprised, to say the least, that anyone would perceive these 1 1/2 pound birds as having such a significant impact on their fish population that they needed to be removed. Hoodies do eat fingerlings, but they also eat many crayfish, aquatic insects, snails, some frogs and tadpoles, and the roots and seeds of some aquatic plants. I can't quantify how many small fish a hoodie might consume in a summer, but I'd be astonished if there weren't more than enough fish to share with the anglers on our lakes.

The recommended removal of the hoodies raises some larger questions. How do we weigh our responsibilities and obligations to the natural world against human values and interests? Are there ethical principles that constrain our use of resources and how we modify the environment? If a species that has lived in our area for thousands of years prior to our recent presence is suddenly perceived as competition, what should be our response? How can we know what is the full ecological role and value of a species? Is a species' ecological role only important if it directly benefits us?

There are many more questions we could ask, none of which I or anyone else can perfectly answer. We are asked every day to contemplate what actions toward the land and water are "good" or "right." How we answer them says a lot about who we are, how deep our love of a place is, how much we are able to see larger communities beyond ourselves, and how much we are able to give.

Regarding the specific issue of the hooded mergansers, I believe they have an intrinsic right to live in their natural habitat. I also believe they pose no significant competition to recreational fishing on any lake in our area. If they did, I'd still say they have an equal right to be here.

Hummingbird Clearwing Moth

While watering our perennial garden one late July day, I watched a hummingbird clearwing moth (*Hemaris thysbe*) extracting nectar from several marsh milkweeds we had planted. This little moth is only slightly bigger than a large bumblebee, but it is so unique that it couldn't possibly be confused with any other type of insect. In a way, it almost looks like a flying crayfish, sans the big pincers, probably because of its banded abdomen and bushy-looking tail.

The tiny thing was utterly unconcerned with my presence, and nectared from flower to flower despite frequently coming within a foot of me. It moved so quickly that I had trouble getting the slow shutter of my digital camera to capture it, but I finally managed to get a number of great shots. On one of them, you can easily see the proboscis projecting into the flower to sip nectar. The clearwings lack scales on large portions of their wings, and on several other pictures one can see the transparent surfaces.

If you're looking for a good identification guide for insects on the Internet, I recommend www.bugguide.net.

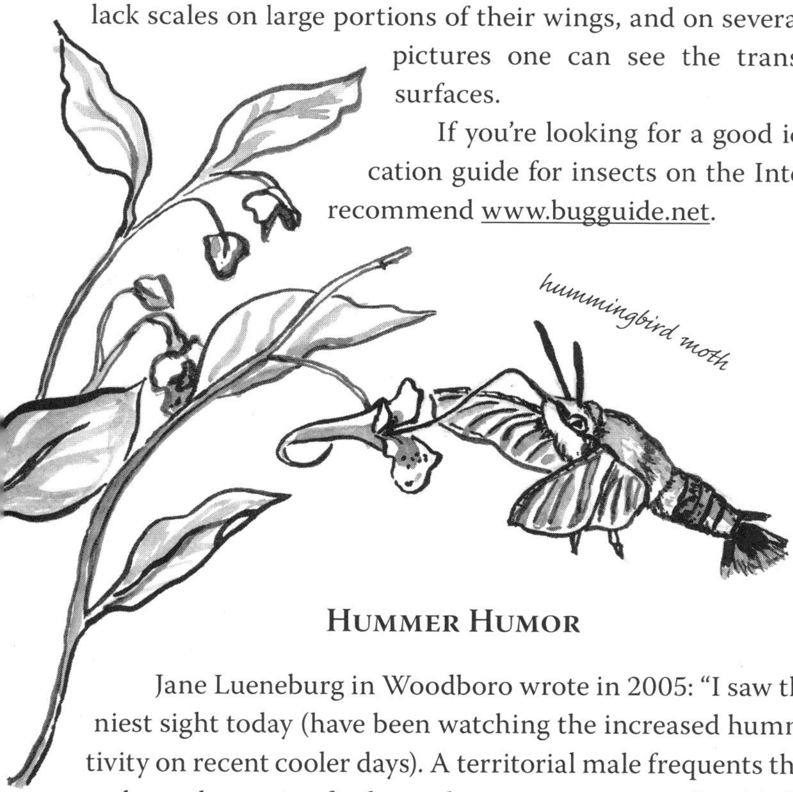

hummingbird moth

Hummer Humor

Jane Lueneburg in Woodboro wrote in 2005: "I saw the funniest sight today (have been watching the increased hummer activity on recent cooler days). A territorial male frequents the same perch on the nectar feeder and scares away any other bird trying to drink. Today I saw a female hanging upside down on the feeder perching ring … looked similar to a nuthatch in the 'head down' position. After quite awhile, she fluttered her wings and righted herself without releasing her foothold on the perch and started to drink. Soon the territorial male came in for the attack and she flipped over backwards again and he flew away. I wonder how long before he catches on to what she's doing!"

Indian Pipe and Pine Sap—Saprophytic Flowers

Two of the more remarkable herbaceous species that emerge in July look more like some odd mushroom than a wildflower, but wildflowers they are. Indian pipe (*Monotropa uniflora*) and pinesap (*Monotropa hypopithys*) have no chlorophyll, and thus fail to photosynthesize or show any green color. Yet, they create a flower and seeds just like any of the other wildflowers currently in blossom.

The difference is that they are saprophytic, meaning they get their nutrients from decaying organic matter. Really, they're more parasitic than saprophytic, because they obtain their food from the roots of other plants via mycorrhizal fungi. The fungi form a bridge that transfers carbohydrates from the photosynthetic plant to the "saprophyte."

Indian pipe is at first ghost-white with pinkish overtones, its flower drooping in a crook like a pipe. After pollination, the flower curves upright, and the entire plant turns black.

Pinesap's flower is typically yellowish, though it can be tan or red. The ½-inch flower nods downward in a cluster with three to 10 other compatriots.

Indian pipe

Kirtland's Comeback

Kirtland's warblers are extremely uncommon in the Northwoods. The only sighting I'm aware of in our particular area was when Pete Dring reported seeing two male Kirtland's warblers near Land O'Lakes on July 3, 1997. Bill Reardon, an expert birder in our area, heard the warblers singing while he was driving down the road with his windows open. Both males were singing in a young jack pine stand, the favored habitat of the Kirtland's. Pete helped band one of the males, while the other managed to escape their nets.

If you're not up on the significance of Kirtland's warbler sightings, they are a federally endangered species with only one known breeding area in the world. The entire worldwide population of Kirtland's warbler nests is in a northern area of the lower peninsula of Michigan and nowhere else. The area stretches 60 by 100 miles, mainly east of Grayling, in the jack pine plains of Crawford, Oscoda, and Ogemaw counties. A few Kirtland's pairs also nest in Kalkaska, Iosco, Roscommon, and Montmorency counties.

For unknown reasons, although large tracts of burned-over

jack pine exist in other areas of the U.P., Wisconsin, Ontario, and Quebec, Kirtland's warblers have not chosen to nest there, though individual singing males turn up now and again. These blue-gray and yellow warblers, just a bit smaller than a house sparrow, rely on Christmas-tree-sized 8- to 20-year-old jack pine forests with low hanging branches that touch the ground for their nesting habitat. Since jack pines will only release seeds from their tightly sealed cones when a temperature of 116°F is reached, this usually means a forest fire has to occur. Hence, as a partial result of our war against forest fires, the bird has been pushed onto the federal endangered list.

Federal and state agencies have managed sections of the Michigan jack pine barrens since 1957 specifically to help the survival of the Kirtland's. Controlled burns, efforts to remove brown-headed cowbirds that parasitize the nests, and planting of nearly 4 million jack pines in 1994 alone on more than 2,000 acres of land assisted in bringing the population up to 633 singing males in 1994. The lowest number occurred in 1987 when only 187 singing males were censused. In 2004, census participants counted 1,341 singing males in Michigan, the highest number ever recorded, and the fourth consecutive year the count was over 1,000!

Kirtland's warblers arrive in early May and depart between August and October for their wintering grounds in the Bahamas. They can be heard singing from mid-May to mid-July, usually from the top of a pine or a high broken stub of a tree. Listen for the clear, loud, and persistent song of the Kirtland's, which sounds like *chip-chip-chip-chery-reep*. They usually forage on the ground and low in trees looking for various insects and ripe fruits in season.

Land Leeches

Under the heading of "Be Extremely Thankful for Small Blessings" comes my newfound knowledge that while we have our share of aquatic leeches, some countries have terrestrial leeches. In southern and southeastern Asia, Madagascar, and South America, some 50 species of land leeches pose serious threats to humans. They live in the trees and on the ground in concentrations as dense as 50 per square yard, and as people and animals walk beneath the trees, the leeches drop on them like rain. I'll spare you further details as I suspect your imagination can fill these in.

I was also impressed to learn that leeches were so popular a treatment for various illnesses that the French people bought an estimated 100 million leeches in 1850 alone. French fashion designers even incorporated leech shapes and color patterns into expensive gowns. In Russia, the over-harvest of leeches was so extensive that in 1848 the state instituted a closed season on leeches and a length limit of 2½ inches for in-season captured leeches. Leeches even reached endangered status in England, Spain, Portugal, Italy, and Bohemia.

In June of 2004, the U.S. Food and Drug Administration approved leeches as medical devices. Leeches are widely used in American hospitals to help heal skin grafts by removing blood pooled under the graft and to restore blood circulation in blocked veins.

Medicinal leeches - *Hirudo medicinalis* - normally make their home in fresh water.

Let Sleeping Logs Lie

In 2004, some friends of ours, standing on their dock fishing on the Manitowish chain of lakes, were approached by a DNR warden and told to "clean up" around their dock. Their legally citable offense was that they had collected tree branches floating down the river, and placed them around their dock for fish habitat. It is illegal without a permit to put tree branches into navigable waters, though it's perfectly legal to remove woody debris if you so choose.

The DNR warden was simply doing his job, but the timing of the incident was impeccable—I was just finishing an article for the UW Trout Lake Station regarding a very important study they are conducting on the introduction and removal of coarse woody habitat along two lakes in our area. The study is producing incontrovertible evidence that trees fallen into the water along shorelines provide superb habitat for fish, turtles, frogs, aquatic insects, and a host of other organisms that feed on them.

The researchers' scientific data will confirm a process that is observed and understood by just about anyone who fishes our waters. Where do anglers typically catch the most fish? Around "structure," which comes in the form of woody debris, aquatic plants, rocks, and so forth. Among numerous functions, these structures provide refuge, an essential source of cover for many aquatic organisms. Nearly all predator-prey fish relationships are focused on the edge of refuges. Here, muskies and walleyes and other predators continually hunt these boundaries. Open water with no structure, on the other hand, has nutrients, but no refuge. Refuge areas are then the hotspots—sanctuaries if you will—for aquatic life.

The researchers don't claim that what they are doing is rocket science. Trees that fall into lakes obviously provide refuge for fish. We have built fish cribs for decades and dropped them in our lakes for this very reason. A simple observation of where the anglers are focusing their efforts on a lake will typically tell you not only where the fish are, but where the prerequisite refuge habitat exists.

So our current regulations on the placement and/or removal of coarse woody debris make not one whit of ecological sense. In the DNR's defense, however, the regulations stem from a legitimate concern for creating navigational hazards, and from the fear that people might dump any number of things in the water while claiming they are creating "fish habitat." Unregulated, humans have historically displayed an ecological ignorance that has compromised our aquatic plant and animal communities again and again.

Removal of fallen trees from wild shorelines owned by the public is illegal, as is the addition of any materials to public shorelands. The predicament emerges on private property. Shoreland owners have the right to remove trees without a permit, but they must get a permit if they want to add a tree or, as in the case of our friends, collect branches that are floating by.

The issue is not one of property rights, but of property responsibilities, an essential component of property rights and true citizenship that is too often forgotten. We focus on our rights, but what are our responsibilities and obligations to the animal and plant communities that live in and along our waterways? And when do we devise public policy to protect them or, in the absence of clear regulations, simply step up to the plate and act in their best interests?

Dead trees often fall prey to social pressures, in that people feel the need to "clean up" their property. Cleaning our house makes sense, but cleaning up our shorelines and our woodlands doesn't. As part of recognizing our responsibilities to the natural community, will we become able to change our attitudes about the manicured shorelines we appear to most highly esteem and learn instead to treasure wild shorelines? If we don't feel comfortable with completely wild conditions, can we value planting native perennials and shrubs that will provide at least a semi-wild landscape?

We all know that one person's mess is another person's treasure. We need to put that in nature's terms. Wild shorelines are beautiful and should be treasured, because they provide the very wildlife most of us came here explicitly to enjoy. Where some people see dead wood, we need instead to see that wood as the very foundation of a vibrant, living community.

When we finally learn to leave the dead where they fall, we will better be able to say we have learned to appreciate life.

Loon Dramas

Russ Gaarder called me on July 21, 2001, with a remarkable loon sighting and story. He and his wife Judy were driving on Hwy. 70 between Sunday Lake and Shishebogama Lake when they drove over the top of something large and brown on the road. They stopped and turned around, and slowly approached what turned out to be a loon chick sitting on the road! Another car stopped, and together they carefully picked up the chick, which was quite feisty, and carried it to the shoreline of Sunday Lake, placing it in some water lilies.

Russ and Judy then called the Northwoods Wildlife Center to get their perspective on what to do. Mark Naniot, the director of rehabilitation at the Center, told them to bring the loon in. The next day, Russ located it along the shoreline and took it to the center where they examined it, estimated it was about three weeks old, and found it was blind in one eye. In the meantime, Judy called around to folks on Shishebogama and found Sharon Snyder, who is the "loon ranger" for the lake. Sharon keeps tabs on the loons, and she said that two pairs on the lake were each missing a chick. The pair on Sunday Lake still had its chick, so the best conclusion available was that the chick had left Shishebogama for some reason and tried to walk to Sunday Lake.

Mark brought the chick to Shishebogama on July 23 to try to release it back to one of the pairs. They went out in Sharon's boat and put the chick on the water near the first pair, which proceeded immediately to attack it. Mark quickly scooped the chick up and headed over to the other nesting pair on the lake. They set the chick in the water there, and the adult pair came up to it and began to dive all around it, as if trying to encourage it to dive as well. The chick never dove, and the adults soon lost interest and drifted away.

In the meantime, an immature eagle sat in a nearby tree observing the drama, likely licking its chops. So Mark took the chick back to the Wildlife Center for the evening rather than leave it exposed to the eagle, and ultimately the chick died. The people involved certainly did everything within their power to help the chick, but for whatever reason, this chick apparently was not meant to survive. It was probably genetically weak. Simply being blind in one eye would make it unable to fend for itself in the exceptionally exacting and demanding world of a loon.

In the world of wildlife rehabilitation, loons are possibly the most difficult of patients. They are typically unable to survive the stress of captivity. Unlike eagles and owls and a host of other birds and mammals, no injured loon has ever been kept in captivity and used in educational programs. Mark says that on average two to three days in captivity is about all that loons can tolerate. The stress of human contact builds up lactic acid in the loons, leading to rapid and fatal muscle and organ damage. The Center has kept loons for as long as 5 weeks, but that's the absolute exception.

Whatever the reason, loons remain very difficult to rehabilitate. Maybe that very wildness within loons is what all of us so cherish.

Loons Killing Loons

During the summer of 2005 Jeff Wilson, a loon researcher in Mercer, reported that there were four observed cases of adult loons killing other adult loons. One death occurred on Clear Lake in Oneida County, an incident that was witnessed by numerous people. The two adults fought by using their beaks and beating one another with their wings. One loon was weakened and climbed onto shore, but eventually went back into the water and was attacked again by the other. The attacker climbed onto the back of its opponent and pecked its head, then held its head under the water until it drowned. The loon washed up on shore about 15 minutes later.

Loon Fidelity

Contrary to common belief, loons don't necessarily mate for life. Though they usually remain faithful from year to year to their nesting lake, they often change mates. At least 20 percent of the loons studied over the last decade by biologists throughout the loon breeding range in North America switched mates annually. In fact, many engage in a practice called "rapid mate switching," most likely a reproductive strategy triggered by nest failure. Switching mates occurs in both males and females, but more so with females.

Losing Loons to High Water

In nature, what benefits one species often is detrimental to another. The state of high waters in rivers and lakes in 2001 made life very difficult for nesting loons. In an early July conversation with biologist Terry Daulton, one of seven field researchers in an EPA/DNR study to establish a population model for loons, Terry said that loons were still sitting on nests on six of 14 of her study lakes that held nesting pairs. On two of these lakes, females had just laid eggs the last week of June. Given the 28-day incubation period, this meant some loon chicks would just be hatching in late July. Typically, loons are on eggs by the middle of May and the chicks hatch between June 15 and June 25.

High water flooded out many of the best nesting sites, causing some loon pairs to forgo any attempt at nesting, or to nest on marginal sites. Some nests washed away in wind and waves or in rising waters. Terry observed 16 failed nests, among them five failures on Trude Lake near the Turtle-Flambeau Flowage, and three on Crab Lake near Presque Isle.

A few of the failures appeared due to predation. On one nesting platform, an animal, likely a raccoon, had swum out to the platform and broken off a portion of it while taking the eggs. Its claw marks could be clearly seen in the Styrofoam. Otters, fishers, bald eagles, muskies, and snapping turtles are also all known predators of eggs and/or chicks.

Several years ago, a study was conducted of chicks with radio implants, which allowed the researchers to follow the chicks throughout a summer season. One researcher followed a radio signal to a fisher's den, while on two other occasions signals were received from something moving along the bottom of a lake—likely from the belly of a snapping turtle or musky. An adult loon (not the parent) was even observed stabbing and killing a one-day-old chick on one lake.

Loosestrifes on the Loose

Purple loosestrife (*Lythrum salicaria*) comes into flower in July along lakes and rivers and in wetlands. If you don't already know how to identify this aggressive exotic, you need to learn to recognize it and then to destroy it wherever you see it. Nasty things can come in pretty packages, and purple loosestrife fits that bill. It's illegal to plant, distribute, sell, or cultivate purple loosestrife in Wisconsin, at the cost of a $100 fine. The cost to the botanical diversity of a shoreline is far greater.

We do, however, have several native loosestrifes that are rather uncommon, very pretty, and worthy of our appreciation. Mary and I frequently paddle the Trout River, and the initial quarter mile of stream has large colonies of swamp loosestrife. Swamp loosestrife (*Decodon verticillatus*) grows in shallow water in muck or peat sediments. The stems reach 6 feet tall, often arching over to touch the water and then rooting at the tip. The leaves are arranged in whorls of two to four, but the beauty of the magenta flowers is the draw. They develop in dense clusters in the axils of the leaves, where the leaves attach to the main stem

Yellow loosestrife (*Lysimachia terrestris*), also known as swamp candles, grows in wet meadows or along shorelines, gracing the water's edge with a plume of small yellow flowers.

Common names often make for confusion. Plants in the *Lythraceae* Family (including the *Decodon* and *Lythrum* genus) belong to the Loosestrife Family. Plants in the genus *Lysimachia* belong to the Primrose Family, but are still referred to as loosestrifes. So we can't condemn the entire family or its namesakes. Stay focused purely on purple loosestrife as the Darth Vader of loosestrifes, and enjoy the others.

Marsh Milkweed

Along many lake and river shorelines, we see beautiful stands of marsh milkweed (*Asclepias incarnata*), their domed, purplish-red flower clusters in partial blossom. The tiny flowers are quite complex, each one surrounded by five clasping hoods that enclose five nectar-secreting horns. The flowers are constructed in a manner that generally ensures that an insect will fly away with a leg or three full of pollen.

If the flowers are not sufficient enough for identification, the plant's narrow, usually opposite leaves, slender seed pods, and milky sap should convince you of its identity.

Monarch butterflies commonly hover about the plants, and lay their eggs on them, just as they do on the upland common milkweed. Hummingbird moths are also known to sip the nectar from the flowers, so marsh milkweed is a wonderful native plant to put in your flower garden. It's remarkably drought-tolerant for a plant that grows in wetlands.

All milkweeds produce a milky, sticky sap that is at least unpalatable and often toxic to bird predators, so a number of insect species, like monarch butterflies, have adapted to feeding almost entirely on milkweeds in order to avoid predation. These insects are typically brightly colored, their colors warning the birds somewhat like a flashing neon sign that says, "Warning! Do Not Eat!" This process, called Mullerian mimicry, depends on birds to memorize the color, associate it with a very bad taste, and then to leave alone any insect displaying that color.

The plant is also not the most palatable to mammals and other birds, only a few of which graze the leaves or eat the seeds. Some birds, like yellow warbler, northern orioles, and alder flycatchers, do use the strong stem fibers for nest construction, but the alkaloid compounds contain cardiac glycosides that just make milkweed plain undesirable.

Humans haven't found much palatable about the plant either, and I've always been surprised that the genus name is *Asclepias*, in honor of the Greek god of medicine, because it really wasn't (and shouldn't have been) widely used for medicinal purposes. The Meskwaki tribe made a root tea "to drive the worms from a person in one hour's time." It's true that the tea drives all sorts of things out, given that it works very well as a laxative and a purgative. But that should hardly rate it the honor of being named after Asclepias.

Other uses were employed by Native Americans. They braided the fibers of the stem to produce a strong cordage used for wampum belts and fish nets. Francis Densmore lived with the Chippewa in the early 1900s and wrote that a decoction of the root was good for bathing a child or for soaking your feet when you're tired. The silky seeds and threads were sometimes used in bedding in lieu of feathers.

American Kestrels

In mid-July 2003, Mary, Callie, and I hiked along the upland edge of the Little Turtle Flowage and kept hearing and seeing several small hawks perched on distant trees. Their call was an even-pitched *kle-kle-kle-kle-kle.* Eventually the birds flew, revealing pointed wings that were swept back and angled at the elbow. Their small size, similar to a killdeer, indicated that the birds had to be either merlins or kestrels. I walked toward one of the trees and the bird held still long enough for me to clearly see a black, vertical sideburn running through the eye on either side of the face, identifying the bird as a kestrel. It soon flew, so I turned and walked toward a white pine where I had seen another bird barely visible in the foliage. I got under the tree and couldn't find the bird, but suddenly it shot from the tree straight out across the upland grasses. Thirty seconds later another bird shot out from within the foliage so quickly that I barely got a look at it before it, too, was well over the grassland.

We eventually counted five kestrels in the area, and while I looked that white pine up and down, I could not find the expected cavity-nesting hole. Kestrels typically nest in old tree excavations left behind by flickers and pileated woodpeckers. They aren't known to ever excavate their own holes.

However, we just weren't looking in the right place. An artificial nesting box was plainly evident in a nearby pine.

We were excited to see the kestrels because, as birds of open-country habitat, they're relatively uncommon in the Northwoods. We see them regularly in the southern part of the state, perched on telephone wires or hover-hunting over fields. In fact, kestrels are the most common North American falcon, breeding throughout North and South American from the Arctic treeline to Tierra del Fuego. But they're a treat for birders in the Northwoods.

Historically known as the sparrow hawk, kestrels do indeed eat songbirds like sparrows, particularly house sparrows in cities, but much of their diet is made up of grasshoppers, crickets, and dragonflies, with an occasional vole, snake, frog, or bat thrown in for a side dish.

Kestrels will use nest boxes set on poles 10 feet or more in the air and facing in toward an open field. Just don't place the kestrel boxes near your bluebird boxes—the bluebirds will thank you.

A Day in the Life of a Mayfly

I had the opportunity in mid-July to give a two-day program at the Bear Paw Inn on the Wolf River, and during one of the evenings, we went to the shoreline of the Wolf and observed a prodigious mayfly hatch. Apparently these were "white Wolf" mayflies, a particularly remarkable species in that they hatch, molt on the fly, mate on the fly, and then die all in the same evening. There was a veritable snowstorm of these mayflies sweeping back and forth along the surface of the Wolf, and numerous trout were rising to nab the spinners that fell to the water after mating. We needed binoculars to clearly see the mayflies in the dusky light, and though it was absolutely impossible to estimate how many mayflies were creating this blizzard, we hazarded a guess of many thousands just on the very small stretch of river we were observing.

A few years later in late June and early July of 2002, Mary and Callie saw large numbers of mayflies scattered on the surface of the Manitowish River. On closer examination, they found that these were the empty husks of the larvae, each with a hole in its back where the "dun" had emerged. They wondered what had happened. Well, here's a thumbnail account of the remarkable life cycle of mayflies.

Mayflies belong to the order *Ephemeroptera*, from the root "ephemeral," an appropriate derivation given that the adults usually live for just one day. In preparation for adulthood, the aquatic nymphs undergo a dramatic

adult mayfly

metamorphosis. Their mouthparts and digestive systems shrink; their sex organs and eyes enlarge; and their stomachs change into an inflatable air chamber. The nymphs then float to the water's surface, where their back splits open and the "dun" emerges, coated with a water-resistant film.

During this time, predators like trout and water striders feed on the duns. The duns that survive the feeding frenzy on the surface then lift off in a slow flutter that attracts insect-eating birds like swallows, phoebes, and flycatchers, along with other predators such as bats and dragonflies. The survivors of the aerial predators flit into the treetops and attach themselves to the undersides of leaves (or possibly your window screens). They then "hang out" for nearly a day while they rapidly experience what amounts to their childhood and adolescence. Their tail filaments grow to nearly twice the length of their bodies; their multi-faceted eyes become ultrasensitive to movement and light reflection; and the female fills with eggs from end to end. The dun sheds its last water-repellent covering, the final vestige of its aquatic ancestry, and the female becomes vividly colored in order to be easily spotted by the male's light-sensitive eyes.

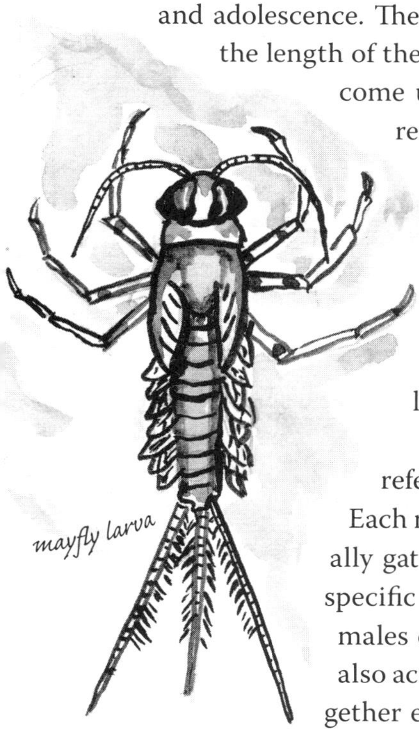

mayfly larva

The final adult stage begins in a form referred to as an "imago" or "spinner." Each mayfly joins a nuptial swarm that usually gathers at sundown. The females emit a specific pheromone, which sexually attracts males of their own species. The pheromone also acts as the glue that keeps the swarm together even when it passes through a swarm of another species. As the mass rises up and down above the water, the spinners copulate in mid-air. Shortly thereafter, the spent males drop into the water to die, while the females, ripe with fertile eggs, plant their eggs in, on, or above the water, depending on the species. They, too, then fall into the water, where they are devoured by surface-feeding insects and fish. The eggs hatch two weeks later, and the tiny larval mayflies begin their year-long (or longer in some cases) aquatic sojourn, undergoing 15 to 30 molts before they emerge as the fleeting but elegant flying adults.

Merlin Nest

My family and I located a merlin's nest while paddling the Manitowish River in July of 2004. Locate may be giving us too much credit, because you could hardly miss it. A full hundred yards before the nest, we could hear continual raucous bird calls, a caterwauling of sounds like you might hear from a flock of crows or gulls. We came around a river bend and saw tall pines along the shoreline, one of which contained what appeared to be a crow's nest in it. The context immediately added up to a merlin nest, and indeed we soon saw four merlins flying back and forth among the pines.

Merlins are well-known for making a racket around their nests, and these four lived up to their reputation. I asked Bruce Bacon, DNR wildlife manager in Mercer, what the noise was all about, and he said it was the young begging for food after they fledged. While the eggs are incubating and after the young have hatched, the merlins stay quiet around the nest. But once the chicks have fledged, pandemonium seems to rule the day.

Most people have never seen a merlin. These small falcons are a species of special concern in Wisconsin, and while no surveys have ever been done on their numbers, Bacon estimates that five years ago, we only had about 30 to 40 nests in the whole state. Today he believes that those numbers have doubled, but merlins are still very uncommon in Wisconsin.

Merlins nest almost exclusively in old crows' nests, which are typically high in a conifer along a lake shoreline or at the edge of a forest or field. They like edges because a merlin's diet consists mostly of songbirds and dragonflies, and to catch them, the merlins need open air space to maneuver. Bacon has seen them take birds as large as mourning doves and flickers, both of which are nearly as big as the foot-tall merlins.

Bacon and several other DNR bird banders have banded dozens of merlins over the last decade, but so far they haven't received a single band return, so they really don't know where the merlins winter and what route they take. By visual observation of the bands, they do know that the same merlins return to the same nesting territories every year, and that their nest success rate is very high—three to four chicks usually hatch and fledge every year from nests.

Complete and Incomplete Metamorphosis—Ch-Ch-Ch-Changes

The metamorphosis of insect larvae into adults is a remarkable process. Most insects, including flies, butterflies, beetles, wasps, ants, and bees, undergo complete metamorphosis, and emerge as a winged adult that bears virtually no resemblance to the larva. Complete metamorphosis includes four stages: the egg, the larva or growing stage, the pupa or transformation stage, and the adult or reproductive stage.

The larval caterpillar lives to eat and grow, essentially acting as "a digestive system on a caterpillar tread, using its six thoracic legs and its ten stubby abdominal prolegs to hold on tightly to its food," writes entomologist Gilbert Waldbauer. The pupal stage is a transitional period where an insect progressively matures into its adult physical characteristics, growing wings, genitalia, and so forth. The adult butterfly or moth is utterly different, bearing colorful wings, owning six legs that serve as landing gear, and in most cases drinking flower nectar from a long, coiled sucking tube. It no longer even has mouthparts for chewing. The adult is specialized to mate and distribute eggs from host plant to host plant. More than 775,000 known insect species undergo complete metamorphosis.

A far smaller group, some 150,000 insect species, undergo incomplete metamorphosis, skipping the pupating stage and going directly from nymph to adult. Dragonflies, grasshoppers, and true bugs, among others, pass through only three life stages: the egg, the nymph or growing stage, and the adult or reproductive stage. Nymphs and adults look and behave relatively alike, a good case in point being dragonflies, which live in the water as nymphs. When they climb out of the water onto a plant stem, they emerge as an adult, leaving their dry nymphal body husk behind.

Shedding Less Light

Lee Andreas sent me the following regarding turning out yard lights at night:

> "For more than 20 years I was the dam tender at Rainbow Dam. Among the many duties of the job was to check on the water level of the reservoir during periods of high water and much rain. These checks came at all hours of the day and night. I remember crossing over the bridge on many hot and muggy evenings to get to the gauge house on the other side.
>
> "There were two dusk-to-dawn lights that illuminated the bridge. State Forest Road D crossed at the dam, and the lights were a matter of public safety. On the hot and humid nights, the insects were drawn to the lights, and the bats were drawn to the easy pickings they had for a meal. At first I admired what the bats were doing to all of the insects that fill our night skies. I would even stop and admire their efficiency, only to slap a few mosquitoes that they did not have a chance to eat.
>
> "Then one morning on my daily routine, I picked up a single wing of a luna moth. No other parts were to be found. I immediately became highly disturbed by what I had in my hand—the wing of the world's most beautiful creature.

I stood there for a few minutes and looked around and became madder by the second. What sadistic S.O.B. would pull the wings off of this marvelous creation? If the late Reggie White or someone of similar stature were standing there and pulling off the other wing, my adrenaline level was such that I would have picked him up and thrown him over the railing into the river. My reference to an S.O.B. was not to a swell old boy, but the original meaning of the term.

"For a few days I stewed and fretted over the manners of others of the race to which I belong. Slowly, rather than in a flash, it came to me. Those wings were not torn off by someone with a low I.Q., but what I had witnessed was the result of bat foraging. The bat lobby and bat lovers will not come out and tell us that bats do such things, but they cannot deny it. A luna moth is an insect. Insects are drawn to artificial lights at night, especially mercury vapor lamps. Bats eat insects without regard to our likes or dislikes."

Turn off those lights.

Mosquitoes, Genghis Kahn, and Other Invaders

It would be fine if we could eat mosquitoes like we can blueberries and raspberries. Our dogs eat them, snapping their teeth at the little whiners whenever the pests buzz them. Given all the disease organisms mosquitoes can carry, I suspect that's not the healthiest way of dealing with them. But try and reason with a dog …

In 2005, we had quite a hatch of tiny mosquitoes that didn't bother buzzing our ear first, but simply went straight for our unprotected skin, like an arrow shot from a bow, and commenced drilling.

I'm always impressed with their instant attentiveness. Their ability to find us within the first five seconds of our appearance outdoors is certainly worthy of respect and admiration. They're extremely good at what they do, little marvels of evolution that they are.

As a naturalist, I always feel compelled to put the best shine on anything natural that I can, given that we humans are adept at trying to eliminate anything that bothers us in the least without looking at the bigger picture. But, I admit it's hard to shine these little skeeters up, even though I know plenty about how important they are as pollinators of plants (males feed only on plants remember), and how valuable they are as food for a huge array of insect-eaters.

They're also equally important as bedevilers of human beings, a role that has led to a host of surprisingly positive endings, depending, of course, on your perspective. Mosquitoes carry malaria, as you likely know, and while human populations usually develop a general resistance to their local mosquitoes, invader forces from far away don't have the same resistance. Thus, mosquitoes have turned back many an invading army that had no business trying to overwhelm a populace. In 1022, the army of King Henry II of England invaded Italy and was defeated by malaria so rampant that it could "in no way be described." Malaria is considered the agent that most probably prevented Genghis Khan from invading Western Europe. The Roman army lost more than half of its 80 thousand-man army in Scotland to a local strain of malaria. The ancient Romans even built a temple on the Palatine Hill honoring the fever goddess, where they prayed for mercy from the killing fevers that sprang up every summer.

The British raised their flag on many lands, but came to describe West Africa as the "white man's grave" due to malaria. Even Alexander the Great, who seemed invincible both to his enemies and to the many innocent populations he conquered, died in 323 B.C. of a mysterious illness that was likely malaria.

Yellow fever borne by African mosquitoes came to the Americas sometime before 1650, probably carried in a water cask on a slave ship. Military campaigns in the New World encountered disaster via mosquitoes. More than half of a 12 thousand-man force sent to take Cartagena, Colombia, in 1742 were felled by the illness. When the French tried to take back rebellious Haiti in 1802, they lost more men to mosquitoes than to enemy forces. Of 29,000 troops, only

6,000 made it back to Europe.

Even French- and German-born popes died of malaria in the eleventh and twelfth centuries, and numerous popes apparently refused to sit in Rome out of fear of contracting malaria there. Many Egyptian mummies have enlarged spleens, which is a symptom of the disease.

The stories abound far beyond this sampling, as do the mosquitoes. And the stories continue, because in the twenty-first century, millions still die every year from mosquito-borne malaria. We're not immune to mosquito-borne diseases in Wisconsin either—mosquitoes now carry West Nile virus in nearly every county of Wisconsin, killing thousands of birds and other critters, and causing illness and sometimes death in people.

I know I think twice about hiking into certain places because of the mosquito quotient. So maybe that's the best "shine" we can give them at present—they help keep land wild—and that's a blessing.

Most Fragrant Flowers in July

What are the most fragrant flowers in July? My Top Five would be:

- Wild rose
- Spreading dogbane
- White water lily
- Marsh and common milkweed
- Horned bladderwort (You'll have to look hard to find this one.)

Moth Storms

When we pulled into a Minocqua gas station in mid-July of 2000, there was a literal blizzard of moths around the lights. I wondered, not for the first time, why these new gas stations have more lights than the average airport landing strip. The insect culprits were the adult moths of the forest tent caterpillars that had been so numerous in May and June. The adult moth was uniformly tan/buff-colored, about 1 to 1.5 inches wide, with a stout short body, scalloped wings, and two oblique darker brown stripes on each forewing.

The good news was that the adult moths weren't feeding. Adults can only mate, lay eggs, and die, and they do all of this in a few days. The bad news was that they were laying eggs. The eggs were cemented together in cylindrical masses with a frothy substance that hardens and turns a glossy dark brown.

Great numbers swarm around lights, hence the attraction to gas stations (they certainly couldn't have been attracted to the prices), and provide yet another reason to turn off yard lights.

Northern Harrier

We see harriers with some frequency over the Manitowish River and in the sedge meadows of Powell Marsh. "Harrier" derives from the sixteenth-century English harien, meaning "to pillage and torment." Thus, we've named one of our foremost military fighter planes the "Harrier," and we somehow managed to attach the term to the marsh hawk as well.

I suppose from the perspective of a vole, the term is apt. Voles comprise 95 percent of the harrier's diet in prime habitat. But vole populations rise and plummet in about four-year cycles. The cyclical lows greatly impact harriers, but in good years, voles far exceed harrier appetites. So it's a cycle of feast and famine. Harriers will also eat grasshoppers, snakes, frogs, sparrows, blackbirds, squirrels, and rabbits. As opportunistic feeders, they're certainly not entirely helpless without voles around.

While hawk identification can be maddening at times, harriers provide one easy field mark. Their large white rump patch is a dead give-away, though you have to be careful not to confuse the rough-legged hawk with the harrier during spring and fall migration. Rough-legs have a white tail with a broad black band toward the tip.

Harriers hunt prey "on the wing," flying with slightly up-tilted wings in a dihedral like a turkey vulture. They cruise low over fields and marshes, often less than 7 feet above the ground, using their superb vision and hearing to locate prey. Their flattened facial disk, along the lines of an owl's, is thought to help them focus sound. They also perch-hunt, hover-hunt, stoop, and soar. In summer, a large hovering hawk over a northern marsh has "harrier" written all over it.

Harriers are one of only a few North American hawks that show sexual dimorphism in plumage. That is, the male and female are different. The males are a pale silver-gray, while the females appear brown above and streaked-brown below. Immatures have a different look as well. They are dark brown above and copper red below.

Harriers are also the only hawk that nests on the ground and in colonies. Nesting pairs often associate in loose colonies of a dozen or more pairs in prime habitat, the nests usually spaced at least 100 yards apart.

Harriers have one other unique trait. They're the only hawk that is frequently polygynous. One male often mates with several females, while each female only mates with one male, an atypical behavior in the monogamous world of hawks. A 25-year study of harriers by the Hammerstroms in Wisconsin showed that 25 percent of the nests were associated with polygynous matings, and that increased polygyny corresponded with high vole populations. Good food makes for good sex, I guess.

During incubation by the female, the male seldom comes near the nest, but will fly by with a captured prey item, triggering the female to fly up. He then drops the prey, and as it falls through the air, the female catches it in her best Willie Mays imitation, then lands and walks back to the nest with it. On one bird hike in the Powell Marsh Wildlife Area just west of the Manitowish, we watched a male drop prey to a female on three occasions. Juveniles will do the same after fledging in July, catching dropped prey in the air.

Harriers prefer wet meadows and marshes, but they also occupy dry upland prairies and fields, often in association with short-eared owls, which take over the predation chores at sunset.

As one would expect of a marsh hunter, the harrier's numbers have declined since 1960 due to the decline in grassland and marsh habitat.

Northern Water Snakes

I lead canoe trips every year along the Trout River, and we always stop at one particular beaver lodge where I check for basking northern water snakes. On one occasion, seven water snakes were hanging out and seemed quite unperturbed by our close presence and discussion. Their dark coloration blended well with the stick construction of the lodge, and if we hadn't looked closely, we would have missed them. That's something to say, given that northern water snakes usually stretch to over three feet long and are heavy-bodied and impressive to behold. If they had been lying on their backs—something I've never seen a snake do—their white undersides with a speckling of bright red half-moons would have given their presence away.

Northern water snakes feed on crayfish, frogs, aquatic insects, and slow-moving fish, but they're non-venomous and don't represent a threat in any manner to humans.

Our long winters explain why 13 of the 21 types of snakes found in Wisconsin reach their northern range limit in Wisconsin. In the Lakeland area, we really only have six types of breeding snakes—the northern ringneck, smooth green, western fox (often called a pine snake), common garter, northern redbelly, and northern water snake. None are the least bit harmful to humans, although most will bite if picked up. But if you pick me up against my will, I'll bite you, too.

Old-Growth Hemlock—A Revolutionary Idea

The Plum Lake-Star Lake State Natural Area is a 561-acre stand of old-growth eastern hemlock, sugar maple, and yellow birch. The oldest hemlock dated in the stand began life 265 years ago, in 1740. It was just a young pup when in 1776 America declared its independence from England, an obscure event I'm sure was lost on everything and everyone who lived in the Northwoods at the time.

While we celebrate some 230 years of independence on July 4, hemlocks may take 250 to 300 years simply to reach maturity, and may live for 400 years or more (the record is 988 years). The 260-year-old in the Plum Lake stand represents a hemlock in middle age.

Because early growth of hemlocks is so slow, trying to correlate age and size can be highly deceptive. Trees less than an inch in diameter may be as old as 100 years, and saplings 2 to 3 inches in diameter may be 200 years old. One 10-inch diameter, pole-sized hemlock was found to be 359 years old! Big doesn't always mean old in the hemlock world.

Eastern hemlock is highly shade tolerant and can survive with as little as 5 percent of full sunlight reaching it year after year. As such, it's the most patient of trees, willing to spend several centuries or more waiting for a gap in the canopy to create a window of sunlight, then racing its fellows for emergence into the sky.

To become even the skinniest of saplings requires exceptional luck and effort for a hemlock. While hemlocks frequently produce good cone crops—one Wisconsin study showed hemlocks producing good or better annual cone crops 61 percent of the time—only 25 percent of the seeds are typically viable. The tiny seeds, only 0.06 inches long, require warm, moist soils (59°F is optimal) for germination, but then only grow an inch or two a year for the first decade. The roots of first-year seedlings extend just half an inch into the soil, making them extremely sensitive to high temperatures and drying.

Of course, this assumes the seedlings get started at all, given that most seeds can't penetrate the layer of leaves and needles that cover the forest floor. Ground fires expose mineral soil, creating ideal conditions for hemlock regeneration, but absent this, hemlocks regenerate best on top of old stumps, mossy logs and tip-up mounds where soil is exposed. These sites eventually rot away, leaving hemlocks propped up on stilt-like roots that make them vulnerable to windthrow.

If a hemlock seedling can get a foothold, then white-tailed deer, snowshoe hare, mice, voles, and squirrels conspire to browse the young shoots in winter. Though hemlock is only ranked seventh in winter food preference for white-tailed deer, a hemlock stand provides ideal cover during winter. Yarding deer, eating five pounds of browse per day per individual, tend to eat themselves out of house and home in their winter yards, eventually browsing available seedlings into oblivion.

The sum of such natural constraints renders hemlock a near ghost on the landscape, representing today only 0.5 percent of the northern forest, a forest in which it was once a dominant force.

The revolutionary idea regarding "management" of hemlock is to leave it alone, even to encourage it, as is now practiced by most state and national forests. Only a few decades ago, the few remaining hemlocks were commonly cut out to encourage the more economically beneficial hardwood species that typically replace them. A century ago, we were busy cutting hemlock primarily for its bark, which contains 10 percent tannic acid. Entire tanning factories ran on hemlock bark.

But rarity tends to increase value, even if the value is merely aesthetic and ecological in a century that so values economics. The soulful experience of walking amidst trees that preceded the formation of our country can't be given dollar value. The pleasure of hearing a host of birdlife like blackburnian and black-throated green warblers defies traditional economics too, though birdwatchers spend more money in the Northwoods than anyone seems to realize.

With immeasurable luck, the pre-Revolutionary War seedlings in the Plum Lake-Star Lake Natural Area and elsewhere will watch over the landscape for another two centuries or more, indicating a revolution in our stewardship of trees that is worth celebrating.

One Good Tern Deserves Another

While paddling with a group on the Turtle-Flambeau Flowage in mid-July 2001, we spotted both black terns and Caspian terns. While black terns are a species of special concern in Wisconsin and are uncommonly seen, Caspian terns are quite a rare sighting, and have been listed as an endangered species in Wisconsin since 1989. Caspians are herring-gull-sized with a black cap, red bill, and a short, slightly forked tail. In the nearly 20 years we've paddled on the Flambeau Flowage, we had never seen Caspians.

Osprey Bomber

Bruce Bacon bands osprey for the DNR, and he told me in 2004 of one of his fellow banders who had an adult osprey drop a fish on his head while he was at the rim of the nest. Adult ospreys and eagles almost always fly a short distance away when banders climb their nests, but this one may have been upset enough that it bombed the bander. There's no way to know if it was intentional, but if someone appeared to be taking my chicks, I might bomb him, too.

Raising the Blue Flag

Our high waters in 2002 led to a profusion of blue flag irises in roadside ditches and wetlands. The "fleur-de-lis" likes its feet wet, so wet summers often dramatically increase growth in ephemeral wetlands. The name "fleur-de-lis," commonly thought to mean "flower of the lily," originated when Louis VII, king of France, adopted a blue flag as the emblem of his house. Over time the "fleur-de-Louis" was corrupted through spelling errors.

The plant's leaves resemble pointed swords. A thick, fleshy rhizome extends horizontally underground, from which clonal stems grow upward to form new plants, explaining why blue flags are usually found in large patches.

Raspberry Picking Time

It's not only the wild blueberries that are ready for picking in July, it's the red raspberries as well.

Our two most common wild plants are black raspberry (*Rubus occidentalis*) and red raspberry (*Rubus strigosus*). Black raspberries have black fruits and nastier prickles on ridged stems, while red

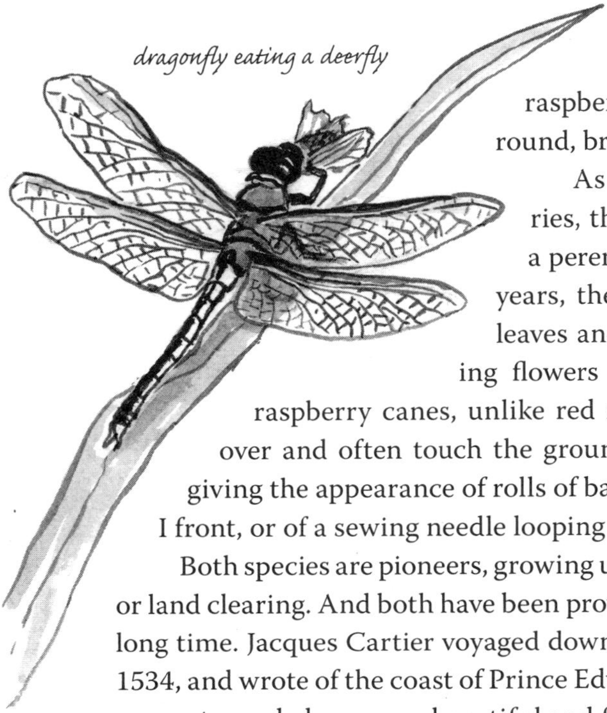

dragonfly eating a deerfly

raspberries have red fruits on a round, bristly stem.

As is the case with blackberries, the cloning stems rise from a perennial base, and live for two years, the first year just producing leaves and the second year producing flowers and fruits as well. Black raspberry canes, unlike red raspberry canes, will arch over and often touch the ground, then root at their tips, giving the appearance of rolls of barbed wire on a World War I front, or of a sewing needle looping through a quilt.

Both species are pioneers, growing up in areas disturbed by fire or land clearing. And both have been providing food for people for a long time. Jacques Cartier voyaged down the St. Lawrence River in 1534, and wrote of the coast of Prince Edward Island: "The land that was not wooded was very beautiful and full of ... raspberries."

In 1616, Samuel de Champlain wrote while paddling the Ottawa River: "We also found it was almost as if God had wished to bestow a gift of some sort on this barren and unfriendly country for the succour and support of its people—that in season the riverbanks were thick with berries of all sorts, including raspberries and blueberries." Later, as he paddled on Lake Huron, he wrote, "For some time we had been eating only one meal a day. Luckily, there was also plenty of blueberries and raspberries. Without them we might have starved to death."

I was surprised to learn that red raspberry is considered by some to be an aggressive and undesirable invader in southern Wisconsin, and in need of controlled management.

That's always a value judgment. When does too much of a good thing become a bad thing? Wild raspberry foragers would probably disagree, including such species as ruffed and sharp-tailed grouse, wild turkeys, American woodcocks, blue jays, veeries, wood thrushes, American robins, gray catbirds, brown thrashers, cedar waxwings, scarlet tanagers, rose-breasted and pine grosbeaks, rufous-sided towhees, fox and Henslow's sparrows, Baltimore orioles, common grackles, purple finches, Eastern and least chipmunks, raccoons, fox squirrels, and, of course, bears.

The bristly thickets provide good nesting and protective cover for a variety of small birds and mammals, and in winter, rabbits and deer happily browse the stems.

Densmore and Smith wrote that the Ojibwe and Potawatomi used a tea from the root for healing sore eyes. Densmore went so far as to say, "These [raspberry and wild rose decoctions] would cure cataract unless too far advanced." Back in 1828, the French naturalist Rafinesque, who wrote *Medical Flora* or *Manual of Medical Botany of the United States,* said, "Raspberries afford delicious distilled water, beer, mead, and wine. Said to dissolve tartar of teeth. Twigs dye silk and wool."

Ripe Cherries

Our black, pin, and choke cherry trees are often laden with fruits in July, and evening grosbeaks, among many species of birds, have a field day. The grosbeaks seem unimpressed with whether the cherries are ripe or not, readily taking green ones, then nimbly separating the flesh from the pit, and dropping the pit beneath them.

Second Nestings

Many species of birds will nest twice in a breeding season, which is a surprise to some, but even more surprising is that they may choose different nest sites throughout the season. In early spring, song sparrows and eastern towhees place their nests on the ground, but when nesting again in late June or July, they build their nests in low shrubs. American robins typically place their first nests of the spring low in an evergreen tree, but build their later nests in a higher site within a deciduous tree.

The thinking on this is that dead grasses provide the best cover in spring before the shrubs and trees leaf out, and as the summer progresses and leaves are fully formed, cover becomes equally good or better higher up.

Latitude has a great deal to do with how many clutches a bird may attempt in a breeding season. Most tropical species can lay eggs over a period of at least four months, whereas species in temperate zones like ours can lay for less than two months, and arctic species may have less than one month. A red-winged blackbird usually has enough time to raise two broods in the Midwest, but has only time enough for one brood in Alberta, Canada. To compensate for their lack of breeding opportunities, birds breeding in higher latitudes typically lay more eggs in a clutch than tropical birds.

Shorebird Migration in Mid-July

If you thought summer was just getting into high gear by mid-July, for many shorebirds, the party is already over. Many species of Arctic-nesting shorebirds are now passing through Wisconsin en route to their wintering grounds in southern South America. It's not unusual to see 10 or more species on a good day in July, such as short-billed dowitchers, stilt sandpipers, solitary sandpipers, pectoral sandpipers, least sandpipers, and Wilson phalaropes.

semi-palmated sandpipers

These early migrants are typically males who arrive on their breeding grounds, mate, and then take off, leaving the raising of the young to females. These male shorebirds win no prizes as family men. A little more than a month from now, the young, only 50 to 60 days old, will begin to pass through our area.

It's a bit baffling why these birds leave the tundra so soon after the breeding season when plentiful food is still readily available. The males don't even wait for the breeding season to conclude before they leave. Their remarkably early departure suggests they have more of a tropical heritage than a northern disposition, even though they nest beyond the treeline in the tundra.

Bane There, Done That

Spreading dogbane is currently in flower in many places where there is full sun and disturbed soil, and it's the only flower I know that can compete with the overwhelming perfume of common milkweed. These two species of flowers together can make you swoon with their sweetness.

If you don't know how to identify spreading dogbane, their red stems, opposite blue-green leaves, and nodding pinkish flowers are distinctive. As one would expect from its name, spreading dogbane readily spreads utilizing horizontal rootstalks to clone itself and occupy new ground.

Interestingly, the beautiful little flowers are nasty traps—not for the long-tongued butterflies that are their proper pollinators, but for smaller flies and moths that get caught by their tongues in the flowers' V-shaped nectaries and can't pull out. I picked a few flowers to see this for myself, and by looking under a dissecting microscope found two insects trapped in one of the flowers—one by its leg and the other by its tongue. They were furiously trying to disengage themselves but couldn't, and thus were doomed to die of starvation or frustration, whichever came first.

Break off a stem and it will ooze with an acrid, milky sap very similar to milkweeds. Monarch butterfly caterpillars are reputed to feed only on milkweeds, but they actually also feed and pupate on spreading dogbanes. Look for the large, yellow-striped caterpillars and green, gold-dotted pupal cases on the plant. In addition, the snowberry clearwing, a sphinx moth that resembles a bumblebee, feeds on dogbane.

Few vertebrates eat spreading dogbane for the same reason that few eat milkweed. The milky sap causes vomiting because it contains cymarin, a cardiac glycoside that is toxic not only to dogs and humans but to livestock and most mammals. Insects that can synthesize this chemical are themselves toxic to most creatures that can't tolerate it. So, like milkweeds, spreading dogbanes rely on their reputation, and on the learned responses of birds, mammals, and other predators, to protect them.

"Bane" comes from the Anglo-Saxon word *bana*, meaning a "murderer or destroyer," and it was applied to a number of plants that are poisonous. Thus, we have fleabanes and cowbanes and baneberries and wolfsbane, all of which have dire consequences for certain species. They could be the bane of your existence if you chose to eat them.

If you're ever in need of some string, the stem fibers of spreading dogbane are long and stringy and can be twisted into strong, durable cordage.

Sturgeon Jumping

Greg Holt from Manitowish Waters regularly observes lake sturgeon jumping on Benson Lake. Benson Lake is little more than a widening of the Manitowish River, yet it seems to hold good numbers of lake sturgeon throughout the summer months. The sturgeon jump most often during the middle of the day, but they jump in the early evenings as well. Greg reported that on one July 4 evening he and his family paddled out to the middle of the lake in order to glimpse some long-distance fireworks, and a sturgeon jumped just 15 feet from his boat.

The adult sturgeons in the Manitowish are old, most dating prior to the building of the Turtle-Flambeau dam in 1926. In May, fishery biologists catch, tag, and strip some of the sturgeon of their eggs when they are spawning in the rapids just below the Hwy. 51 bridge northwest of Manitowish Waters. The largest spawning female that the DNR has caught is a 75-inch, 140-pounder. Tens of thousands of sturgeon fingerlings have been released above Benson Lake during the 1990s in hopes of restoring a younger generation of sturgeon. In the meantime, the closest thing we have to watching a whale breach in the Northwoods is watching a sturgeon jump, so if you're paddling the Manitowish, take your time going through Benson Lake and watch for sturgeon.

Late Summer Wildflowers

Late July brings a riot of wildflowers to sunny roadsides and lakeshores. In open, sunny areas, look for wild bergamot, heal-all, fireweed, spotted knapweed, goldenrods, yarrow, mullein, evening primrose, tansy, yellow and white bush clover, daisy fleabane, asters, oxeye daisy, tall buttercup, black-eyed Susan, closed (or bottle) gentian, and orange hawkweed.

In the wetlands, look for blue vervain, swamp milkweed, water parsnip, water hemlock, monkeyflower, arrowhead, yellow and white water lilies, pickerelweed, sweet flag, bur reed, bulrush, wool grass, blue-joint grass, wild rice, and more.

You can still find a few wildflowers in pine woods: look for pipsissewa, wintergreen, one-flowered wintergreen, pyrolla, and Indian pipe in flower.

Red-berried elder (*Sambucus pubens*) provides a burst of color right now with its clusters of red berries.

Heal-all (*Prunella vulgaris*), or self-heal, is very common right now in open woods as well as fields and roadsides. A European import, the light-purple irregular flowers of the heal-all have an unusual lip. Because of the lip, the plant was supposed to cure mouth and throat diseases, according to the ancient Doctrine of Signatures, which stated that the shape of a plant was nature's, or God's, signature regarding its medicinal use.

One early herbalist wrote that there was no herb in the world better at healing wounds than heal-all. Others used it for headaches, internal bleeding, bruises, diarrhea, and mouth and throat ulcers. Modern herbal practitioners ascribe little value to the plant, though one source says it has antibiotic qualities.

Vulgaris means "common," an appropriate title for such a generalist. It's interesting that the word "vulgar," to which we now ascribe the definition of ignorant or crude, came from a word that originally meant "common" or "popular."

Swimming Sandhill Cranes

Terry Daulton called me on July 30, 2002, to ask if I knew anything about the ability of sandhill cranes to swim. She and her husband Jeff had just watched two juvenile sandhills swim about 100 yards across their bay. As the juveniles exited the water and walked up onto the shore, two adult cranes flew over and one landed next to the young cranes.

Was this unusual behavior? This is where a good personal library comes in handy. If you can't be smart, own good books. I skimmed through sections of the book *The Cry of the Sandhill Crane* by Steve Grooms and found just what I needed:

"Sandhill crane chicks can swim, and are quite buoyant and comfortable in the water. The buoyancy is useful, for many greater sandhills nest in marshes, with the nest protected from predators by a moat of water."

So swimming is not unusual. But why would the birds have chosen to swim—couldn't they have flown? Chicks typically begin to fly in 10 weeks, so I needed to count backward to when they normally hatch. Cranes usually are present in our area by the beginning of April, and we conduct our statewide crane count in the middle of the month, expecting that migration is generally concluded by then and cranes are situated where they intend to stay. So, if we conservatively say that cranes should be on nest by May 1, and incubation takes 28 to 31 days, hatching should typically occur around Memorial Day. Terry saw the swimming chicks at the end of July, about 9 weeks after the likely hatch date, and a week or so before they typically fledge.

Interestingly, crane chicks are "nidifugous" (nest-fleeing) birds. Their wings develop slowly, but their legs develop rapidly. A crane chick can walk within a day of hatching and run when two days old.

Trust Lands

I led an old-growth hike on the Van Vliet Hemlock stand in Vilas County in August of 2005. Because the site is owned by the Board of Commissioners of Public Lands (BCPL), I had the opportunity to tell a bit of the agency's story. The BCPL manages about 80,000 acres of Trust Lands remaining from nineteenth century federal land grants to Wisconsin. The agency was established to accept nearly 10 million acres of land granted by the federal government to support public education and infrastructure development in the state.

The land grants fell into two main categories. Educational land grants included the sixteenth section of each of the state's nearly 1,500 townships—the "school section." These lands were almost all sold and the proceeds invested for the long-term benefit of public education. Other educational land grants were used to promote colleges "related to agriculture and the mechanic arts," resulting in lands given for "land grant colleges." These lands are now in use by numerous state colleges and universities.

Transportation land grants were made to support the development of roads, canals, and railroads. Much of this land was simply transferred by the BCPL directly to railroad companies, which were allowed to sell the lands as they chose. Nearly four million acres of lands were granted to the railroads in Wisconsin. Other land grants were used to build connecting roads between military forts, such as Fort Crawford in Prairie du Chien, Fort Winnebago at Portage, Fort Howard in Green Bay, and Fort Wilkins in the U.P.

Swamp land grants were also accepted by the BCPL for the express purpose of draining the lands for agriculture. Those lands were divided in half by the legislature in 1865, with the proceeds from one portion to be used to create a permanent Normal School

Fund to support the training of public school teachers.

The long and short of it is that the BCPL sold millions of those acres to create the Trust Fund that in large part has helped finance school districts and municipalities throughout Wisconsin to the tune of more than $346 million in the last 25 years.

The remaining lands are managed for sustained timber production and forest conservation. Most importantly, some of these lands are the best remaining examples of natural communities we have left in Wisconsin. Nearly 20,000 acres have outstanding qualities that could give them state natural area status.

The Van Vliet hemlock stand is one such site, containing a managed, old-growth hemlock-hardwood stand with scattered super-canopy white pines. The BCPL owns numerous other old-growth parcels that also represent this rare age-class—all of which, in my humble opinion, deserve immediate designation as state natural areas. At the least, they should be placed into a deferred/reserved status.

The BCPL office is in Lake Tomahawk on Hwy. 47, and staff members there can help in recommending sites to visit.

When It Rains, It Pours

The big news in early July 2000 was the amount of rain that fell on the Northwoods. Our gauge in Manitowish showed about 3 inches of rain, while reports of 7 inches or more in Oneida County were common.

Besides into basements, where does all that water go? Here's the breakdown:

1. Evaporation from the leaves and stems

When rain falls, the wetted surfaces of leaves, stems, soil, and rocks immediately begin losing water to evaporation. In heavily vegetated areas, a large quantity of the rain is intercepted by branches and stems of plants. In a deciduous forest and in mature croplands, 10 to 30 percent of the annual rainfall is evaporated before it even reaches the soil.

2. Transpiration out through the leaves.

Transpiration is the means by which all plants expel water from their leaves during photosynthesis. Water is taken up by roots from the soil, moves up the trunks as sap, and is transpired through the stomata, which are thousands of tiny holes on the underside of every leaf. An acre of corn expels 11,000 to 15,000 liters of water per day into the air. A single large oak tree gives off nearly 150,000 liters per year. Transpiration accounts for even more water loss than evaporation.

3. Into the soil

While all soil can absorb rainfall, the rate varies according to the soil type. Sandy soils, for instance, have a high rate of absorption, while clay soils have a low rate. Termed the "infiltration capacity," this absorbency rate declines during a rainstorm as the soil gets saturated, much like a sponge that can only hold so much water. Any rain that tries to enter the ground in excess of the infiltration capacity accumulates on the ground surface. The overland flow increases where the land surface is compacted. Our most extreme compaction is accomplished through the imposition of acres of asphalt. In extreme cases, up to 100 percent of the rainfall can travel as overland flow.

4. Into rivers and lakes through groundwater

Rain that infiltrates into the soil may reach the groundwater, from whence it is slowly discharged to streams and lakes. The base flow in a river is due to groundwater entering the stream channel. During periods of no rainfall, water levels go down, but river water still continues to flow because much of that water is coming from groundwater. The Manitowish River, for instance, is called a perennial river rather than an intermittent river, because it continues to flow even in times of no rainfall. An intermittent river dries up and becomes a "wash" during prolonged dry spells.

If you thought the July 2000 rain was extraordinarily intense, remember the storms in 1993 that led to massive flooding in the Midwest, breaking all records. New London, Iowa, had the most intense rainstorm of them all—6.5 inches of rain fell in 15 minutes! People claimed they could hardly breathe while the rain was falling.

Aquatic Flowers

I paddled the Bear River with a group of people during the last week in July of 2003 and the early-flowering aquatic plants were blossoming in profusion. Pickerelweed and white and yellow water lilies were most prevalent, but swamp milkweed and wild roses dotted the shorelines, cattails and bulrushes emerged in flower from the shallows, and wild rice was just starting to flower in the enormous beds that the Bear is known for.

While I admire the beauty of aquatic flowers, I also admire their remarkable ability to adapt. They live with their roots continually submerged in water, in widely varying water levels, and they must adapt to currents or waves that tug and tear at them every second of every day.

How do they do it? First, they have to breathe. The stems and leaves of emergent plants like pickerelweed, cattail, and arrowhead are laced with spongy tissue, called aerenchyma, that allows oxygen to flow down to the roots, while also making the leaves and stems buoyant and able to rise and fall with changing water levels. Look at the stem of a white water lily and you'll see four air tubes running the length of the stem, acting as the ductwork that moves oxygen to the roots and carbon dioxide back to the surface.

To hang on in the current, the roots of most aquatic plants form an interlocking network, an elaborate weaving in the sediments, that holds both the plants and the sediments in place.

To prevent their leaves from tearing in the wind and waves, floating-leaf plants have evolved a leathery texture with a thick cuticle that protects the upper leaf surface and sheds water to prevent them from becoming submerged. With a magnifying glass, you can see the stomata, the small air holes that cover the upper leaf surface and exchange gases. Submerged plants use an opposite strategy, producing flexible and often finely divided leaves that reduce resistance to water currents. The leaves have no waxy cuticle on their surface so that gases can be exchanged in the water. That's why when you pull a submerged plant like the ribbony wild celery out of the water, it collapses into a limp mass, but in the water it spreads out and is buoyant.

Get out those flower guides and try to put a name to some of the aquatic flowers. "Give things the dignity of their names," writes Natalie Goldberg. "When we know the name of something, it brings us closer to the ground. It takes the blur out of our mind. It connects us to the earth. It makes us more awake."

I recommend the book *Through the Looking Glass: A Field Guide to Aquatic Plants* (Susan Bormen, et al). It's a straightforward manual, written for the amateur, and it offers excellent line drawings.

Marsh Love Potion

White and yellow water lilies are now in flower and are easy to identify even by their leaves. The large leaf of the white (*Nymphaea odorata*) water lily comes to a right angle in its notch (remember "right-white"), while yellow (*Nuphar variegata*) water lily leaves are more oval and rounded at the notches.

Why would water lilies have evolved leaves the size and shape of dinner plates? They are almost certainly an adaptation to surviving nasty weather. Round, smooth-edged shapes provide the least resistance to wind and wave action. The tough, waxy surface of the leaf presumably also evolved to resist water and hail penetration. Note that the stomata (breathing pores) appear on the topside of the leaf, rather than the underside as is common in most plants.

Sometimes a strong wind will pick up the leaf and turn it over, revealing a red underside on the white water lilies. The red pigment is thought to help raise leaf temperatures slightly, thus increasing transpiration.

Individual flowers only live a short period of time. The bisexual flowers operate in a unisexual manner, the female parts opening before the male to prevent self-pollination.

Shortly after fertilization, the flower closes, its stem coils, and the flower head withdraws underwater. The seeds take about a month to mature inside a fleshy fruit. The fruit eventually breaks off, floats to the surface, and releases the seeds. The seeds then sink and germinate the following spring, reaching maturity three years later.

The most remarkable historical usage of white water lilies that I've read about was their use as a love potion. For the love potion to work, the flowers had to be picked during a full moon, though the pickers had to wear earplugs to prevent being bewitched by the local water nymphs. The dried flowers were then worn as love talismans.

Feel free to try this. I think it may have more likelihood of success than an ad in the "Personals" section of the newspaper, plus there's no agonizing over how to describe yourself as the catch of the year. And it's free! The one hitch—how do you explain why you're wearing a bunch of dead flowers?

Bog Orchids

I led a paddle trip on a lake near Sayner on July 29, 2005, and while we were there to look mostly at the wild rice, I also spotted two species of orchids in the bog mat surrounding the lake. One, the tall white bog-orchid (*Platanthera dilatata*), was about 18 inches tall with small, very fragrant white flowers. The other, known as the small northern bog orchid (*Platanthera obtusata*), was about half that height, with small greenish-white flowers.

The tall white bog-orchid was most impressive, its brilliant white flowers standing well above the bog mat and gleaming in the sun. Their luminescence served as the inspiration for the other common name given to this species—bog candles.

Back in June, Mary and I were biking in the Bayfield Peninsula and stopped at the Bark Bay Slough State Natural Area. As we looked over the water and the adjoining bog, we first saw literally hundreds and hundreds of the tall red flowers of pitcher plants, and then we noticed dozens of smaller magenta-colored flowers that we couldn't quite identify from a distance with our binoculars. So we took our shoes off, and walked carefully into the pleasantly cold bog. To our delight, we found the purplish flowers were dragon's-mouth orchids (*Arethusa bulbosa*), an orchid we rarely see. Still, as rare as they seem to be in Wisconsin, I was quite surprised to learn that in the patterned peatland complexes of northern Minnesota, dragon's-mouth populations can number in the tens of thousands.

Just a week later, I trekked along with a friend in a large bog complex near Springstead, and luck struck twice—the bog supported good numbers of dragon's-mouth orchids as well.

The beauty of the dragon's-mouth is its pink lip with rose-purple splotches. The lip curves downward and has a crest of fleshy yellow bristles running down its center, and though I've no idea what the tongue of a dragon looks like, this would be a marvelously imaginative rendering. Arethusa was a beautiful water nymph in Greek mythology, and the flower fits the image, with a pretty face that looks like it has upright ears. Some wildflower enthusiasts go so far as to say that the dragon's-mouth is the most beautiful flower in all of North America.

Numerous other orchids grow in bogs, including the common pink lady's slipper, grass pink, and rose pogonia, all of which typically flower in June. Wisconsin supports some 42 species of orchids, and many call the bogs home. If you've never walked in a bog, you might give it a try. Be sure to take a partner along. Sometimes you can step through the bog mat and put yourself in a bit of a pickle, but the potential finds can be worth the risk.

bee at rose pogonia

How Forests Heal

On July 30, 1999, a windstorm toppled and/or snapped an estimated 100,000 trees in Vilas County, leaving a great deal of sadness in its wake, as well as work. Many people lost big old pines that are not replaceable within a human lifetime. Sites that held an aura of age and dignity due to the presence of the old trees now looked entirely different, almost unrecognizable. The feel of such places changed, and that was a very significant loss.

But from the perspective of a forest seedling or sapling, the blowdown offered great opportunities. The question is what species will thrive in the openings left behind by the destruction, and the answer depends on a host of physical and biological factors.

One physical factor is the amount of sunlight that can now reach the forest floor. Some sites lost only a few trees among many, leaving relatively small gaps in the forest canopy. Most woodlands have an understory of seedling and sapling trees that are "waiting in the wings" for just such gaps. Sugar maple and eastern hemlock seedlings may wait 100 or more years in the shade, barely gathering enough sunlight to survive and remain the same size year after year. Some saplings of hemlock only 2 inches in diameter have been found to be 200 years old!

They have the patience of Job, biding their time until a hole in the canopy opens. Once sufficient sunlight penetrates, a race ensues to see which branches penetrate the sky first.

This process is called "gap phase reproduction," and species that can tolerate full shade, like hemlock, basswood, sugar maple, and yellow birch, employ this strategy in the competitive world of a shaded, older forest.

Other sites suffered near or complete blowdown from the storm, opening the entire forest floor to sun. Here, surviving seedlings and saplings will face stiff competition from seeds that blow in, are carried in, or are still viable in the soil from previous years. Species that thrive in full sunlight and disturbed conditions, like popple (quaking aspen and big tooth aspen), jack pine, white birch, and red pine, have a big edge in taking over a stand. These trees are the pioneers of the forest, building upon cleared land in the toughest of circumstances.

Consider other factors that determine what survives and what doesn't. White birch repopulated much of the burned-over lands of northern Wisconsin in the early part of the century, because it germinates very well on exposed mineral soils. However, it's small seeds have a devil of a time piercing the leaf litter on unburned forest floors, so we see little germination and reestablishment of white birch today. But let a fire consume that layer of duff, and white birch can dominate. I doubt whether we will ever again allow fires of such quantity and quality, without which white birch faces imposing competition with limited prospects for success.

Most deciduous tree species vegetatively reproduce when knocked down. White birch and basswood clumps are common in the Northwoods, the vase-like growth form originating from sprouts off the stump of the parent tree that died. Unfortunately, none of our conifers will resprout from a stump, though the branches of white cedar that has tipped over can take root to form a line of new trees.

Popple may be the most adept tree of all at vegetative reproduction. Cut an aspen stand and the roots of each tree will "sucker," sending up new shoots from the old roots all around the stump. Aspen's prodigious growth, often 3 feet or more per year, frequently outpaces the competition, regenerating a clear-cut forest into trees 20 feet high in a relatively short period. So those popple woods that fell to the storm are very likely to resprout popple.

Which trees take hold may be a matter as simple as what species has seeds present. After the big cuts of white pine at the turn of the century, the Northwoods saw few white pine for many decades, in significant part because there was little seed source.

Even the presence of seeds doesn't ensure success. Hemlocks often germinate on fire-scarred sites, but they may not survive due to browsing by deer and rabbits. Red oak might enter a site if not for their acorns whetting the appetites of deer and squirrels.

Even if seeds are present and no predation occurs, do the right temperature and moisture conditions exist for germination and seedling survival? A drought year would work strongly against hemlock, which thrives in moist conditions. A very cold winter and spring might favor species like balsam fir that can tolerate intense cold and heavy snows.

Soil conditions are another factor. Our soils typically favor species that tolerate dry conditions, because our sandy loams percolate water through them like a colander with big holes, which is in large part why we grow such beautiful pines and so little corn.

One way or another, we will have the "weedy" species to thank for pioneering our largest blowdowns, and thus healing the wounds. In forest succession, where species of trees, shrubs, and wildflowers continually and gradually replace one another, the pioneer species must do the initial work. They are replaced over time by species that can live in their partial shade (the intermediate species), and finally by species that can live in full shade (the climax species).

Seldom does the successional path lead to old growth climax forests. Nature inflicts disturbance—from fire to blowdown to disease to insects—all too often.

The colonization of each blowdown site will be a unique opportunity to study how our forests heal themselves after such powerful injury. One study of sugar maple estimated that 4,000 seedlings spring up every year under a mature sugar maple, totaling over one million seedlings in the life of a 350-year-old tree. Out of those, about 50,000 lasted into the second year, some 1,400 made it 10 years, 35 grew over 20 feet tall, two reached 150 years old, and only one was lucky enough to reach full maturity. So there's an enormous amount of mortality in the understory as well as the canopy.

I encourage schools and public and private landowners to watch, measure, and record this regrowth. It will give all of us a glimpse into the healing arts practiced by trees.

A Damming Controversy

I attended the 2003 annual meeting of the Manitowish Waters Lake Association and listened to a presentation by two DNR biologists regarding problems associated with how the Rest Lake dam is operated on the Manitowish River and chain of lakes. The biologists spelled out a series of dilemmas caused by fluctuations in the downstream river depth and flow. These problems result from either holding water back to fill the upstream chain of lakes, or rapidly dumping water out to drop the chain during times of high water or during the winter drawdown. The focus of their discussion was on the remnant population of sturgeon that is left in the Manitowish River, and how altering the release and storage of water could potentially help restore this population.

Some quick background: The chain's water level is rapidly lowered 3½ feet in October so that property owners do not need to take out their docks over the winter. There is no other stated reason by the dam owner, XCEL Energy, for this drawdown. XCEL receives no value from this drawdown or from stored water during the summer. Once the ice has gone off Rest Lake, planks are put in the dam to hold water back and fill the chain up to the desired level, while still allowing a bare minimum of 50 cubic feet per second (cfs) of water to go through the dam.

From a human standpoint, the problem is clear—downstream property owners are regularly flooded out or left high and dry, depending on how water is stored and released by the dam. In the spring, snowmelt waters flow unimpeded through the dam and flood downstream areas until the moment the ice goes off Rest Lake. Then the water is held back to fill the chain. At that moment, floodwaters immediately begin to recede and often within a few days the downstream river will drop 2 to 3 feet.

In October when the drawdown occurs, the downstream river rises several feet and again floods many people's properties, sometimes overflowing their docks and flooding basements.

From a natural history standpoint, the problem is less easily measured. In a dry spring, the little water available is held back to its maximum potential, and the river depth goes way down. The sturgeon then either can't make it up to their spawning area, or may get left high and dry on the rocks they are spawning on, in which case they must be physically dragged to deeper water.

If we get a big rain in the spring after the sturgeon have spawned, the high water is released over the dam in a large pulse in order to keep water levels even in the chain, resulting in a flood surge that scours the sturgeon eggs off the rocks.

Of course, the impact of such fluctuations must go well beyond the sturgeon and affect other species, though none of us knows just what the effects might be since no long-term studies have been made of the Manitowish system.

The meeting brought out a lot of fears of the unknown, and fear usually fuels anger and suspicion. Comments were made like these:

- Since sturgeon aren't fished by most people, what do we need them for? Get rid of them. Who cares about sturgeon?
- Since the DNR doesn't have long-term data from when the dam was built in 1887, how do we know that sturgeon haven't always been in such low numbers? (Currently only about five 80-year-old or older females are spawning each spring.)
- Since the downstream property owners bought their property after the dam was built, they should have known better. It may be a problem, but it's their problem, and it's their fault they bought into it.
- There is no problem. It's all a fabrication by the DNR, which, as we all know, is the Evil Empire and can never be trusted.

Not a soul brought up the idea that whatever would be best for the river and the lakes is what we should do.

The discussions continued through 2005, and the lake associations maintained their stance that no changes were necessary. The DNR finally proposed changes in the dam flows in February of 2006, but as of this writing, the issue remains in limbo.

I'm genuinely worried about what will transpire, and I'm praying that our love of this place will ultimately guide us to do what's best for the river and the natural community it supports. I'm praying that our discussions won't continue to degenerate into an us-versus-them shouting match, or a which-side-of-the-dam you live on feud. I'm praying we finally come together and rise to the occasion.

Too many times such issues have caused great discord and harmed the relationships within a community of people. I don't believe any of us wants that, so we must try to fully listen to and understand one another, and ultimately practice the best form of stewardship we can for the lakes and waters that we so love.

common loon
adult and chicks

August

Let your imagination drift away from the Earth into those yawning depths where galaxies whirl like snowflakes in a storm. From somewhere out there among the myriad galaxies, imagine looking back to the one dancing flake that is the trillion stars of our Milky Way. Galaxies are as numerous as snowflakes in a storm!

—Chet Raymo, *Skeptics and True Believers*

Birds often seem strangely absent in August. In fact, the birds are still here (except for very early migrators), but they lose most of their desire to sing once their chicks have fledged from their nests. By mid-August, territorial boundaries loosen or are erased altogether, most pair bonds go the way of high school romances, and birds start hanging out in mixed flocks.

I love quiet, but not silence. Kobayashi Issa, a sixteenth-century haiku poet, wrote that birds "sing the music of heaven in this world." I've been asked many times whether birds sing for pure joy. No one will ever know, but I know they bring joy to me. Joseph Wood Krutch wrote: "The ornithologist who has convinced himself that bird song has 'nothing to do' with joy has not taken anything away from the robin. Ornithology notwithstanding, the robin continues to pour forth his heart in profuse strains of unpremeditated art."

W. Warde Fowler said in 1895: "So of all the sounds which wild nature brings to the human ear, [bird] songs are the most powerful in their contribution to our happiness. Men high and low, rich and poor, have always felt this, and always will feel it."

For me, there's always a sadness to August that counterbalances the exuberant joy of spring. The choir has had its curtain calls, and the concert has diminished to only a few solo voices singing backstage.

Where Have All the Birds Gone?

We tend to see far fewer birds in August. Most northern birds undergo what's called a "post-nuptial molt." All adult birds undergo a molt at least once a year. The post-nuptial molt is perfectly timed to coincide with the time when food is most plentiful, the energy demands of nesting are over, and the energy demands of migrating have yet to begin. Most birds molt their wings and tail feathers symmetrically and in pairs, enabling them to maintain the ability to fly. Still, they seem to prefer to lie low and remain relatively secretive during this time period.

On the other hand, many waterbirds—loons, grebes, ducks, geese, swans, and most cranes and rails—lose all of their flight feathers at the same time, grounding them for a short period. In order to avoid predation, they become very secretive, spending most of their time in shallow water hidden in the tall cattails, sedges, and grasses that so beautifully grace our waters at this time of year.

Aristotle's Views on Migration

Our youngest daughter Callie is a Grecoophile—a lover of all things having to do with Ancient Greece, and she often discusses with us the theories of some Greek philosopher or another such as Aristotle. However, Aristotle was not only a philosopher. He was also considered the greatest scientist of his time. No doubt he was, but when I decided to go to Aristotle's writings to see what he thought about migration, I found he had more than a few "unusual" ideas, nearly all of which were accepted as truth for more than 2,000 years, until studies in the 1800s disproved them:

Aristotle understood that some birds migrate, and specifically noted such behavior in pelicans and cranes. However, he wrote:

"A great number of birds also go into hiding ... Swallows, for instance, have been often found in holes, quite denuded of their feathers, and the kite on its first appearance has been seen to fly from out some such hiding-place ... the stork, the owzel, the turtle-dove, and the lark, all go into hiding ... the thrush and the starling hide."

Aristotle also believed in transformations, writing that the European redstart, a common summer bird, simply changed into the European robin, a bird that migrates south into Greece for the winter, while in reality the redstart leaves Greece to winter in Africa.

Medieval Europeans amplified the notion of transformation. When seeing small, black-and-white geese appear in the winter (birds that had migrated from the Arctic), they named them barnacle geese, somehow determining that they grew from tubular, "goose-necked" barnacles that cling to floating driftwood.

We've clearly come a long way in our understanding of migration, but when I see a black-bellied plover, I'm still left in awe of the many mysteries of migration, and how little we yet know.

Beating the Heat!

Lord, it was hot in August of 2001. If I'd wanted to live in Georgia, I would have moved there a long time ago. I knew that whining was unbecoming, and that in January, we'd all be daydreaming of those wonderful days last August when we were swimming all day long. But there's a limit to all good things, and we exceeded it that year. I must admit, though, that there were some advantages. We ate ripe tomatoes from our garden in late July, a record for us.

With all those warm feathers serving to insulate them, what do birds do to beat the heat? We were closely observing an eagle during the heat, and it clearly had its beak open. It was almost certainly panting, though we couldn't see its chest heaving as we would with a dog. Birds have no sweat glands, so birds utilize their respiratory tract to lose heat. Songbirds pant, while non-songbirds, like the eagles, rapidly vibrate their upper throat and floor of their mouths, a process called the "gular flutter."

Large soaring birds also lose heat by soaring in the afternoon thermals. I led three trips on the Turtle-Flambeau Flowage that August, and each day we saw numerous eagles and osprey soaring, possibly in an attempt to beat the heat.

Batesian Mimicry

No, this isn't a bunch of folks making fun of me (though it's been know to occur). Since monarch butterflies eat the bitter-tasting juices of milkweed and spreading dogbane, they have earned the respect of predators, which generally leave them quite alone. Somewhere and somehow along the evolutionary wheel of adaptation, the viceroy butterfly came to look almost exactly like the monarch, and thus through its mimicry, it also is disdained by predators, though it would likely taste just fine. This mimicry was first described by the naturalist H. W. Bates, no relation, who was later honored by having the process named after him.

Northwoods Time Travel

Jim Bokern and I co-led a canoe/kayak trip down a portion of the Bear River in August of 2001. What is most remarkable about the Bear is that it appears fundamentally unchanged over the centuries in its course and character, still flowing quietly and circuitously through wild rice marshes, sedge meadows, and occasional pine uplands.

Despite its diminutive size, the Bear has a rich history, once having served as a major artery in the fur trade by transporting traders and trade goods to the two fur trading posts in Lac du Flambeau.

It's difficult to imagine long, heavily laden birch-bark canoes plying this shallow river, but so they did, and in significant numbers over the course of nearly two centuries. Unfortunately, prior to the fur trade, it's impossible to say how much the Sioux and Ojibwe, and the native people before them, may have used the river. No written records remain from that time, so the river holds its own secrets from times earlier than the late 1600s.

However, in the early 1800s, numerous traders and explorers wrote journals that we can read today to get a sense of the character of the rivers and the people's lives. Amateur historians used to have to dig to access these journals, but now Jim Bokern, in coordination with the North Lakeland Discovery Center, has put together a Website called "Digital Time Travelers" that makes it very easy to read the journals. Journals from Malhiot in 1806, Stevens in 1824-1841, Doty in 1832, Allen in 1832, Hall in 1832, Cram in 1840, Gray in 1846, and Norwood in 1847 are all available to read. This exceptional Website is accessible through the Discovery Center's home page at www.discoverycenter.net. Click on "Links" to access it.

Quoting from the Website: "Digital Time Travelers is an interdisciplinary experience that integrates the study of both cultural and natural resources. All research is based on the analysis of 18th and 19th century Wisconsin and the Upper Peninsula of Michigan. The sponsors of the Digital Time Travelers Program Jim Bokern, Ryan Christianson, and the North Lakeland Discovery Center hope to partner with other interested people in documenting the unique cultural and natural resources of the Northwoods while following centuries-old canoe routes and portages. We are hopeful that these web pages and experiences will create a broad forum to promote discussion, debate and achieve new levels of understanding regarding the early natural and cultural resources. The final product of Digital Time Travelers will be a web site that will allow users to navigate the north woods with a virtual canoe trip supported with journals, research, images and observations of its creators."

Peak Berry Time

We picked our first blackberries on August 8, 1997, and there was a host of blackberries yet to come ripe. Blueberries could still be found in significant numbers, while raspberries were just about gone by.

Thimbleberries were ripe as well. The salmon-colored berries make a good jam. Some find the berries tart, but they taste pretty mild to me. Look for shrubs 3 to 6 feet tall with large maple-like leaves located usually in open rocky woods and along shores. Thimbleberry is a far-northern shrub, found most often in boreal forests, so we're at the southernmost edge of its range here in the Lakeland area.

Rattlesnake Plantain

While camping in early August 2004, Mary, Callie, and I found dozens of the orchid rattlesnake plantain in flower beneath a stand of old-growth hemlocks. Three species occur in our area, but the one we saw exclusively was lesser rattlesnake plantain (*Goodyera repens*), the smallest of the three species. Interestingly, rattlesnake plantain will grow in conifer bogs, on mossy cliffs and rock ledges, and in dry to moist upland forests. But their essential requirements for life are cool, nutrient-poor, acidic soils in full to partial shade, which are pretty much the polar opposite of those of most plants, which prefer life in warm habitats with nutrient-rich soil. This orchid doesn't do well when the living is too easy.

The small white flowers require magnification by a hand lens in order to be seen well enough to be appreciated. A hood extends over the flower's lip, giving it the appearance of an open bird beak.

The rosette of dark green leaves is mottled with white or pale green reticulation along the veins. With an active imagination, a snake-like skin might be envisioned, hence the name.

Others say the name derives from the curative powers of the leaves when applied to snake bites. Mrs. William Starr Dana, in her 1893 book *How to Know the Wild Flowers,* wrote that "the Indians had such faith in its remedial virtues that they would allow a snake to drive its fangs into them for a small sum, if they had the leaves on hand to apply to the wound."

In his 1775 volume *The History of the American Indians*, James Adair wrote: "When an Indian perceives he is struck by a snake, he immediately chews some of the root, and having swallowed a sufficient quantity of it, he applies some to the wound ... For a short space of time, there is a terrible conflict through all of the body, by the jarring qualities of the burning poison, and the strong antidote; but the poison is soon repelled through the same channels it entered, and the patient is cured."

The question with such writings is always how does one separate folklore from fact? Any volunteers out there willing to serve as a test case?

I didn't think so.

I like Thoreau's simple appreciation of a rattlesnake plantain leaf: "It looks like art."

Blowdown Normalcy

The August 9, 2005, windstorm that blew down hundreds of trees at the North Lakeland Discovery Center and Camp Jorn in Manitowish Waters offered a good example of a "normal" blowdown in the Northwoods. We can reach this conclusion because we have a good idea of how frequent and extensive blowdowns were prior to settlement, due to the work of two ecologists, Charles Canham and Orie Loucks.

Canham and Loucks studied original surveyor records, and noted that by 1850 surveyors were required to record the tracks of tornadoes and windstorms they encountered along survey lines. These paths are commonly called "windfall" or "fallen timber" in their records. In general, the surveyors recorded the bearing of a blowdown and its position along survey lines, mapping the outline of each blowdown on their sketch maps.

Canham and Loucks exhaustively examined the surveyor's notes and maps for the nearly 16 million acres of the pre-settlement hemlock-hardwood forests of northern Wisconsin. They concluded that catastrophic winds maintained 17 to 25 percent of the pre-settlement landscape in younger forests. Thus, up to one-fourth of the Northwoods was recovering from blowdowns at any given time. That's a lot of wind and a lot of fallen trees.

The storm that hit Manitowish Waters, then, was part of a blowdown pattern that has been impacting the Northwoods for many hundreds of years. I don't know what the estimated size of the blowdown was at the Discovery Center and Camp Jorn, but I'd be surprised if it was more than 40 acres, making it a smaller than average blowdown for the Northwoods.

The trees that blew over were those most susceptible at the time, and, obviously, those that were hit by the highest winds. Susceptibility of an individual tree to windthrow is a function of four things:

- the characteristics of the tree
- the site
- the surrounding forest structure
- the nature of the storm system

A lot of big pines came down in Manitowish Waters. That makes sense given that they were taller than the surrounding trees, and given that their roots were fairly shallow and weak in the sand soils of the area. These factors made them relatively easy to knock down.

The Value of Blowdowns

It's typical to use words like "disaster" and "devastation" to describe the destructive aspects of powerful storms. But if we consider that ecological disturbances are really agents of change, and not disasters, then the language of destruction is inappropriate.

Clearly, there's a sense of loss and sadness and often a sense of waste associated with a blowdown. I have certainly felt that way, and I've been particularly emotional if I had a personal connection to the forest that was hit.

But we also need to ask the ecological question of whether blowdowns actually damage a forest community. And the answer is no. Certainly there are individual trees that are killed, but the word "damage" implies that there is evidence that the blowdown in some manner harmed ecosystem processes, significantly reduced the number of species, or reduced their average abundance.

If the truth be known, just the opposite is true. Blowdowns typically create increases in diversity and abundance of both tree and herbaceous species.

Blowdowns also cycle nutrients more quickly through fallen coarse woody debris and increase habitat for an array of species that utilizes standing snags or fallen logs. A proportion of older trees are replaced with younger trees, and canopy diversity typically increases.

If a blowdown only affects a patch within a larger forest, its long-term effect on the whole forest will be slight. And from an ecological perspective, this is beneficial. Consider that mortality is always taking place in a forest; thus, a pulse of downed trees can be viewed as normal and positive. The openings that are created will fill with herbs, shrubs, tree seedlings, and saplings, and will be alive with birds and mammals. Nothing goes to waste—opportunity only increases as change occurs.

A true old-growth forest is not uniformly old. Our pre-settlement forests were a mosaic. Patches of different species and age-classes created a biologically diverse landscape, though one clearly dominated by old trees.

Blowdowns aren't forces of devastation as much as they are the arbiters of sometimes subtle and sometimes profound change. We may feel devastated by what we see as loss, but the forest endures, as does its wildness. Blowdowns are simply examples of the power and drama of the natural world. They are forces and places that demonstrate the wildness of nature, as well as its restorative abilities.

Brown Pelican Saga

In the July section of this book, I reported the sighting of an adult brown pelican on Big Sand Lake near Phelps. Sadly, the pelican was found dead on July 30, 2002.

But the story of brown pelicans in the Northwoods didn't end there. On August 4, 2002, Larry Mirkes on Mercer Lake in Mercer telephoned and laughingly told me to come get the brown pelican on his lake before it ate all the fish. He said his boat was still in the lake if I wanted to come see it.

Fifteen minutes later we were walking out on his pier when the brown pelican flew right in front of us and out of sight around a bend in the shoreline. We hopped in Larry's boat and tried to follow, but it was gone. We searched along the shorelines for 10 minutes or more, and were getting discouraged. Where, after all, can a bird with an 8-foot wingspan hide? Then suddenly it was nearly overhead and wheeling into a nearby bay to land. It stayed on the water for a minute, and from studying its markings, I could determine it was clearly an immature brown pelican. Then it was up in the air and flying directly at us in the boat. If brown pelicans were known to attack boaters, I would have been diving for cover. Fortunately it turned and flew some 30 feet off our bow, skimming over the water.

During the next 10 minutes, it performed three more close flybys, and we were able to observe it twice as it tucked its wings in from a height and plunged into the water for a fish. Both times it came up to the surface, extended its neck straight up and seemed to be swallowing something.

I left shortly thereafter with the pelican calmly preening itself on a floating swim dock some 50 yards down the shore from Larry's pier.

Naturally, I immediately posted my sighting on the Wisconsin BirdNet, an e-mail listserve that functions as a sighting bulletin board and bird discussion forum for Wisconsin birders. Naturally several birders drove to Mercer the next morning to see the pelican and, naturally, it was gone.

Just where would a brown pelican go, given that brown pelicans are coastal saltwater birds from Florida that have no business hanging out on inland lakes in Wisconsin?

That night (August 5) I listened to a phone message from Jim Rice saying he had seen a brown pelican earlier in the morning on Pike Lake, which is located on Hwy. 70 about 15 miles west of Minocqua). The bird was flying around several fishing boats as if it knew that it could get a handout or might be able to steal a meal.

Could this have been the Mercer Lake bird? From Jim's description, the pelican appeared to be an immature, like the bird seen on Mercer Lake.

But the trail got cold. No news of any kind came in until a week later when an immature brown pelican was reported on Lake Redstone in Sauk County, northwest of Reedsburg. The bird was seen on August 7, and again on August 11.

Birders along the way got worked up, because rarities are exciting events. They fire the imagination and humble us with unanswerable questions. To be graced where you live with a bird that belongs more than 1,000 miles away is quite a gift.

The Archer

In August, wetland flowers festoon our lakes and rivers in an array of colors. Few of these aquatic species are more interesting than arrowhead, though arrowhead displays a less showy flower than many of our more vain species. Arrowhead flowers grace river edges and lakeshores from late July through early August. The male flower displays three silky-white petals arranged in whorls of three high up on a separate stem. The female flowers also bloom in whorls of three, but lower on the stem and clustered inconspicuously in a head.

The leaves offer the quickest key to identification, though their extreme variability can make differentiating between arrowhead species difficult. Submersed plants typically develop narrow, ribbon-like leaves that look like a long, flat grass, while emergent plants display broad, arrow-shaped leaves, with sundry divergences in between. We host numerous species of arrowheads, the leaves varying dramatically from grass-leaved arrowhead (*Sagittaria graminea*) with its narrow to broad spoon-shaped leaves, to the broad-leaf arrowhead (*Sagittaria latifolia*) with leaves true to its name—shaped like perfect arrowheads.

Arrowhead can grow in several feet of water completely submersed, or up on muddy banks. The leaves appear to adapt themselves to the water levels—the ribbony leaves offer the least resistance to a water current, while the broad leaves offer the most photosynthetic surface area.

Sagittarius is, of course, the archer, and the image of his sharp arrows gave rise to the genus name Sagittaria.

Small 1- to 2-inch potato-like tubers form at the end of long subterranean runners that originate at the base of the plant. These can be harvested by using a hoe or rake to free them from the mud. Gathered by the Ojibwe in the fall, then strung and hung to dry in the wigwam, the tubers were later boiled like potatoes. People were eating arrowhead tubers 3,000 years ago according to studies in the western U.S. In the far East, arrowhead is cultivated as a crop along the margins of rice paddies.

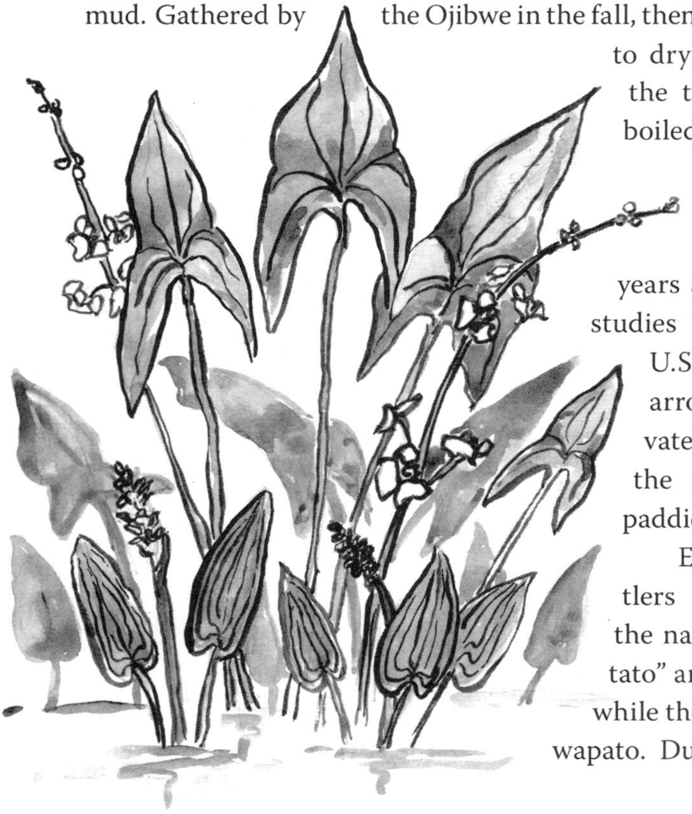

European settlers gave arrowhead the names "swamp potato" and "duck potato," while the Ojibwe called it wapato. Duck potato refers to arrowhead's delectability as a waterfowl food. Tundra and trumpeter swans dig out the tubers and eat the small, flat seeds. Black ducks, gadwalls, mallards, pintails, wigeons, wood ducks, canvasbacks, and an array of other waterfowl help themselves at the arrowhead table too, though the tubers may be buried too deep at times to root out. Muskrat and beaver also relish the tubers, and even porcupines venture into the water to eat the leaves and stems. Beds of arrowhead leaves also offer shelter and shade for fish.

Arrowhead leaves transpire water very efficiently, and are often blamed for drawing down water levels in seasonal reservoirs and pools. However, if you're trying to restore a shoreline or aquatic plant bed in front of your property, arrowhead has a wide tolerance of pH, grows on a variety of sediments and in a variety of water levels, and removes phosphorous from the water and sediments. Planting the tubers usually leads to rapid clonal growth. For a combination of beauty, wildlife value, and ecological utility, arrowhead can hardly be beat.

Canada Geese—
A Love Affair Gone Bad

I've been a part of numerous indignant conversations in which Canada geese have been castigated not only as a nuisance, but as a problem requiring their immediate removal. These discussions are ironic in that it was only a decade ago that people in the Northwoods were literally thrilled to see more geese nesting in our area. Due in large part to the public's desire to see more geese, efforts were made by the DNR from the mid-1980s to the mid-1990s to import geese from southern Wisconsin and Green Bay to our area, and I don't know of a single person who wasn't applauding the effort. Our overall habitat, when kept wild, is relatively poor for geese, and there was little legitimate concern for their growing too large in number.

The geese were released in major water bodies and marshes like the Powell Marsh, Willow Flowage, Rainbow Flowage, Little Turtle Flowage, and Turtle-Flambeau Flowage. We saw very little increase in local populations until the mid-90s when populations started to take off.

What happened?

Well, for one thing, the geese were often protected and fed by locals. In the town of Mercer, lots of us used to feed flocks of geese that hung out by the Mercer School. Because the school is located in town, the geese were effectively inhabiting a wildlife refuge, safe from hunting and most predation. In our desire to see more geese, we provided them a refuge for over a decade and fed them more corn than an average hog might have wanted, all of which spelled population increase.

Then there's the fact that geese are grazers, as you probably well know. As housing has increased in the last decade, so has their favored habitat—otherwise known as lawns—for grazing. All this newly developed private property wasn't lost on the very intelligent geese, which soon learned that private land acts as a de facto refuge area. I don't expect geese can read, but they sure seem to understand what all those "NO HUNTING" signs mean.

Eventually, folks who were very happy to see a squadron of 30 geese on the Turtle-Flambeau Flowage became equally unhappy when they saw 100 geese. For many people, that fine line between the right number and too many had been crossed.

Before we get too carried away about the evil geese, it's important to realize that the problems people experience in southern Wisconsin will never occur here unless we make the same mistakes they made down there. Given all our county, state, and federal forest lands, I can't imagine that we will ever come remotely close to converting our landscape into a lawnscape or farmscape, which the geese in southern Wisconsin have found to be the penthouse of habitats.

We need to breathe slowly and calmly about this, and do the right things to stem the population growth of the geese. Taking appropriate measures isn't rocket science. Four things need to be done now. First, stop feeding the geese (and the ducks and anything else that will walk up on your dock or your land and use it as an outhouse)! This is a simple decision, based on the knowledge that humans don't know what we're doing when we begin feeding large herbivores.

Second, geese like to land on water and then walk up on land, but they don't like walking through shrubs. They're a bit chunky, after all, for strolling through a hedge. So maintain whatever shrubbery you have along your shoreline and plant additional shrubs to fill in the gaps. These can be low shrubs that allow you to see over them. Ideally, they should provide a buffer zone of 10 feet or so to discourage the geese, but even a narrow strip of shrubs can be very helpful.

This is, of course, what most of our shorelines naturally looked like before we arrived, and what our shorelines still look like where they have been kept wild.

Third, sell the lawnmower, or at least reduce it from the size of a farm tractor to something small and difficult to push, which will discourage you from the time-honored tradition of manicuring land that was meant to be forest. I'm not saying you should get rid of your entire lawn. Lawns are great for children to play on, for picnics, and other activities. But so are the woods. And the geese won't come to play or feast with you.

Lastly, either hunt your land yourself or let someone else hunt it for geese. The early goose season opens September 1 and runs until September 15. This season was expressly created to take local breeding geese, because migrating geese don't start coming our way until at least mid-September. (The migrant goose season runs from September 17 to December 17.)

It would be a crying shame if we lose our appreciation for the beauty and grandeur of a flock of geese because we can't stop planting lawns or feeding wildlife that doesn't need to be fed. I will always want to view geese as American naturalist Henry Beston experienced them: "I saw a flock of geese flying over the meadows along the rift of dying, golden light, their great wings beating with a slow and solemn beauty, their musical, bell-like cry filling the lonely levels and the dark. Is there a nobler wild clamor in all the world?"

Celestial Events

- August 6 marks true mid-summer, the halfway point between ice-out and ice-up.
- We're down to 14½ hours of daylight on August 7, 14 hours of daylight as of August 18, and by August 28, daylight will grace us for just 13 hours and 30 minutes. We will continue losing about 3 minutes of sunlight per day.
- The peak Perseid meteor showers occur around August 11 or 12. You can expect to see about 75 meteors per hour.

Approach of the Red Planet

At magnitude –2.9, Mars dominated the southeastern night sky in August of 2003. On August 26 and 27, the red planet came closer, though only by a little, to Earth than at any time during the last 60,000 years, at least according to one source. Other sources indicate anywhere from 2,000 to 100,000 years.

Every 15 to 17 years, Mars appears almost this large as it passes closest to the earth while it is also nearest to the Sun. During August of 1971 and September of 1988, it appeared almost as large as it was in 2003. For some perspective, the late August 2003 show represented only one of five occasions (at most) that any of us will ever see Mars so clearly in our lifetimes.

By close to Earth, astronomers mean that Mars was a mere 34.4 million miles away (and "only" 206.65 million miles from the sun).

Chickadee Mating Song

What specific song does a male chickadee sings to attract a female? Well, the *Stokes Guide to Bird Behavior* describes eight different songs and calls. Nothing's ever easy, even for a bird. Among the most common songs is the *fee-bee* song, a clear, whistled two-note phrase, the first note higher than the other. This song is often given by the males to establish and maintain territories, and is the song most closely associated with mating. The *chickadeedeedee* call appears to be a social contact call, keeping the flock together even when they can't see one another.

The *tseedeleedeet* call, a sputtering phrase with the accent on the last syllable, is used by both males and females during territorial skirmishes. The *dee-dee* call is repeated in a scolding fashion and also indicates territorial displeasure. This call often leads to a chase through the trees to run off the intruder. A breeding territory averages about 10 acres in size, but by this time of year, the territories are no longer defended.

All-Terrain Predators

Few organisms give people a worse case of the heebie-jeebies than daddy longlegs. Their size and suspended body hanging low between their arched legs tend to stimulate shrieks and shakes from otherwise normal adults.

For the more scientific among you, daddy longlegs belong to the order *Opiliones*, which is not in the class Insecta. Daddy longlegs have eight legs, lack antennae, and have a two-part body—unlike true insects, which have six legs, antennae, and a three-part body. The daddy longlegs' eight legs are delicate and break off easily, though their loss appears to affect them very little and may in fact serve as a defense against predators, since the separated legs will twitch awhile in a manner that distracts the predator and allows the daddy longlegs to high-step it away. The second pair of legs is the longest of the four pairs, and contains sense organs that tell the daddy longlegs where food and danger may be, as well as informing it about things humans will probably never understand.

Daddy longlegs populations peak in the summer. In the spring, babies hatch from eggs laid at the end of the previous summer. They must molt six or more times until they are fully grown and sexually mature. Then they mate, and the female deposits her eggs in damp soil or in cracks in decaying wood. The male stands over the female, protecting the female under his tent of long legs, while she lays the eggs. Then the adults die, the entire cycle in temperate climates like ours only lasting one season. However, some species may overwinter as youth and then molt into adults in the spring.

Daddy longlegs have paired glands at the sides between their first and second legs that contain a bad-smelling fluid. This odoriferous concoction appears to act as a deterrent to some predators, though other predators don't seem affected at all. The daddy longlegs prefer humid places because they need water constantly and dry out rapidly in direct sun. They are both scavengers and predators and apparently have very poor vision, which may account for their tendency to traverse over humans who get in their way.

If looked at closely, they look like some strange robot from a Star Wars movie, and no doubt they have been the inspiration for more than a few science fiction creatures. Their long legs enable them to cruise rapidly over difficult terrain in a manner our military forces would like to emulate. Maybe some day a clever engineer will figure out how they cover so much ground so effortlessly, and design the ultimate all-terrain vehicle, inspired by the daddy longlegs.

Defining "Healthy" Forests

In 2004, 25 Wisconsin legislators asked the White House to transfer management authority of the 1.1-million-acre Chequamegon-Nicolet National Forest to the DNR because the preferred master plan alternative reduced the annual cut from 167 million board feet to 130 million board feet. Rep. Don Friske (R-Merrill) was quoted as saying, "We are very concerned about set-asides that are being made in the plan for passive management in the name of enhanced recreation. We do not believe that the proper middle ground has been found. Active management in the CNNF has been the key to achieving healthier forests since these two forests were first established in the 1920s."

There are numerous issues to address in that statement given that the CNNF is among the most heavily harvested of all our national forests, but the statement that most interested me was the implied truth that if forests aren't actively managed, they aren't healthy. I've heard this said by many people over the years, and nothing could be further from the truth. If the concept was true,

we would have no choice but to describe the pre-settlement forests of Wisconsin as unhealthy because they were unmanaged—something I can't imagine anyone suggesting.

The core issue is the definition of a "healthy" forest. Is health defined as producing maximum growth in the shortest period of time? Or is health defined as producing the maximum biodiversity over long time frames appropriate to species that can live 500 years? Is health determined from a human use standpoint, from a landscape ecology standpoint, or from some value in between?

Another issue involves which model one chooses to employ. Some view forests through an agricultural model, while others use an ecological model. An agricultural model sees forests in the same light as gardens, thus concluding that we should manage forests just as we manage gardens or farms. But comparing the health of a forest to that of a healthy garden utilizes productivity as the measuring stick, and there's far more to forest health than maximum productivity. Thinning carrots and pulling weeds makes a "healthy" garden, but I don't know anyone who would argue that equivalent forest plantations are healthy ecosystems.

"A stand of trees is not a forest," wrote E. C. Pielou in her book *The World of Northern Evergreens*. "The regrowth of trees is not the same thing as the renewal of a forest."

Leopold wrote 60 years ago: "A system of conservation based solely on economic self-interest is hopelessly lopsided. It tends to ignore, and thus eventually to eliminate, many elements in the land community that lack commercial value, but that are (as far as we know) essential to its healthy functioning."

Please understand that I am not endorsing the either/or dichotomy of managed versus unmanaged forests. Health in forests is every bit as complex a concept as it is in humans. Health is more than the absence of disease or the production of maximum growth. Health is a continuum of factors and processes that can only be measured over the centuries-long life span of forest ecosystems. Forests require the death and dying of many individual trees in order to sustain the conditions necessary for literally thousands of life forms. Health includes issues like diversity, stability over time, and self-renewal.

Managed forests can be quite healthy, as can unmanaged forests. I'm simply calling for the obvious acknowledgment that nature can manage itself in good health with or without our involvement.

Double-Crested Cormorants

Jeanne and Tom McJoynt reported on August 24, 1998, that a pair of double-crested cormorants were perched high in trees on Cathedral Point in Trout Lake. A few days later Dean Acheson reported a cormorant sitting on a light pole in front of Save-More in Minocqua. The question they both had was: Where did the cormorants come from?

Cormorants nest in large colonies in only a few places around the state. Green Bay, islands off Door County, the Mead Wildlife Area in Marathon County, Green Lake, the Crex Meadows Wildlife Area in Burnett County, and Gull and Eagle islands in the Apostle Islands are the known nesting rookeries. There are no nesting sites reported in the Lakeland area.

So where did these cormorants come from? Cormorants are known to raft up in big numbers in fall on Chequamegon Bay, prior to migrating. A few cormorants are commonly seen every summer on the Turtle-Flambeau Flowage. As for where these individuals came from, and what they were up to, that remains a mystery. The best speculation was that they were non-breeders and/or juveniles simply out exploring.

Fall Tenting

In 1997, I noticed quite a number of trees in the Lakeland area infested with what appeared to be a webbed tent over the tips of many leaves, the tents sometimes as big as several feet long. These constructions were the work of the fall webworm (*Hyphantria cunea*), a species of tiger moth from the family Arctiidae. Tent caterpillars build similar looking web-tents in trees, but their webs are usually built in the forks of branches, while fall webworms' nests are built at the tips.

The web-building culprit is the larval caterpillar stage of the fall webworm. They build the tents around the leaves they are eating, living in the web nest for four to six weeks before forming a cocoon, usually in bark crevices or under leaves on the ground. Here they will pupate through the winter. In spring the adults emerge, mate, and the female lays her eggs on the leaves of food sources for the larvae, almost always deciduous trees like ash, cherry, willow, and apple. The eggs hatch in 10 days into caterpillars, and around we go again. Fall webworms are common, fluctuate in number every year, and are of little consequence in our region.

If you poke around in their webs, you should find droppings and sometimes the molted skins of the caterpillars that undergo five molts before pupating.

Yellow warblers are one of the main predators of the webworms, along with two species of hornets.

Mosquitoes

I don't usually root for an early August frost, but early August of 2000 provided us with enough mosquitoes to give new definition to the words "blood donor." We were blessed the previous three years with minimal mosquito numbers. Say what you like about poor winters (and there's a lot to be said), the upside of minimal snowloads, early springs, and low water levels is a diminished mosquito crop. Our heavy July and early August rains in 2000 changed all that, so we moved fast and exposed little skin.

Autumn brings many blessings, not the least of which is mosquito-free hiking. Of course, it's important not to whine louder than the mosquitoes attacking you. This is life in the Northwoods, after all.

Feather Combs

On a hike in 2002, we found the remains of a great blue heron recently torn to pieces by a predator. I picked up one of its feet and examined its four toes closely (three toes forward, one rear). The middle toe was 4 1/2 inches long, and the claw had "pectinations"—teeth like a tiny comb—along its outer edge. This adaptation is apparently useful in combing out parasites and straightening out the bristles of feathers. The first and second toes were the only ones that had partial webbing between them, probably to aid in supporting a bird as big as a heron in soft mud and sand. The long back toe makes perching in trees possible.

But what I found most intriguing—and perplexing—was the fact that the back toe had one knuckle joint, the right front two knuckles, the middle toe three knuckles, and the left front four knuckles. I suspect there's a logical explanation for this, but I'm at a loss to explain this varying flexibility of the heron's toes.

Fireweed

Fireweed's hot-pink flowers bloom in August all along roadsides. Not to be confused with purple loosestrife, which grows in wetlands, fireweed flourishes in dry, poor soils and on ground that has been burned over. While hiking along Maine's Allegash River in 1857, Henry David Thoreau wrote about fireweed: "At the edge of some burnt land, which extended three or four miles at least ... [was] an exceeding wild and desolate region ... covered with charred trunks, either prostrate or standing ... and there were great fields of fireweed on all sides, the most extensive I ever saw, which presented great masses of pink."

In 1944, Lewis Gannet wrote in the New York Herald Tribune: "London, paradoxically, is the gayest where she has been most blitzed. The wounds made this summer by flying bombs, are still raw and bare, but cellars and courts shattered into rubble by the German raids of 1940-41 have been taken over by an army of weeds which have turned them into wild gardens.

"There is the brilliant rose-purple plant ... [that] Americans call fireweed because it blazes wherever a forest fire has raged ... It sweeps across this pock-marked city and turns what might have been scars into flaming beauty."

Fisher Family Life

Fishers would fail to pass current tests for having family values. The males disappear after mating and offer no help with raising the young, while the females spend nearly their entire lives pregnant and raising young.

The female gives birth on average in late March, typically to two to three kits, then she breeds again within 10 days. She utilizes delayed implantation to forestall the birth of her kits until the following March. Implantation usually occurs in late February, followed by a 30-day gestation period.

The female selects the den and almost always chooses a hollow tree in which to raise her kits, usually an old heart-rotted aspen.

The kits are born completely helpless, with their eyes and ears tightly closed, and they're only sparsely furred. Biologists theorize that giving birth to such small and helpless young is quite adaptive for the females because it allows them to hunt while pregnant, unburdened by heavy fetuses.

The young develop rapidly with the mother nursing them, but they remain quite helpless for several weeks, often not even standing up until they are three weeks of age, and not opening their eyes until seven weeks have passed. The kits are completely dependent on their mother's milk until they are eight to 10 weeks old. After two months, they typically begin to learn how to climb, and it's not until they are at least three months old that they begin to show interest in hunting. In most cases, they're unable to kill independently until they are at least four months old.

Use of the natal den usually ceases within two months, though the dens may be utilized off and on for a month or so after that. Studies of radio-collared fishers have shown that juveniles remain in their mother's territory into the winter, often avoiding their mother, and by one year of age they all disperse to establish their own home ranges.

By fall, the male kits are clearly longer and heavier than the female kits, and eventually the male becomes much larger than the female. Males weigh from 7 to 12 pounds, averaging nearly twice the weight of adult females.

Fishers: A Piece of the Biological Puzzle

Some folks get quite worked up about fishers, blaming them for every ill on the land. I view them, however, as just another predator among the foxes, coyotes, raccoons, minks, weasels, wolves, otters, and the rest.

Wisconsin always had good numbers of fishers until trapping and logging led to their extirpation from the state in 1932. Many other states, from New York to California, experienced the same population declines and eventual extirpation. The last native fishers were reported in Michigan in 1932, while the last reliable reports of fishers in Montana and Idaho came in the 1920s. Remnant populations could be found only in small areas of Maine, the White Mountains of New Hampshire, the Adirondack Mountains in New York, the vast wetlands of northern Minnesota, and scattered regions of the Pacific coastal mountains.

Many states reintroduced fishers to reestablish a native mammal and to reduce high populations of porcupines, one of the favorite foods of fishers. Montana reintroduced fishers in the late 1950s; Vermont in 1959; Oregon in 1961; Idaho in 1962; and West Virginia in 1969.

Eighteen fishers from New York and 42 from Minnesota were released in Wisconsin in the Nicolet National Forest between 1956 and 1963. In Michigan's U.P., 61 fishers were reintroduced between 1961 and 1963.

In Canada, fishers were reintroduced in Nova Scotia in 1947, in Manitoba in 1972, and in Alberta in 1990. Thus the fisher now successfully lives throughout much of its historic range, a great success story by many people's standards.

In Wisconsin's Northwoods, the DNR estimates that we have a population of one fisher for every two square miles. Fishers are relatively easy to trap, and we have a very successful trapping season in the fall.

One question that remains elusive is: What was the historic biological control on fishers? Wolves are really the only animal that can kill them with relative ease, although large bobcats can take small fishers (but large fishers can take small bobcats, so that's a wash).

Fishers are roundly blamed for lows in grouse and snowshoe hare populations, but a classic understanding in wildlife ecology is that prey species populations control predator populations, not the other way around. The grouse and hare cycles will continue to go up and down whether fishers are here or not, as they certainly did in all those years when fishers weren't present in Wisconsin. Today, with only one fisher for every two square miles, there's just too much ground for them to cover to have a dramatic impact on grouse populations.

Fishers will also take chipmunks, squirrels, rabbits, and even a fawn now and again, and they typically go into winter well fed on all the deer gut piles left in the woods after hunting season. There's also evidence that they will climb nest trees of endangered and threatened birds and take young birds or eggs, and that's of great concern. But that's what an opportunistic predator does, and we have to learn to live with that.

They'll also steal berries from your berry patch, but so will every fruit-loving bird we have, as well as coyotes, foxes, and the neighbor's kids.

Nature knew what it was doing long before we arrived, and it continues to do quite well for itself despite our continual introduction of non-native invasive species, and all the other ills we throw at it. Native biological diversity is something to celebrate, and the fisher belongs as one of the original pieces in the native biological puzzle.

Feeding Teenagers

In 2003, the fully-fledged eagle chick in the nest across the river from our house continued to beg piteously for food well into August, even though it was perfectly capable of catching its own. Its cries started at first light and lasted for several hours.

Fledging doesn't necessarily mean independence for birds, any more than getting their driver's license means teenagers will be leaving home anytime soon. Every year, we watch a number of young songbirds around our feeders—including rose-breasted grosbeaks, evening grosbeaks, and purple finches—that sometimes feed independently and sometimes beg for food from their parents.

I'm unsure how long parents continue to feed their fledged offspring, and the amount of time certainly varies according to species. But I have found some amazing statistics regarding feeding of the chicks while they're still in the nest. Raptor parents like eagles bring back single large prey items to the nest and tear them apart for their young. On the average, they bring a fish every few hours. However, songbird parents typically haul food back to the nest hundreds of times per day. One eastern phoebe with four chicks made 8,942 visits to her nest over 17 days, an average of 526 flights a day. I don't know if that's some kind of record, but it should be. No parent should have to work that hard.

Some birds carry more than one prey item back to the nest, and thus have to leave the nest fewer times. Tree swallow parents average 19 prey items per nest visit, many of which are still alive, and all carried in their mouths. A brood of five chicks will be fed an average of 8,000 prey items per day, which amounts to a bucketful of insects. Hopefully most of these are mosquitoes and deerflies.

Puffins, which nest along the Atlantic coast, carry up to 50 small fish at a time in their bills for their brood of young, though how they manage to catch the last few fish with their bills already full remains a mystery.

Nearly all songbirds feed high-protein insects to their young, except for the finches—goldfinch, purple finch, house finch, siskins, crossbills—which feed their young lower-protein seeds.

I'd never thought about bringing water back to the nest, but common ravens deliver water to their young in their beaks. How other Northwoods birds deliver water, if in fact they do, is unknown to me. I have read of the sandgrouse, a bird of deserts and dry grasslands in Africa and Asia, which actually transports water to its young in its belly feathers. The feathers soak up water like a sponge. The parent stands erect when it returns to the nest, and the chicks drink from a groove down the middle of the belly feathers.

Frost in August

We had two consecutive nights of light frost on August 13 and 14, 2004, and another light frost on August 21. None of the chilly nights killed the tomatoes in our garden (we covered them), or other susceptible plants around us, but the frosts certainly served notice to all organisms that they better complete their life cycles, adapt quickly, or get out of town.

A Mighty Wind

A significant number of area trees blew down during a major storm on August 14, 2000. I was shocked when I drove into the Kemp Natural Resources Station and saw the number of old-growth hemlocks scattered about like toothpicks. I had just helped to lead an old-growth hike there for Nicolet College on August 5, and all the participants were wowed by the beauty of the Kemp stand. Tom Steele, the station's director, estimates that they lost about 25 percent of the trees.

The good news is that sunlight will now reach forest floors that had been in shade for a very long time, seeds will germinate, and the understory will become vibrant. The bad news is that while old trees are replaceable, they certainly won't grow back within human life spans. To lose 250-year-old trees is like having a museum swept away by a tornado. To allow the process of forest succession to work its slow magic and eventually reestablish an old-growth stand may take 500 or more years. The loss, while natural and expected as part of normal forest disturbance, is painful and difficult to accept.

Lee Andreas, a retired forester in Woodruff, noted in a letter to me that the outbreak of forest tent caterpillars may have helped save many area trees from toppling in the storm. The trees with the least amount of leaf surface offered the least resistance to the winds, translating into fewer losses.

Lee also observed that the species suffering the greatest losses were aspen, balsam fir, paper birch, and red maple. These short-lived, fast-growing trees seem particularly susceptible to windthrow. However, Lee added that the winds were equal-opportunity destroyers, able to damage all species.

He noted that red oaks and sugar maple seemed to suffer the least damage, a lesson for homeowners planting trees around their homes.

Goshawk in Action

I was privileged one August to observe something I've never seen before—a goshawk capturing a wood duck in the air and taking it down. I was canoeing with a group on a portion of the Wisconsin River, when what I thought at first were two wood ducks came careening through the air, one right on the tail of the other. They passed right in front of us, giving me barely enough time to think that the second bird didn't look much like a duck, then they veered upriver. I heard a loud thwack as they entered some trees. In the canoe behind me, John Burlingame said he saw the hawk capture the woodie, drop it to the ground, then swoop to the ground, hover over it, and stare at John, as if to say, "This is mine—don't even try to take it."

The hawk had to be a goshawk, because no other hawk of the forest has the speed and size to bring down a large duck. Only the goshawk has the bulk and power of a buteo and the killing skills of an accipiter.

Why Flock?

In August, we often play host to a flock of grackles that descends upon our feeders. Where do they suddenly come from? Members of the blackbird family "flock-up" in late summer and early fall. By winter, roosting flocks of a million or more blackbirds (including starlings, grackles, red-winged blackbirds, and other blackbird family members) will congregate in fields in southern states.

Flocking-up is typically a pre-migratory behavior, engaged in after territorial behavior has ended and the young-of-the-year have fledged. Birds are now free to socialize. Flocking is usually thought to occur as a means of providing greater safety and more eyes to spot food sources. The safety theory works only for low-flying daytime migrants who need to escape predators. But many high-flying and nighttime migrants flock as well, so the theory has holes in it.

The "many eyes" theory also has limited applicability. Many species don't fly in flocks, instead flocking-up during migratory stopovers. Many species come together to form loose aggregations that forage in a host of sites and by a variety of means. Given the varying appetites and approaches to eating, it's unlikely that many eyes are all that helpful.

It's possible that flocking helps birds find their migration routes. Older birds that have completed migration may help lead the juveniles in the flock that are unfamiliar with the pathway.

Many studies have tried to link flock configuration with aerodynamic efficiency—geese flying in a V-formation supposedly are more aerodynamic. It's entirely possible that flying in formation reduces drag on each individual, but studies conflict on whether this is actually true.

Birds that flock together show "social facilitation," meaning that the behavior of one member of the flock often induces the rest of the flock to behave in the same way. If one bird flies up in alarm, they all leap up, or if one starts preening, they all start preening. It's peer pressure taken to the extreme, if you want to put it in human terms.

Most remarkable is the ability of flocks to fly synchronously, twisting and turning only inches apart as if they had practiced these maneuvers for years in a dance hall. Interestingly, researchers have observed that the leadership of the flock changes, seeming to sweep through the flock along one edge. Although not well understood, the instantaneous reactions within a flock to one another are a visual marvel.

Truth is, no one can really say why birds flock. Some researchers believe many birds may be drawn to one another instinctively, exhibiting a social gregariousness that meets some unidentifiable need. Maybe, like humans, they just enjoy one another's company.

Goldenrods

The golden plumes of goldenrod (*Solidago* sp.) dominate the roadsides and open fields of late summer and early fall. Some 50 species clothe the Northwoods, many of which are botanical nightmares to try to identify, so I recommend enjoying their beauty and skipping the cataloging.

The genus name *Solidago* means "to make whole," while the Ojibwe called the family *gizisomukiki*, which translates as "sun medicine." Goldenrods have been used historically to treat so many illnesses that it is like modern-day ginseng in its history as a cure-all.

Goldenrods are one of the most important fall nectar flowers for bees, and though goldenrods have been widely blamed for hay fever, they have nothing to do with it whatsoever. Instead, their buddy ragweed deserves all the credit. Goldenrods have been named as the state flowers of Nebraska and Kentucky.

Avian Adventurers

On August 13, 2002, John Spickerman reported seeing a great egret feeding on the Gile Flowage just south of Hurley (Mary actually saw one there on the same day as well). Then on August 24, Mary, Callie, and I got close and lengthy looks at a great egret feeding on the Powell Marsh. Its snow-white plumage dramatically contrasted with the dark mud flats where it was feeding.

Great egrets are almost as large as a great blue heron. They have long, yellow bills, and black legs and feet.

While great egrets are not as rare a sighting as the brown pelican that wandered our way a few weeks before this, I've only seen a great egret on two other occasions in our area during the last two decades. They're an uncommon nesting resident of southern and far-western

Wisconsin, but they aren't known to nest in northern Wisconsin. Where they do nest, however, they often nest in large numbers—a rookery in Horicon Marsh hosted more than 200 nesting pairs until a windstorm knocked the nest trees down a few years ago.

Great egrets are known to wander northward after nesting. One source writes that egrets can turn up almost anywhere in the summer, often traveling hundreds of miles north from their spring rookeries. We undoubtedly saw one of these adventurers.

Bye Bye Birdies

With the first frost looming on the horizon in August and the resultant plummeting of insect populations, insect-dependent birds start to move south.

The neotropical species, those that fly the farthest, are typically the ones that leave the soonest. Species like Nashville, yellow, northern parula, and chestnut-sided warblers often head off for South America in early August. Last to leave are the warblers that migrate only as far as the southern U.S., species like palm, pine, and yellow-rumps.

Other insect-eating neotropical migrants like swallows, flycatchers, and vireos also begin migration early in August, and the small hawks and falcons, like Cooper's and sharp-shinned hawks, kestrels, and peregrines, begin to pass through in late August.

A Jewel of the Wetlands

We have a large stand of jewelweed flowering below our house in the moist soils separating the wetlands from the uplands. Hummingbirds work the tubular flowers during the day; at dusk, hummingbird moths take over the nectar patrol. Both types of hummers pollinate the flowers by picking up grains of pollen from the top front of one flower and depositing them on the next. I wonder if the ever-territorial hummingbirds prevent the moths from utilizing the flowers during the day, forcing the moths into crepuscular (dusk and dawn) feeding behavior.

Jewelweed eclipses most definitions of a "weed." The "jewel" part of the name is most apt, because of the spurred flower shape and orange color. Some folks see the dangling flowers as jeweled earrings, while others see jewelry in how the edges of the leaves sparkle with drops of water after a rain.

The fruit pods give it another set of names, from "touch-me-not" to "poppers." The pods pop open when touched, the outer covering uncoiling like a spring and shooting the seeds 4 to 5 feet through the air.

These succulent plants grow to 5 feet tall and are supported by hollow stems that seem to hold as much water as the wet soils in which they grow. Their shallow roots can only grab moisture just below the surface, so jewelweed wilts and dies quickly in a drought or at the first hint of frost.

For those of you susceptible to poison ivy, boil the leaves, stem, and flowers of jewelweed in water until the water turns deep orange. Or crush the stem and just apply the fluid. Many people swear by the decoction as a cure for the evil ivy.

Landscaping for Birds

Many fruiting shrubs come ripe in August, so birds must be happy campers. As insect populations decline with frosts, fruits become all the more important. If you want to encourage birds and other animals to frequent your yard for fruits/berries/seeds, consider planting what I think are the top 10 native wildlife shrubs:

- Blackberry (*Rubus* sp.)—97 users
- Blueberry (*Vaccinium* sp.)—53 users
- Dogwoods: gray (*Cornus racemosa*), silky (*Cornus amomum*), red-osier (*Cornus stolonifera*), round-leaved (*Cornus rugosa*), alternate-leaved (*Cornus alternifolia*), or bunchberry (*Cornus canadensis*)—90 users
- Elderberry (*Sambucus canadensis*)—79 users
- Holly, northern (*Ilex verticillata*)—36 users
- Viburnums: nannyberry (*Viburnum lentago*) and maple-leaved viburnum (*Viburnum acerifolium*)—25 users
- Serviceberry (*Amelanchier canadensis*)—58 users
- Sumac, staghorn (*Rhus typhina*)—50 users
- Thimbleberry (*Rubus parviflorus*)—unknown # of users
- Wild cherries: pin, choke, black (*Prunus sp.*)—81 users

Listening Point

In 2002, I spent several days in Ely, Minnesota, at a conference that celebrated wilderness writers, and Sigurd Olson in particular. We were given a tour of his home in Ely and his Burntside Lake cabin, a site that he named "Listening Point." Sig wrote many fine essays, but may be best known for his essay bearing the same name. In "Listening Point," he describes the importance of this rocky peninsula to him:

> "From it I have seen the immensity of space and glimpsed at times the grandeur of creation. There I have sensed the span of uncounted centuries and looked down the path all

> life has come. I have explored on this rocky bit of shore the great concept that nothing stands alone and everything, no matter how small, is part of a greater whole.
>
> "I named this place Listening Point because only when one comes to listen, only when one is aware and still, can things be seen and heard. Everyone has a listening-point somewhere. It does not have to be in the north or close to the wilderness, but some place of quiet where the universe can be contemplated with awe."

Here's hoping you have found a listening point.

Migration Habitat

Summer is short enough, but in case we don't recognize its decline, the appearance of migrating birds serves as a reminder of how fleeting it really is.

For most songbirds, the best viewing is in the willow and alder shrubs around the shorelines of lakes and rivers. In a study of migrating songbird habitat in Park Falls, Wisconsin, researchers found that songbirds use a mosaic of 15 habitats during migration, but that wetland habitats (sedge meadows, alder shrub, and willow shrub) attracted more individuals and species than all other habitats combined.

Nature Conservancy Purchases Tenderfoot Forest

On August 30, 2005, Governor Doyle and DNR Secretary Hassett came to the Northwoods to announce The Nature Conservancy's (TNC) purchase of 971 acres of the Tenderfoot Forest, an absolutely exceptional parcel of land and water. The acquisition will protect nearly four miles of undeveloped lakeshore on three wild lakes and more than 500 acres of old-growth hemlock-hardwood forest. In fact, Tenderfoot contains the largest remaining expanse of old-growth forest left in private ownership in Wisconsin

The significance of a purchase like this is profound, because over the past 100 years, old-growth forest has been reduced to one-quarter of 1 percent of its original size in Wisconsin. To restate that for emphasis, 99.75 percent of all of the original pre-settlement forest in Wisconsin was cut, leaving us with forest communities that, while regrown, are by no means restored—a crucial distinction. The restoration of old-growth hemlock-hardwood forest (hemlock, sugar maple, yellow birch, basswood) like that found on the Tenderfoot Forest will take centuries to achieve, and it will occur only where we stop harvesting the young forests that regrow.

TNC bought the property from the Rahr family, which has owned and cared for it for 120 years. The family, in its great generosity, donated more than $1 million of the value of the land to the Conservancy to ensure that the land and waters are protected for future generations.

State officials came here to celebrate the Rahrs' vision, because TNC was awarded a $2.1 million state Stewardship Fund grant for protection of the Tenderfoot Forest. This is a prime example of what the Stewardship Fund program was designed to accomplish, and why the Stewardship Fund is absolutely necessary to maintain. One has only to look along the shorelines of many nearby developments to see how the Rahr property could have been carved up and gated off had it been sold.

The Conservancy will open the property for public recreation, including canoeing and kayaking on two lakes, motorized boating on Tenderfoot Lake, hunting for whitetail deer and ruffed grouse, and fishing. There will be several miles of hiking trails and extensive opportunities for enjoying pristine, wild lakes and undeveloped shoreline.

Visiting Tenderfoot will be a unique outdoor experience. Visitors will need to use a public dock on Palmer Lake, across the water from the preserve, and paddle or motor in to the site. Access by foot will be through the Ottawa National Forest, but no linking trails exist at the moment.

The Conservancy committed to raise $2.4 million in private

funds to complete the acquisition and management of Tenderfoot, and for other conservation efforts in northern Wisconsin. TNC's private fundraising will more than double the amount awarded by the Stewardship Fund.

One last note on the Stewardship Fund: TNC has protected more than 10,600 acres of significant natural areas throughout the state with the help of the Stewardship Fund, and has matched those funds with $8.5 million in other public and private funds. Without the matching funds that the state provides, The Nature Conservancy and other land trusts could not afford to buy and conserve spectacular natural areas like Tenderfoot. Since it was established in 1989, the Stewardship Fund has helped conserve more than 300,000 acres of land in 71 of Wisconsin's 72 counties.

I've been to the property several times, and I'm overjoyed that such a property still exists, that it will be conserved, and that the public will have the chance to walk in such a beautiful forest.

Nighthawk Migration

August 20 usually marks the day to go out around dinnertime and see if nighthawks are passing through. Nighthawks continue to pass through our area until the second week of September. They are one of the first birds to leave us in the late summer, and they are among the last migrants to return in the spring—we seldom see them until late May.

Keep an eye peeled skyward in the early evening hours for the darting flight pattern, which is often referred to as moth-like. The nighthawks' diet consists almost entirely of insects, so they, like warblers, head south early or face the dire consequences of starvation.

The Sounds of Silence

The master plan for the Northern Highlands State Forest designates 2,000 acres in the Bittersweet Lakes area (Bittersweet, Prong, Oberlin, and Smith Lakes) as a no-motor area. I've heard arguments against this that hinge on how unfair it is to restrict any type of access to a public area. The underlying belief seems to be that all users of all types should be permitted in all places at all times and that restricting use means a "closing down" of an area.

I understand the arguments, but I see it differently. The designation to restrict some usages in certain areas generally occurs because of use conflicts, where one type of recreational use can't co-exist with another or where co-existence would mean such a reduction in enjoyment for a particular recreational user group that it would effectively exclude it. Restricted designation also is implemented, though rarely, as a means of protection for rare plants and animals from potentially destructive human disturbance.

We've exercised such use designations in our cities for a long time, fully understanding that we need to separate conflicting uses such as industrial factories and residential areas, heavy truck traffic and suburban neighborhoods, and so forth. But while we accept a wide array of use zoning in our cities, problems often arise when we apply the same principles to public lands and waters. The issues are fundamentally the same—certain uses are simply incompatible with others.

Oneida and Vilas counties contain 2,447 lakes, covering 162,300 acres. The NH-AL State Forest plan lists eight wilderness, no-motor lakes; 45 wild lakes; and 10 public, no-motor lakes or springs—a total of 63 lakes. Of the 900 lakes within NH-AL boundaries, this amounts to 7 percent of all NH-AL lakes. Within Vilas and Oneida counties as a whole, the 63 lakes comprise a little over 2 percent of all lakes.

The lakes chosen for designation are also small lakes—average sizes are 25 acres for wild lakes, and 50 acres for wilderness lakes. All of these lakes have some significant botanical or wildlife values that should be, at least by my value system, protected.

As for rivers, all rivers in the NH-AL are open to motorboats, including the stretch of the Manitowish River that flows through the Manitowish River Wilderness Area.

I support the designation of additional lakes as no-motor, because a very large percentage of people come to the Northwoods to canoe, kayak, hike, bird-watch, sit on the end of piers, watch sunsets, and other quiet activities. They aren't elitist or non-democratic or any other name that's been thrown at them. They simply would like to have a reasonable percentage of areas where they can experience silence.

Many people come here in order to relax, and peace and quiet obviously plays an instrumental role. Rather than closing down lakes, I see no-motor designations as a means to open up lakes to a quality of use that seldom can be experienced in the Northwoods, and which will only become harder to find as our population continues to increase. An added and essential benefit is that many species of plants and animals benefit from minimal human disturbance. Their needs must be taken into account, too.

My hope is that we can all come to accept that silence is an important commodity, that it's relatively rare these days, and that it ought to be valued and protected. The total multiple-use concept only works for a minority of user groups. Much as I'd like to have our woods and waters be used for all things by all people at all times, this is simply not possible, nor desirable, nor right.

Old Growth and Bladderworts

Chad McGrath and I led a hike in 2001 into three old-growth forests in Iron County. The first site we visited, Frog Lake and Pines State Natural Area, provided an example of a true pinery, its poor soils supporting a mix of mature red and white pines.

As one heads north in Iron County, the soil improves, altering the upland forest communities in the general direction of hemlock-hardwoods. We next hiked into Moose Lake Hemlocks, a 40-acre stand dominated by Eastern hemlock and yellow birch. Further north, we explored the Island Lake Hemlocks, a stand again governed by mature hemlocks.

Our group may have been as impressed by the extraordinary growth of purple bladderworts (*Utricularia purpurea*) on Frog Lake as the ancient trees. The exquisite purple flowers ringed the entire shoreline of Frog Lake, the blossoms likely totaling in the thousands. That's an exceptional number, given the ranking of purple bladderwort as a species of "special concern" in Wisconsin.

Bladderworts are insectivorous plants, consuming zooplankton and other tiny aquatic creatures. Any zooplankton living in Frog Lake must live in constant fear of being "swallowed up" by the colonies of bladderworts, though I doubt that zooplankton have much conscious awareness, much less a sense of fear.

50 Years Dormant

David Hoffman of Eagle River was staying on Black Oak Lake at a cabin that has been in his family since the early part of the twentieth century. On the mantle of the fireplace rested a large western pinecone. The cone is much larger than any we have in the Midwest, and it had been closed tightly for at least 50 years—an apparent memento from someone's trip out west long ago. For a joke, David put it outside on the path leading to the house where a family member was bound to see it upon their arrival the next day.

It rained that night, and when David looked at the cone the next day, it had opened up, astonishing him. How can a cone suddenly become "active" after 50 or more years? But that wasn't the end of the story. He left it in the sun that day, and it closed back up.

I called Tom Steele, director of the Kemp Natural Resources Station, and a forester by training, and he said he wasn't surprised. Many conifer cones are "hygroscopic," meaning they attract or absorb moisture from the air and then open up, an adaptation that probably evolved to help them disperse their seeds during the most favorable weather for distribution and germination. In the dry West, it makes the most sense for a pinecone to open when there's moisture available for germination and wind for dispersal. Tom suggested thinking of it as a sort of a meting out of seeds to fit the best environmental conditions.

Still, for a cone to mechanically function after sitting on a mantel for 50 years boggles the mind. If David puts the cone back on the mantel, will his great-grandchildren be able to observe the same trick 50 years from now? At what point will the cone lose its ability to open and close?

Purple Loosestrife

Purple loosestrife is in full bloom in wetlands during early August. Purple loosestrife grows 3 to 7 feet tall with a dense bushy growth of one to 50 stems. A single stalk may produce 100,000 to 300,000 seeds annually. Mature plants with 50 shoots produce more than two million seeds a year! The seeds remain viable in the soil for many years. If seed proliferation isn't enough to scare you, purple loosestrife's large, woody taproot has fibrous rhizomes that form a dense mat and spread vegetatively to produce clonal shoots. Purple loosestrife displaces native wetland vegetation and can overrun literally thousands of acres of wetlands and almost entirely eliminate open water habitat by choking waterways.

Every year I try to sound the alarm for residents to take up arms (actually, shovels work better) against this invader. It's time to do so now, before the plants go to seed. Dig the roots and place the entire plant in a plastic garbage bag to be added to the landfill. Avoid leaving behind any of the root, because it can resprout.

Introduced in the 1800s from Europe as a garden perennial, purple loosestrife was first seen in Wisconsin in the early 1930s. It's now widely dispersed throughout the state, and I've seen it on rivers like the Manitowish and Trout, as well as in wetlands like those near the DNR fish hatchery in Woodruff. It is illegal to sell, distribute, or cultivate purple loosestrife in Wisconsin, as well as 24 other states.

The DNR recently introduced a species of beetle that specifically feeds on loosestrife. These insects hold the ultimate key to controlling the purple loosestrife population at a manageable level. Individuals can raise the beetles in the spring and release them along their shorelands in the summer. Contact the DNR to participate.

Red Squirrels—To Kill or Not to Kill

Wally Krueger on Carlin Lake told me he had a red squirrel on his property with a white tail. Since Wally had been waging war on his red squirrels, shooting them with his .22 rifle, he noted that the red squirrel seemed to be waving his tail like a white flag, as well it should have been.

Wally and I talked for a while about the value of shooting red squirrels, the question being whether shooting is a successful means of removing them from one's property. I don't know for sure, but I suspect killing them is a never-ending battle that most folks ultimately lose. The reason is that the habitat around most people's homes is prime real estate for red squirrels, given all the usual bird feeders and free food available. Thus, to shoot the territorial pair of red squirrels on your property merely opens the door for another pair to replace them on your highly desirable turf. One friend of mine shot 42 red squirrels one fall before he gave up. It's probably best just to learn to live with a pair and appreciate their behaviors. We're in their territory, after all.

Invasion of the Shoreline Snatchers

I've started to take note of how often and where I see reed canary grass (*Phalaris arundinacea*) growing, and I believe this extremely aggressive grass may be every bit as invasive in wetlands as purple loosestrife. In southern Wisconsin, reed canary grass often forms monotypic stands in disturbed wetlands. The UW Arboretum in Madison has acres of it, which Arboretum managers have no idea how to control. After visiting those stands, I started looking for it here in the Northwoods, and I've been taken aback by how much is growing in places I don't recall ever seeing it before.

Reed canary grass is a native grass, but a European strain of the grass has essentially assimilated the native strain. Lakeshores, streambanks, marshes, and exposed moist ground like roadside ditches are prime sites for canary grass, particularly if the site has been disturbed in any manner. Planted for erosion control, it certainly accomplishes that purpose by stabilizing shorelines, but its ability to crowd out virtually every other species along a shoreline makes it highly undesirable. Once it's established, it's nearly impossible to remove.

Canary grass seems to be sneaking in under our conservation radar, and I think we better start paying attention.

Roadside Riot

August provides us with few woodland wildflowers, but makes up for this negligence by offering a riot of roadside flowers. The list runs long: wild bergamot, common Saint. John's-wort, black-eyed Susan, tansy, aster, butter-and-eggs, bush clover, daisy fleabane, evening primrose, goldenrod, hawkweed, oxeye daisy, mullein, common milkweed, Queen Anne's lace, spotted knapweed, fireweed, spreading dogbane, birdsfoot trefoil, yarrow, and others. Many of these flowers are quite hardy and will last well into September. Nearly all of the roadside flowers are annuals that grow tall and robust in order to be pollinated, then send thousands of seeds skyward in hopes of pioneering new sites come next year.

One of my favorite roadsiders is wild bergamot (*Monarda fistulosa*). The flower and leaves smell wonderfully pungent, and the lavender flowers seem to spread their many tubular petals exuberantly in a wild burst. *Fistulosa*, the species name, means "full of pipes," in reference to the long florets. The fragrance apparently is similar to that of bergamot oranges from Bergamo, Italy, and gave rise to the plant's genus name. For you tea lovers, the flavoring of Earl Grey tea comes from bergamot oranges.

Hummingbirds, butterflies, and bees like bergamot. As for humans, the aromatic leaves can be made into a strong tea, while American Indians are said to have boiled the plant with sweetflag (another aromatic plant) and bone marrow to make a hair dressing. One source says that both the leaves and blossoms can be used fresh in salads or as a flavoring for meat. The dried petals and leaves make great ingredients in potpourris.

Bee balm (*Monarda didyma*) is the southern relative of wild bergamot. It's not pollinated by bees, but rather was once used to soothe the sting of bees. Another name is Oswego tea, apparently from its use as a tea by American Indians in the vicinity of Fort Oswego, New York. The Indians used it to treat chills and fevers, and after the Boston Tea Party, settlers widely used this tea as a substitute for imported varieties.

Migration Magic

In mid-August of 2003, I hiked a section of eastern shoreline along the Rainbow Flowage and observed at least seven species of shorebirds probing for food in the mud flats. I was able to identify five of the species: lesser yellowlegs, long-billed dowitcher, pectoral sandpiper, semi-palmated plover, and spotted sandpiper. The first four are long-distance migrants from the Arctic on their way to Central and South America, while the spotted sandpiper breeds from southern Missouri all the way to the Arctic Circle and may winter only as far south as the Gulf States. The other two shorebird species were quite distant and defied my best attempts to identify them.

More than 500 North American species will migrate this fall, all seeking more dependable food supplies and willing to risk all. For many, the journey will far exceed our simple thought of a straight-line, here-to-there, north-to-south jaunt. Most young-of-the-year have no adults to lead them and can only blindly follow an instinctive urge to fly a particular direction for a certain length of time. They'll follow the stars by night and the sun by day, somehow adjusting for the movement of both bodies across the sky. They'll utilize magnetic fields, landmarks, and possibly even low-frequency sound waves generated by winds and surf. As Scott Weidensaul, author of *Living on the Wind,* writes: "Propelled by an ancient faith deep within their genes, billions of birds hurdle the globe each season, a grand passage across the heavens that we can only dimly comprehend and are just coming to fully appreciate."

I can't imagine juvenile shorebirds, only four months old, flying from the Arctic circle to the tip of South America and landing right where their kind have landed for thousands of years, but so they do.

Fall migrants pose a difficult identification challenge because most have molted into their winter plumage, but the appreciation of their flight only grows easier the more you know about them. There are no farewell parties for our breeding species, no hullabaloo send-offs. One day you'll notice the absence of their sound or visual presence, and wonder when they left, and where they went. In the meantime, their more northern compatriots will be bustling through, visible only for a short window of time to those who watch for such events.

Keep an eye skyward if you can. Think of the incredible stories that migrants could tell, like the Alaskan bar-tailed godwit that eats so much prior to migration that it forms thick rolls of fat comprising up to 55 percent of its body weight. When it finally can't stuff in another insect, its body undergoes an astounding change—the kidneys, liver, and intestines shrink to a fraction of their usual size. Then when the wind is strong and right, they jump into the air and fly non-stop to New Zealand, over 6,000 miles away, at least a four- to five-day flight even with their wings and the wind propelling them at a minimum of 45 miles per hour. Godwits can't land on the ocean or they'll drown, so once aloft, there's no return.

Most migration stories are more fathomable than the godwits, but none should fail to kindle your admiration and amazement.

Low Water Levels and Shorebirds

Water levels were way down in August 1998. The Turtle River became more trail than river in parts. In fact, one canoeist told me he pulled his canoe half a mile through a portion of the Turtle.

Low water levels can have their upside, however. While leading a group of sea kayakers on the Rainbow Flowage, we were treated to some very low, nutrient-rich water that exposed extensive mud flats rich in birds. At one muddy beach, six great blue herons and a sandhill crane were lined up probing the muck for invertebrates, while an array of shorebirds and gulls scavenged around them. We saw several Bonaparte's gulls among the more common ring-billed gulls, and the shorebirds were positively friendly, allowing us within 15 feet without flying.

Shoreline Restoration

Dave and Sandy Hipp on Stone Lake in Manitowish Waters invited me to their home in August of 2004 to see the shoreline restoration work they had completed that spring. They utilized "deltalock" bags—rubberized bags filled with soil that the plants can grow through—to convert a very steep, eroding drop-off along their shoreline into a more moderate slope where plants can grow and hold the soil.

It was the first time this method had been used in Vilas County, and it was the result of several years of planning and shared expenses with Vilas County Extension. Dave said the method is frequently utilized in Europe but is relatively new to the U.S.

The Hipps stacked the bags, overlapping them like shingles, along their shoreline in November. Then in May, they planted a variety of herbaceous and woody shrub species between the bags. The bags were then finally coated with a slurry compound made of shredded bits of newspaper that contained two species of native grasses.

They watered the grasses, herbs, and shrubs all summer. The result was an intact shoreline that is effectively resisting erosion, and also looks very nice. The bags are permanent and don't decompose. The plants establish their roots right through their thin skin, so the bags act like rocks in resisting wave action, but also permit plants to thrive.

The restoration will hopefully serve as a model project for others who wish to stop continued erosion along steep-banked shorelines.

Snappers Hatching

Lots of people see snapping turtles lay their eggs in June, but very few of us ever get to see the hatchlings emerge from the nest. On August 26, 2005, however, Gary and June Beier on Ike Walton Lake in Lac du Flambeau got to witness the event.

Gary says he was looking out his window when he noticed what looked like leaves moving on his driveway, but there was no wind. He went out to take a look and found several baby snapping turtles about the size of silver dollars crawling across the asphalt. He got a bucket and put them in it, then found the nest hole next to the driveway where the turtles were emerging. Over the course of an hour, 27 snappers scrambled out of the gravel!

Gary carefully put them all in the bucket, took them down to the lake, and released them into the water. Two quickly turned around and burrowed back into the sand along the shore, but all the others swam out into the water to face whatever challenges might await them.

Snappers lay 30 to 80 eggs, which typically incubate for 60 to 90 days, depending on the soil temperature. A cool summer delays hatching, sometimes so far that the hatchlings overwinter in the nest. Hot, dry summers hurry the process along, which seems to have been the case at the Beier household.

High incubation temperatures also produce more females, while low temps yield more males, so I suspect Gary and June's snappers were disproportionately female.

Turtles take a long time to mature into adults compared to most animals. I don't have a figure for snappers, but Blanding's turtles take 17 to 20 years to reach sexual maturity.

Socializing Loons

Loons begin gathering in pre-migratory social groups in August, and we see assemblages of varying sizes every year. Smaller groups are most common, like the group of 14 common loons swimming together that Mary, Callie, and I saw on Star Lake on

August 7, 2004. At one point, they began tremoloing back and forth, creating a wild chorus of agitated beauty. People do sometimes see large aggregations of loons, particularly on the bigger lakes in our area like Trout and Fence.

Sometime in early July loons lose their hormone-driven territoriality and decide it's time to hang with the gang. It's also true in July that non-mated bachelors flock together in neutral buffer zones between established territories in what may be the equivalent of a frat party. Whether loons in a group are mated or unmated is very difficult to determine without the ability to identify individuals by their leg bands. One source says that perhaps 20 to 30 percent of adults fail to breed and spend the summer in loose flocks socializing and feeding.

This mid-summer social flocking soon leads to pre-migratory flocking. Yet one year on the Turtle-Flambeau, there were still two pairs of loons sitting on eggs in early August. Their nests had been preyed upon twice, and they were attempting a third incubation. So loons can be at a variety of growth and behavioral stages in August, and researchers continue to try to sort it all out.

Actual migration won't begin until late September, peaking in the latter half of October. In August, most chicks haven't reached adult size and have yet to fledge. Fledging occurs about 75 days after hatching, so if we take June 15 as an average hatch time, most chicks don't fledge until the beginning of September.

Lake Study Says to Leave the Dead

[Reprinted from an article I wrote for the University of Wisconsin Center for Limnology in August, 2004.]

As a sign that sanity can exist amidst apparent chaos, many people hang little plaques above their disarrayed desks that say things like, "A messy desk is a sign of productivity," or "Clutter is a sign of a creative genius." Whether that's true for office desks is debatable, but a team of researchers from the UW-Madison Trout Lake Station is working to prove a comparable analogy in nature—that "messy" lake shorelines with downed trees all along their rims are nature's sign of productivity and creative genius.

Their research is triggered by the realization that human development along northern lakeshores is rapidly stripping away the dead trees and other natural debris that had been common to lake ecosystems since the last glaciers departed 10,000 years ago. Scientists have long thought that woody shoreline habitat was critically important to aquatic food chains, but exactly how important to specific organisms has never been demonstrated.

With the clock ticking as more and more shorelines are developed, the UW researchers are trying to accurately determine how fallen tree trunks and branches, or "coarse woody habitat," affect insect, frog, and fish populations. To do so, they've been given the unique scientific opportunity to manipulate the entire shorelines of two undeveloped lakes in the Northern Highland State Forest north of Minocqua.

What makes the study even more unusual is that one of the lakes, Camp Lake, is naturally divided into two separate basins, while the other lake, Little Rock Lake, is hourglass-shaped and has been separated at its narrowest point by two heavy curtains. Thus, researchers are able to manipulate the shoreline of one basin on each lake while leaving the other one natural for use as a reference, or control, for the experiment.

Three of the researchers, Greg Sass, Anna Sugden-Newberry, and Matt Helmus gave me a boat tour of both lakes in mid-June to demonstrate what whole-lake manipulations look like. We began in Little Rock Lake, where researchers had installed an impermeable barrier nearly two decades ago to separate the two basins. While similar in its natural state in most ways to Camp Lake, Little Rock historically had a high density of downed trees along its shoreline. In 2002, the researchers removed trees from the north basin, leaving only the trees that were too buried in the sediments to be moved.

Little Rock's south basin, however, was left alone, where its high number of naturally downed trees give it a wild appearance, a look that many shoreline owners might consider "messy" or "chaotic."

Data collected in the north basin has shown dramatic changes in the basin's fish populations and their behaviors. The biggest change has occurred in the population of yellow perch. Perch numbers have dropped to nearly zero, because yellow perch usually deposit their sticky eggs over submergent vegetation or submerged brush and branches in shallow water. Bass predation upon them has also increased due to the lack of woody habitat for the perch to use as a refuge. Thus, the absence of toppled trees in the water appears to have the potential to severely reduce perch populations.

The largemouth bass population has also suffered as the yellow perch have declined. They've had to switch from eating yellow perch, a favorite prey item, to eating more of a terrestrial diet. Rather than looking out into the water for their supper, they now look up to the surface in hopes of finding insects or frogs or snakes on the surface of the water. Stomach analysis has shown that the bass are even eating rodents swimming along the shore. The net result: The growth rate of largemouth bass has significantly declined, and their long-term reproductive success may be at risk.

Camp Lake, only a mile west, provided the researchers with the opposite opportunity for manipulation. Camp Lake historically had a very low number of naturally downed trees along its shoreline. In March 2004, trees were hauled in and placed on the shoreline ice of its south basin. Each tree was placed about 10 meters apart all the way around the 40-acre basin. When the winter ice melted, the trees, which included an array of species and sizes and shapes, sank into the water. The north basin, which is connected to the south basin by a tiny channel, was left in its natural state—a "clean" shoreline with very few downed trees.

In the south basin, the impacts were immediate. As we motored along, Sass pointed to the many trees lying in the water along the shoreline: "Next to every new log that we put in the water, there's now a largemouth bass nest, and sometimes two. And if you look in the branches of the trees in the water, there's a mass of toad eggs in nearly every one."

Sass swims the shoreline every week with snorkeling and scuba gear to count and mark the largemouth bass nests. Several years of prior baseline research by Sass and others had shown that fish seldom moved between the basins. So while connected, the basins acted as if they were two separate lakes. But now the fish were migrating through the channel and into the south basin to nest, presumably because of the better habitat provided by the downed trees. In contrast, very few bass now nest in the north basin.

Helmus explains that the woody habitat provides a substrate for plants like algae and aquatic insects to latch onto for use as a home and for food. The tangle of branches further acts as a protective refuge for insects and small fish. "These trees are where the action is," says Helmus. "The little fish hide inside, but every once in a while get chased out, and then a predator will have a meal. The trees create refuge areas, and become hotspots for aquatic life."

Most anglers already know this. To find fish, one usually has to find structure, some kind of architecture in the water like aquatic plants or downed trees that provide cover and food. "In shallow lakes, open water has nutrients and plankton, but typically little refuge," says Sass. "Most of the predator-prey relationships are focused on the edge of refuges in these lakes."

We watch as a loon pops up and dives again and again near our boat, actively fishing. Loons sometimes use floating woody habitat along shorelines as a platform for building their nests, and they certainly know to fish around the wood. So do great blue herons, mergansers, kingfishers, otters, and other fish-eaters and insect-eaters. Turtles line up to bask on the logs. Dragonflies and damselflies perch on the branches.

Yet, dead and downed wood still gets a bad rap. We talk about getting rid of the "dead wood" in an organization. We think of death as the end of being of value or service, but it turns out that even in death, a tree has a life of its own. While everyone sees the same shorelines, not everyone understands them.

"Coarse woody habitat is a natural occurrence," says Sugden-Newberry. "It's part of being in the Northwoods. If you move up here and have lakeshore property, you have to treat it differently and look at it differently than city property. Just because trees are in the water, doesn't mean they are debris or going to waste. They're a living community."

So, it turns out cleanliness is not next to Godliness, at least along lakeshores. "One learns a landscape finally not by knowing the name or identity of everything in it, but by perceiving the relationships in it," wrote Barry Lopez. Sass believes that if people knew the effects of the changes they were making along their shorelines, many people would manage their property differently. "Wood is critical to spawning success for many fishes," Sass says. "It's an interaction that has gone undisturbed for thousands of years."

"We need to look with an ecological lens," adds Sugden-Newberry. "We don't see that what we do on land affects aquatic life." Shoreline owners not only reduce coarse woody habitat by removing fallen trees, but also by thinning and removing trees and shrubs from along the shoreline to improve their view of the water, thus greatly reducing the amount of wood that can ultimately fall into the lake. An earlier study on northern lakes estimated that it would take 200 years to replace the downed trees that have been removed from nearly all developed shorelines. Another study in Ontario aged trees that had accumulated in a lake and found the average age of logs was 443 years. Some logs had been in the water for as long as 1,000 years, demonstrating that trees will provide extremely long-term habitat in our lakes if we simply leave them alone.

"It's frustrating," laments Sugden-Newberry. "We can change our shorelines quickly, but it takes a very long time for them to recover. And that's hard to manage."

Submerging Grebes

One August, we watched a family of five pied-billed grebes repeatedly demonstrate their unique ability to simply submerge in water. These birds are sort of the U-boats of the avian world. It's as if they simply pull their own plug and sink. The explanation is that they can reduce their buoyancy by expelling air from their body and feathers. They're uncanny and amusing to watch, often surfacing under a decking of water lily leaves with only their head protruding. The juvenile pied-billeds sport a brown-and-orange-striped head that would give them a rather dashing look if their feathers didn't stick out this way and that. They look like they just got out of the shower, which is an appropriate look for a bird nicknamed, among other things, "the hell-diver" and "the water-witch."

Why the name "pied-billed"? The word pied means "having patches of two or more colors" (with reference to the black and white plumage of the magpie). The bill of this little grebe is chalky white with a dark ring around it, so it's considered "pied-billed."

Turtle Body Shop

The Northwoods Wildlife Center in Minocqua rehabilitates a wide array of injured animals, but one of their more interesting tasks involved the reconstruction of a painted turtle. Mark Naniot, the Center's licensed rehabber, glued a turtle's shell back together after it had been shattered by a car. The turtle itself was fine, but needed a patch job with super glue, auto body putty, and some sanding to its shell in order to resume its normal life.

Underwater Prairies

Mary, Callie, and I paddled the headwaters of the Manitowish River one mid-August, putting in at the boat landing on Hwy. B, and fighting wind and waves through High Lake and Rush Lake to Fishtrap Lake. We were most taken by the initial channel that leads from Hwy. B to High Lake. Unlike the warm August waters of most shallow channels, the water was clear and cold, reflecting its origin in headwater springs. Luxurious beds of aquatic plants cordoned the channel, the crystal waters providing an unclouded view of their long stems emerging from the sediments. River ecologists and writers have often referred to the aquatic plant zone as an "underwater prairie," and seldom have we understood the descripton as clearly as we did in the headwaters of the Manitowish.

Submergent plants anchored in the sediments grew to varying

heights under the water, while some plants like bladderwort simply drifted rootless in the water column. Other emergents like water lilies and watershield floated their leaves on the water's surface. Pickerelweed stood a foot above the water, while bulrush and cattail grew tall enough to create lengthy shadows.

The underwater prairie community is analogous to forest communities. Whenever I take people on forest walks, I talk about the basic ecological concept of layering. Forests tend to be "richer" with more layers, including low herbaceous species, tall herbs, short shrubs, tall shrubs, short trees, and tall trees. Insects, birds, and mammals feed, mate, nest, and find cover at varying levels of the forest, so as a general rule, the more layers, the better.

The same holds true under water. The underwater prairie with a rich array of vertical layers presents the widest range of habitat options for a host of creatures. If you can get past the typical "yucky weeds" reaction, it's also quite beautiful.

Water Action Volunteers/Adopt-a-Lake

If you live on a river or lake and want to get involved in measuring water quality, evaluating shoreline habitat, looking at aquatic insects, or considering a whole gamut of characteristics of the water you love, two state programs are worth your time and attention. The Water Action Volunteers program, cosponsored by the DNR and Wisconsin Extension, trains people to monitor streams and rivers. Contact them in Madison at (608) 264-8948 or via the Web at www.clean-water.uwex.edu/wav/.

The Adopt-a-Lake program, sponsored by the Wisconsin Lakes Partnership, works with everyone from school kids to lake associations. Contact them at (715) 346-2116 or via their Website www.uwsp.edu/cnr/uwexlakes/adopt-a-lake.

Both programs bring science down to earth, and engage regular folks in the hands-on, feet-wet exploration of their lake or river. The data generated is compiled and used as a baseline to monitor changes over time. These quantitative measures are exceptionally helpful in turning subjective observations into objective, comparative data that we can use to accurately assess changes that many of us feel are occurring in our lakes and rivers.

If you belong to a lake or river association, give these folks a call, have them come speak to your group, and maybe train your membership to monitor the water and shorelines. It's personally educational, socially valuable, and just plain fun.

Watershield

I was asked once about the football-shaped leaves found among lily pad colonies—whether they crowd out the white and yellow water lilies, and what one could do to get rid of them.

The questioner was describing a plant called watershield, a native aquatic plant that is commonly seen growing near or among water lilies. Watershields are easily identified by the slippery clear gel that encases much of the plant, and by the fact the leaf stalks attach to the middle of the leaves.

What good is watershield? The stems, leaves, buds, and seeds of watershield are eaten by numerous waterfowl, while the leaves provide shelter and shade for a host of invertebrates and fish. In other words, watershield provides most of the same beneficial services that water lilies do. They grow in large clonal colonies like water lilies, and differ most in how demure their flowers are compared to the regal aspect of water lilies.

Thus, from a general ecological perspective, watershield is as desirable as water lilies, and should not be removed in any manner. In any case, it's illegal to remove aquatic plants from public waters. If they're crowding out water lilies, that's the way of the world. Lilies often crowd them out, too. There's likely some competitive advantage they are enjoying in a particular water body that makes them best adapted to the site.

Wetland Ferns

Ferns are not my botanical specialty, but there are two ferns that you should see with some regularity if you're out canoeing.

Royal fern is common to river and wetland edges, and is easily identified by its rounded elliptical leaves that look more like a locust tree than a typical fern. Its fertile spore-bearing stalk appears in July and is still evident in August. I've seen royal ferns commonly along Rice Creek and the Bear River, among other sites.

Sensitive fern also grows along wetland and river edges, and is also easily identified by its broad unfern-like leaves. Notice the center stem, or stipe, of each leaf, and how the leaflets are winged as they attach to the stipe. This characteristic is hard to write about, but is easily observed. Sensitive fern is very sensitive to cold, dying back with the first frost; hence, the plant's name.

Two Wild Edibles

From the woods, I like the leaves of the common wood sorrel (*Oxalis sp.*). They have a lemony flavor and can be an excellent addition to salads, or the leaves can be steeped for a citrusy tea. "Oxalis," from the Greek *oxys*, means "sour," while "sorrel" comes from the Old High German *sur*, which also means "sour." Indeed, the leaves are sour, but pleasantly so. Use wood sorrels with discretion—if eaten excessively, they are said to inhibit the absorption of calcium.

From the bogs, look under the tiny (¼-inch) leaves of creeping snowberry (*Gaultheria hispidula*) for their pure white berries, which taste like juicy wintergreen Life Savers. I've never tried the leaves, but they are said (in *Peterson's Guide to Edible Wild Plants*) to make an excellent wintergreen-flavored tea as well.

Wisconsin Wildlife

I often am asked to speak to groups that aren't from Wisconsin, and they always want to know what makes Wisconsin remarkable biologically—what are the keynotes to our state? My answer is that Wisconsin's plant and animal communities are wonderfully diverse because three major ecosystems collide here: tall-grass prairie; the east-central deciduous forest (oak-hickory-sycamore); and the northern transitional forest (what we call the "Northwoods," including white and red pine, hemlock, yellow birch, and others). The Canadian boreal forest just touches into a few areas of northern Wisconsin, so we get a number of species also appearing here at the southernmost edge of their range.

Because of the habitat diversity this represents, we are graced with the following:

- 408 bird species (400 native, eight introduced)
- 19 amphibian species (12 frogs and toads, seven salamanders)
- 35 reptile species (snakes, turtles, lizards, all native)
- 72 mammal species (69 native, three introduced)
- 159 fish species (145 native, 14 introduced)

Plant species range over 2,600, and I wouldn't want to hazard a guess on the insect species, though I'm sure a good estimate exists.

Our biodiversity is exceptional, though to try to learn all the species probably represents many lifetimes of work. I'm continually humbled but always excited by the complexity of it all.

When I'm asked to describe the biological keynotes specifically for the Northwoods, I always fall back on the four "Ws"—water, woods, wildlife, and winter. I'm tempted to add a fifth keynote, though it fails to begin with a "W," and that is beauty. I spend as much of my time as I can in a kayak on our rivers and lakes, and as the aquatic flowers bloom in August's profusion, one can only be captured by the beauty of our lake country. John Muir wrote, "No synonym for God is so perfect as beauty," and in late summer on a wild river, my whole heart beats in agreement.

Wild Rice in Flower

Mary, her sister Nancy, and I paddled a portion of Rice Creek one late August just above Island Lake, and found acres upon acres of wild rice just coming ripe. For a while, the creek channel actually became lost in the waves of rice stalks; then we were suddenly out again onto open water.

Archaeological evidence suggests that wild rice has been an important food for native people in the upper Midwest for more than 2,500 years. The "wild rice district" of Minnesota and Wisconsin was frequently spoken of by the French missionaries as a land of plenty where rice seemed inexhaustible, as did the fish and waterfowl that lived in the shallow lakes and rivers. Rice beds extended from north-central Minnesota near the headwaters of the Mississippi to the western shore of Lake Michigan, supporting an estimated 30,000 people. Fur traders ate and traded for the rice, relying on it to get them through the long winters.

Today, wild rice occupies about 20,000 acres in Minnesota and around 6,000 acres in Wisconsin, comprising the greatest concentrations of wild rice in the world.

While European wheat is now the staff of life for most Midwestern Americans, wild rice is our native staff of life, the only cereal grain native to North America. A member of the grass family, like corn, wheat, oats, barley, and millet, wild rice stores proteins, fats, and carbohydrates in the seed, providing superior nutrition.

Wild rice is also a top-flight food highly favored by just about every species of duck, swan, or goose known, as well as by a number of songbirds.

Look for wild rice to be coming ripe at the end of August. Wild rice beds ripen gradually, so the bed can be riced over the course of several weeks. Ricing is remarkably easy to do when the rice is ripe. The seed heads "shatter," meaning the seed simply falls from the plant when tapped.

If you've never tried ricing before, be sure to check with the DNR to see when the season is open, and to determine whether you need a license for the area in which you intend to rice.

Transition

By the end of August, there's usually a change in the air that's palpable. The wind has more of a bite and it carries that wonderfully rich smell of autumn that we all can recognize but can never quite describe. Change has come, and it's picking up speed. What passes for summer in the Northwoods has escaped again despite our every effort to hold on to it.

The transition is as much emotional as it is physical. As summer dies, we're reminded of how precious and short life is. It's time to let summer go and honor the bittersweet energy of autumn. It's time to start the shift inward toward winter.

Red-Winged Blackbirds Return to Manitowish

March 2, 1997
March 23, 1998
March 24, 1999
March 6, 2000
March 21, 2001
March 26, 2002
March 24, 2003
March 24, 2004
March 27, 2005
March 24, 2006

The 10-year average for the return of red-winged blackbirds is March 20.

American Robins Return to Lakeland Area

March 25, 1997
March 28, 1998
March 27, 1999
March 17, 2001
March 25, 2002
March 23, 2003
March 20, 2004
March 28, 2005
March 25, 2006

The nine-year average for the return of robins is March 24.

Canada Geese Return to Lakeland Area

March 2, 1998
March 20, 1999
March 2, 2000
March 20, 2001
March 19, 2002
March 20, 2003
March 22, 2004
March 28, 2006

The eight-year average for the return of geese is March 15.

SIGHTINGS

Community Sightings of Note – Firsts and Unusuals: 1997

3/17/97: Roger Dorsey spotted a kingfisher on Gilmore Creek near the Rainbow Flowage. Sam Robbins writes in his book *Wisconsin Birdlife* that most spring kingfisher arrivals occur between April 10 and 25 in northern Wisconsin, so Roger's sighting is quite early. Robbins notes, however, that winter kingfisher records do exist for 56 counties, including Vilas, so kingfishers occasionally remain in the Northwoods all winter when they can find running water.

3/29/97: Linda Thomas from Sayner called with sightings of cowbirds (no celebration there), and most remarkably, an eastern meadowlark.

3/29/97: Darlene and Robert Kiesgen saw hooded mergansers on the Manitowish River just out of Boulder Lake.

Community Sightings of Note – Firsts and Unusuals: 1998

3/8/98: Bob and Bev Michaels, who live on the Tomahawk River near Minocqua, noted their first sighting of a kingfisher.

3/27/98: Janet Alesauskas reported bluebirds arriving in Lake Tomahawk.

3/28/98: Russ Jacobson on Booth Lake called with his first sighting of grackles.

3/28/98: I paddled a stretch of the Manitowish River, and turned up Canada geese, wood ducks, ring-necked ducks, hooded mergansers, mallards, and green-winged teal. I was mystified by a species of songbird singing consistently in several stands of big pines along the river, and finally figured out that brown creepers were in full voice. A literal army of redpolls (hundreds) swarmed our feeders, so numerous they made the ground look like it was moving. Juncos made their arrival, too!

3/28/98: A gadwall was mixed in among the geese, mallards, and ring-necked ducks at Powell Marsh.

3/31/98: Jack Bull of Winchester called with a first sighting of a red-tailed hawk.

Community Sightings of Note -- Firsts and Unusuals: 1999

3/3/99: Mark Brandt watched a varied thrush in the Woodruff DNR parking lot. The Lakeland area seems to get one of these lost western birds every winter.

3/8/99: Mary found the first open pussy willows on the marsh below our house.

3/14/99: The Manitowish River opened below our house today. We had been out skiing on it just two days earlier, and the ice had looked good, which only shows how quickly conditions can change. On another note, Mary, Callie, and I saw a lone snow bunting while skiing on Powell Marsh.

3/24/99: Bob Kovar spotted a crow in Manitowish Waters with a white tail, a gray middle, and a black chest and head. He laughingly pondered whether it might have been eating the carrion of an albino deer, but we both agreed it was more likely a case of partial albinism.

3/27/99: Bev and Bob Michaels observed common mergansers on the Tomahawk River.

3/31/99: Linda Thomas spotted two tree swallows in Minocqua.

3/31/99: Marv Babic of Mercer reported three killdeer.

3/31/99: Bill Bender on Dead Pike Lake reported the first sandhill cranes.

Community Sightings of Note – Firsts and Unusuals: 2000

* First week of March: Jack Bull from Winchester found eight sets of shed antlers in early March, while noting that several bucks were coming to his feeder and still had their antlers intact.
* Roger Genschow reported a merlin stalking his bird feeder on Squirrel Lake near Minocqua.

3/2/00: Roy Mollen called with the sighting of an osprey on the Big St. Germain River, an exceptionally early arrival date for an osprey.

3/2/00: Terry Daulton heard a winter wren off Popco Circle Road in Mercer.

3/3/00: Exceptionally warm weather in the last three weeks of February brought about early migration for a number of birds. In Manitowish, we had our first American tree sparrow, European starling, Canada goose, belted kingfisher, and common goldeneye.

3/4/00: It was certainly a time of contrasts. Our feeders were still loaded with winter finches in early March. An ornithology class from UW-Madison stopped by our house and saw evening grosbeaks, pine grosbeaks, common redpolls, a purple finch. They also spotted a boreal chickadee and a flock of bohemian waxwings. As the week progressed, we had arctic nesting species feeding alongside red-winged blackbirds, an unusual juxtaposition!

3/5/00: Grackles and mallards returned to Manitowish,

3/7/00: Peter Dring near Land O'Lakes observed mourning cloak and Compton's tortoise shell butterflies. He also observed an osprey, eight hooded mergansers, and two rough-legged hawks that day.

3/13/00: Our dogs came in with the first wood ticks of the year!

3/18/00: Terry Daulton of Mercer reported the first woodcock.

3/19/00: Mary, Callie, and I saw a flock of at least 100 snow buntings in the Powell Marsh. We also watched a red fox sitting at a possible den site.

3/24/00: A family hike on the Powell Marsh yielded sightings of sandhill cranes, tundra swans, ring-necked and pintail ducks, and numerous rough-legged hawks.

3/25/00: Dorothy Bendrick called with a sighting of 20 eagles sitting on the ice of Little Rice Lake in Boulder Junction. The convention included 12 adults and eight immatures that sat for an hour or more in small groups all facing Dorothy's house! They were all gone by 5 p.m. that afternoon and didn't return. I suspect Dorothy was baking fish for dinner that afternoon.

3/25/00: Chip and Georgia Wulff observed a loon appear on Sunday Lake, precisely timing its arrival with the ice going off the lake.

3/26/00: Another family hike on the Powell yielded wood ducks, hooded mergansers, blue and green-winged teal, and scaup on the open water, while snow buntings were still working the iced-up portions of the marsh. The big event of the day for us was hearing a northern shrike singing from the willow tangle along the dikes. It was the first time we had ever heard a shrike sing.

3/27/00: Ada Karow from Lac du Flambeau called with the first sighting of 18 common mergansers.

3/27/00: Roger Ganschow also reported a flock of common mergansers immediately arriving on Squirrel Lake as the ice went off.

3/28/00: Jack Bull called with the first-of-the-year sighting of three killdeer on a road near Winchester.

3/31/00: Linda Thomas observed first-of-the-year tree swallows along Little Arbor Vitae Lake.

3/31/00: The spring peepers and wood frogs began chorusing from a vernal pond near our home in Manitowish in the afternoon.

Community Sightings of Note – Firsts and Unusuals: 2001

*A northern shrike had our bird feeders staked out for nearly all of March.

3/3/01: Ken Meine of Hazelhurst observed a great horned owl sitting 20 feet up in a tree next to his house. He'd been wondering why the crows were raising such a racket for the last few days near his place.

3/3/01: We finally got a flock of pine siskins in at our feeders in Manitowish. Their presence broke up the monotony of the 100 or more goldfinches that mobbed our feeders daily.

3/13/01: Kathy Vogt reported a wood duck on Little Horsehead Lake in Presque Isle.

3/16/01: Elinore Sommerfeld reported that an eagle pair was sitting on a nest on Upper Gresham Lake.

3/16/01: Annette Tellefson watched a barred owl sitting in a tree all day long outside her house. Two ravens eventually landed and sat "feather-to-feather with the owl!" she reported.

3/18/01: Hans and Linda Delius watched 14 eagles sitting in trees around the open water on Horsehead Lake.

3/19/01: Evening grosbeaks appeared at our feeders in Manitowish.

3/26/01: Mary Adams had starlings appear, and watched a northern shrike eating suet at her feeder! Usually a shrike is eating the bird that was eating the suet.

3/30/01: Mary Perkins reported a blue-phase snow goose among a flock of Canada geese loafing on Sturgeon

Lake in Manitowish Waters.

3/30/01: I paddled a section of the Manitowish and saw hooded mergansers and geese on the river. Later Mary and I saw four trumpeter swans, two adults and two cygnets, near our home on the Manitowish River.

3/31/01: Donna Schrameyer in Hazelhurst had good views of the first osprey of the year.

Community Sightings of Note – Firsts and Unusuals: 2002

*Tom Burnette in Hazelhurst had white-winged crossbills at his feeder since early March. Sandra Wenzel in Sayner had red crossbills for most of March at her feeder.

*I received two reports of common redpolls being found dead near feeders in March 2002.

*Karen and Jim Cramer in Boulder Junction had red crossbills at their feeders in March, as well as a red-headed woodpecker. Red-heads are considered uncommon winter residents in central and southern Wisconsin. As acorn eaters, red-heads usually find northern Wisconsin much too snowy for ground foraging. Their presence was a good indicator of just how snowless the 2001-02 winter was until March.

3/3/02: The Manitowish River opened up below our house on February 19, an exceptionally early opening, but then it froze over again today.

3/4/02: Bob Kovar in Manitowish Waters watched the mating of a pair of eagles that nests on his property. They mated on the branches of nearby trees, not on the nest itself. Most eagles copulate repeatedly over many days right up to egg-laying to ensure the fertility of the eggs.

3/8/02: Edie Burtch in Woodruff watched a barred owl eating a rabbit on her deck. She noticed the owl in the late morning, and it remained until late afternoon. Her husband then threw the remains of the rabbit off the deck and into the woods. The next day the dead rabbit and the owl were back on the deck, the owl apparently finding the deck a comfortable dining area. This time her husband threw the rabbit out onto the ice on the lake. The next day the barred owl was perched on their gas grill, apparently looking for the old rabbit, or maybe a fresh one!

3/12/02: Gene Somers from Presque Isle reported a northern shrike at his feeder. This was the first report I had of a northern shrike in our area this winter.

3/18/02: The first migrating songbirds to return to the Manitowish area arrived and were...ta, da, ta, da... starlings. Oh, well.

3/24/02: John Spickerman on Ike Walton Lake in Lac du Flambeau observed a sharp-shinned hawk eating the redpolls at his feeder.

3/25/02: Ada Karow in Lac du Flambeau reported the first yellow-bellied sapsucker of the year in our area.

3/29/02: June Schmaal had a barred owl overlooking her deck feeders along Johnson Lake in Arbor Vitae. The owl seemed completely acclimated to human presence, not spooking when June walked right under it.

3/30/02: Goldfinches were molting into their spring plumage – Callie said they looked like they had a bad paint job.

Community Sightings of Note – Firsts and Unusuals: 2003

*Jim Hoppe in Hazelhurst had a great horned owl nesting right in his yard, and the crows were after it in a big way. Crows hate great horned owls for a very simple reason – the great horneds fly into their communal roosts at night and take them one by one for dinner.

*Cora and Roy Mollen in St. Germain e-mailed with a wonderful sighting of an ermine, saying it "comes to try to feast on our hanging suet bag. He has to leap from the tree trunk onto the suet and takes many a tumble while trying. Once in a while he manages to hold on and eat."

3/2/03: We had our first European starlings find our feeders – oh joy. The good news is they left again.

3/13/03: Ken Boleen on Rice Lake sighted a pine grosbeak, his first for the winter. Pine grosbeaks were a rare commodity this winter.

3/15/03: Ed Stenstrom in McNaughton reported he had up to 34 mourning doves feeding at his place. Mourning doves used to be very hard to come by in the winter, but they now seem to be everywhere.

3/17/03: Nancy Doxsee got an eyeful in her first-ever sighting of a wolf. Two wolves crossed Hwy. 51 right in front of her, then stopped just off the shoulder of the road and watched her watching them.

3/17/03: We observed common goldeneye below the Rest Lake dam.

3/22/03: Cindy Carpenter called from Chicago to give us northerners a heads up that sandhill cranes were flying over the city and heading northward.

3/22/03 Our sightings included a rough-legged hawk at Powell, grackles at our feeders, and six trumpeter swans and three hooded mergansers on the Little Turtle Flowage.

3/24/03: Common mergansers and ring-necked ducks put in their first appearance on the Manitowish River.

3/24/03: Brian Ackley in Lac du Flambeau watched a ruffed grouse come to his bird feeder and eat millet and cracked corn.

3/25/03: Joanne Dugenske has a summer home in Springstead, but called from Illinois to say that she had seen 19 loons on a chain of lakes in Antioch, Illinois, and advised us to keep a heads-up.

3/26/03: Mary and Callie saw a northern harrier and five sandhill cranes on Powell Marsh.

3/29/03: Missy Drake on Round Lake in Boulder Junction had a varied thrush feeding among flocks of juncos and goldfinches at her feeder.

3/29/03: Dan Carney from Woodruff took a bird-watching drive to a boat landing on the Wisconsin River in McNaughton. He saw an Eastern phoebe sitting on a post, as well as an array of waterfowl, including black ducks, hooded mergansers, buffleheads, ring-necked ducks, scaups, and great blue herons.

Community Sightings of Note – Firsts and Unusuals: 2004

* Bev Engstrom in Rhinelander sent me a photo of a white-headed chickadee that had been visiting her mother's feeders for two winters.

* Janeen Clark on Little Ten Lake in Lac du Flambeau observed a barred owl perching off and on near her house for several weeks in early March. The owl must have had some local hunting success, because Janeen described how after one swoop for prey, the owl, "perched looking at me and opened and closed its mouth a couple of time, and out popped a pellet." (On average, owls regurgitate two pellets each day, each pellet emerging about 6½ hours after a meal.)

* In mid-March, Jack Bull in Winchester had a snowshoe hare leap up into his deer feeder and help itself to the corn.

3/15/04: David and Sharon Lintereur began tapping their 200 maple trees in Lake Tomahawk, though the sap run began slowly due to less-than-ideal temperatures.

3/17/04: Marian Brim in Jacksonville, Illinois, reported about 100 common loons gathered in a bay of the Illinois River near Havana, Illinois. Marian also noted that the wintering bald eagles on the Illinois River near Meredosia, Illinois, left that week and headed north.

3/18/04: Kay Lorbiecki in Presque Isle photographed a partial albino common redpoll visiting her feeder. The redpoll was all white, but had retained its red cap.

3/18/04: Rolf Ethun in Manitowish Waters photographed a saw-whet owl that had been hanging around his deck. At one point, Rolf observed the saw-whet and a gray squirrel sitting nearly nose-to-nose on a branch. I'm not sure what squirrels think of saw-whets, or vice versa, but obviously these individuals struck a momentary peace.

3/21/04: The Manitowish River opened below our house, despite continuous cold weather.

3/25/04: Gary Ruesch on the Rainbow Flowage watched a pair of adult red fox walk into his yard and lie down on top of the snow. In short order they began playing, wrestling, chasing one another onto the ice, jumping on one another, and in general frolicking in the snow for some 20 minutes. They finally laid back down, and eventually wandered off.

3/27/04: We observed our first grackles, purple finches, and northern harriers in Manitowish.

3/27/04: John Spickerman watched a flock of killdeers near Saxon in Iron County.

3/29/04: Gary Garton in Rhinelander saw seven sandhill cranes flying overhead.

3/29/04: Jack Bull watched a rough-legged hawk scavenging a dead deer.

3/29/04: Mary Madsen in Presque Isle had a meadowlark feeding on sunflower seeds beneath her feeders, an odd sighting given that grassland species don't spend much time in the Northwoods.

3/31/04: Gary Ruesch on the Rainbow Flowage watched an otter walk through his yard and out onto the ice. The otter began chewing at the ice and eventually made a hole and dove in. Gary could actually see it swimming under the ice. It came back up onto the ice, dove back in a second time, and emerged soon thereafter with a large bullhead in its mouth. Several dives later, it brought up another 10-12-inch bullhead, and ate half of it before diving back in and swimming away.

Community Sightings of Note – Firsts and Unusuals: 2005

*Ken Drawz reported a barred owl visiting his yard during daytime hours north of Mercer. It perched in a red pine about 30 feet from his deck and apparently was quite interested in his red squirrels. Ken watched it one day as it "seemed to go to sleep but in reality was keeping a close watch on the red squirrel which was up in a maple 75 to 100 feet away. Squirrel watched owl, and owl seemed uninterested until squirrel decided to make a run for it down the tree. Owl took off and almost got squirrel as it hit the snow and went under near a tree trunk. Owl did not get its meal."

*John Bie had a pair of red-bellied woodpeckers at his feeders just south of Woodruff. This is uncommon enough, but John says the pair has stayed year-round for the last three years, and nests somewhere nearby. One of the chicks frequently came to his suet feeder last summer. This is news indeed – I'm not familiar with anyone else in the area reporting a nesting red-bellied woodpecker. John left a number of old and dead white birches standing on his property, and he suspects that's where they are nesting.

*In mid-March, John Kresey on Springstead Lake observed a saw-whet owl sitting for more than an hour about 10 feet from his feeder. He watched as a curious gray squirrel clambered over to within two feet of the saw-whet, apparently quite interested in what this little owl was doing in its territory. The saw-whet never budged.

*John also put out a loon nesting platform for several years, and has devised a roof guard of chicken wire to keep eagles from stealing the eggs. John also feeds corn to deer, and as a result has 30 to 40 wood ducks come in every spring to his feeder, where they scrounge corn that has fallen on the ground.

3/25/05: The Manitowish River opened just a day after we had been skate-skiing along its periphery (never trust rivers to be ice-covered), and within a few hours, we heard our first Canada geese of the spring.

3/29/05: Colleen Matula saw an Eastern kingbird near Saxon in Iron County.

3/29/05: Bill Bender in Manitowish Waters had a merlin fly into his window and knock itself silly, allowing Bill to get extensive up-close looks at the merlin before it gathered its wits and flew off.

3/31/05: At dusk, Mary and I watched two woodcock doing their aerial dance in a wetland opening.

Community Sightings of Note – Firsts and Unusuals: 2006

3/6/06: John Spickerman reported seeing nine trumpeter swans on the Manitowish River by the Hwy. 51 bridge. John also watched a northern shrike stalk his feeders in Lac du Flambeau this morning.

3/10/06: Mary caught the very brief mating of the two eagles that nest across the river from us. We were sitting at our dining table and Mary was scanning through the window with her binoculars, when she suddenly said, "Get your binoculars!" I was back in 5 seconds, just in time to see the eagle already dismounted and leaving the nest. No romance wasted here!

3/10/06: Starlings appeared in our yard, the likely benefactors of the strong southerly winds and 45°F temperatures.

3/11/06: Temperatures hit 50°F, and the snow was melting so quickly that it looked like someone deflated it. There was still plenty of snow in the woods, however. I snowshoed in the afternoon, and there was at least a foot on the ground.

3/12/06: Ryan Brady reported a great day of hawk-watching at the Northern Great Lakes Visitor Center near Ashland. His four-hour total count of 80 bald eagles was the third highest in the site's history. He also tallied a single-day site record of six golden eagles, including four adults and two subadults.

3/13/06: After three straight days of mild weather and melting snow, a blizzard blew in creating white-out conditions in Manitowish. This was the first real blizzard of the 2005-06 winter for us, dropping 22 inches of snow. It came complete with a few flashes of lightning and peels of thunder. Any birds that came north on the strong winds and warm temperatures the day before were no doubt seeking therapy.

Frog Phenology

April signals the beginning of frog courting in northern Wisconsin. By mid-May, the crescendo of chorusing frogs and toads can amaze you. Love knows no bounds. The male who sings loudest may have the best luck attracting the girls, so volume control isn't part of the plan.

Northern Wisconsin typically provides habitat for eight frog species and one toad species. Two factors trigger the emergence of hibernating frogs: frost-out/ice-out and temperature. Spring rains that occur near frost-out and ice-out typically rev the migration of early spring frogs into gear.

All Wisconsin frogs and toads require water for breeding. Note how the early breeders call from ephemeral waters, while later breeders use permanent waters. Deeper, permanent waters warm up much more slowly than temporary, shallow ponds and marshes. Given that water temperature greatly affects breeding, it makes sense that early breeders would utilize the shallowest waters.

But vernal (temporary) ponds represent a real roulette wheel. When wood frogs, spring peepers, chorus frogs, and leopard frogs move to these ponds to breed, they engage in a race to breed, hatch their eggs, and have their tadpoles transform into terrestrial frogs before the water dries up. It's a gamble that eliminates predators like fish, but it also ups the chances in a drought year of being caught high and dry before the tadpoles can develop lungs.

Here's the general phenology for northern frogs and their habitat:

Species	Breeding Period	Habitat
Wood frog	late April to early May	vernal pond
Spring peeper	late April to late May	vernal pond/marsh
Chorus frog	late April to mid May	vernal pond/marsh
Leopard frog	early May to early June	lakes/streams/marsh
American toad	early May to early June	shallow waters
Eastern gray treefrog	late May to June	trees/shrubs near water
Mink frog	June	cool, permanent water
Green frog	June to mid July	all permanent water
Bullfrog	mid June to July	all permanent water

Frogs in April

4/23/97: Spring peepers began singing in Manitowish.

4/29/97: Chorus frogs began singing in Manitowish. I also watched numerous wood frogs all clasped together in one writhing lump in a little ephemeral pond.

4/5/98: Spring peepers and wood frogs began their choral courting.

4/20/98: Leopard frogs were gurgling away in shallow marshlands. Their "song" is best likened to the sound of stomach acid, a sort of growling, rumbling indigestion.

4/7/99: Spring peepers and wood frogs began calling in the Manitowish area.

4/2/00: Woody Hagge and family heard leopard frogs on Foster Lake in Hazelhurst, an exceptionally early date for leopard frogs.

4/24/00: We heard our first chorus frogs.

4/14/01: Spring peepers and wood frogs began chorusing in the Mercer/ Manitowish area.

4/26/01: I did my first DNR frog count of the year and had spring peepers chorusing at all 10 locations. I also heard a few leopard frogs on Whitney Flowage, a rather early observation. The next day, Callie and I heard leopard and chorus frogs chorusing out on the Powell Marsh.

4/30/01: Toads began trilling.

4/16/02: Wood frogs, spring peepers, and chorus frogs began chorusing.

4/7/05: We heard our first spring peepers and wood frogs – this is very early for them!

4/12/05: I heard my first chorus frogs.

4/10/06: Spring peepers and wood frogs began calling in Manitowish.

Loons in April

4/5/97: Woody Hagge watched three adult loons fly low over Foster Lake, the first loons reported in the area.

4/7/99: Linda Thomas from Sayner called with the first sighting of two loons on the Wisconsin River, apparently awaiting the opening of our local lakes.

4/9/99: Ron and Lois Hine on Lake Towanda, Uwe Wiechering on Diamond Lake, and Russ Gaarder on Sunday Lake all e-mailed me with sightings that day of the first loon on their lake.

4/1/00: Diane Shay reported the first loon on Verna Lake in Arbor Vitae. Many loons were still in transit! A posting on the Wisconsin BirdNet from April 1, and another two days earlier, reported counts of up to 136 loons staging on Lake Monona and Mendota in Madison. Unlike typical ice-outs in later April when loons seem to magically appear at the exact moment the ice lets go, the early ice-out (March 25) on many area lakes seemed to have come even too early for the loons. Many open lakes were still awaiting the return of "their loons" a week later.

4/8/01: Art Barlow saw four common loons arrive on the Wisconsin River near his property in Rhinelander. In past springs, Art has had dozens of loons "stack up" while awaiting the opening of lakes.

4/21/01: Karen Kappell spotted a pair of loons on Wild Rice Lake, shortly after ice-out.

4/21/01: Chuck and Joan Schell had loons return to Blue Lake.

4/17/02: Jane Lueneburg reported a pair of loons returned to a 35-acre lake in Woodboro – the ice went out that night and the loons were there by 5:30 a.m.

4/18/02: Jim Sommerfeldt observed two loons on Middle Sugarbush Lake in Lac du Flambeau.

4/19/02: Bob Cayze watched ice-out take place on White Sand Lake around 1 p.m. and by 4 p.m., two loons had taken up residence.

4/18/03: Ada Karow in Lac du Flambeau reported the first loon on Mitten Lake.

4/12/05: Ed Marshall reported the ice went off Squaw Lake west of Minocqua on April 10, and two days later he heard his first loon.

4/13/06: The first loons were reported on several area lakes.

Sightings

Community Sightings of Note – Firsts and Unusuals: 1997

4/1/97: Pete Dring had both a male cardinal and song sparrows appear around his home in Land O'Lakes. Pete also measured the amount of water that the snowpack actually contained that day. He found 5.5 inches of water in 12 inches of snow. A light powder snow, in contrast, usually holds about 1 inch of water for every 10 inches of snow.

4/2/97: Linda Thomas in Sayner reported the first killdeer and geese.

4/2/97: Ada Karow watched a fox sparrow at her feeder in Lac du Flambeau, and she heard a male saw-whet owl calling.

4/2/97: Pete Dring observed a morning cloak and Milbert's tortoiseshell butterfly. Morning cloaks and the tortoiseshells are members of the anglewing family, a group of butterflies that overwinter as adults in our area.

4/3/97: Jack Bull watched two beaver kits feeding on the ice with two adult beavers on Plum Lake in Sayner. Last year's kits will be pushed out of the lodge later this spring when the new young are born.

4/3/97: Mary and I saw our first killdeer and northern harrier in Manitowish.

4/4/97: Ada Karow observed a yellow-bellied sapsucker.

4/4/97: Mary saw a sandhill crane flying down the Manitowish River, and song sparrows were singing in our yard in the morning. I took my first canoe trip of the year on the Manitowish and saw numerous mallards, hooded mergansers, wood ducks, Canada geese, and common mergansers. The most numerous birds by far were robins feeding all along the exposed muddy and icy shores of the river.

4/6/97: Jana Jirak observed an Eastern kingbird near the Rainbow Flowage in St. Germain, a most unusual sighting given that this neotropical migrant usually doesn't arrive back in northern Wisconsin until mid-May. They winter from Colombia south to Argentina and Chile.

4/6/97: Mary and I found our first flowering hazelnut. Cowbirds and tree sparrows arrived at our feeders.

4/10/97: Pete Dring in Land O'Lakes saw the first phoebe of the season.

4/13/97: Mary and I watched two flocks of tundra swans silently fly over our house. It's difficult to imagine a sight more beautiful than a flock of sun-lit white swans against a brilliant blue sky.

4/15/97: Pete Dring reported the first yellow-rumped warbler of the season, and noted that the first male catkins on alder were producing pollen that same day.

4/21/97: Tree and cliff swallows returned to Bob Kovar's home in Manitowish Waters. One tree swallow was already sitting in its nest box.

4/25/97: Mary and I observed our first hermit thrush and snipe of the year.

4/25/97: Bonnie Drozdzik observed 16 loons all swimming together on a patch of open water on Lake Gilmore near the Rainbow Flowage. The ice went off most of our lakes a few days later, but prior to that waterbirds were confined to the few areas that held open water.

4/28/97: Mary and I saw our first greater yellowlegs on the Powell.

4/29/97: Swamp sparrows began singing in Manitowish.

Community Sightings of Note – Firsts and Unusuals: 1998

*In early April 1998, Donna Schrameyer

from Hazelhurst found ten or more redpolls dead in her backyard over a two- or three-day span, the likely victims of salmonella poisoning.

* Donna was also one of numerous people who reported black bears visiting their feeders in early April. The bears, in their usual nimble and gentle manner, knocked over her feeders.

4/2/98: Sue Whitfield watched a pair of kingfishers mate on her property in St. Germain.

4/2/98: Deer ticks were already numerous.

4/2/98: Mary Goldthorpe from Lac du Flambeau reported a tom turkey eating sunflower seeds and corn under her bird feeder. At that time I wrote this: "Usually a sighting like Mary's of a "southern" bird can be dismissed as an anomaly or as a released bird, but wild turkeys have greatly increased in population and range in southern and central Wisconsin, so it's possible we may begin to see more turkeys attempting to pioneer the north country." Now in 2006, turkeys are seen rather commonly.

4/3/98: Gary Milanowski reported a dozen or more woodcocks doing their evening sky dance at the North Lakeland Discovery Center.

4/4/98: Mary and I observed our first sandhill crane of the year flying down the Manitowish River.

4/4/98: Tag alder, hazelnut, and silver maple came into flower in Manitowish.

4/5/98: Fox sparrows appeared in Manitowish, along with a flock of brilliantly colored evening grosbeaks.

4/5/98: While paddling a section of the Wisconsin River, Jeff Richter and I managed to kick up hundreds of geese, mallards, common mergansers, and scaup, along with a few hooded mergansers and wood ducks. Three tundra swans gave us a fly-over, and we had at least 15 separate sightings of muskrats, the most either of us can ever remember seeing in a short two-hour paddle.

4/6/98: We heard the first winnowing snipe overhead in Manitowish.

4/8-9/98: Area lakes opened up very early. Most ice went out during this two-day period.

4/15/98: Mark Zanoni of Three Lakes observed numerous yellowlegs (unsure if they were greater or lesser yellowlegs) along the mud flats of the Manitowish River.

4/17/98: Linda Thomas from Sayner reported first sightings of phoebes, flickers, white-throated sparrows, and yellow-bellied sapsuckers.

4/17/98: Rosie Richter from Mercer saw a trailing arbutus in flower, the first flower of the year in our upland pine forests.

4/19/98: White-throated sparrows returned to our feeders.

4/20/98: Mary and I took our inaugural sea kayaking trip on the Turtle-Flambeau Flowage and saw many birds, but the standouts included a dozen or so yellow-rumped warblers flitting along the shoreline, numerous winter wrens singing their hearts out, and pied-billed grebes diving and calling from a host of marshy locations. If you're not familiar with the pied-billed's call, it's raucous and singular. I still like Pete Dring's easily recalled description. He says they sound like they're laying a square egg: *Ow, ow, ow, ow, ow. . ow . . . ow . . . . Ow!!*

Community Sightings of Note – Firsts and Unusuals: 1999

* Eagles typically lay their eggs around April 1. Hatch occurs around May 1.

4/2/99: Song sparrows, wood ducks, cranes, and hooded mergansers found their way to Manitowish.

4/3/99: Juncos and tree and fox sparrows arrived in Manitowish.
4/4/99: Phil Williams called with the first sighting of a bear, wandering across his driveway on North Turtle Lake in Winchester.
4/7/99: Pete Racey observed 30 or more common mergansers on Stone Lake.
4/8/99: Dick Rust observed hundreds of white pelicans on the Wisconsin River just south of McNaughton. The wild rice marshes on the Wisconsin River that are visible from Hwy. 47 south of McNaughton are worthy of a stop anytime you pass them this time of year. The site attracts great numbers of waterfowl, including hundreds of tundra swans every year.
4/8/99: Jack Bull in Winchester spotted two vultures.
4/9/99: Tree swallows were back on the Little Turtle Flowage, as were two ospreys.
4/12/99: Mary and I hiked out on Powell Marsh and saw our first-of-the-year greater yellowlegs, shovelers, American bittern, and marsh hawks. Mary also saw a woodcock that same day in the marsh below our house
4/12/99: Audie Mellenthin from Presque Isle reported a trumpeter swan on Oxbow Lake.
4/15/99: We finally stopped over at the Folsom Cranberry Marsh on Little Trout Lake in Manitowish Waters, where Bob Kovar had been telling us for two weeks that a flock of tundra swans were loafing and feeding. Remarkably, they were still there, 23 of them, feeding comfortably amidst significant numbers of bufflehead, goldeneye, geese, hooded mergansers, wigeons, common mergansers, and mallards.
4/20/99: In Manitowish, our first white-crowned sparrow arrived.
4/25/99: Mary and I saw our first flowering trailing arbutus and hepatica. If your trailing arbutuses are oddly short on fragrance, give them a good misting with water and the wonderful aroma should emerge. The suggestion comes courtesy of Mary Beth Kolarchek of Manitowish Waters.
4/26/99: In Manitowish, our first white-throated sparrow appeared.
4/30/99: Judy Rice reported two white pelicans on Amik Lake.

Community Sightings of Note – Firsts and Unusuals: 2000

* Audrae Kulas on Little Gibson Lake and Donna Schrameyer of Hazelhurst e-mailed during the first week of April to comment on how the ground looked like it was "moving" because of the huge numbers of juncos and redpolls passing through.
4/1/00: Teena Orling reported seeing a male cardinal on the eighteenth fairway of the Timber Ridge Golf Course in Minocqua. Being from St. Louis where cardinals are common, Teena was particularly pleased to get a look at this beautiful species that seldom wanders as far north as Minocqua.
4/1/00: Mary and I visited Little Trout Lake and saw very sizable flocks of common mergansers and goldeneye, as well as numerous marsh and rough-legged hawks. A turkey vulture also sailed directly over our heads near Powell Marsh.
4/2/00: Bob Kovar, the manager of a cranberry bog on the north end of Little Trout Lake, watched 15 tundra swans dabbling near the shoreline. It seems fair to say that Little Trout attracts more than its share of migrating waterfowl and should be on the list of sites for birders to watch in the spring.
4/2/00: That afternoon we kayaked with friends Chad McGrath and Mary

Jo Sloane on the Turtle-Flambeau Flowage and saw numerous eagles, buffleheads, hooded mergansers, wood ducks, and Canada geese.

4/3/00: A host of first-of-the-year sightings were happening, but I could hardly see across the river through the snow squalls. Our feeders and the ground beneath them were loaded with birds. We had evening grosbeaks and redpolls left over from the winter, and additional large numbers of juncos, tree/fox/song sparrows, red-winged blackbirds, grackles, and starlings. Smaller numbers of house finches, pine siskins, and American goldfinch, along with our resident blue jays, hairy and downy woodpeckers, chickadees, mourning doves, and nuthatches rounded out the army. It was a bit of a zoo out there!

4/4/00: Bob Burge observed a hen turkey in his yard on Boot Lake in Springstead.

4/5/00: Jack Bull of Winchester watched a spotted fawn come to his deer feeder. He estimated the fawn to be roughly two months old.

4/10/00: Bob Kovar reported that 30 or more tundra swans were on Little Trout Lake. Last year, a similar-sized flock chose to do the same during our similarly early spring, waiting for several weeks before launching for their Arctic nesting grounds.

4/14/00: Rolf Ethun saw a yellow-rumped warbler in the Boulder Junction area, the first warbler I heard tell of that year.

4/15/00: Jean Long reported a deluge of common redpolls at her feeders. Several other folks called with similar numbers of redpolls. These little armies of redpolls seem to come through in early spring every other year, feed voraciously for a week, and then move on.

4/17/00: Bev Van Goethem of Hazelhurst had an early male bluebird in her sumac.

4/18/00: Kent Collett observed how robins survive the bitter cold and ice that April can serve up. Kent was hiking along an open stream near his Park Falls home when he saw bird tracks in the snow leading to the water's edge. There, robins were shaking leaf debris looking for insects and eating bugs from along the edge of the water.

4/21/00: Don and Greta Janssen e-mailed with the sighting of a female white-winged crossbill coming to their feeder in Woodruff.

4/24/00: In Manitowish, we first heard or saw phoebes, flickers, and white-throated sparrows. That same day on Powell Marsh, we saw the first greater yellowlegs of the year as well as 11 hawks in the air at one time, nearly all hover-hunting.

4/26/00: We heard our first American bitterns, hermit thrush, and snipe.

4/30/00: We found our first hepatica and trailing arbutus in flower.

Community Sightings of Note – Firsts and Unusuals: 2001

4/1/01: Jack Bull in Winchester reported having a lone redpoll at his feeder, the only redpoll reported to me in our area all winter.

4/1/01: Terry Daulton and Jeff Wilson heard the first sandhill cranes of the year calling on the Turtle-Flambeau Flowage

4/9/01: Rosie Richter reported the earliest sighting of a pair of bluebirds just north of Mercer.

4/10/01: Art Barlow reported tundra swans on the Wisconsin River near McNaughton.

4/11/01: Peter Dring observed tree swallows near Land O'Lakes.

4/13/01: Pete Dring observed golden-crowned kinglets, white-crowned sparrows, chipping sparrows, and hermit thrushes, the first of these species reported this year.

4/13/01: Audrae Kulas had fox, tree, and song sparrows return to her feeders, as well as a red-bellied woodpecker.

4/16/01: Chuck and Joan Schell in Minocqua reported a yellow-bellied sapsucker and phoebes. They also had mallards that came up from the lake and ate their birdseed on the ground.

4/16/01: A post by Paul Bowman to the Wisconsin BirdNet described red-necked grebes seen on Stacks Bay on Lake Minocqua.

4/16/01: Joan and Chuck Schell spotted a pine warbler at their feeders on Minocqua's Blue Lake.

4/17/01: Allan Schrank, a smoke spotter for the DNR working in the Squirrel Hill fire tower, watched two turkey vultures hovering just a few feet outside his tower window. That could be unnerving!

4/17/01: Barb Schrank observed five turkeys crossing Squirrel Lake Road.

4/20/01: Dan Carney discovered yellow-rumped warblers and ruby-crowned kinglets on the Bearskin Trail near Harshaw.

4/20/01: Barn swallows returned to the Manitowish River.

4/21/01: We heard snipe winnowing on the Manitowish.

4/23/01: Mary and I spotted several greater yellowlegs on Powell Marsh. In a study of contrasts that evening, it was snowing and blowing wildly outside, but spring peepers and wood frogs were singing at the top of their lungs all the while.

4/25/01: Gary Ruesch viewed nine white pelicans loafing on the Rainbow Flowage.

4/25/01: Jack Bull watched a bobcat ambling down South Turtle Lake Road in the mid-morning, apparently oblivious to his presence as he walked toward it.

4/26/01: Leatherwoods, aspens, willows, red and silver maples, hazelnuts, and alders were all in flower.

4/27/01: I took my first swim of the year in the Turtle River, upside down in my kayak. Need I say it was unplanned? Yes, the water was COLD.

4/29/01: We heard black-and-white warblers and black-throated green warblers while hiking at the Plum Lake/Star Lake State Natural Area.

4/29/01: Rosie Richter reported the first Baltimore oriole at her feeders just north of Mercer.

4/30/01: Trailing arbutus and hepatica were in flower in Manitowish.

Community Sightings of Note – Firsts and Unusuals: 2002

4/1/02: Jacky Sell in Winchester found cougar tracks in her son's yard. They took measurements and pictures to verify their identification.

4/5/02: Betty Roe in Manitowish Waters reported that a dozen white-winged crossbills had been present at her feeders for the last three weeks.

4/7/02: Jane Lueneburg in Woodboro reported an osprey sitting on nest on Stag Lake, 8 miles west of Rhinelander.

4/8/02: Cora and Roy Mollen on the St. Germain River observed: "A group of newly-come buffleheads put on a fascinating display for more than a half hour. The routine went like this. All dive. All rise. Then scoot across the water together at lightning speed with bodies held almost out of water. This was repeated over and over. Amazing."

4/9/02: Jack Bull in Winchester reported seeing snow buntings migrating back through our area on their way north.

4/11/02: Jane Lueneburg in Woodboro observed the first fox sparrows, juncos, and tree sparrows.

4/11/02: Dan Carney in Minocqua reported the first yellow-bellied sapsuckers and chipping sparrows, and still had dozens of redpolls coming to his feeders.

4/11/02: Mary and I heard our first woodcock peenting below our house in Manitowish. We also saw a flock of 18 bohemian waxwings at Mary's father's house in Wausau. They were eating the fruits from a neighbor's flowering crab tree, then coming into his yard and picking up pieces of ice, apparently for drinking water.

4/11-12/02: Dave Picard in Lake Tomahawk reported the first tree swallows and winter wrens.

4/13/02: Linda Thomas in Sayner reported the first bluebirds and white-throated sparrows, and heard a loon flying over, undoubtedly looking for open water and finding none.

4/14/02: Jim Cramer in Boulder Junction observed northern flickers and a flock of 50 or more robins.

4/14/02: Audrae Kulas saw a fritillary butterfly in the Rhinelander area.

4/14/02: Mary, Callie and I walked Powell Marsh and saw at least four pairs of sandhill cranes, mallards, Canada geese, black ducks, wigeons, shovelers, wood ducks, hooded mergansers, green-winged teal, and numerous eagles. The highlights were a flock of 40 or more snow buntings, and three species of shorebirds – killdeer, greater yellowlegs, and pectoral sandpipers.

4/15/02: We kayaked a short stretch of the flooding Manitowish River, and saw 33 species of birds, including 11 species of ducks, trumpeter swans, a flock of snow geese, bald eagles galore, a northern shrike, tree swallows, Eastern phoebes, kingfishers, flickers, yellow-bellied sapsuckers, great blue heron, and the highlight – a yellow-rumped warbler. Every corner of the river held another flock of ducks. After five months of mostly feeder birding, this was heaven.

4/15/02: Howard Johnson watched two wolves cross Bobcat Lake at 7:30 in the morning, 3 miles south of Minocqua, and walk right in front of his dock.

4/15/02: Cora Mollen opened a birdhouse on her St. Germain property and found it packed with dried mushroom caps. Some squirrel had apparently planned some gourmet winter dining.

4/16/02: Mary and Callie saw of flock of eight white pelicans on Powell Marsh. In the late afternoon, the pelicans were gone, but a flock of tundra swans had replaced them.

4/17/02: Leatherwood came into flower in Rhinelander.

4/17/02: Dan Carney watched three turkeys wandering about in the Hazelhurst area. Dan also saw canvasbacks on the water that day.

4/17/02: Scott Kimball saw a pair of pine warblers and noted that they like peanut butter.

4/17/02: Jim Sommerfeldt on Middle Sugarbush Lake in Lac du Flambeau had a bear destroy his feeder.

4/20/02: Mona Wiechmann in Manitowish Waters found a sharp-shinned hawk on her deck that had lost a battle with her window.

4/20/02: Darrell and Lyla Thornton observed a flock of cormorants on Amik Lake.

4/21/02: We heard snipe winnowing on the Little Turtle Flowage during a snow flurry.

4/22/02: We saw our first turkey vultures near Presque Isle.

4/22/02: Scott Kimball in Boulder Junction observed a pair of red crossbills apparently involved in courtship – Scott was able to walk to within 5 feet of the female.

4/28/02: Dan Carney observed a gray-cheeked thrush in his Hazelhurst yard. The bird eventually entered his garage and Dan had to capture it to get it out. Gray-cheeks nest in far northern Canada.

4/29/02: Marilyne Haag observed three vultures perched in a tree outside her home in Boulder Junction, and they stayed through dinnertime. This is not usually a good sign.

Community Sightings of Note – Firsts and Unusuals: 2003

4/7/03: John Spickerman reported a tufted titmouse at his feeder! These birds are relatively common in southern Wisconsin, but seldom are seen in the Northwoods.

4/10/03: Parker Sharp observed a varied thrush at his feeders on Papoose Lake in Manitowish Waters.

4/12/03: In Manitowish, we saw our first turkey vulture and heard our first winter wren singing.

4/12/03: Linda Thomas reported the first osprey of the year standing on the power pole nest that is easily seen just off Highway 47 south of Lake Tomahawk.

4/13/03: Sally Hegeman in Boulder Junction spotted a saw-whet owl perched on the handle of her snow shovel, where it remained for about half an hour.

4/14/03: Pete and Carolyn Dring in Land O'Lakes observed a pair of red-breasted mergansers sitting on a nest, and saw their first dragonfly.

4/15/03: Pete and Carolyn watched a flock of tree swallows winging over their lake, as well as seeing a northern flicker and yellow-bellied sapsucker.

4/16/03: Susie Breiten noticed two hummingbirds flying around her deck! She quickly concocted some sugar water nectar, filled up her feeder, and placed it outside, but by then the hummers had departed. The next morning the nectar was frozen. Hummers don't usually return until around Mother's Day, so Susie's sighting was exceptionally early.

4/18/03: Ada Karow in Lac du Flambeau reported the return of white-throated sparrows.

4/18/03: We observed a common snipe rummaging around under our feeder, a quite unusual behavior for a snipe.

4/18/03: Ginny Sparkowski and Natalie Gleffe in Woodruff/Minocqua watched a great blue heron spear and swallow a small mammal, ID unknown.

4/19/03: Jack Bull in Winchester reported seeing a wood thrush.

4/19/03: We nearly ran over a woodcock that was standing in the middle of the road on our way to Powell Marsh. At the marsh, most notable were 12 sandhill cranes, a pintail duck amongst a flock of mallards and ring-necks, and several yellowlegs, species unknown, usually the first neotropical shorebird to return to our area.

4/21/03: We observed at our feeders probably two dozen fox sparrows, as well as a bevy of tree and song sparrows, juncos, purple finches, eight evening grosbeaks, goldfinches, mourning doves, blue jays, and a noisy collection of blackbirds – rusties, brewer's, red-wingeds, cowbirds, and grackles.

4/22/03: Gary Ruesch on the Rainbow Flowage observed 30 tundra swans, and a day later, a flock of 75 common mergansers.

4/23/03: Dr. Chomingwen Pond observed a flock of about 60 swans resting on Lake Shishebogama in Minocqua. She wrote, "They apparently tucked their heads under their wings for a snooze, for what we saw most of the time was mounds of white feathers on the blue waters of the lake." She wasn't sure of their identification, but a flock of this size was almost certainly tundra swans migrating through on their way to their Arctic nesting grounds.

4/25/03: Gary Ruesch on the Rainbow Flowage reported watching 10 bald eagles sitting single file along the edge of the ice just before the ice went out.

4/25/03: White-crowned sparrows showed up at John Campbell's feeders in Minocqua.

4/28/03: Jo Duller on Diamond Lake had a yellow warbler at her feeder.

4/28/03: Chuck and Debra Smith in St. Germain reported pine warblers in their yard.

4/29/03: Suzanne Denney watched a bobcat on Squirrel Lake Road near Winter Park. Mary and I finally saw our first-ever bobcat a few weeks earlier, crossing Highway 51 in the morning.

Community Sightings of Note – Firsts and Unusuals: 2004

* Turkeys are becoming relatively common up here. Rick Jolen called on 4/13 with the sighting of a hen turkey on old Hwy. 70 in Minocqua. Janeen Clark reported seeing a turkey crossing Hwy. 70 West in Minocqua near Wal Mart on 4/14. Linda Thomas saw two turkeys at the Woodruff Senior Center on 4/16. Jack Bull watched two turkeys cross Powell Road in Manitowish Waters on 4/26.

4/2/04: We took our first paddle of the year on the Manitowish River, and saw our first wood ducks and common mergansers.

4/3/04: A sharp-shinned hawk sat by our feeders.

4/4/04: Another paddle on the Manitowish turned up our first belted kingfisher. Mary and Callie heard sandhill cranes the same day on a hike near Powell Marsh.

4/5/04: Song and tree sparrows appeared at our feeders, and we saw a kestrel, turkey vulture, goldeneyes, and shovelers the same day on a trip up to Ashland.

4/5/04: Bruce Bacon in Mercer reported a white-throated sparrow.

4/5/04: Fox sparrows arrived in large numbers during the first 10 days of April. Ada Karow on Mitten Lake in Lac du Flambeau observed a flock at her feeders, along with her first phoebe of the year. Mary and I had a dozen or more show up at our feeders the next day.

4/6/04: Ospreys returned to the nesting platforms along Hwy. 47 north of McNaughton. Jane Lueneburg had the great good fortune of watching sandhill cranes in a farmer's field engage in their courtship dance. They "pranced around with much head-bobbing and dipped – sometimes all the way to the ground. One would jump in the air and also partially flap his wings. It's the first time I've ever seen the sandhills dance in person...and I was thrilled."

4/6/04: Kay Lorbiecki in Presque Isle was watching her large flock of common redpolls at her feeders when a merlin swooped in and tried to take one. Kay wrote, "The redpolls vaporized, leaving the merlin standing on the ground five feet from the window. He looked around for maybe five minutes, hopped up on a birch log and wondered where his mid-morning snack went."

4/10/04: Laurie Timm had both tree and fox sparrows at her feeders. Juncos arrived everywhere it seemed around the same time.

4/11/04: Dave and Sharon Lintereur pulled their maple syrup taps after gathering 1,200 gallons of sap, burning nine cords of wood, and ultimately making about 24 gallons of syrup.

4/13/04: Dan Carney observed his first yellow-rumped warbler on the Bearskin Trail, along with golden-crowned kinglets, common snipe, and hermit thrushes.

4/14/04: Arnold Sawatske had a male cardinal coming to his feeders in Presque Isle.

4/16/04: Dan Carney observed his first northern flicker, wood-pewee, and yellow-bellied sapsucker, and found a pair of Eastern phoebes already on nest.

4/18/04: I buried my car in the mud on Circle Lily Road right before a monster thunderstorm rolled in, but I did get to hear my first winter wren of the year as I walked out with thunder rumbling all around me. There are silver linings in just about everything.

4/19/04: White-throated sparrows appeared at our feeders, and I heard our first American bittern in the marsh the same day. I need some help on the following sighting. A fellow in the U.P. reported seeing a big ball of earthworms where a culvert goes under the road and into some water. He estimated he could fill two 5-gallon buckets with them. Does anybody have any explanation for this?

4/26/04: Tracy Janeczko watched a pine warbler eating sunflower seeds at her feeder in Manitowish Waters.

4/26/04: Janet Akey observed two swans on Lynx Lake, the first she had ever seen in 13 years of living on the lake. Shortly thereafter, a loon swam up and chased the swans off!

4/27/04: Dan Carney birds regularly along the Bearskin Trail south of Minocqua, and reported seeing three horned grebes.

4/29/04: Dan Carney observed palm warblers, great crested flycatchers, and veeries, and a day later saw Nashville warblers.

Community Sightings of Note – Firsts and Unusuals: 2005

* Spring came on remarkably fast in 2005. In the phenology of human events of spring, three important milestones occurred: We left our windows open overnight for the first time on 3/27/05; ate our first lunch out on the deck while soaking up sun on 3/28/05; and hung out our laundry to dry for the first time on 4/3/05. After a long winter, these events are always thoroughly appreciated!

* Mary Madsen e-mailed me with the following story: "We have enjoyed watching the antics of an otter as it comes out of the lake up onto the ice for a short jaunt & a roll in the snow, before diving back into the hole of open water. We also knew that our resident pair of eagles were watching him too. The other day we came home to see the pair of eagles feasting on otter. After awhile, their fledgling joined them. When there was barely anything left, 2 more young eagles (not fully mature) also stopped for a bite to eat. At one time there were four of them 'picking' remains. By the next day, all that remained were a few tufts of fur, and plenty of tell-tale tracks in the snow. I'm not liking our eagles quite so much these days, but it is nature's way!"

4/1/05: Colleen Matula saw golden-crowned kinglets in Boulder Junction, and a chipping sparrow the next day.

4/1/05: At Manitowish, we heard our first song sparrows.

4/2/05: Fox sparrows appeared in Manitowish.

4/2/05: Jeff Wilson and Terry Daulton heard sandhill cranes near the Turtle-Flambeau Flowage.

4/3/05: Zach Wilson observed a northern harrier.

4/3/05: I paddled a section of the Manitowish and saw my first blue-winged teal of the year. Mary saw the first turkey vulture of the year also.

4/4/05: Phil and Nancy Williams reported that Rock Creek near Winchester was full of common and hooded mergansers, as well as buffleheads.

4/4/05: Bob Kovar observed great blue herons near Manitowish Waters.

4/4/05: Mary, Callie, and I walked the dikes at Powell Marsh and at one point watched 17 hawks in the air, 15 of which were rough-legs.

4/4/05: Laurie Timm reported the first kingfisher of the year near Witches Lake.

4/5/05: We saw our first osprey of the year sitting on one of the nests along Hwy. 47 near McNaughton.

4/5/05: Dave Holmes watched a northern shrike snap an insect out of the air like a flycatcher on Powell Marsh.

4/5/05: Mary Madsen watched three flocks of tundra swans fly overhead, "low enough to hear the rustle of their wings." She estimated they totaled around 100 swans. She also watched two flocks of sandhill cranes fly overhead.

4/5/05: Dave Koch observed two trumpeter swans sitting on the ice along the Trout River. He and his son listened as they trumpeted numerous times, then produced a garbled trumpeting like "a deep throated bullfrog." Dave's son could still see them and said they were trumpeting with their beaks underwater! I have no explanation for that.

4/6/05: Dave Holmes reported the first yellow-bellied sapsuckers and golden-crowned kinglets of the spring. Jack Bull reported the first flicker of the year in Winchester.

4/7/05: Bruce Bacon watched wild turkeys engage in courtship behaviors near the Little Turtle Flowage in Mercer.

4/8/05: We observed our first ring-necked ducks and heard our first pied-billed grebe on the Little Turtle Flowage.

4/8/05: Bill Bayer watched three tom turkeys wander through his yard on the north end of the Turtle-Flambeau Flowage.

4/8/05: Dan Carney had turkeys in his yard in Hazelhurst, and watched the male displaying to the two hens. He also reported the first winter wren of the year.

4/9/05: Out on Powell Marsh, we watched a flock of 20 or more snow buntings landing on the rotting ice. We also saw our first green-winged teal of the year, as well as a flock of nine tundra swans.

4/10/05: The ice went off many lakes in the area today. Woody Hagge reported that the ice went out on Foster Lake in Hazelhurst, one week ahead of the 32-year average. On 3/26, he measured 21.5 inches of ice on Foster. Two weeks later, the ice was gone, by far the quickest melt since Woody has kept records. Woody noted that even the loons were caught off guard. They didn't return until two days later.

4/11/05: John Firnett on Spider Lake had a male cardinal singing at his feeder.

4/12/05: The first leatherwood shrubs came into flower in Rhinelander. Several folks reported their first mosquitoes buzzing them – sad, but true.

4/14/05: Dave Holmes reported two short-eared owls flying at Powell Marsh.

4/17/05: Dave Holmes observed the first bittern of the year on Powell.

4/17/05: Janet Alesauskas reported the first yellow-rumped warblers of the year in the Lake Tomahawk area.

4/17/05: Amber Roth reported seeing a scissors-tailed flycatcher! The bird was fly-catching in an open field along Hwy. 51, just two miles south of Manitowish.

4/18/05: Dan Carney reported the first hermit thrush this year in the Hazelhurst area.

4/23/05: A rarity sighted this month was a northern mockingbird. It was seen at the home of Nancy Skowland at Powell in Iron County. A few years back Nancy had a painted bunting at her house, so there must be some strange energy convergence going on at her place that the birds love.

4/23/05: The first white-throated sparrows returned to Manitowish.

4/25/05: Leatherleaf came into flower, despite the cold.

4/26/05: Dave Holmes observed a greater yellowlegs on Powell Marsh.

4/30/05:Migration is all about timing. The three weeks of cold weather that followed our initial warm spell this April held down insect hatchings, and the consequences for birds were substantial. Marge Gibson, an exceptional wildlife rehabilitator in the Antigo area, wrote: "We have received many purple martins and swallows starving due to the cold temperatures and lack of insects. Many swallows are being found dead in nest boxes as well...Out of 16 pairs of a local colony, I have 10 birds in and 2 died on site during the night."

Fish Spawning Phenology on the Manitowish River

Species	Timeframe	Substrate/Habitat
Burbot	Jan-March	gravel
Northern pike	early April	silt/detritus/flooded vegetation
Walleye	mid-April	gravel/cobble
Yellow perch	early May	silt/detritus/flooded vegetation
Musky	early May	silt/detritus/flooded vegetation
Suckers (white)	mid-May	gravel/cobble
Greater redhorse	mid-May	gravel/cobble
Sturgeon	mid-May	gravel/cobble
Black crappie	late May	silt/detritus/flooded vegetation
Largemouth bass	late May	sand/gravel/vegetated areas
Smallmouth bass	late May	sand/gravel/vegetated areas
Rock bass	late May	sand/gravel/vegetated areas
Bluegill	late May	sand/gravel/vegetated areas
Yellow bullhead	early June	sand/gravel/vegetated areas
Pumpkinseed	early June	sand/gravel/vegetated areas

Note: Northern lakes and rivers have a very compressed spawning period compared to the southern part of the state

Hummingbird Arrival in May

5/11/97: Linda Thomas from Sayner called with the first sightings of ruby-throated hummingbirds.

5/8/98: Hummingbirds returned to Lee Snow's home in Harshaw. But most of us were kept waiting until 5/15, a few days later than their traditional return over Mother's Day.

5/5/99: Ron Winter in Boulder Junction and Carolyn Kutz in Winchester reported the first hummers of the year. We observed our first hummer in Manitowish on 5/10.

5/2/00: Uwe Wiechering on Diamond Lake won the prize for the first reported hummer in the area. Ron Winter of Boulder Junction saw his first hummers on May 3, and added that he saw his first tourists on May 4, though he failed to identify the species.

5/6/01: Darleen Kiesgen in Boulder Junction and Ron and Kris Wiltzius on Wyandock Lake reported the first hummers.

5/6/02: Howard Johnson in Minocqua observed the first hummingbird.

5/8/03: Bob and Darleen Kiesgen in Boulder Junction and Joe Tennessen in McNaughton reported the earliest return of hummingbirds.

5/10/05: We saw our first hummer in Manitowish.

Average date of return is May 7. To follow the migration of hummingbirds north, log on to www.hummingbirds.net.

Jean Long from Arbor Vitae e-mailed me with a fun sighting: At her birdbath, she twice watched a hummingbird fly through the spray of water thrown up from a bathing rose-breasted grosbeak. She concluded that hummers take showers, not baths. I remember a few years ago getting several letters and calls from people who were watering their lawns with a hose and had hummers fly purposely back and forth through the spray. As a result, I agree with Jean. Hummers take showers.

Baltimore Oriole Arrival in May

5/11/97: Linda Thomas from Sayner called with the first sightings of northern orioles.

5/11/98: Linda Thomas in Sayner reported the earliest oriole. To show how dates can vary even in nearby areas, "our" orioles in Manitowish didn't return until 5/19.

5/7/00: Jim and Karen Kramer in Boulder Junction reported the first Baltimore orioles. The same day, Dan Carney from Hazelhurst watched Baltimore orioles taking tufts of old cattails to build their nest.

5/10/01: Eileen Gottwald in Springstead and Jim and Lois Kruse in Hazelhurst both had orioles return to their feeders.

5/7/02: Mary Ash had a Baltimore oriole at her feeder. I was inundated with calls from excited feeder-watchers in May 2002. There were more rose-breasted grosbeaks and Baltimore orioles visiting area feeders than I have ever seen. We had nine Baltimore orioles and at least eight rose-breasted grosbeaks at one time. My best guess as to why so many birds appeared at feeders was the insect hatch failed to materialize in the first half of May, which left the birds extremely hungry.

5/8/03: Bob and Darleen Kiesgen in Boulder Junction reported the earliest return of orioles.

5/14/03: Bob Kovar in Manitowish Waters noticed orioles had returned that day, so he set whole oranges out on his deck to cut open, but was interrupted by a phone call. When he got back, three orioles were pecking at the whole oranges, apparently so hungry they couldn't wait for them to be quartered.

5/5/04: The first Baltimore oriole was reported in Lac du Flambeau.

5/9/05: Grace Wanta on the Turtle-Flambeau Flowage reported the first Baltimore orioles.

Average date of return for Baltimore orioles is May 8.

Indigo Bunting Arrival in May

5/18/97: Grace Wanta on the Turtle-Flambeau Flowage reported an indigo bunting eating sunflower seeds from beneath her feeder.

5/10/99: Chuck Schell reported indigo buntings in his yard in Minocqua.

5/8/00: Mary Ann Michaelis of Manitowish Waters observed indigo buntings at her feeder.

5/8/01: Ron and Kris Wiltzius on Wyandock Lake reported the first indigo bunting.

5/18/03: Mary and I had a pair of indigo buntings at our feeders in Manitowish.

5/12/04: Bob Metz on Fence Lake in Lac du Flambeau had two indigo buntings arrive, the same day they arrived at our feeders. Indigo buntings were unusually cooperative at feeders this spring. Laurie Timm observed 10 males and a few females at her feeders, while another caller reported seven males in her backyard.

Average date of return for indigo buntings is May 12.

Rose-Breasted Grosbeak Arrival in May

5/15/98: Rose-breasted grosbeaks returned to Manitowish.

5/5/99: We saw our first rose-breasted grosbeaks in Manitowish.

5/8/00: We had our first rose-breasted grosbeak return to Manitowish.

5/1/01: Jack Bull in Winchester and Jim and Lois Kruse in Hazelhurst reported the first rose-breasted grosbeaks.

5/6/02: Betty Liebert in Lac du Flambeau reported the first rose-breasted grosbeak.

5/9/03: Audrae Kulas reported the first rose-breasted grosbeak at her Woodboro home.

5/6/04: Nancy Skowlund in Powell reported the first rose-breasted grosbeak in the area.

5/7/05: Laurie Timm reported the first rose-breasted grosbeak in the area.

Average date of return for rose-breasted grosbeaks is May 7.

SIGHTINGS

Community Sightings of Note – Firsts and Unusuals: 1997

*Spring arrived very slowly in 1997. That's the nicest way I can describe the five consecutive days of snow squalls we had from May 12 to May 16.

5/3/97: We heard our first leopard frogs.

5/8/97: White-crowned sparrows finally returned to our feeders.

5/12/97: Alice Esterl had two male western tanagers show up at her feeders in Springstead, and they remained until May 19. The regular range of western tanagers extends eastward only to the Black Hills of South Dakota. Wisconsin sightings in any given year are very rare, and only one pair has ever nested in Wisconsin, back in 1903. The western is unmistakable. As Alice says, it looks like a big goldfinch with a red head.

5/14/97: Two Harris sparrows showed up at our feeders, the first time we ever saw this species in Manitowish. They are an uncommon migrant through Wisconsin, and usually only make a very brief appearance before heading for their nesting grounds in northern Canada.

5/17/97: Ada Karow from Lac du Flambeau called with sightings of a black-and-white warbler and a Nashville warbler.

5/19/97: Ann Harding from Lake Tomahawk reported seeing blackburnian warblers.

5/21/97: Ada Karow from Lac du Flambeau called with sightings of a Cape May warbler.

5/24/97: Jackie Johnston observed a pair of scarlet tanagers east of Lake Tomahawk on Hodstradt Lake.

5/25/97: Elaine Kotlarek from Arbor Vitae wrote with sightings of many birds at her feeders, including Swainson's thrush and gray-cheeked thrush.

5/26/97: Lee Snow counted sightings of 64 species of birds in Harshaw, including warblers like magnolias, American redstarts, black-throated greens, golden-wingeds, and Nashvilles. Lee used 12-power binoculars to help get positive IDs on birds.

5/26/97: Ada Karow reported a brown thrasher.

5/30/97: Ada Karow heard her first whip-poor-will, and reported a family of raccoons living in her wood duck box. You'd think an adult raccoon would be way too big to get through the entrance hole, but raccoons seem capable of just about anything.

5/30/97: Amber Roth identified 47 species of birds in a Hazelhurst area yard and adjoining neighborhood, including 10 species of warblers. That's a great example of how rich our bird life is during the final weeks of migration in late May.

Community Sightings of Note – First and Unusuals: 1998

*We had a remarkable spring, or early summer if you like, given the warm temperatures! The reversal from the last two springs would seem to indicate we had lost 10 degrees in latitude. There have been entire summers (does 1993 ring a bell for anyone?) when we didn't experience the warm weather we had this year in April and May. Flowers blossomed anywhere from three to five weeks ahead of last year.

*Don and Greta Janssen reported a merlin nesting near them on Tomahawk Lake again in 1998. They also had a loon nest near their cottage with three eggs in it, a rather rare occurrence.

5/3/98: We spotted goldthread in flower.

5/4/98: Toads began trilling.

5/4/98: Trilliums flowered in Rhinelander, and lilacs blossomed at our home.

5/6/98: Black ash and pin cherries flowered in Manitowish.

5/6/98: Linda Thomas saw purple martins on Little Arbor Vitae.

5/7/98: In Manitowish, pine siskins and yellow warblers returned.

5/8/98: Gaywings came into flower.

5/8/98: White-crowned sparrows arrived at our feeders.

5/10/98: Ovenbirds, brown thrashers, black-and-white warblers, black-throated green warblers, and spotted and solitary sandpipers all returned to the Manitowish area.

5/10/98: We found bog laurel, bog rosemary, starflower, bellwort, and cottongrass in flower.

5/11/98: Linda Thomas heard whip-poor-wills calling in Sayner.

5/12/98: Jennifer Mikulich of Manitowish Waters noted that the first Canada goose goslings appeared on Powell Marsh, and that ring-necked ducks were also nesting.

5/13/98: Bob Kovar of Manitowish Waters had orioles return, while Mark Pflieger from Harshaw reported a ruffed grouse nest with 12 eggs in it on his property.

5/14/98: Samaras were falling off the silver maples, and tiger swallowtail butterflies appeared.

5/15/98: Families of goslings were swimming on the Powell Marsh, and Eastern gray treefrogs began "singing."

5/15/98: Common yellowthroats and gray catbird returned to Manitowish.

5/15/98: Wild calla blossomed.

5/16/98: Bunchberry flowered.

5/16/98: Deerflies and horseflies bit us.

5/17/98: We took our first swim. (The water was warm!).

5/17/98: Nannyberry, hawthorn, and rock cress all came into flower.

5/18/98: Canada mayflowers were flowering everywhere.

5/18/05: Veeries and Eastern kingbirds arrived in our area.

5/18/98: Mary and I took a long sea kayak tour on the Turtle-Flambeau Flowage. We saw thousands of dragonflies, usually in "kettles" of a hundred or more in little bays. When the mosquito hatch hit, they were well-received by the dragonflies.

5/27/98: Mary and I saw six painted turtles laying eggs on the abandoned railroad track across from our home in Manitowish.

5/28/98: Though this isn't a sighting, and I refrain from political rantings and ravings as often as possible, I must report that a public hearing in Mercer on personal watercraft ended in a vote of 76 to 16 in favor of limiting jet ski hours to 11 a.m. to 3 p.m. daily. Hurrah!

Community Sightings of Note – Firsts and Unusuals: 1999

5/1/99: Leatherleaf came into flower in the bogs on May 1.

5/2/99: I saw yellow-rumped and black-and-white warblers, though I had been hearing the yellow-rumps for at least a week prior to that.

5/3/99: The next day I heard my first black-throated green warbler, meaning that many of the early warblers had returned by the beginning of May. Ada Karow of Lac du Flambeau heard the first whip-poor-will of the spring calling through the night.

5/3/99: Juneberries came into flower.

5/8/99: Pin cherries came into flower.

5/8/99: We heard our first sedge wrens in a nearby wetland.

5/9/99: We heard our first yellow warblers and ovenbirds in Manitowish.

5/12/99: Choke cherries came into flower.

5/14/99: Gary Ruesch watched 14 eagles sitting together on a shoreline of the Rainbow Flowage. The Rainbow only has three active eagle nests, so it's likely the eagles were gathering because a fish spawn was taking place.

5/14/99: Our apple trees and lilacs bloomed, a very early date for these species up here.

5/15/99: Toads and Eastern gray treefrogs began singing.

5/16/99: Black cherries came into flower.

5/28/99: Ed Marshall reported 25 white pelicans on Squaw Lake near Lac du Flambeau.

Community Sightings of Note – Firsts and Unusuals: 2000

* An American elk, a close cousin of white-tailed deer, was seen three times in early May in our general area - once in Woodboro, once on Fish Trap Road in northeastern Price County, and once near our home at the Hwy. 47 bridge in Manitowish (though not by us). Elk are not "supposed" to be over our way. They were released well west of here in the Clam Lake area several years ago. Sounds likely that this one was on a walkabout.
* Art Berhnardt watched a bald eagle take too big a fish on Trout Lake and

have to swim it back to shore. As Art wrote, the eagle was "looking for all the world like an Olympic swimmer doing the butterfly stroke. The shoreline was at least a quarter of a mile away, but the eagle soon was on the beach ripping and devouring large chunks of flesh from a defunct seven or eight pound walleye. A pair of loons was attracted by the commotion, and came quite close to see what was going on."

* Betty Walters reported 18 goslings trailing behind an adult goose. The 18 young likely represented three families that had joined together.
* Ann Hanson from Sugar Camp had 47 redpolls die at her feeders from salmonella poisoning in the last three weeks of April and into May.
* Our most unusual sighting in Manitowish in early May was a yellow-headed blackbird under one of our feeders eating sunflower seeds. Tha's a first for us in our 17 years here. Numerous mornings we've also awakened early to the repetitive *coo-coo-coo* of a black-billed cuckoo in the sedge marsh below our house.

5/1/00: Leatherleaf came into flower in the bogs near us. White-crowned sparrows showed up at our feeder as well.

5/2/00: We had a brown thrasher at our feeder.

5/3/00: We saw our first black-throated green warblers and yellow warblers.

5/3/00: We canoed a portion of the Manitowish and had good numbers of pectoral sandpipers, solitary sandpipers, and greater yellowlegs working over the exposed mud flats along the riverbanks.

5/3/00: Leatherwood came into flower.

5/4/00: Wood anemone blossomed.

5/4/00: Eastern gray treefrogs and American toads began singing, as did ovenbirds.

5/5/00: A hike along a wetland yielded firsts of Nashville warblers, sedge wrens, swamp sparrows, and a catbird.

5/5/00: Juanita and Ike Lanz wrote regarding the bittersweet pleasure of having merlins nesting near their house on Papoose Lake. Given that merlins eat songbirds, their local birds are likely singing the blues rather than their territorial songs.

5/7/00: Mary Ann Michaelis of Manitowish Waters watched a scarlet tanager at her birdbath.

5/7/00: June Schmaal on Johnson Lake in Arbor Vitae heard a male cardinal.

5/7/00: Jim and Karen Kramer in Boulder Junction saw chestnut-sided warblers and common yellowthroat warblers.

5/8/00: Blueberries and calla lilies came into flower.

5/9/00: Peggy Allen of Woodruff observed male and female cardinals near Howard Young Hospital.

5/14/00: Bog rosemary and bog laurel were in flower in a bog on the Raven Trail, while goldthread blossomed under hemlocks in the uplands.

Community Sightings of Note – Firsts and Unusuals: 2001

* Red admiral butterflies were abundant this spring. They typically vary in number from year to year, migrating north in the spring on strong southerly winds. They lay eggs on stinging nettles, their host plant. It's one of the few good things I can say about the plant, though I'm told stinging nettles can make a good wild food when boiled. You can easily identify a red admiral by the large, showy, orange-red band that splits its forewings (the upper wings).

5/2/01: Ada Karow in Lac du Flambeau heard the first whip-poor-will.

5/4/01: Peggy Allen spotted a pair of merlins using a dead pine for a perch near Howard Young Hospital in Woodruff.

5/5/01: Dan Carney observed golden-winged and Nashville warblers on the Wisconsin River, and yellow, chestnut-sided, palm, and pine warblers on the Rainbow Flowage. Dan also saw a catbird, ovenbird, and varied thrush that same day.

5/7/01: Jean Long in Arbor Vitae reported the first scarlet tanager.

5/10/01: Jan Gresmer on Big Crawling Stone Lake reported the first catbird.

5/10/01: A male Harris sparrow fed on sunflower seeds under our feeder. He stayed a couple days and then moved on.

5/16/01: The sturgeon spawned on the Manitowish River. Redhorse were also spawning that day, and numerous eagles lined the river to partake in what must have appeared to them as a table set for a king.

Community Sightings of Note – Firsts and Unusuals: 2002

5/1/02: Peggy Trotalli observed eight horned grebes on Trout Lake.

5/1/02: Dan Carney watched 40 to 50 yellow-rumped warblers at Goodnow Springs.

5/2/02: Jack Bull in Winchester watched his first kestrel of the year.

5/3/02: Bob Kovar in Manitowish Waters observed five tundra swans on one of the cranberry marshes in the area.

5/3/02: Jeff and Rosy Richter in Mercer had a yellow-headed blackbird and a white-winged crossbill in their yard.

5/3/02: Mary Ash in Lac du Flambeau saw a blackbird in her yard that had a completely white head.

5/5/02: Dan Carney observed a palm warbler and savannah sparrow near the Rainbow Flowage. A white-crowned sparrow appeared at our feeders in Manitowish.

5/6/02: Ken Bovine on Rice Lake in Mercer had a male cardinal singing at his house.

5/6/02: Two Harris sparrows arrived at our feeders in Manitowish.

5/7/02: Therese Klausler in Powell watched sandhill cranes walking near the Sandy Beach boat landing for several days as if they owned the place.

5/8/02: Ron Winter in Boulder Junction observed his first Baltimore oriole. Arleigh Ashton in Boulder Junction watched her first hummingbirds of the year come to her feeder. The temperature was 34°F, which is tough sledding for hummers.

5/9/02: Audrae Kulas had a Cape May warbler come to her suet feeder.

5/10/02: Sally Hegeman in Boulder Junction observed a brown thrasher.

5/11/02: Lois Kruse in Minocqua had the privilege of watching a pair of sandhill cranes do their courtship dance.

5/11/02: Audrae Kulas observed a juvenile gray jay on her property. Gray jays nest as early as late February, so young of the year flying this early in May is quite possible.

5/11/02: We watched an American bittern for 10 minutes as it fed in the flooded meadow just 20 feet below our deck.

5/12/02: Jim and Nancy Skowlund in Powell had a Harris sparrow at their feeder.

5/12/02: Mary Voelz in Minocqua watched a yellow-headed blackbird at her feeder for several days.

5/12/02: Jim and Lois Kruse watched a female scarlet tanager working on their suet feeder.

5/12/02: Ada Karow in Lac du Flambeau had eight white-throated sparrows in her yard.

5/12/02: We watched numerous double-crested cormorants flying and swimming along the shoreline of Lake Superior at the mouth of the Presque Isle River.

5/13/02: We saw a marbled godwit and our first yellow warbler in Powell Marsh, plus a solitary sandpiper below our house.

5/13/02: Dixie McCaughn in Arbor Vitae watched a male and female scarlet tanager in her yard.

5/15/02: Jeff and Diane Zanski on Squaw Lake had two indigo buntings and two orioles at their feeders.

5/16/02: Bob Kovar watched a lesser golden plover on one of the cranberry marshes in Manitowish Waters.

5/16/02: Angie and Joe Skroback listened to a whip-poor-will for an hour in the morning on Clear Lake in Manitowish Waters.

5/16/02: Audrae Kulas had two juvenile gray jays coming in to her feeders.

5/17/02: Carolyn Dring in Land'O'Lakes had a Harris sparrow and several savannah sparrows at her feeders.

5/18/02: Carl Foleberg in Winchester called to report an indigo bunting at his feeder for the last three days.

5/20/02: On three consecutive nights, Bob Kovar in Manitowish Waters drove up his driveway and found a whip-poor-will sitting in the same place in the middle of the dirt road, its red eyes gleaming in his headlights. This was just after dark, and Bob guesses that with our cold nights, the whip-poor-will was absorbing the radiant heat from the driveway. Later in the evening, the whip-poor-will was always gone.

5/20/02: Linda Thomas from Sayner called to say the loons were now nesting on Plum Lake.

5/21/02: Carol Hartman in Presque had her first male indigo bunting come to her feeder. So did Jack Bull, except his indigo bunting ate from his hummingbird feeder, as did a black-capped chickadee. What do you put in those feeders, Jack?

Community Sightings of Note – Firsts and Unusuals: 2003

5/3/03: Dan Carney observed a least sandpiper and a greater yellowlegs, two shorebirds, on Bearskin Creek.

5/3/03: Kay Lorbiecki in Presque Isle watched her first common green darner dragonfly of the year.

5/5/03: We observed our first palm, yellow-rumped, and black-and-white warblers on a hike along the Manitowish.

5/5/03: Dan Carney watched his first alder flycatcher near Hazelhurst, and two days later saw his first Nashville warbler.

5/8/03: Art Bernhardt observed a red-necked grebe on Trout Lake.

5/8/03: Joe Tennessen watched a cardinal sitting in a pine tree while he sat in the dentist's chair in Woodruff.

5/8/03: Mary and I heard toads trilling in Manitowish.

5/10/03: Dan Carney in Hazelhurst observed black-and-white warblers and American redstarts.

5/10/03: Al and Julie Hillery had white-crowned sparrows at their feeders, a first for them.

5/10/03: We had rose-breasted grosbeaks and orioles return to our feeders in Manitowish.

5/11/03: We had a red-bellied woodpecker visit our feeder, only the second time we've ever had one at our house.

5/11/03: Diane Shay in Arbor Vitae had ruby-throated hummingbirds return despite the monsoon weather.

5/12/03: Dan Carney in Hazelhurst saw his first black-throated green warblers and pine warblers. Annamarie Beckel in Woodruff watched a Cape May warbler feeding on her suet, and had orioles and hummingbirds return the same day. Ada Karow in Lac du Flambeau heard her first whip-poor-will of the year.

5/13/03: Dan Carney in Hazelhurst had golden-winged warblers, chestnut-sided warblers, and ovenbirds. Eric Stark watched a red-headed woodpecker on a tree behind his feeder in Manitowish Waters.

5/14/03: Rita Bonderski in Hazelhurst watched a just-returned oriole sitting on her old outdoor water pump handle.

5/14/03: Diane Steele observed a pair of merlins likely working on a nest in a tall pine along the shoreline of Trout Lake.

5/15/03: Bridget Hornburg on Bolten Lake near Lac du Flambeau watched a bald eagle land near a loon's nest, scare away the loons, and start throwing around the nesting material with its beak. Whether the eagle got any eggs wasn't clear.

5/15/03: Paul Goetz in Lac du Flambeau heard a cardinal singing in his yard and found the male cardinal eating seeds under his feeder.

5/15/03: Kathy and Bob Teska in Arbor Vitae had an albino squirrel visit their yard.

5/15/03: Ada Karow in Lac du Flambeau observed a common yellowthroat warbler along the shore of Mitten Lake.

5/15/03: We heard Eastern gray treefrogs.

5/16/03: Dan Carney had his first blackburnian warbler, as well as seeing his first family of goslings.

5/17/03: Dan Carney watched a Wilson's warbler, magnolia warbler, catbird, and warbling vireo among others at Goodnow Springs off the Bearskin Trail.

5/17/03: We saw our first cedar waxwing in Manitowish.

5/18/03: Mary and I saw a lesser golden plover on Powell Marsh. We also observed a loose flock of five American bitterns flying together, a very unusual sight.

5/19/03: Dan Carney heard his first great-crested flycatcher, and watched an indigo bunting and scarlet tanager in his binoculars at the same time. If he could have added an oriole in there too, he'd have experienced just about as much color as an eye can take.

5/22/03: Lynn Reed observed a yellow-headed blackbird near the Boulder Junction Post Office, a very odd place for a yellow-headed to be hanging out!

5/23/03: Dan Carney in Woodruff watched a hummingbird collecting lichens to build its nest.

5/23/03: Janeen Clark on Little Ten Lake in Lac du Flambeau described seeing a "feast of color" that songbirds were providing for her. Between the buttery yellow of goldfinches, the brilliant orange of Baltimore orioles, the deep blue of indigo buntings, and the sunset red of scarlet tanagers, she sounded like she was in heaven.

Community Sightings of Note – Firsts and Unusuals: 2004

* Our cold and wet spring delayed many natural events, from leaf-out to spring flowering to bird migration. The positive side was that spring, which often seems to arrive and depart simultaneously, was a long-winded affair this year. The cold slowed insect hatching, and kept more birds for longer periods at our feeders than nearly any other spring I can remember.

5/1/04: White-crowned sparrows appeared in Manitowish.

5/5/04: Dan Carney spotted black-throated green and black-and-white warblers south of Minocqua.

5/6/04: Dan saw a northern waterthrush and ovenbirds, both warblers, in the same area south of Minocqua.

5/6/04: Nancy Skowlund in Powell reported eight wood ducks that regularly come up to eat corn at her feeders.

5/7/04: Dan Carney found a Swainson's thrush and a vesper sparrow on his daily hike.

5/8/04: We saw our first Baltimore oriole in Manitowish. On a hike in Powell Marsh, I saw my first killdeers, long-billed dowitchers, lesser yellowlegs, Savannah sparrows, and sedge wrens, along with bitterns and rough-legged hawks. Two of the killdeers hopped repeatedly over each other for several minutes, in the killdeer version of leapfrog. I assume they were engaging in part of a courtship ritual, though I can find nothing in the literature about such behavior.

5/9/04: Dan Carney reported a chestnut-sided warbler, dozens of Cape May warblers in spruce trees, an American redstart, and an orange-crowned warbler.

5/9/04: Jack Bull in Winchester had a red-bellied woodpecker visit his feeders.

5/9/04: Blackflies hatched.

5/9/04: We observed a blue-headed vireo, ovenbirds, and pine warblers galore in the big pines of Frog Lake State Natural Area.

5/10/04: Rolf Ethun reported a relatively tame female bobwhite quail at his feeder near Manitowish Waters. Bobwhites nest far south of here, so this bobwhite was likely released by someone training their dogs to hunt quail.

5/10/04: We had a catbird eat the oranges we put out for the orioles.

5/10/04: Toads began trilling.

5/12/04: Bob Metz on Fence Lake in Lac du Flambeau had a pair of red-headed woodpeckers at his feeders.

5/13/04: Mary Ash in Lac du Flambeau had scarlet tanagers arrive at her feeders along with six indigo buntings. Barbara Schmidt reported that a northern parula warbler hit her window.

5/14/04: Joe and Angie Skroback on Clear Lake in Manitowish Waters had bluebirds, orioles, evening and rose-breasted grosbeaks, and red-headed woodpeckers at their feeders. Most remarkably, they also reported a painted redstart, a bird that nests in the desert Southwest.

5/14/04: Dan Carney kept spotting warblers – golden-winged, common yellowthroat, Wilson's, and black-burnian.

5/15/04: Rosie Richter in Mercer had a brown thrasher at her feeders.

5/16/04: Jeff Richter in Mercer watched a sharp-shinned hawk take a male goldfinch at their feeder.

5/17/04: We had a first-ever sighting at our feeders – a male bobolink eating sunflower seeds! Bobolinks are grassland birds, and the only place I see them in the Northwoods is in Powell Marsh, where they nest in the immense sedge/leatherleaf meadows. I also traveled to Ashland that day, and saw a flock of dunlins and a flock of marbled godwits on Chequamegon Bay, along with a flock of common terns.

5/18/04: On a hike in Powell Marsh, I observed a flock of semi-palmated plovers and dozens of lesser and greater yellowlegs. I saw three families of geese with at least six goslings each, the goslings little more than bundles of bright yellow feathers. Ten turtles were lined up in a row on the east bank of a dike basking in the sun. Nearly all of the turtles appeared to be Eastern spiny softshells, a relatively uncommon species in the Northwoods.

5/23/04: A caller from Minocqua watched a northern mockingbird eating oranges from her feeder. Northern mockingbirds are quite uncommon visitors to Wisconsin, much less the Northwoods. Their nesting range extends into northern Illinois, and only a few records of nesting mockingbirds in Wisconsin have been confirmed over the last 50 years. This mockingbird apparently was quite aggressive, driving off the Baltimore orioles that considered the oranges their property.

5/28/04: We observed both American golden plovers and black-bellied plovers on the mud flats of Powell Marsh last week. Both birds are remarkably beautiful, nest far up in the Arctic, and were a bit late in leaving for their breeding areas.

Community Sightings of Note – Firsts and Unusuals: 2005

* Many birds were still making their way back to the Northwoods as of mid-May. It was a cold and wet spring for the most part, not in the least bit conducive to migration.

5/6/05: Barn and cliff swallows returned, but their lives were difficult, given the fact that very few insects had hatched.

5/7/05: Dan Carney called with first sightings of magnolia warblers in the Hazelhurst area.

5/8/05: Dan Carney reported firsts of American redstarts, black-and-white warblers, ovenbirds, parula warblers, and chestnut-sided warblers.

5/8/05: We heard our first black-throated green warblers.

5/9/05: Toads began trilling in Manitowish.

5/10/05: Bob and Sherlene Schmidt reported a cardinal at their feeder in Winchester.

5/11/05: Joanne Dugenske reported a small flock of blackburnian warblers flitting along the water's edge on Stone Lake in Springstead.

5/16/05: With the long-awaited return of the sun came a number of birds: Yellow warblers, catbirds, our first orioles, the first hatch of goslings, horned larks, and my first-ever sighting of a lark sparrow on Powell Marsh. Lark sparrows are a bird of the grasslands of southwestern Wisconsin, and while many sparrows are not particularly attractive, the lark sparrow is a strikingly beautiful bird.

June Phenology Appendix

Sightings

Community Sightings of Note – Firsts and Unusuals: 1997

* Deerflies and horseflies hatched out late in June. They apparently don't feel dizziness from endlessly flying in circles around our heads. Both species like to go for the highest spot on you, so wearing a hat can be helpful in keeping them off your head. I suspect we should be appreciative of their exceptional flying abilities. They are exceptionally fast and elusive, but it's hard to appreciate something that wants to take a large chunk out of you. The bite of the female horsefly is particularly nasty and is done by a series of cutting and piercing stylets that can penetrate horse hide. By contrast, human skin must be like slicing through butter.

Community Sightings of Note – Firsts and Unusuals: 1999

* Frank Fassino watched a mature eagle on Echo Lake in Mercer swim some 800 feet to shore doing a perfect breaststroke. Or maybe it was more of a butterfly stroke, the way the wings swept through the water. Crows dive-bombed the eagle as it made its way, but the eagle persevered and pulled itself up on dry land behind some vegetation. Frank sneaked around to get a closer look at it, but it flew away as he approached. Curiosity led Frank to the spot where the eagle had beached, and there stretched a 22-inch-long redhorse that Frank estimated weighed more than five pounds. It is little wonder this eagle couldn't get airborne with its meal.
* Jim Moore spotted a sow bear with four cubs crossing the road near Powell Marsh. The average litter in our area is now triplets for bears. It used to be that in poor habitat, sows seldom mated until they were five years old, but the average age in our area is now 3½ , with 20 percent of sows mating at 2½.

Community Sightings of Note – Firsts and Unusuals: 2000

* While I was hiking in June with Bob and Diane Diederich on their Pike Lake property, they pointed out to me an active osprey nest perched on the top of a large boulder in the middle of the lake! An adult flew back and forth from the nest and circled over our heads for a while. Osprey like to nest at the top of the landscape, usually perching precariously at the very top of large trees, though I've seen them occasionally on top of posts only 15 feet above the water. Still, I'd never seen a pair nesting only 5 feet above the water, much less on a boulder. Usually nest sites low to the water don't last long because anglers will anchor just off from the nest, or birdwatchers will gawk too closely. But the Pike Lake shoreland owners apparently respect this pair's need for personal space. They're to be congratulated!

Community Sightings of Note – Firsts and Unusuals: 2001

* Chuck and Carol Berigan live west of Minocqua and have have been visited frequently by bears over the years. They've learned to set up a "bear-friendly" feeder, a simple platform feeder that the bears can knock over easily, and which can be set back up in a snap. But they reached their limit when their motion light went on, and as they tell it: "We checked the yard, and sure enough, there was a bear. In fact, not one bear but FOUR! There was a large (mother) bear with what appeared to be a yearling and two cute little cubs. Momma was taking great pains to show her brood the proper technique for licking up spilled sunflower seeds. It certainly was refreshing to see good 'family values' being taught to the youngsters. After romping around our backyard for about 15 minutes, the group headed off down the path into the woods." Chuck and Carol have "decided to surrender," and have pulled in their bird feeders. They run a resort, and bears and visitors don't always mix.
* I joined a group of teachers in mid-June for a visit to the Cathedral of the Pines in the Nicolet National Forest. This site may be the finest remaining stand of old-growth white pine in Wisconsin, and for an added touch, it has a large great blue heron rookery at the top of the pines. We sat near the rookery without disturbing it and listened

to the remarkable sounds of the adults feeding the voracious young. Most of us have heard the incessant sounds of begging baby birds emanating from a songbird nest. Well, multiply that sound to reflect the large size of the heron young, and then multiply again by a factor of 90 for the number of nearby nests, and you will have a sense of the cacophony. I highly recommend a visit. The site is near Lakewood, just west of Hwy. 32.

* Art Bernhardt observed a mallard drake with a purple head rather than a green head. Sometimes a certain light on feathers can make them appear different colors, but Art swears that in his 60 years of birdwatching he's never seen a mallard like this one.

* Carole Goetz of Lac du Flambeau e-mailed me with a theory on the "purpose" of our forest tent caterpillar outbreak. She felt that because of the nearly complete defoliation in some areas, that seedlings and saplings on the forest floor were the beneficiaries of an additional month or more of sunlight, thereby generating a growth spurt. She asked my opinion, and I would agree entirely with her regarding the effect, though ascribing a "purpose" through our human eyes to any wildlife activity can get us quickly into dark waters. I'd love to see a study comparing understory growth during "normal" summers to understory growth during a forest tent caterpillar summer.

6/1/01: Donna Schrameyer in Hazelhurst saw her first newborn fawn. She also watched a hummingbird take a bath in her birdbath – I'd think they would spray water all over the place with the speed of their wings.

6/3/01: Al and Julie Hillery watched a brown doe with her new white fawn out on their bog. The next year on May 31, they reported that they watched a white doe with her brand new brown fawn.

Community Sightings of Note – Firsts and Unusuals: 2002

* Janeen and Bob Clark in Lac du Flambeau wrote of leaving their windows open at night and being serenaded to sleep by the spring peepers, tree frogs, trilling toads, and wailing loons – "Who could ask for more?" they asked. Indeed.

* Carol Pfister in Lac du Flambeau e-mailed to describe several experiences with bears on her deck ripping apart her bird feeders and enjoying a sunflower seed dinner. One yearling bear just laid on its side and lapped up the seeds on the deck.

Community Sightings of Note – Firsts and Unusuals: 2003

* Chuck and Marianna Boyd live on the Manitowish Chain, and sent me an e-mail appropriately titled "Strange Buddies." They noticed a crow sitting on a bare pine branch some 70 feet from their window, and immediately noticed a mature bald eagle sitting less than two feet away. Chuck watched them just hanging out for five minutes, and when he walked to a different window, he saw that another crow was sitting on the same branch as the eagle but only a foot away. All were seemingly enjoying one another's company. He opened the door to get a photo, but as so often happens, the birds spooked and took off.

* Dave Gajafsky e-mailed me with a sighting of a cougar not far from McCormick Lake in Hazelhurst. He was quietly riding a motorscooter when he came upon the cougar standing in the trail, and observed it clearly for about 20 to 30 seconds.

He described it as about 6 feet long and 30 inches tall at the shoulder, with a long curving tail and a small head.

* Lon and Ginny Sherman from Land O'Lakes observed a large female bear with five cubs trailing along behind her in single file on Hwy. M near Trout Lake.
* Sharon and Dave Lintereur in Lake Tomahawk observed a barred owl chick, and wrote that it "sounds like a steam whistle when it wants food." Barred owls can make some of the strangest noises...the kind of noises you don't want to hear at night if you listen to ghost stories.

Community Sightings of Note – Firsts and Unusuals: 2004

* Louise Sachs on Fence Lake watched a pair of orioles eating suet from her feeder for a month, a behavior certainly not usually associated with orioles. Maybe they're on the Atkins Diet.

6/23/04: Judy Sattersten reported seeing a cougar cross the road in front of her on Hwy. 51, north of County H. A few seconds later, she saw a white deer standing by the side of the road acting in a very agitated manner. Judy felt strongly that the deer understood it was being hunted.

6/26/04: Mary and I watched white pelicans on the Fox River in De-Pere perform a choreographed feeding behavior. Ten birds or so would swim into a circle and then all charge toward the center, and when the circle was nearly closed, simultaneously dip their bills under the water to catch fish. This corralling behavior is something I've read about, but never observed, and it was fascinating to watch.

Community Sightings of Note – Firsts and Unusuals: 2005

* Water levels were very low on many lakes and rivers in the area, and remained that way throughout the summer. The water levels caused some recreational problems, but more importantly, they left many beaver dams and much aquatic plant habitat high and dry, and in general caused a variety of problems for animals that live in the riparian zone.
* Janeen Clarke on Little Ten Lake in Lac du Flambeau reported watching a yellow swallowtail butterfly drinking from her hummingbird feeder. It drank so much she wondered how it could still fly! Perhaps the butterfly should have been referred to Butterflies Anonymous.

July Phenology Appendix

Sightings

Community Sightings of Note – Firsts and Unusuals: 1997

* Martha Griffiths from Minocqua reported that a female grouse with chicks attacked her car as she turned into her driveway. The hen grouse flew at the car with her wings flapping, and the Griffiths hastily withdrew in the face of the surprise attack.
* Lee Snow from Harshaw wrote with a sighting of a pair of red crossbills and one of their young at her feeder. Red crossbills very rarely breed in Wisconsin. In his book Wisconsin Birdlife, Sam Robbins is only able to confirm two nests with eggs in the entire history of the state, though he suggests they are probably a

more widespread breeder than records indicate.

7/21/97: Elizabeth Stone and her family observed seven adult loons gathered together on Squaw Lake apparently just socializing. Adult loons are often seen in groups beginning in late July as their territorial instincts lessen. Sometimes unmated adults gather even earlier in the year.

7/28/97: We picked our first wild raspberries.

Community Sightings of Note – Firsts and Unusuals: 1998

* An Antigo birder wrote in to the Wisconsin BirdNet that she had watched three barred owls repeatedly plunge their feet into Moose Lake while in flight. They were about 10 feet off shore, and though none were seen to catch anything, it appears that they were fishing.
* Sally Hegeman from Boulder Junction called with a sighting of three black-capped chickadee chicks feeding one another chunky peanut butter from her feeder.
* Jack and Barbara Bull in Winchester have attracted an unusual array of birds to their home for years by feeding scrap meat at their feeders. In July, they lured in one of the most unlikely species of bird one might see at a feeder – turkey vultures. Two vultures enjoyed the daily soup kitchen at the Bulls'. Since turkey vultures are an uncommon summer resident in northern Wisconsin, their visit was particularly noteworthy.
* Cora and Roy Mollen had a fly-in at their birdbath in St. Germain. Over the course of 20 minutes, three young and two adult rose-breasted grosbeaks, two chickadees, two blue jays, a red-eyed vireo, a robin, and two yellow-bellied sapsuckers all took turns splashing about, while numerous goldfinch disdained the crowds and came back later.
* Jean Powell reported seeing black-backed woodpeckers on a dead red pine in their woods in St. Germain.

7/3/98: I led a canoe trip down the Manitowish, and we began the trip by watching a pair of very large snapping turtles mating in the river. They floated with the current, rolled over numerous times, flapped their arms, separated, and came back together. For turtles, they seemed to be having a very good time. The books say that snappers mate most frequently in the spring and fall just after and just before hibernation, but these two must have been illiterate. Snappers finish laying their eggs in late June (nests usually average about 25 eggs), and young usually emerge from late August into the fall, though some may overwinter in the nest.

Community Sightings of Note – Firsts and Unusuals: 1999

7/10/99: We picked up 3.4 inches of rain in Manitowish, while areas north of us received as much as 8 inches of rain along with extreme winds that leveled trees in long swaths.

Community Sightings of Note – Firsts and Unusuals: 2000

* Cora Mollen from St. Germain reported finding a dead bald eagle in perfect condition in her woods back in March. The adult was lying on its stomach with its head turned to the side and had no external signs of injury. Luckily, it had a band on one of its huge gold talons. She brought it to the DNR for testing, and received word in July that the eagle had been banded as a nestling in 1973, giving it a very full life of 27 years.

  It's very rare that eagles in the wild live this long given all the mortality factors that exist in the natural world. Fifteen years is considered a good long life for an eagle in the wild. Ron Eckstein, wildlife manager from Rhinelander and bander of most of the eagles in the Lakeland area, said the eagle (a male) died of electrocution. Remarkably, it was still in breeding condition, though it had slightly elevated lead levels.

* John and Jane Kafura from Lac du Flambeau observed a hummingbird nest and the two young being fed by the female in the nest. At only an inch to an inch-and-a-quarter in diameter (about the size of a half dollar), hummingbird nests are easily concealed. Typically the female lays two pinto bean-sized eggs, incubates them for 16 days, and the young fledge three weeks later.

  John also noted that a female hummer slammed into their window. John picked it up, saving it from becoming a possible snack, and held it until it revived 15 minutes later and flew off.

* Juanita Lanz found a dead mourning warbler below a window on her deck on Papoose Lake. Juanita mentioned that she had never seen a mourning warbler before. I don't see them very often either, but it's not because they're rare. Mournings are listed as a fairly common summer resident of northern Wisconsin. They're just very secretive. They hide in the low, dense vegetation of young forests, and nest in clumps of nettle or jewelweed, where most folks don't mess around. They stubbornly refuse to respond to "pishing" or "squeaking," and they have legitimately earned their reputation as "skulkers."

* Pam Schoville, who lives on a 35-acre lake in Hazelhurst, sent me a picture of a loon resting on her swimming raft, something loons aren't known to do. Now if she can snap a picture of it doing a swan dive off the diving board, she'll make the cover of *Audubon*.

* While we're on loons, Bette Brandenburg told the story of the time she and her husband were returning from an errand, only to hear the most awful sounds and wails coming from their lake. They hurried to the shore and saw two adult loons in a battle with an eagle in the water. The loons were swimming under and around the eagle, which was desperately flapping and flopping its way toward shore. Bette thought the loons were striking at the eagle underwater. Eventually, the eagle made it to land and disappeared behind a fallen tree. Bette was greatly concerned that the eagle had taken the loon's chick, but they spotted the chick a little later on the other side of the lake. I suspect the eagle had a large fish, and that's what they were fighting over.

Community Sightings of Note – Firsts and Unusuals: 2001

* Harold Freund watched chipping sparrows catch forest tent moths and fly with them back to their nests, apparently feeding the moths to their young. Hopefully, they had a lot of young to feed.

7/12/01: Linda Hunt observed a male and female hummingbird mating on her feeder. When they were done, the female hung upside down from the feeder, and was still doing so when she called. I have no idea as to the function of this behavior, but I suppose it's healthier than smoking a cigarette.

7/27/01: Diane and Bob Diederich observed an avocet on Pike Lake! That's a great sighting – I've only seen avocets in southern California, and never in Wisconsin. Avocets do migrate through Wisconsin, and they usually stir up quite a bit of excitement among birders when they're seen.

Community Sightings of Note – Firsts and Unusuals: 2004

- George and Linda Tanner identified a northern waterthrush in front of their cottage on Crawling Stone Lake. They saw two or three young birds with the adult, and theorized that it was flight school time, and their yard was where the young were getting launched into the world. The northern waterthrush is an uncommon warbler that nests often in the root systems of fallen trees less than a foot above pools of water. In my wanderings over the years, I've yet to see one.
- Mary, Callie, and I kayaked a stretch of the Manitowish River and paddled within 20 feet of a great blue heron that didn't move a muscle while it was fishing. It was so still, and we were so close, that Callie and I began wondering if it was real. It never did move until after we were well past it. I've often called herons the Zen yoga masters of the avian world. Their complete concentration and ability to remain absolutely transfixed is highly enviable.
- Jim Ferguson watched a female common merganser with 21 youngsters in tow behind her on Lake Tomahawk. There are two likely explanations for this large family size: One, another female may have laid her eggs in this female's nest, a form of intraspecific brood parasitism that is relatively common among ducks, particularly those that nest in cavities. Given the shortage of suitable cavity nesting sites near water, some females are driven to take this measure. Since ducks don't defend the immediate vicinity of their nests, it's relatively easy to parasitize their nests.

  The second possibility is that the female adopted additional chicks after the mother of those chicks disappeared. Common mergansers on average lay 8 to 11 eggs, so two family groups may have joined under the banner of one adult.

7/16/04: The eagle chick that Mary and I watched grow up in a nest across the river from our house fledged this day. Eagles chicks take anywhere from 70 to 98 days to fledge, and since eggs are typically laid around May 1, this one appears to have done well.

7/24/04: Northern lights were pulsing.

Community Sightings of Note – Firsts and Unusuals: 2005

- Jack Bull observed the very unusual sight of two trumpeter swans feeding in a ditch beside Chaney Lake Road just over the Wisconsin border into Michigan. The swans were apparently unafraid of the people who were stopping along the road to observe them, and simply continued feeding on plants in the ditch.
- Nancy Pilmonas on Little Manitowish Lake reported that she and her husband Ray were sitting outside about 8 p.m. when they saw a fisher attack a fawn! They ran to try to rescue it, but the fawn had gotten away from the fisher and disappeared. Later, a fawn returned to the spot where the attack had taken place and bedded down for the night.
- Donna Roche in Lac du Flambeau wrote, "My sighting is a pileated woodpecker eating the berries of a serviceberry tree. I was alerted to this action by his 'happy' calls to another bird nearby. It was very strange to see a large woodpecker swaying while holding onto small branches and delicately plucking

berries with his large bill. I've shared these delicious berries with other birds before, but never expected any woodpecker, let alone a pileated, to accomplish such a feat."

7/10/05: Jim Moore reported seeing a short-eared owl sitting on the ground in Powell Marsh. He and his wife Barb watched it for five minutes or so. Short-eared owls are ground nesters, and seeing one in mid-July suggests that a pair could be nesting. Short-ears are rare nesters in the Northwoods, so this could be a significant finding.

7/18/05: Callie and I had an unusual sighting, or more like an unusual listening, while walking along one of the dikes in Powell Marsh. As we were slowly poking around, we heard a continual series of guttural squawks and quacks that sounded somewhat like ducks, but unlike anything I could recall ever hearing. The sound was coming from just over the edge of a dike that was protected from view by tall grasses. Thus we couldn't see the critters, nor they us. We eventually came to an open spot where we could look back down the dike to where the sound was coming from, and immediately an American bittern flew up, while another remained hunched in the grass trying to use its cryptic markings to hide from us. So we had been listening to a very animated discussion between two bitterns, though what they could feel so strongly about is well beyond me.

7/19/05: Dave Holmes reported: "Powell Marsh continues to be more interesting. Saw the adult Virginia rail again this morning, in the same spot as yesterday. It pops out of the weeds onto the dike road (eastmost of the 3 Powell entrances) about 75 feet south of the gate. It's quite bold, and has been giving me a good long look before running back into the grass. Went back this evening about 6 p.m. and saw roughly 15 shorebirds on the mud flats in the main pool (again at the eastmost entrance). The group contained greater and lesser yellowlegs, least and pectoral sandpipers."

7/20/05: Laurie Reek, who lives near Booth Lake in the town of Minocqua, observed three fishers eating raspberries in her raspberry patch just 30 feet away from her house. The fishers foraged in and out of the patch for many hours, chattering to one another much of the time. One was smaller than the other two, suggesting a young-of-the-year getting its first taste of red raspberries.

7/21/05: Marylyne Haag in Boulder Junction reported observing hummingbirds mating. A female hummer was perched on a tomato cage in her garden while a male hummer was flying in short pendulum swings nearby. The female flipped backwards so she was belly up, and he mounted her. He fluttered his wings briefly, then it was over.

7/30/05: Callie, Mary, and I observed two short-eared owls in flight on Powell Marsh, the first time we'd seen the owls on Powell this year.

Sightings

Community Sightings of Note – Firsts and Unusuals: 1997

* Lee Snow from Harshaw reported a remarkable sighting of two juvenile red-necked grebes on a pond near the corner of Hwy. 47 and Cty. K. Red-necked grebes are rare Wisconsin summer residents, nesting in only a few scattered locations throughout the state, though they are relatively common in Minnesota.
* Bunny Weisendanger from Manitowish Waters wrote me with her records of loon nestings on Powell Marsh. Bunny began keeping records in 1987, and she has recorded a territorial pair on the marsh every spring. In six of those 10 years Bunny has also seen loon chicks with the adults. The Weisendangers are "loon rangers" for Project LoonWatch, a program coordinated by the Sigurd Olson Institute in Ashland.

Community Sightings of Note – Firsts and Unusuals: 1998

* Ironwood trees (or hop hornbeams if you prefer) are dropping their seeds in August. Each seed is wrapped in an air-filled sac, and each of these bladders is attached to a flower-like bouquet of seeds that falls from the tree. I know of no other tree in our area with a similar manner of wrapping and packaging their seeds.
* In mid-August, Carne Andrews in Boulder Junction watched several mallards jumping straight up into the air to pick and eat blackberries. She said it looked like they were on pogo sticks.

8/23/98: Val and Bob Hitt observed a hummingbird interaction that I've never seen or heard of. A hummer consistently flew up behind a female (or juvenile – they're unsure which) that was perched on a coneflower, pulling with its beak on the head feathers of the bird on the coneflower. The accosted bird would let its feathers be pulled, then spread its wings and flutter them without flying. The birds did this over and over for 15 minutes or more.

8/26/98: Gary Rausch on the Rainbow Flowage reported 14 double-crested cormorants swimming and perching on stumps on the flowage.

8/29/98: Gary later called with the sighting of a hundred or more nighthawks over the Rainbow.

Community Sightings of Note – Firsts and Unusuals: 1999

* Roy Mollen of St. Germain watched a mother duck and five ducklings walk by him at the clubhouse on the Plum Lake golf course. He commented to someone who works at the course that the family was rather small. The employee responded by saying that it had been larger at one time, but he had seen a loon on two different occasions swim up behind the ducklings, drag one of them under the water, and drown it. The loon didn't eat the ducklings, but simply killed them.
* Bernie Langreck and Peggy Bronsberg reported the sighting of 10 sandhill cranes feeding together on the far southwestern end of the Turtle-Flambeau Flowage. Mary and I saw eight sandhills feeding together on the Powell Marsh a week earlier, and the next day we got a call from Bob Kovar of Manitowish Waters who had seen 13 together the previ-

ous day on the marsh. Cranes, like many birds in late summer, come together in social flocks to feed, loaf, and roost together. Several thousand can typically be seen in October at crane "hotspots" like Crex Meadows and the Sandhill Wildlife Area.

* Mary received a call from a gentleman who was cutting a tree in his yard that apparently served as the nesting site for a family of flying squirrels. He watched as the adult squirrel transported each of the five babies to a nearby empty birdhouse, gliding down while carrying one at a time to their new home.
* Jack Bull from Winchester called with questions regarding all the chipmunk tunnels on his property. I used the opportunity to research them a bit and found that burrows may be used for many years and are of two types – simple and extensive. The simple systems are often merely one or two tunnels with a widened terminal end. Extensive systems consist of a more complex plan of tunnels that may be 20 feet or more in length and from 1 to 3 feet below the surface. These are usually 2 inches in diameter and end in a nest that can be as large as 17 by 24 inches. The nests are usually full of stored food, which the chipmunk utilizes over the long winter.

8/27/99: Nadine Kovar of Manitowish Waters observed a Wilson warbler at her thistle feeder.

Community Sightings of Note – Firsts and Unusuals: 2000

* Marylyne Haag in Boulder Junction reported a pair of red crossbills at her feeder. Crossbills very seldom remain in Wisconsin through the summer, though they have been known to "irrupt" some summers in other states. They are the epitome of unpredictability. We usually consider ourselves very fortunate to see them in winter, so Marylyne's rare sighting is quite significant.
* Jack Bull of Winchester observed a very curious behavior. He watched a chipmunk catch and eat a grackle under his feeder. Chippies are known to eat insects like grasshoppers and cicadas, and in his book *Mammals of Wisconsin*, Hartley Jackson notes that they are reported to eat small mice, young birds, and birds' eggs. But catching and consuming a grackle, a bird significantly bigger than a chipmunk, seems most unusual.
* The Northern Lights made an appearance on several evenings around August 11. I got up at 3 a.m. one of the mornings and saw the display. It was the same night of the Perseid meteor shower, so I was able to watch both meteors and Northern Lights at the same time, a most unusual stroke of luck.
* John Noble and Chris Dobbe in Arbor Vitae reported watching a cecropia caterpillar eating the foliage on one of their apple trees. The caterpillars can reach 4 inches in length, and the wings of the adult moth can span 6 inches, making it larger than a hummingbird!
* Val and Bob Hitt from Boulder Junction observed a hummingbird caught in a spider web! One wing was tangled in a "rope" of webbing, and a large spider was moving toward it. Val and Bob figured the hummer had touched a thread of the web, and as it flapped its wings, it twisted the webbing into a rope. They dashed onto the porch, cut the webbing, and the hummer flew off. They later saw it at one of their hummingbird feeders trailing a wisp of spider web behind it. I've heard of hummers "velcroed" to the burs of

burdock, but not in spider webs.

* Phil and LaRoy Tannah reported a badger in their yard eating sunflower seeds and corn. It was unafraid of them and actually laid down on the ground while it ate the seeds for over half an hour.
* We had an immature sharp-shinned hawk visiting our feeder over the last three weeks. It sat right outside our window, directly above one of the tube feeders, and simply waited. We watched and waited right along with it for what seemed like a very long time, with no results for our vigilance. However, I found the feathers of several songbirds on the ground around our feeders, so I assume the sharpie had some success.

Community Sightings of Note – Firsts and Unusuals: 2001

* Russ Gaarder observed the following: "Two or three weeks ago I was walking down our road when a rabbit came running down the middle of the road towards me, ran within 3 ft. past me, and continued down the road. I thought this was rather odd behavior until I saw that a fisher was chasing it – about 40 yards behind the rabbit. The fisher veered to the side of the road when it saw me but continued chasing the rabbit. They both went around a corner so I don't know the outcome of the chase." Remains of snowshoe hares are the most common items found in studies of the intestinal tracts and scat of fishers. So, Russ' remarkable observation of a rabbit being chased by a fisher is likely an event that occurs all the time in the natural world.
* Audra Kulas wrote to describe how the ruby-throated hummingbirds appear to know that she is the source of their food and signal her when she's not efficient enough in her job: "I don't know how much is coincidence, or how well the hummingbirds can see through our windows, but the following has happened twice this year. I check the feeders (3 of them) daily & usually have to replace at least one each day, but twice I have not checked soon enough apparently for the hummers. The first time I missed checking, a hummer hovered outside the living room window long enough to cause me to check the feeders; one was empty. This week, I was sitting at the computer and one of them came to the window and once again, hovered. As long as the feeders are filled, this hasn't happened."
* Casey Skvorc on Big Lake in the Cisco Chain watched an eagle swim some 600 feet to shore, rowing with its wings. Likely, the eagle had misjudged the size of fish it was attempting to fly off with and, being greedy, refused to let it go. Its choice required a swim, but the resultant feast certainly should have made up for the indignity.

Community Sightings of Note – Firsts and Unusuals: 2002

8/23/02: A flock of 18 nighthawks passed through Manitowish, our first sighting of any nighthawk movement.

8/25/02: Jim and Barb Moore spotted 24 sandhill cranes on Powell Marsh. We went out a bit later and observed 22, all of which at one point gracefully leapt into flight, a sight as lovely as one can ever hope for. Sandhills "stage" beginning in August, coming together in large social groups as they gradually wander southward.

8/30-31/02: Bunny and Willie Weisendanger observed 28 sandhill cranes and 15 great blue herons on Powell Marsh.

Community Sightings of Note – Firsts and Unusuals: 2003

* Audrae Kulas reported a pair of ravens bringing their three young in to Audrae's feeder. Audrae fed them seeds and bread, and every morning the ravens were out in the yard awaiting their benefactors.
* Karen Loichinger observed 10 adult loons gathered together near her home on Buckskin Lake.
* Jane Lueneburg reported that her husband saw a rabbit or hare lying on its back in a shallow depression of sand and wiggling with its legs straight upward. Jane says her sister reports having seen the same behavior in southern Wisconsin. Well, it could just be rabbits break-dancing. But I suspect they were dust bathing to discourage parasites and maintain oils in their fur.
* Sharon and David Lintereur had a pair of red-headed woodpeckers and Baltimore orioles eating choke cherries in their yard. We don't often think of woodpeckers as feeding on fruits, but indeed they do, including berries from species like buckthorn, wild cherry, grape, dogwoods, holly, Virginia-creeper, poison ivy, elderberry, and even blackberry.
* Mary and I hiked a stretch of beach along the Rainbow Flowage, and among the many eagles, ducks, and gulls was one lone black-bellied plover, a strikingly handsome black-and-white male.
* Jack Bull in Winchester reported several interesting sightings. First, Jack had a family of crows coming to his feeders and eating sunflower seeds. Earlier in the summer he was putting out cat food cans filled with bacon fat, egg yolks, and the like (Jack doesn't want heart disease, but he's happy to give it to the crows), and the adult crows would pick up the cans and fly away with them, presumably feeding the contents to their hungry youngsters.
* Second, Jack had a black squirrel eating the moose antlers he has mounted to the exterior of his house, which he found quite annoying. That's quite a common behavior for squirrels and mice, though usually they choose a cast-off set in the woods, not someone's mount.
* Third, Jack learned how to keep ants out of his hummingbird feeder. He took the insect repellant "Off" and doused the wire that he uses to hang the feeder. Apparently, ants don't like DEET any better than mosquitoes.
* Finally, on August 23, Jack heard a loud thump on his window, and found an ovenbird that had broken its neck. Ovenbirds are in the warbler family, and the fact that a deep-woods bird like this hit a window indicated to me that warblers had begun their move south.

8/2/03: Karen Johnson called with the sighting of a cougar emerging from the woods and slowly crossing Fallon Road off Hwy. K in Manitowish Waters. Karen watched it from her bike for 5 to 10 seconds before it melted back into the woods on the other side of the road.

8/25/03: Michele Bergstrom reported thousands(!) of nighthawks flitting over the Eagle River downtown area, wheeling and dipping on their migration south.

Community Sightings of Note – Firsts and Unusuals: 2004

* Raspberries came ripe rather late. Callie, Mary, and I picked a quart or so for pancake embellishment on August 7. Some folks were still picking blueberries into August, which is also several weeks late. Blackberries came ripe rather late, too. We picked our first ripe ones on August 22.

8/26/04: Sharon Lintereur in Lake Tomahawk observed several Harris's sparrows while she was stacking some wood. Harris's are very uncommon to begin with, but if they show up at all, they usually aren't seen until later in September and into October.

8/27/04: Ron Winter in Boulder Junction reported the following remarkable sighting: "This morning we were privileged to observe a northern goshawk take a crow at our feeders. The hawk must have hit the crow just a few moments before I first looked, as the crow was struggling hard, on its back with both feet of the hawk on the crow's torso. The crow was flapping its wings and pecking back at the hawk. In a couple of minutes the hawk had a fifty-cent-piece-size hole in the crow's breast. The crow then quit struggling (probably dead). The hawk held its stance for about another minute, then to my amazement flew off with the crow through the trees ... It was – I've been struggling for the correct word here, I'm not a writer – gruesome isn't what I want either. It was just as it was. That's how nature is ... I was just too enthralled to even grab a camera."

Community Sightings of Note – Firsts and Unusuals: 2005

* Chomingwen Pond in Minocqua wrote to me about hummers: "Are other hummingbirds as smart as mine? My feeder hangs just beyond the edge of my picture window, and I cannot always tell when it is empty. So when the hummingbird can't get lunch there he (or she – it used to be only a male but this morning it was a female) faces the picture window, flies close to it and hovers sideways across it before heading off to other sources of sustenance. And they act that way only when the feeder is empty. One early spring a hummer gave me that message in late April before I had put the feeder out, since Mother's Day is the usual start of the hummingbird season. I chided him for expecting lunch when he showed up two weeks early without advance notice!"

8/7/05: Marty Wambsganss on Lake Minocqua reported seeing a green heron standing on his dock. "I could get quite close and watch it hunt for and capture a fish ... I was surprised that it stayed around as long as it did and was not frightened by me. It may be that it was a juvenile as it had a white-streaked chest. Two days later, I saw two green herons on the dock."

8/8/05: Gary Rusch on the Rainbow Flowage reported a gray squirrel that was laying out flat in his bird bath to escape the 90°F heat, proving that we're not the only species that suffers in the heat.

8/11/05: I paddled with a group on the Rainbow Flowage and we discovered that it was down 8 feet from its normal level. The good news associated with such low water is that hundreds of acres of mud flats have been exposed for migrating shorebirds. One birder reported observing 12 species of shorebirds on the southeastern end of the flowage, including some heavily sought after species like buff-breasted sandpiper and American golden plover.

8/14/05: Darwin Wile reported water levels had dropped on Powell Marsh, exposing some significant mud flat areas. In only a few minutes of birding, Darwin and his daughter identified several shorebird species foraging in the mud – greater and lesser yellowlegs, Baird's and least sandpipers, pectoral sandpipers, and killdeer.

INDEX

alder, tag, 77
aquatic flowers, 316-317, 379-380
archaeological survey, 113-114
arrowhead, 337-339
ash, mountain, 138
aspen, 77, 129-130, 149-150, 181-182
ATV, 174-175
aurora, 23
badgers, 180-181
bass, 374-378
Batesian mimicry, 330
bats, 297
bear, black, 125-127
beaver, 25-26, 252-253
Beltane, 117
bergamot, 369
bird, bands, 128
bird, beaks, 128-129
bird, divorce, 65-66
bird, feathers, 93
bird, song, 160-161, 177-179
bittern, American, 55
blackberries, 138, 332
blackbird, red-winged, 32, 200
bladderwort, 235, 365-366
blowdown, 258-261, 319-322, 333-335, 354-355
blueberries, 257-258
bluegills, 241-244
Board of Commissioners of Public Lands, 313-314
bobcat, 28
Brockway Mountain Drive, 130
brood amalgamation, 179-180
bryozoa, 249-250
buds, 26-27
bunchberry, 202
bunting, indigo, 152-153
bunting, painted, 151
butterflies, 38-39, 44-45, 95
calla, wild, 189-190, 202
caribou 28
caterpillars, forest tent, 170-171, 227-231, 299-300
catkins, 129-130
cherries, 205, 307
chickadee, black-capped, 20-22, 200, 342-343
chipmunk, 61, 105-106
cisco, 291-294
clear-cuts, 181-182
coarse woody debris, 283-285, 374-378
condors, 190-191
Conservation Congress, 95-97
conservation easements, 265-266
coot, 55
cormorant, double-crested, 347
Cornell Lab of Ornithology, 98-99
courtship feeding, 266-267
cowbird, 194
coyote, 28
cranberry, high-bush, 202
crane, sandhill, 58-59, 70-72, 97-98, 100, 162-163, 312-313
crayfish, rusty, 240-244
creeper, brown, 60
Crex Meadows, 74
crossbills, 63
crust snow, 27-28
daddy longlegs, 343-344
dam, Rest Lake, 322-325
deer, white-tailed, 28, 31, 76, 175, 207
dog days, 267
dogbane, spreading, 235, 309-310
dogwoods, 137
dove, mourning, 95-97
dragonflies, 94, 196-197
drumming, 115-116
ducks, 127
dutchman's breeches, 139-140
eagle, bald, 55, 72-73, 85, 192-195
eclipse, lunar, 67-68
eclipse, solar, 66-67, 179
economics, 132-134
ecotourism, 132-134
egret, great, 357-358
elderberry, 138
emblem birds, 198-201
equinox, 58
ferns, 381-382
finch, 64, 65, 93, 202, 266
firecrackers, 175-176

fireweed, 349
fisher, 350-352
fledging, 202-203
flocking, 355-357
flooding, 79-81, 102-103
flowers, fragrances, 225-226
flowers, imperfect-perfect, 151-152
fluke, parasitic, 164-168
fly, black, 182-184
fly, deer/horse, 250-251, 273, 274
fly, friendly, 230-231, 275
flycatcher, great-crested, 210
fogbow, 206-207
forget-me-nots, 207
fox, red, 28
frogs, 82-83, 95, 108-109, 146-147, 164-168, 208-209, 223-224, 271
global warming, 43-44, 83-84
goldenrods, 357
goose, Canada, 73-74, 180, 195, 200, 339-341
goshawks, 168-169, 355
grebe, pied-billed, 245, 378-379
grosbeaks, 63, 64, 156
ground nesters, 138-139, 214-215, 272
grouse, sharp-tailed, 74-75, 274
gull, Bonaparte's, 81
hare, snowshoe, 28
harrier, northern, 85, 300-302
hawks, 48-49, 85-86, 123-124, 130-132, 217, 262-263
hazelnut, 77
heal-all, 311-312
health, forest, 344-347
heat, 329-330
hemlock-hardwood forest, 302-304, 361-363
hepatica, 136
heron, great blue, 166, 209-210, 270, 348-349
highest use, 171-175
hummingbird, ruby-throated, 134-135, 140-142, 217, 262-263, 279
ice, 19, 20, 56-58, 86-87, 88-90
Indian pipe, 279-280
iris, blue flag, 235, 305
jack-in-the-pulpit, 211-212
jay, gray, 54
jewelweed, 358-359
juneberry, 138, 181, 205
kestrel, American, 291
kinglet, ruby-crowned, 191-192
landscaping, 260
leatherwood, 77-78
leeches, 203-205, 282-283
lily, white water, 317-318
longspur, Lapland, 90
loon, common, 60, 87-90, 124, 217-219, 246-247, 264-265, 285-288, 373-374
loosestrifes, 288-289, 367
lupines, 201
lynx, 28
Lyrid meteor shower, 75
mallards, 221-22
Manitowish River, 19, 247-249, 269-270
maple syrup, 35, 91-92
Mars, 342
mayflower, Canada, 147-148
mayfly, 292-294
mergansers, 215-216, 277-278
merlin, 38, 85, 294-295
metamorphosis, 295-296
migration, 31-35, 93-95, 119-122, 148-149, 328-329, 358, 361, 370-371
milkweed, 289-290
mistletoe, 237-238
mole, star-nosed, 106
molting, 328
moonbow, 251-252
moose, 28
mosquito, 231-232, 297-299, 348
moths, 40-41, 219-221, 278-279, 296-297
mountain biking, 41
mouse, 105-106
nests, 59-61, 63-65, 98-99, 138-139, 187-188, 193, 214-215, 233, 272-273, 307-308
nighthawk, 362
nightshade, dwarf enchanter's, 268-269
Northwoods Wildlife Center, 232
Ojibwe, 91-92, 113-114
old-growth, 302-304
oranges, 223
orchids, bog, 318-319
osprey, 86, 305
otter, 37
ovenbird, 224-225

owls, 22, 23-24, 48-49, 50-51, 54, 55, 78, 100-101, 114-115, 157-158, 211
peanut butter, 100
pelican, 101, 262, 336-337
perch, yellow, 241-244, 374-378
phenology, 43-44, 52-53
pine sap, 279-281
pine, 173-174, 226-227, 366-367
pitcher plant, 236
planets, 154
plantain, rattlesnake, 332-333
play, 29-30
pollen, pine, 226-227
Porcupine Mountains, 41
prairie chickens, 101-104
radar ornithology, 45-46
rail, sora, 161-162
rain, 314-316
Raptor Education Group, 232-233
raspberries, 138, 305-307
raven, 29-30, 36, 60, 155
recreation, 46-47
redhorse, 192
redpoll, common, 63, 103
redstart, American, 122
reed canary grass, 368-369
rice, wild, 383-384
robin, American, 32, 56, 185
rose, wild, 225, 234-235
salamanders, 94
salmonella, 49-50
sandpiper, spotted, 66, 77
shoreline restoration, 372-373
shrew, 105-106
silence, 363-365
siskin, pine, 64
skunk cabbage, 61, 104-105
slopes, 99
smelt, rainbow, 241-244
snakes, 154, 302
snowberry, 382
snow depth, 20, 48-49
snow fleas, 53-54
soils, 159-160
solstice, 234
sparrows, 107-108
spirit, 51-52
squirrels, 22, 28, 48, 61, 82, 233, 368
starling, 32
strawberries, wild, 169
sturgeon, 310-311
swallow, 60, 248
swans, 42-43, 56, 65, 109-110, 169
tanagers, 162, 184-185
temperature, 27
Tenderfoot Forest Preserve, 361-363
terns, 254-256, 304-305
The Nature Conservancy, 361-363
thimbleberries, 138, 332
thrush, hermit, 200, 276-277
trailing arbutus, 136-137
Trust Lands, 313-314
turtles, 56-58, 212-214, 373, 379
veery, 200
v-formation, 110-11
viburnum, maple-leafed, 128
voles, 105-106
Voyageurs, 269-270, 330-331
vulture, turkey, 85
walleye, 241-244
warblers, 85, 99-100, 154, 195-196, 281-282
watershield, 381
waterspout, 186-187
waxwing, cedar, 263-264
webworm, fall, 347-348
whip-poor-will, 236-237
Whitefish Point Bird Observatory, 123
willow, 77
window treatments, 62-63
wind pollination, 142-143
wing-droop-fluff display, 155-156
winterberry, 137
wolf, 28
wolverine, 28
woodcock, American, 55, 124-125
woodpecker, ivory-billed, 143-146
woodpeckers, 115-116, 135
wood sorrel, 382
wrens, 60, 112, 239-240

Order Form

Telephone: Call (715) 476-2828 Fax order: (715) 476-2818
E-Mail order: manitowish@centurytel.net
Postal order: Manitowish River Press, 4245N Hwy. 47, Mercer, WI 54547
www.manitowish.com

Check the following books that you wish to order. You may return any book for a full refund, no questions asked, as long as it is still in good saleable condition (in other words, still like new — thank you.)

Title (Books by John Bates)	Price	Qty	Total
Trailside Botany	$14.95	_____	_____
A Northwoods Companion: Spring and Summer	$14.95	_____	_____
A Northwoods Companion: Fall and Winter	$14.95	_____	_____
River Life: The Natural and Cultural History of a Northern River	$24.95	_____	_____
Graced by the Seasons: Spring and Summer in the Northwoods	$14.95	_____	_____
Graced by the Seasons: Fall and Winter in the Northwoods (10/06)	$14.95	_____	_____
Other Books by Manitowish River Press:			
Heartwood (by Mary Burns)	$9.95	_____	_____
North Country Moments (Cliff Wood) (SPECIAL PRICE! 50% OFF)	$7.50	_____	_____
Subtotal			_____
Sales Tax: Please add 5.5% for books shipped to Wisconsin addresses (Subtotal x 1.055)			_____
Shipping: Media Rate: $2.50 for the first book, and $1 for each additional book. Priority Mail: $4.50 for first book, $2.00 for each additional book.			_____
		TOTAL	_____